THEIR PATRIOTIC DUTY

The Civil War Letters of the Evans Family

of Brown County, Ohio

EDITED BY ROBERT F. ENGS *&* COREY M. BROOKS

ORIGINAL TRANSCRIPTIONS BY JOSEPH SHELTON EVANS, JR.

FORDHAM UNIVERSITY PRESS

New York 2007

Library of Congress Cataloging-in-Publication Data

Their patriotic duty : the Civil War letters of the Evans family of Brown
County, Ohio / edited by Robert F. Engs and Corey M. Brooks ; original
transcriptions by Joseph S. Evans, Jr.—1st ed.

   p.   cm.

Includes bibliographical references and index.

  ISBN 978-0-8232-2784-6 (cloth : alk. paper)

  1. Brown County (Ohio)—Social life and customs—19th century.

  2. Evans, Andrew, 1809–1879—Correspondence. 3. Evans,
Samuel, 1834–1910—Correspondence. 4. Ohio—History—Civil War,
1861–1865—Social aspects. 5. United States—History—Civil War,
1861–1865—Social aspects. 6. Brown County (Ohio)—Biography.
7. United States. Army. Ohio Infantry Regiment, 70th (1861–1865)
8. United States. Army. Colored Infantry Regiment, 59th (1864–1866)
9. Soldiers—Ohio—Brown County—Correspondence. 10. Evans
family—Correspondence. I. Engs, Robert Francis. II. Brooks, Corey
M. III. Evans, Joseph S.

F497.B8T455 2007

977.1'7960410922—dc22

                2007039175

Printed in the United States of America
09 08 07   5 4 3 2 1
First edition

In Memory of Joseph Shelton Evans, Jr.

CONTENTS

Acknowledgments *ix*

Editors' Note *xi*

Evans Family Tree *xiii*

Introduction *xv*

Maps *xxv*

"I Have Seen the Elephant": February 1862–April 1862 *1*

"We Can Endure": May 1862–April 1863 *21*

"The Duty Imposed Upon Us": May 1863–November 1863 *134*

"Forced into a Responsible Position": December 1863–November 1864 *220*

"I Am Ready for Them to Give Up": January 1865–April 1865 *313*

"To Lay Aside All Prejudice"?: May 1865–January 1866 *346*

Epilogue *389*

Timeline *395*

Bibliography *399*

Index *403*

ACKNOWLEDGMENTS

During the decade and a half in which this project germinated, many people have contributed to its realization. Most important, of course, has been the Evans family. Today, many are widely scattered from their ancestral home in Brown County, Ohio, but they are all descendants of the individuals the reader will meet in the pages that follow. Central to our success was the late Joseph S. Evans, Jr., who made the initial transcriptions of the letters and to whom this book is dedicated. His daughter, Ann Guise, invited Bob to take on the role of editor and has been quietly supportive over all the years it has taken.

Those who care about the preservation of Ohio history—the staff of the Ohio Historical Society and Archives—were most helpful. They generously assisted Bob during his visits to the Archives and did copying and mailing of original letters that faded or seemed illegible.

More than a dozen research assistants aided Bob before Corey joined as co-editor. Most valued in the early years of transcription and analysis was Brandon Hersch. Able assistance was also provided by Daniel Wolf, John Paul Remorenko, and Michael Sanders.

Many colleagues have contributed suggestions and insights. James McPherson was enthusiastic about the idea when first introduced to the letters. Barbara Savage, Drew Faust, and Charles Rosenberg contributed insights on everything from format to Civil War soldiers' literary habits, to nineteenth-century rituals for describing deaths of loved ones to those who were absent, such as soldiers like Sam Evans.

Many friends and associates helped refine our work by "test flying" our transcriptions of letters in classroom settings and incorporating the Evanses into their own scholarly work. Feedback from Scott Nelson and Carol Sheriff, David Henkin, and Martin Burke helped us refine the editing and explanatory footnotes. Thanks also to Rachel Bernard, Daniel Immerwahr, and Ariel Ron, who used our transcriptions in their class at San Quentin State Prison. Bob's past and present graduate students also contributed editorial suggestions and read lengthy portions of the manuscript. They include Rob Gregg, Jeffrey Kerr-Ritchie, James Johnson, and Ricardo and Angela Howell. Deborah Broadnax provided invaluable aid of all sorts; Tayrn Kutish unraveled many technical mysteries for us.

We are especially grateful to Randall Miller and Paul Cimbala for their support and encouragement throughout this effort. We also wish to thank Robert Oppedisano, Nicholas Frankovich, and the very able staff of Fordham University Press for the guidance and editing that has brought this volume to publication. It has been a remarkable collaboration for the two of us. Each of us has learned from the other, and we both have grown as a result.

Robert F. Engs and Corey M. Brooks
Philadelphia, Pennsylvania, and Berkeley, California
June 2007

EDITORS' NOTE

The editors have striven to be faithful to the meaning and style of the original writers.

The word *sic* is added, inside brackets, only when necessary for clarity.

Original spelling has been retained except when the original spelling is indecipherable to a normal reader. In this case, the intended meaning is inserted in brackets after the original word.

Punctuation and typography have been modernized according to these conventions:

Commas have been added in mid-sentence where needed for clarity.

Periods have been added at ends of sentences.

Capitalization has been added where needed for clarity.

Dashes are retained only where they were used in the original.

Underlines have been removed, because of the inconsistency in the frequency and significance in their uses by the letter writers.

Salutations and conclusions have been formatted to appear uniform on all letters.

EVANS FAMILY TREE

Thomas and Elizabeth Evans—emigrated from North Wales, settled near Philadelphia, Penn.

John Sr. (1737–1802) married Hannah Griffith (1738–1816) in 1760

John Jr. (1770–1858) married Mary Housh (1775–1863)
(moved from Baltimore County, Md., to Mason County, Ky., in 1792, relocated to Brown County, Ohio, in 1800)

Andrew (1809–79) married Mary Hiett (1815–93) in 1833
Andrew's siblings: Abraham, Benjamin, John, Thomas, Amos, William, Hannah, Laban, Diana, Griffith

Amos (1819–1863)* married Angeline Wilson
Children: Jane (born 1844), Laban (born 1847), John, Jacob, Griffith, Naomi

Samuel (1834–1910) married Margaret Shelton (1849–1929) in 1867

William H. (1835–1914) married Maria Games (born 1853) in 1867

Samuel and William's siblings:
Abraham   (1835–62, William's twin)
Indiana   (born 1837), married George W. Early in 1857
John B.   (1841–63)
Amos A.   (1843–64)
Mary   (born 1845), married Walter Grierson in 1873
Isabella E. (born 1849), married John Hawk in 1872
Ann D.   (1851–66)
Joseph H. (1854–92), married Louisa Dragoo
Lee A.   (born 1858)

*Andrew's brother Amos's death year is presumed, based on his disappearance from army, and all other, records after that date. Amos's birth date was estimated to within a year, based on subtracting the age listed for him in the 1860 Manuscript Census. The same procedure was used to estimate the birth years of Amos's children Jane and Laban.

INTRODUCTION

The Civil War letters of the Evans family, presented in *Their Patriotic Duty*, offer rich, variegated, and insightful portraits of Civil War life in the Midwest. Specifically they reveal to us the world of middling rural folk from Ohio, a group that sent tens of thousands of their husbands, brothers, and sons to battle, and whose own lives at home were also inexorably changed by the war.

The Evans letters possess many rare qualities that will make them a rich source for students of the Civil War at all levels of scholarly inquiry. There are hundreds of compilations of Civil War letters for Northerners and Southerners, usually letters of soldiers to loved ones at home. Less plentiful, and more often from Southern whites than Northerners, black or white, are letters to absent soldiers from wives and families describing the difficulties that the war brought to those left behind.[1] We know comparatively little about life on the Midwestern home front during the war.[2]

The Evans collection is unusual, though not unique, in that it contains *both* sides of the correspondence—those at the front lines and those at home—of an Ohio white family whose collective lives intersect with many major currents and issues of the Civil War era. The letters offer insight into the home front lives of Midwesterners, who supplied hundreds of thousands of Union troops. They explore many of the central themes of the Civil War era: the meaning of the Union—and one's duty

---

1. See for examples of Northern collections, Judith A. Bailey and Robert I. Cottom, eds., *After Chancellorsville: Letters from the Heart, the Civil War Letters of Private Walter G. Dunn and Emma Randolph* (Baltimore: Maryland Historical Society, 1998); and Richard L. Kiper, ed., *Dear Catherine, Dear Taylor: The Civil War Letters of a Union Soldier and his Wife* (Lawrence: University Press of Kansas, 2002).

2. For example, Paul Cimbala and Randall M. Miller, eds., *Union Soldiers and the Northern Home Front: Wartime Experiences, Postwar Adjustments* (New York: Fordham University Press, 2002), looks at soldiers from New England, Pennsylvania, even Iowa, but lacks an essay on the key states of the Ohio Valley. Another volume of essays about the Civil War home front, Joan E. Cashin, ed, *The War Was You and Me: Civilians in the American Civil War* (Princeton, N.J.: Princeton University Press, 2002), contains an essay addressing the Ohio Valley; Joseph Glatthaar, "Duty, Country, Race, and Party: The Evans Family of Ohio," 332–57, discusses Samuel and Andrew Evans, but focuses primarily on how the war shifted their filial relationship. This volume introduces readers to many more members of the Evans family, their neighbors, and the issues confronting them on the home and war fronts.

toward it; the evolving definition of those things for which it was worth dying; the impact of war on life and work on the home front; the restructuring of familial and community boundaries as a result of the war; the reconfiguration of political allegiances and beliefs; and the evolution of white racial attitudes as slavery disintegrated and black soldiers helped win the war for Union. We can follow this intriguing saga because one of the Evans sons—Samuel—had the foresight to periodically bundle up his letters from home and send them back for "safekeeping" with fellow soldiers returning to Ohio on furlough. The family in Ohio saved these letters *and* the ones he wrote from the war front. They give us an extraordinarily informative and detailed picture of how the war connected people and their concerns, although these people were separated by hundreds of miles.

Samuel's daughter Katherine Evans kept the letters in an old shoebox in the family home, rereading them over and over. Kate gave the letters to Wendell Evans (Sam's grandchild and an engineer by profession) when she entered a nursing home in 1981. Wendell mailed them to another of Sam's grandchildren, Joseph Evans (also an engineer), who had the letters transcribed. Joe sent the letters back to Wendell, who donated them to the Ohio Historical Society Archives in 1984. He also wanted to transcribe them and prepare an edited version as a gift to the Evans clan's grandchildren. Mr. Evans consulted with the staff of the Historical Society; they suggested he find a professional historian to help him.

Mr. Evans shared that suggestion with his daughter, Ann Guise of Philadelphia. She responded, "Oh, Daddy, I know an historian!" Ann's family and my own were members of a babysitting co-op in our University City neighborhood. I somewhat grudgingly agreed to take a look at the letters, having no idea of the richness and breadth of the collection I was about to encounter. Thus the exchange of bottle warming and diaper changing in the past has led to the most intriguing and rewarding editing project of my career.

—*Robert F. Engs*

Description of the Collection

From the collection we have selected and annotated 254 letters. Some two dozen letters in the collection were illegible; another twenty-one were repetitive or uninformative. Most are from the family patriarch, Andrew Evans (91), and from his eldest son, Samuel (103). There are also letters from Samuel's brothers, John, William, and Amos, as well as letters from younger sisters, a cousin, and a few other friends and acquaintances.

The letters draw the reader into the full and textured lives of a Midwestern family suffering the dislocations caused by the war, but also experiencing the many sorrows and occasional joys of rural life in mid-nineteenth-century America. Most of the Evans family lived in Huntington Township, Brown County, Ohio, near the small town of Ripley on the Ohio River. In the Civil War era, this was "Copperhead" country, with many residents descendent from ex-Southerners who had migrated across the river from Kentucky. We learn of the surprise and confusion as farm boys went off to war as volunteers to search for adventure and some, after 1863, to avoid the stigma of being drafted. Samuel Evans, a miller and blacksmith, is one of the two chief correspondents in the collection. Sam, still a bachelor at age thirty, impulsively joined the army while accompanying his younger brother, John, a sergeant in the 70th Ohio Volunteer Infantry, back to his unit. His impetuous act incurred the displeasure of his father, Andrew. The evolving and maturing relationship between Andrew and Samuel is a central theme that holds the collection of correspondence together. Their letters offer a dialogue between generations, viewpoints, and contrasting experiences. They also reveal poignant changes over time. Andrew evolved from a critical father admonishing an errant son who had essentially run away from home, to being an outraged patriarch who comes near disowning Samuel when the latter accepted appointment in a black regiment, to a proud father addressing an equal as he congratulates Sam on his role in the destruction of slavery and making the Thirteenth Amendment possible. Conversely Sam grew from a defensive and apologetic prodigal to a confident, assertive man, proud of his choices and fiercely loyal to the Union cause, although he was surprisingly ambivalent about the proper boundaries of black freedom.

The letters immerse us in the troubled world of the southern Ohio home front. We encounter Sam's grown siblings—Abraham, William, John, Indiana, and Amos—as well as the younger ones, Mary, Isabella, Ann, Joseph, and Lee. We also meet Sam's flirtatious and outspoken cousin, "Little Jane," daughter of Andrew's brother, Amos. The Evans family was not entirely typical, in that Andrew, who was sometimes called "the Squire," was a local leader and one of the more prosperous men of the county. Nevertheless he had not risen so high that he did not still work his own farm with the help of his sons and a few hired hands. The family's associations introduce us to a whole variety of men and women of the time. Southern Ohio contributed thousands of men to the

Union cause, but it was also a hotbed of Southern sympathizers. As a consequence, "Vals" (supporters of Clement Vallandigham), "Butternuts," and "Copperheads" or "Cops" make frequent appearances in these letters.

We acquire a sense of the tragedy that the Civil War brought to people already beset by the uncertainties of weather, disease, and death. The letters begin in February 1862 with the departure of sons Samuel and John for service. Then in April they experience the battle of Shiloh, the first major battle in the West, from which Sam wrote that he had "seen the elephant"—Civil War terminology for experiencing battle. The carnage at Shiloh was the first experience of both sides with the bloody gore that would characterize battles like Antietam, Gettysburg, and the Wilderness. As gripping as the Evans sons' descriptions of that battle are, equally poignant were the crises confronting folks at home. The handling of dead soldiers was still haphazard. Wrong bodies got sent home and it became necessary to open the coffins upon arrival to assure that the correct corpse was inside.

Letters concerning Sam's military experience with the 70th Ohio Infantry and, later, with the 59th USCT constitute about half the collection. Most of his service was spent as part of an occupying army. We learn about the tedium of picket duty and camp life and the problems of illness and death, often results of exposure to the Southern climate and poor sanitary conditions. Sam's civilian skills served him well as he was appointed armorer and blacksmith and also ran a mill for his Ohio regiment.

Sam spent most of the war in West Tennessee around Memphis and LaGrange. He helped construct fortifications for the Union, supervising the "contraband" slaves who did the work. Sam also learned to handle recalcitrant former rebels within Union lines as well as the sometimes corrupt, sometimes incompetent officers in his own army. Moreover, because Sam was stationed primarily with the Union occupying army rather than with battlefront units, and because he later commanded a black company, his correspondence gives us insights about a South different from that described in most Union soldiers' letters.

In May 1863 Sam shocked his family and infuriated his father by volunteering to serve with the newly organized United States Colored Troops. Father Andrew writes he "would rather clean out S__thouses at ten cents pr day" than take such "a degraded position." Sam was less of an idealist than some men who volunteered for the "Negro Service."[3] He was more typical of his race and region, citing practical reasons for his choice. He pointed out to Andrew that the benefits of becoming an officer included getting a horse—"you have never walked as many miles as I have"—and argued that using black troops would save white men's lives. Nevertheless Sam believed in the legitimacy of emancipation and came to celebrate the manliness of his black soldiers. The ongoing dialogue between Andrew and Samuel about his service with black troops is another unifying theme in the letters. It culminates with Andrew's support of not only black soldiers and emancipation but also the radical idea of black male suffrage as well.

Sam's black regiment participated in only two substantial engagements during the war, in June and July of 1864: the Union defeat at Guntown, Mississippi (better known as Brice's Crossroads) and the Union victory at Tupelo, Mississippi. Sam missed the first because of a foot injury. His unit spent most of 1864–65 in the boring, but sometimes deadly, task of patrolling Union lines. Sam described the progress of his black soldiers but also recounted the terrible toll in sickness and death that camp life caused among these troops, as it had done earlier to those in the 70th Ohio.

Similar problems of morbidity and mortality beset the Evans family at the home front throughout the war years. Just as they adjusted to the horrors of war, son John was forced home due to illness contracted in camp. His gradual decline and death in 1863 provide another of the continuing leitmotifs of the collection. During the course of the letters, Andrew Evans loses three of his adult sons to illness, but none died in battle. In fact the only two adult sons to survive were both away with Union troops during most of the correspondence. In addition Andrew's mother, a young daughter, a grandchild, and several cousins died during these years. The efforts of the correspondents to reconcile each other to these losses provides us with a moving sense of how death was handled in Civil War America and the role of their Christian beliefs in the grieving process.[4]

Even as the letters reach an emotional low point with the illness and death among loved ones, other themes emerge. One is the social and

3. See for example, Robert F. Engs, *Educating the Disfranchised and Disinherited: Samuel Chapman Armstrong and Hampton Institute, 1839–1893* (Knoxville: University of Tennessee Press, 1999).

4. See an excellent exploration of this theme in Drew Gilpin Faust, "The Civil War Soldier and the Art of Dying," *Journal of Southern History* 67, no. 1 (Feb. 2001): 3–38.

political atmosphere of wartime Brown County. Letters tell of community and even family fissures as residents divided over the war. Amos reports the presence of many deserters in the county. Feisty sister Ann asks Sam to come home and "thrash" some of their "Val" neighbors. Andrew and Sam exchange remarkably articulate—and intensely partisan—letters about the importance of the Union and its survival, their antipathy to Copperheads, and their fury at Clement Vallandigham, the Copperhead Democratic candidate for governor of Ohio in 1863.

The Evanses had been lifelong Democrats. In these letters they offer remarkably insightful analyses of the wartime Democratic Party, of Lincoln, and of the new national unity party, the "Union Party." Changes in tone and style suggest that they occasionally borrowed passages from broadsides and pro-Union publications like the Union League pamphlets, but their sentiments are the same when they are clearly using words of their own.

During this period, Andrew was elected to the Ohio state legislature from Brown County. He grumbled that his duties as a legislator in Columbus kept him from home too much, but he was intrigued by the less parochial world of the state capital. His letters from Columbus enrich the collection with their observations about his fellow representatives and the politics of conducting the war at the state level. Back at home in Brown County, there were periodic panics about the incursions of Confederate cavalry raider John Morgan, who managed to evoke fear and cause "refugeeing" all the way to Lake Erie.

The political turmoil in Brown County is highlighted by an exchange of letters between Sam and the most memorable female character in the collection, Jane Evans. Jane was about twenty years old and daughter of Andrew's brother Amos. At age forty-three, Amos had volunteered to serve with 89th Ohio Infantry (the same unit as that of Andrew's son William and his son-in-law George Early). This was one of the Ohio units of the Army of the Cumberland that accompanied Sherman on his March to the Sea. Amos, however, was not among them. He almost immediately became ill and, by 1864, had disappeared. (He may have fallen off a hospital ship in Nashville. He is listed in the army records first as "missing," and then as a deserter, but he never returned to Ohio nor was he ever heard from.) Jane had been initially an enthusiastic supporter of "all my boys at war." The disappearance of her father may have provoked her growing opposition to the war. In her September 1864 letter to Sam, Jane called for peace and an end to the draft, noting her disgust at identification of the Union cause with emancipation: "If you was fighting for the old Union as it was I would be in for it. But such a union as some of you are trying to make of it. I can not hold up for it. I would not mind freeing the negroes if they could be sent off and not come back here again."

Jane's letter infuriated Sam. His response is the most vitriolic in the collection. "You had better procure you a lower garment usually worn by [the] male sex, but seldom by the female. It is very much more convenient for your new business than that of your sex. . . . You say too many hard things of [Lincoln] for a young lady of your caliber." There are no more letters from Jane in the collection, at least in part because Andrew circulated a copy of Sam's scathing response among his Brown County Unionist friends.

The final segment of the letters, from the fall of 1864 through January 1866, traces the conflicting emotions of the folks at home and at war as final victory and meaningful peace seemed to elude the North. Andrew and Sam followed the war and exchanged commentary rather similar to that of modern sports fans following their favorite teams and playmakers. They took pride in the success of Ohio units, especially those with the armies of Ohioans Grant, Sherman, and Sheridan. They disparaged the Army of the Potomac with its spoiled Eastern officers, but stayed remarkably supportive of failed, but Democratic, General George McClellan— until he ran for president against Lincoln.

These exchanges between Andrew and Sam highlight another of the more interesting features of the letters: both soldiers in the field and citizens at home were badly misinformed about the course of the war. In the collection, Richmond is incorrectly reported as "fallen" at least four times before the actual event; the same is true for much reviled Charleston. Andrew finally resorts to adding "if true" after his accounts of reported battlefield events. (The thorough annotation of the letters by the editors will enable readers to distinguish factual information from rumors.)

This problem of misinformation was especially painful to the Evanses because son Will was with Sherman's army in Georgia. The North was subject to the wildest rumors about Sherman's whereabouts after he left Atlanta in November 1864. On at least one occasion, Will was mistakenly reported dead and Andrew delayed his mailing to Sam until son Amos could go to town for the latest casualty lists.

In the 1864 letters we also get to know Amos Evans, the third most frequent contributor to the collection. Amos was about eighteen when the war began. He was the son who was most expressive about his Christian faith and his ambitions for the future. He was left to take care of his mother and younger siblings when Andrew went to the legislature in Columbus. "I have been forced into a responsible position in our family and I hope I may be enabled to prove worthy of trust. It is not my desire but I am not to be my own to choose. God has so ordained it." Tragedy once again struck the Evans family. In November 1864 Amos died; his death was undoubtedly hastened by having to take on the entire burden of running the family farm in the absence of his father and his older brothers. Amos had been suffering—like so many people around Brown County in these letters—from "trouble with his lungs." His condition had caused him to fail his physical examination for the army earlier in the war.

While mourning the loss of yet another family member, Andrew and Sam celebrated Grant's victory over Lee but quickly again had to turn to mourning, this time because of the assassination of Lincoln. Andrew hoped that Andrew Johnson would punish the South, but Sam feared that he would "Tylerize" the Union Party (i.e., convert it to Democratic Party positions as Tyler had tried to do to the Whig Party in the 1840s; the Evanses knew their political history).

As the collection draws to an end, Sam was assigned to the new Freedmen's Bureau and sent home succinct, bitter assessments of former rebels and of the plight of freedmen. Andrew was defeated for reelection by Copperheads, but celebrated that "all the military camps in Ohio . . . will soon produce Corn & potatoes, instead of Soldiers." In January 1866 Andrew was forced to report the death of Ann, the most spirited of the younger daughters. He concluded the letter with a plea to Sam to return home, observing, "Our family is so small now, two girls and two little boys all told. You may imagine that we feel lonesome, and desire the presence of those living of our family." The Evans letters end with this entry by Andrew. Samuel returned to Ohio in the spring of 1866.

When we began the editorial process, we envisioned a much longer introduction and epilogue, coupled with lengthy chapter headings alerting the reader to key issues in the letters that followed. Instead we have chosen to limit our editorial intrusions, preferring that characters from the letters should speak for themselves as much as possible. Annotations after the individual letters serve to identify people named and provide context for the reader. The epilogue provides a brief account of the postwar lives of the Evans family that the reader will have come to know so intimately over the course of these letters.

—*Robert F. Engs and Corey M. Brooks*

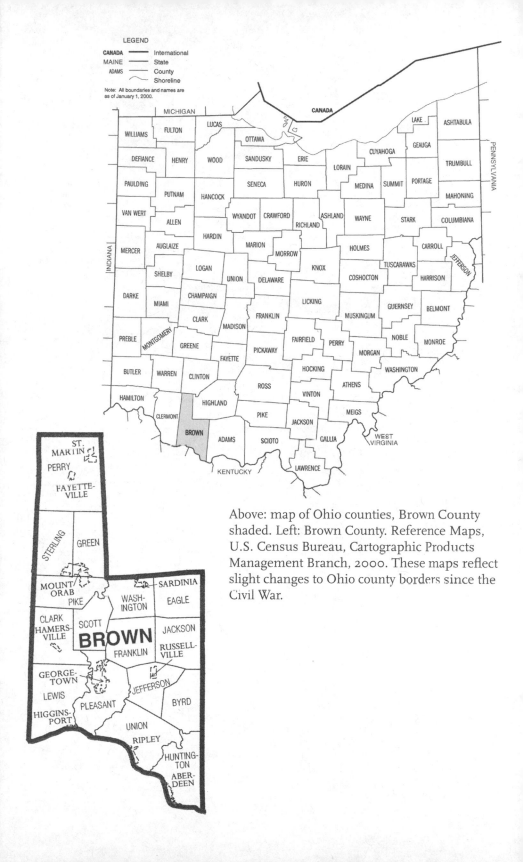

Above: map of Ohio counties, Brown County
shaded. Left: Brown County. Reference Maps,
U.S. Census Bureau, Cartographic Products
Management Branch, 2000. These maps reflect
slight changes to Ohio county borders since the
Civil War.

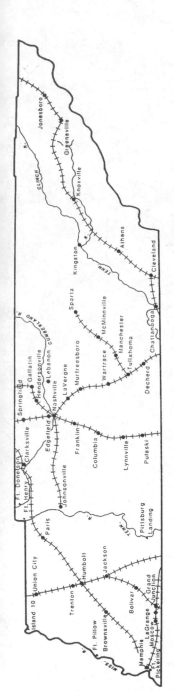

Above: key towns and railroads in Tennessee during the Civil War. From *Slavery's End in Tennessee, 1861–1865,* by John Cimprich. Copyright 1985 by the University of Alabama Press.

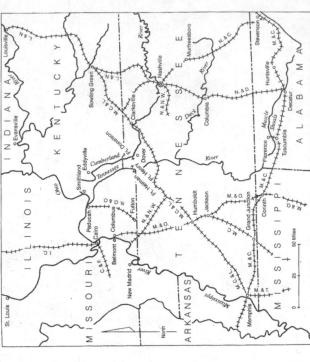

Right: The Western Theater, 1861–1862. Map by Louis S. Wall. From *Forts Henry and Donelson: The Key to the Confederate Heartland,* by Benjamin Franklin Cooling. Copyright 1987 by the University of Tennessee Press.

THEIR PATRIOTIC DUTY

"I Have Seen the Elephant"
February 1862–April 1862

≫ WILLIAM H. EVANS TO SAMUEL EVANS ≪
Aberdeen, Ohio / February 19, 1862

Dear Brother,

When I got home the news of your departure had already reached them. Mother was crying very hard but I reconciled her to some extent. Father looked very sad but said little. The most of our kindred grieved much. Cal was the most completely beaten I ever saw her.[1] She wept bitterly. Enough of this now.

Brother, I enclose to you a necessary writ to continue me your agent to transact any of your business. If I have to collect by law I wish to have authority that will empower me to do so. I have already entered on my duty assigned [collecting outstanding debts to Sam]. I will see that your affairs are attended to. We will miss you much. Your place will be hard to fill. I hope you will take proper care and beg for promotion. I know you can get it if you will only try. Tell John to be careful and don't expose himself unnecessarily.[2] Be brave and right and God will cross in your efforts. Please sign the enclosed and start it right back that I might proceed immediately. I write in great haste as you may perceive, not as good at such as you.

Love to all in hopes of victory,

W.H.E.

P.S. I will write more when you tell me where you are. Love to all the boys, a big fight, a grand victory, distinguished promotion, and safe return.

1. Cal was Samuel's girlfriend at the time.
2. John was one of Samuel's younger brothers, serving with Sam in the army.

Paducah, Ky. / February 26, 1862

Dear Father,

As we are idle this morning I thought that I could do as much good writing as anything else. You may inquire why I went to war. The following are the principal reasons—1st because I wanted [to], 2nd I did not like to see John go without I was along,—3rd I thought I ought to go,—4th I was doing no good at home,—5th was not satisfied without. I do not want you to think I went because I was not treated [well] at home or because I thought so. I went without any coaxing. I thought that the way I went the best because I did not want to "advertise." If I had told the folks at home, not many of them would have been willing, and perhaps would have felt worse than they did. I have no doubt some of the folks were a little astonished when they found I was gone. Let this suffice.

We (John and I) are well except some color. It has been raining a great deal since we left Ripley and the camp was very very poor flat country. We have not seen a corn stalk since we have been here. We were out on battalion drill yesterday in the evening dress parade. This is the only drilling we have done since we came here. This place is surrounded by a breastworks. Five of our men work on it every day, or five from each Co. It looks like it would be hard to get over. There are a great many Ohio boys here. The 26th, 47th, 53rd, 70th, 71st, 77th [regiments] are all here.[1] Some Indiana troops and some Illinois also here. Yesterday a great many of the guns taken at Fort Donelson arrived here, some 7,000 stands of all kinds, nearly all muskets of old style.[2] We have received our accoutrement, but not our guns. No one knows where we will go but some think we will go down to Columbus [Kentucky].

We have just heard [that] 200 secesh prisoners were brought to this town and are now under guard. We don't know where they are from. We have plenty to eat such as it is. Our bread, pilot bread is not very good.[3] We have potatoes, rice, hominy, sugar, coffee, salt. David Games and Will Simpson have been in the hospital since we have been here but are better. John Mc has been selected for hospital cook.[4]

Direct your letters to Paducah, Ky., Co. F. 70th Regiment, Ohio [Volunteer Infantry] care Capt. Blackburn. Give my love to all.

Yours truly,

Sam E.

1. For an explanation of military organization, see James M. McPherson, *Ordeal by Fire*: Vol. 2, *The Civil War* (New York: Alfred A. Knopf, 1982), 172–74.

2. Just ten days before, on February 16, General Grant gained a major Union victory at Fort Donelson on the Tennessee River about seventy miles southwest of Paducah. This victory would enable the Union armies to control the Cumberland River, forcing Confederate evacuation of Middle Tennessee and thus allowing Union forces to capture their first Confederate state capital, Nashville, Tennessee. Also, valuable equipment, guns, and rations were captured along with about thirteen thousand prisoners. McPherson, *Ordeal by Fire*, 224–25.

3. Pilot bread was another term for hardtack.

4. These men were neighbors of the Evanses.

⇾ ANN D. EVANS[1] TO SAM ⇽
Ripley, Ohio / March 1, 1862

Dear Brother Saml,

I take my pen in hand to write you a few lines. Big John got a letter from you today.[2] Sarah and Nancy came over this evening and are here yet. Sam, we have a hen house pretty near done. Ibby [Sam's sister Isabella], got the song you sent her. She says she can't sing it. Sam . . . [you don't] get any popcorn if you don't come over and get some. We are parching some. We have not had a letter from India [Sam's sister Indiana] for a week. She was well as common. Grandmother is well as common. The rest of the folks are well. I have not much news to tell you. Sam, I wish you were nearer home and I would come and see you. I wish this war was ended and all the boys could come home and more. George Jameson has been to see John twice since he has come home. I must close. Give my love to all.

Good by,

A.D. Evans

1. Ann was about eleven years old at the time this letter was written; this accounts for her language being much less sophisticated than that of the other writers.

2. Big John is probably a relative on Andrew's side of the family.

⇾ WILL TO SAM ⇽
At Home / March 4, 1862

Dear Brother,

I have just received a letter from you date Feb. 26 with power of Attorney fixed up all right. I was very glad to hear from you indeed. It was so long before we got any news by letter. Yesterday morning was the first arrival of mails since you left. I received yours of the 21st as it arrived, being there to settle with the Trustees. I made out a bill of $11.20 for Township services and it was accepted. I will present your claim of $25 at next annual meeting of the Board. Shall I just present the claim total without itemizing? But if it is necessary to set forth price, can you give me the price per item?

I ordered your gun home and got it last Friday and in good order. I got an offer of $10 today. I will take it if I cannot get more. The bid is cash. Your books were sorted and laid up before ordered. . . . Have had several good days for grinding. I ground all that came and have partially fixed the dam. I have advertised your claims for collection. I have made a list of your accounts with [nothing] subtracted; I will not alter your book[s] in any way. . . .

Went up to see Cal yesterday and gave her the news—was glad to hear from you, she said—and has written to you. She said if she had been at Ripley you would not have gone. . . .

Candidates are out. Fulton, Martin, and Waldren Candidates for re-election. I. I. Scott's out for trustee. Tarbell, Waldren and Campbell are for Township Clerk.[1] . . . Father is out for squire.[2] . . .

G. W. Early received a letter from Aaron Long Monday last,—he's at Louisville, Ky. in the hospital—has been in the service since December, won honors but didn't tell where. . . . I received a letter from . . . Samuel R. Hiett.[3] . . . He speaks of having quite a hard time since [he] has been in Dixie. He says at Camp Young . . . all the Regiment took diarrhea of chronic form. . . . He says their hospitals are wretched things—he says 'twould make one's heart bleed to see what treatments [are] given their Brave Volunteers. Four have died in his Camp. . . . I send you $1.00 worth of stamps.

Yours in hope of safety,
Wm. Evans

1. The two men Will names as "Waldren" here were probably J. C. and P. W. Waldron. Both of these men show up periodically throughout the letters.

J. C. Waldron worked as a farmer in Huntington Township. A lifelong Democrat, he served in many political positions over the course of his life. In 1863 Andrew Evans defeated him in a race for justice of the peace.

His younger brother P. W. commanded the 3rd Independent Battery of the Ohio National Guard for two years (this is mentioned in later letters). Like his brother he was a Democrat, serving for many years in local office.

2. By "squire" Will probably is referring to the position of justice of the peace for Huntington Township, in which capacity Andrew had earlier served for twelve years.

Andrew's opponent, Alexander Grierson, was an English-born man who immigrated to America in 1836. At the time of this race Grierson was thirty-seven years old and Andrew Evans was fifty-two. Josiah Morrow, *History of Brown County Ohio* (Chicago: W. H. Beers & Co., 1883), Biography Section, 156, 164–65.

3. Sam Hiett was Sam Evans's first cousin. Hiett was Sam's mother's maiden name.

⇢ GEORGE W. EARLY TO SAM[1] ⇠
At School
March 6, 1862

Dear Sam,

Thinking that I would be pleased to hear from you I concluded to write you a small script of such thing as my mind happens to dictate at present: The ground is nicely covered with snow, and more still falling, but getting warmer, I think will turn to rain soon (if not before). My school is quite small this kind of weather, but very pleasant. Only from ten to fifteen per day. My school will be out next week, and then I will be free for a while. till I can find something to do, and if I can't find any thing to do I will go to war as soon as I can find a comfortable place for my family.

East Fork is quite a lonely place to me.[2] So much so that I long to leave. Cousin Jane is still as clever as ever and Big Jane too.[3] I was up there last night, but had no Sam with me to help on the sport. I have to go alone now. How do you like a soldier's life? What Brigade are you in? Who is your General? What kind of guns have you? &c&c. Tell me as near all of it you can when you write. if you please.

Home at night

Not having time to finish my letter at school, I will finish at home tonight. I know nothing very special to tell unless it be that Old Mary Ann Flangher and Wm Wilson were married last night, also Nat Swerengen (or something of the kind) to Betty White. They (the last two) ran off I think, for I saw them going up the Creek this morning, had been to Esqr Sheltons, perhaps—Go It Boots—Now for town news, I am not very well posted in town matters. [one line illegible] I was at town last Saturday night and saw most of the Sisters, that is, those are in the habit of attending and they looked very much like they used to, perhaps not quite so gay. Somewhat the worse on account of your absence, at least I thought so!

Sam, there is something wrong in Clark Temple, but not to convict myself, I will say no more at present, but will from time to time communicate to you some of the "ups and downs" for I think they will occur, but I will be sorry.

I got a letter from Aaron Long two days since, and he is at Louisville in the Hospital. He did not say what was the matter.

We are all well as common. Every one about is well as common. Tell the boys to write to me. Nels & John McNight write any how. I will write as often as I can. I wrote to John B. Evans some time ago but have not read an answer.

More anon,

From brother[-in-law],

G. W. Early

1. George (G. W. Early) was married to Sam's younger sister Indiana. They were two and four years younger than Sam respectively. George was a school teacher before the war.

2. The Evans homestead was located on the East Fork of Eagle Creek. Byron Williams, *History of Clermont and Brown Counties, Ohio* (Milford, Ohio: Hobart Pub. Co., 1913), Vol. 2 Biographical, 211.

3. The name Big Jane appears several times in these letters. There were two older Jane Evanses in the Ripley vicinity, but the context of the letter does not enable us to determine which one, if either, is the person being referred to as Big Jane. Big Jane should not be confused with Cousin (or little) Jane who was Sam's first cousin.

⋙ ANDREW TO SAM ⋘
Home / March 9, 1862

Dear Sam,

I received yours of the 26th Feb on the 4 Mar. John's of the 28, to George was received on the 8th & John's of the 2nd March was received yesterday evening. Six days from date is about the time we receive your letters. John's letter to your mother brings us the sorrowful, but not unexpected, news of your sickness; I thought, your knowledge of yourself, and your condition would have admonished you, not to take so rash a step, at any rate at a time when there was no necessity for such a step to be taken, the regiment was more than full, at the time entered it, & there were 130,000 more men in the field than the President asked for: and for a raw recruit to enter the service for immediate active duty, in the enemy's country in an unhealthy place, this, taking it all in all, looks to me more like you acted under the impulse of the moment, and that you let Uniforms of officers and soldiers, the fife & drum, tempt you to do an act that you would consider rash, under cool and less exciting circumstances. I am far from charging you with not going through patriotic motives, and have no fears but that you would make a good soldier if your health and condition would permit. But you should have remembered the old maxim "it's hard to make a whistle &c" and calculated the depth of water before you plunged in. Soldiers who are only able to fill a place in the hospital are a burden to the Government, & to their fellow soldiers. Enough of this.

Sam if you are living, and unable to do duty, and no prospect of a speedy recovery, you had better get leave to come home and regain your health if possible, for there is but little chance where you are[.] Have the Surgeon to examine and pronounce you unfit for duty. We are about in usual health, have very unsteady weather, we had the highest creek in 14 years (except the big flood) on the next day after you left, and have high creeks twice since, our creek road is almost impassable, it did no damage on our premises only to take the hog pen fence and spoil the road, the mill-dam stood up to it.

A. B. Gilbert's dam is about half gone. Sugar making has been dried up for a week[.] We have quite a cold spell, it is warmer now & sugar water running finely, we have made 193 lbs of sugar and 3 gal of molasses, many of our neighbors have failed to get granulated sugar. But we have not failed in a single case, most of it has been very pretty. Will is making poor progress in collecting your claims, he has made so many things to do, he is not doing any of them, he calls in once in a while and stays all night, he is electioneering for assessor. Abe is about as he was when you left.[1] John Mitchell, Tho Sharp & Will Davis are candidates for Township Treasurer, Tarbell & J. B. Campbell Jr for Clerk, BB Lawwill, John Case Jr, I. C. Mitchell for Constable Saml Canon, W. G. Heitt & W. H. Evans for Assessor.[2] Peggy has been attending a "protracted" [revival] meeting at the ridge ever since yesterday week ago, not returning yet; I just received a letter from Jake Bottner from Lebanon, Ky, he has recovered from his sickness & is fit for duty. The troops have all left that place but the 8th Ky and the sick. Over 900 sick there on the 2nd. I will close this evening with the Cal news.

Evening: Misses Mary Carpenter and Cal Campbell are here on a short visit. They are looking very well. They say there have been no new arrivals or departures in Aberdeen recently. John Carpenter expects to go to his regiment this week. Bill has not returned from Lodge yet. Tad, Pat & Burke are just gone to gather water.[3]

We would be glad to hear from you often & in return some of us will write to you or John three or more times pr week. You have the love and respect of us all. The families of the soldiers in your Regt from this neighborhood as well. Tell Wm Anderson that his case is adjourned to the 29th March at 10 O'clock & perhaps they will try to get his deposition before that time. Old Mitton did not appear nor send counsel, hence the adjournment.

Truly your Father,
Andrew Evans

1. Abraham is William Evans's twin brother. They are two years younger than Samuel. Abraham had practiced medicine at Pleasant Hill, Indiana, for about a year, when illness forced him to return home in the spring of 1861. Morrow, Biography Section, 158.

2. This W. H. Evans who is running for assessor is Samuel's brother William.

3. Tad is a nickname for Samuel's brother Amos, who is about eight years younger than Samuel. Pat and Burke were hired hands in the Evans farm. For more about James Burke, see note on his letter of March 13, 1862 (next letter in the collection).

⇾ JAMES J. BURKE[1] TO JOHN B. EVANS ⇽
Aberdeen / March 13, 1862

Friend John,

I have just received and in haste I commence a reply. I cannot see why you have not received more letters than you have. The Squire has written to you twice. Will has sent a dollar's worth of stamps to Sam. Amos has written also and I sent you a letter this week too and I must say on the part of your friends here they are very anxious that you receive a letter every week nay every day and will take great pleasure answering every one you write to us. The whole fault lies in mail. I have been finding fault with it for the last six months. It was a source of great pleasure to your parents and brothers and sisters to hear you were well and that Sam was getting better and I fervently hope and pray that he will soon be as strong as ever. Tis true he is missed by all and since you left Ripley the times are lonesome enough. Will is now in bed and he has plenty measles. They broke out yesterday and I think he is doing fine. You may get those letters that have been written to you and if so you will get the latest news about here.

I have no doubt those sheet iron crackers you spoke about would be hard to masticate. You want me to hug all the girls for you. Now you know John my hugging propensities have not yet developed themselves. I will gladly obey a soldier's command and will concentrate all my abilities on the performance of that grand design and as to bringing my lips in contact with theirs, oh glory, John, I cannot refuse if they are willing.

Today we heard Manassas was taken, if that be true then I think you will be home again at harvest and then you can hug and kiss yourself.[2] Mary is at my elbow while I write this and she says she is sorry you have not received her letter and that she will write to you tomorrow and to Sam. This is a mistake she has not written yet but will. It is getting late now and soon will be bed time. I must tell you however that my brother John has enlisted. He is in 19 Reg at Indianapolis, Indiana. If you come across him he will be glad to see you. I wish you had a snifter of the Squire's brandy, I think it would soften your sheet iron. You know what, I will now conclude hoping you will return again safe and sound and remember me to Sam and tell him to take care of himself and write soon and oblige your friend,

James J. Burke

1. James Burke worked as a field hand for the Evanses. Apparently he was friends with John and Sam. The only other letter in this collection from him is one written to Sam on April 8, 1862. There is also a brief note from him at the bottom of (Sam's sister) Mary's letter of June 1, 1862. Andrew's letter of July 3, 1862, and Jane's letter of July 7, 1862, reveal why there are no other letters from Burke.

2. Burke's war news was incorrect. There was no engagement at Manassas around this time, and when the two armies did meet there on August 29–30, 1862, it was a resounding Confederate victory.

⋙ SAM TO ANDREW AND MARY EVANS (MOTHER) ⋘
Gothier Hospital, Paducah, Ky / March 16, 1862
Dear Father and Mother,

We are yet in the hospital at this place and cannot tell when we all will get away. We are all on the mend. The measles have [illegible] me. They got into my kidneys or back and caused me a great deal of trouble. Our surgeon says that I have not yet taken the least cold, it's all the regular course of measles. I might say that my hearing is not very good yet. I think it is getting better slowly. This makes the eighteenth day I have had the measles and have eaten but little since. I have no appetite to eat. It is now improving. Our boys, nearly all if they continue to improve, will be able to go to the regiment this week, toward the last of it.[1]

We heard yesterday our regiment was at Savannah up on the Tennessee River. The report is that there are 75 regiments near that place. There has been nothing received directly from 70 since it left. None here has received a letter from any of the boys since they left. All the letters that come here for any of the boys here are forwarded to the regiment. Not one of us has received a letter since the regiment left. This I don't like very well. I cannot tell whether you get our letters or not. I thought I would keep track to see if you would get some of them. I would like very well to hear how you are all. I hope you are all well and are enjoying life as well as opportunity affords. We get but little news here of any kind. There is nothing of importance here to write—all quiet here—no talk of a fight near here. I have got to see a great many gun boats since I have been here. This is a very flat swampy country. Much like an ague country.[2]

Tell all my brothers and sisters to be good boys and girls. Tell my Lee "Howdy" that I would like to see him. Give all the folks my love and respects, accept a good share for yourselves.

I remain your son,

Sam

1. Disease killed twice as many Union and Confederate soldiers as died in combat. Sickness hit especially hard during soldiers' first year with thousands of men from varying backgrounds crowded together, creating a very contagious environment. Soldiers (especially those from rural areas) who had never been exposed to measles, mumps, or tonsilitis were quickly afflicted with these typically childhood sicknesses. While these diseases were hardly ever fatal, they could greatly reduce a particular regiment's ranks for several weeks. More harmful diseases such as dysentery, typhoid, and pneumonia were abetted by the hot climate and poor sanitary procedures. McPherson, *Battle Cry of Freedom: The Civil War Era* (New York: Ballantine Books, 1988), 487–88.

2. Ague is "a nonspecific term for chills and fever, often, but not always, occasioned by malaria." Webb Garrison, with Cheryl Garrison, *The Encyclopedia of Civil War Usage: An Illustrated Compendium of the Everyday Language of Soldiers and Civilians* (Nashville: Cumberland House, 2001), 7.

⤜ AMOS A. EVANS TO SAM ⤛
Aberdeen, Ohio / March 28, 1862

Dear Brother,

I have never written a letter under circumstances like the present—four of us—Mother, Mary, Ibby, and Joseph are down with the measles.

Will has just recovered and Ann is now taking them. Lee and Myself have no symptoms of them yet. Father is tending to them all—he is rather overtasked. We all have quite enough to do—more than we can do.

We rec'd a letter of [the] 26th from John last night the only one since he left you—he was well at that time, 24th. George rec'd one from you also. He stopped and read it. Grandma's came on [the] 26th. We perhaps get all you write in about six days after written. We are very much discouraged since you seem to get none of ours but—we still write as often as ever. John states that Blackburn has offered his resignation—but not until they got up a petition with about two-thirds of the [company] names annexed asking him to do so—you certainly will get news from them sooner than we do and it is no use for me to repeat his letter.[1]

We will get the lower field fenced against hogs tomorrow if it don't rain. The ground has been too wet until now to plow or any thing of the kind. Spring work is going on at a good rate. Your mill has still done all the grinding that came in. The shop has blowed out—I have not been any where since the measles broke out so thick here. They and the whooping cough are all over this township. Peter Waldron's child died a few days ago. J. McCauley lost one of his also.

. . . Candidates are superabundant and are at work industriously for power. "Invincible and Invisible," (Burke and J. Campbell), are giving each other fits in the *Bee* and *Argus*.[2] Let 'em rip and tear. Wendell Phillips got egged at the opera house in Cincinnati this last week while making a speech. The police did not try to stop the row.[3]

. . .

I and all the family would much rather you would come home until you get able for duty. Don't punish yourself for the cooks, but come right along as Col. Blair says and make yourself at home. If not write often— and take care of yourself.

Yours,

Amos

P.S. excuse this writing and the quality of the speech for my hand is too sore to write and my mind is dull.—

1. Blackburn was the captain of Sam's company, F of the 70th Ohio Volunteer Infantry.

2. The *Bee* and the *Argus* were two Brown County newspapers.

3. Wendell Phillips was the acclaimed abolitionist who argued for emancipation as a Union war goal. Cincinnati, situated on the Ohio River directly across from Kentucky,

was notorious for its hostility toward both blacks and abolitionists in the antebellum period.

❧ SAM TO ANDREW ❧
Paducah, Ky / March 30, 1862

Dear Father,

I received your letter from you on the 26th date 19th, which gave considerable satisfaction it being the first letter I have seen from home since Will's first. Was very sorry to hear the measles had got into the family but I hope they will not serve any of them that have them quite as bad as they did me. To tell the truth they nearly fixed me. I have got about again but do not feel very stout yet. The cough attending measles caused a hemorage on my lungs, but it was very slight and was not hard to stop. It only lasted two days. It was six days after I was taken sick before I was broken out, as soon as they went in my cough commenced getting better. And then my kidneys took it. I was bound in the bowels all the time and took considerable physic to start them. Dr. Philips was in to see me after I was sick about a week; he told me not to start my bowels as long as it could be helped. If they were he said it would weaken me so that I could not be able to move myself. Consequently I took his advice. Every one that had measles and took physic ran into diarrhaea as he had said my case would do. Every person with one exception that has died since I have been [here] from the effect of measles, they would think they were well; the first thing they would know they were taken down by lung fever or pneumonia and down they would sink. I have been exceedingly careful of myself about taking cold and the like.

I do not like what we have to eat much but since I have got able to get out I had something better. David is my right hand partner, and since Simpson Games and Dragoo have left, his is the only man with whom I had any former acquaintance. I believe him to be a number one man. He and I got some washing by an old negro woman. She lives with the owner of the hospital that we were in—he said he would do all he could for the sick. The old negro would bring us milk, beef soup, chicken soup—we were to get a good share after we got able to walk out. We went to the house and we would get whatever thing we wanted to eat. Our surgeon (Crain) said dried peaches were good for us—we could get the best for 6 2/3 cts pr. pound and we got the old Darky—All we had to do was to complain of our fare at the hospital and we were sure to get something good to eat—we got a can of blackberries that went pretty well on bread. We did not have to pay anything for what the old darky did for us.

I think that I will be able as soon as I can get to the Reg't for duty. You say you think I had better get a furlough. There is not much chance for that here now as furloughs are about played out. If I had tried hard for one I could have as easily got one as some that did. At least one that gone up in our country ought not to have had one.

Nearly every day the calvary bring us some secesh prisoners in. Tennesseans who were being pressed into the southern army have ran off and come to this town.[1] There are now about 500 of them here and Ethridge is here to head and guide them. They want to form themselves into a Reg't and make Ethridge their Col. I saw him yesterday; he is a mighty fine looking man and mighty full of jokes. He can keep a crowd laughing all the time. I think you were mistaken about Island No. 10 being taken.[2] It was not taken at last accounts though we had the same report that you had. There was a soldier killed by the explosion of a box of cannon cartridges, secesh cartridges taken at Clarksville. He was smoking a cigar and some of the fire fell into the box. If the powder had not been damp quite a number would have been killed. There is a great deal of property here taken at Fort Henry. Donelson [has] bad water and stinks.

You said Burke, Amos, Mary have all written to me. I have not reccived a single letter from any of them. Your's and Will's are the only [ones]. Tell all who have written to me that I will answer as soon as I rcceive them or have an opportunity to. I have written a great many letters since I have been sick. I have not heard a word from John since he left in way of letter or any thing in particular from him. I heard yesterday [that] all of our Co were well and were lying in camp about 12 miles from Savannah [Tennessee] on the Tenn River.

I will close. Give my love to all. And accept my best wishes for your welfare at home and believe me,

big soldier boy,

Sam

P.S. There are some mistakes in spelling but I will not now correct them

1. Tennesseeans were divided in their loyalties during the war. Many from East Tennessee (an area with relatively few slaves, Andrew Johnson's territory) supported the Union. Hundreds, as exemplified by the men Sam describes here, fled to Northern lines and volunteered to fight for the Union.

2. Island No. 10, on the Mississippi River near the Tennessee-Kentucky border, was a Confederate stronghold blocking access to the lower Mississippi by Union gunboats. Sam is correct in advising his father that it had not been captured as of March 30. It did not fall until April 8, 1862. McPherson. *Ordeal by Fire*, 2:229–30.

⇒ JOHN TO SAM ⇐
Pittsburgh, Tennessee (near Savannah) / April 1, 1862

Dear Brother [Sam],

As I have not heard anything from you since I left you, I thought I would write. It may be that you will get it. We are now camped in the woods about four miles from the river. It is a beautiful place and I believe it is a healthy one. Anyhow the boys are most all getting better since we have been in camp here. We expect to leave this place before long and go back on the railroad to a little place called Corrinth, where Rebbles have been making brest works of cotton barbs and cutting trees down all around them. We learned that they have about 80,000 out there. We have about the same amount of Inf, 16 Batteries Artillery, 5 Regt. Cavel.

This is all report. I can't say that it is reliable. I have read several letters from home since we arrived here and I have four for you. I got one for you from Will before I received any myself. I opened it to hear from home. It has $1.00 worth of stamps in it. I would send them all to you if I was sure you would get them. The folks at home are all well or were when the last was written. I heard that you were bleading at the lungs. If this be true, I want you to go home as soon as you can. I also heard that all the rest of the boys have gone home on a thirty day furlough. If you are able, I want you to do the same.

[This is the only page of this letter, the subsequent pages were not preserved.]

⇒ MARY EVANS (SISTER) TO SAM ⇐
Home / April 4, 1862

Dear Brother,

This is such a nice evening I thought I would write to you as I have not been able to write for a while on account of the measles. We have all had them but Tad and Lee they have not taken them yet. We are all getting better, pretty near well. We all got through without a Doctor. Abe has the measles now. Will is staying with him. He was better this morning. Will said he thought Luna was taking them instead of the lung fever.[1] Burke's and Little Jane's letters from John came to hand this morning dated the 24th of March. Pap wrote John a big long letter last Sunday; he says he will write to you next. Sam, it looks so lonesome up to the shop and mill without you. We seldom ever hear the sound of the anvil, only when Pop has a little business there. The boys are finishing gathering corn and fodder. Joe is able to be with them today. Cal Swisher is living at George's. She came there last Saturday and took the measles this week. She says that she has had them; if she has they are the French kind. India has not taken the measles yet and I cannot tell whether she will have them or not. Sam! Burke & Tad went up the hill the first day of April to fool the girls and Jim made a fool out of himself. He was coming down the hill in a fidget, fell down and stoved up his hand and knee, but they are getting well. John said for us to save him some sugar. We have a big cake moulded in a skillet. We will save it. I think it will be as much as both of you can eat. Some of the peach trees are out in bloom here and look so like spring. I suppose you soldiers know what the Secesh lands look like by this time. We have not made any garden yet. Part of it is plowed and the rest was too wet.

. . . Sam, Lee is as fat as a little pig. Pap kissed him for you and he laughed and said he would like to see Sam and John. Pat took sick Monday and has been doctoring for the measles but they have not come out yet. He says they must be the Stern wheeled measles, he says Peggy give them to him. Pap went up to old Johny Hietts today to get seed oats but they had none threshed, only what they saved themselves. . . . Will Simpson brought your clothes home when he came from Paducah. Sam, Will said he thought you would come home with them. Burke is writing to John. Write soon.

From your sister,
Mary Evans

1. Luna was the daughter of Will's twin brother, Abraham, and his wife, Eliza. Morrow, Biography Section, 158.

⇒ S. H. MARTIN TO SAM ⇐
Aberdeen, Brown County Ohio / April 4, 1862

Mr. Samuel Evans it being some time since i saw you i imbrase this opportunity to write you a few lines i am well and hope this few lines will find you the same Sam i would like to hear from you i want you to write to me and let me no how you like solgering i understand your company left you at paduca to take care of the sick so i dont supose you have kild ary se sesh yet but i hope you will fix some of them yet an live to get back to old huntington we cant do well without you. . . .

i expect a tight race betwen the old Squire and Click grearison and the would have not a bin if the Sqire wuld have offerd for it he just sed he would serve if they elected him Sam i will send a ticket with the particulars Sam your mother and the children have all had the measles you have had them to i under sand

i think soldiering must agree with John i undesand he ways 215 Sam i want you to write to me and give me all the particulars give my respects to all my friends

Excuse bad ritting and spelling

S.H. Martin

[Most of the Evans family were excellent spellers. Not all of their correspondents were. This letter, transcribed without corrections, is of interest both for its content and style of composition.]

⇢ JAMES S. BURKE TO SAM ⇠
East Fork, Aberdeen / April 8, 1862

Friend Samuel,

Having bought a new pen and the first use I put it to is to write to you. I hope these [words] will find you enjoying the best of health as they leave all your friends here except Lee. The measles have made their appearance on him. I think he will have them easy enough, all but the cough; it is rather wearisome. Well, one of the most important items of this epistle will be the election: the old trio of Trustees go on as usual, David Tarbill [sic, Tarbell] as Township Clerk; he left Campell along way in the shade.[1] . . . Assessor Sam Cannan (Will [Sam's brother] got 87 votes . . .). Your father ran for justice against Alexander Grierson. The latter got a 180 and the Squire 165 or 170. We done our best to have the man of our choice elected but our opponents had whiskey, lying and unfairness against us. Big John is in my estimation a consumate fool and I think he glorys in it. There are some more who are not much better. This is all I believe I can say about the election.

Miss Jane Curtis is laid up with the measles, I have not seen her yet. Bill is grinding tonight, has plenty of water and wheat. He don't like the trip up Salt River very well, especially on bad boats.[2] One consolation to him, he has plenty of passengers to go with him. The ladies of Aberdeen look blooming and hearty. I have seen several during the past week. They, I think, anticipate a hasty return of those they cherish and whose memory is always dear to them and I hope from the bottom of my heart that it will not be long until you are all at home again and that peace will hereafter bless you. It has been raining today and is yet tonight which makes walking very hard. I hope you will excuse my mistakes and that you will condescend to write to me and let us know all the news and be sure to take good care of yourself while I remain your

Sincere friend

Jas S Burke

1. Dave Tarbell was another perennial Democratic candidate for local office. His last name is spelled in a variety of ways through these letters. Carl N. Thompson, comp., *Historical Collections of Brown County, Ohio* (Piqua, Ohio: Hammer Graphics Inc., 1969), 667–68.

2. The expression "to go up Salt River" meant to go into political oblivion.

⤷ JOHN AND SAM TO FATHER ⤶
Camp Chila [Shiloh?] / April 10, 1862

Dear Father,

I know you have heard that we have had a great battle here and will get a more minute description of the battle than I could possibly give.[1] The battle commenced about day light on sabbath morn right in front of our camp, not more than 200 yards from our tents. Our brigade commenced the fight. We drove them back on center but they flanked us on the right and left and we were forced to fall back on account of not having any reinforcements in time. They drove us back from our tents, took what suited them and threw the rest out in the rain. There were several of our boys wounded but none killed in our Co. Pres[ley] Lane was shot in the leg, Sawyer in the arm, Shelton in the shoulder. Joseph McDaniel's fore finger on his right hand was shot off. A ball struck Sam's cartridge box—mashed it all in. A grape shot hit him in the neck; a buck shot went through his hat but he was not hurt much. A musket-ball cut my blouse on the right shoulder, a buck went through my left sleeve but they got no meat. Sam has better luck than I. He is truly a brave man. He slept in the rain two nights but he is as well as common. There were several killed out of our Regt. Our field officers are all brave and true men and deserve great praise for their good conduct in battle. None of them were wounded. Col. Loudon & Maj[.] [McFerren] had their horses shot under them.[2] The boys are all tolerably well. I will let Sam write the rest.

Your Son,

J B Evans

Well, Squire, John has given me the privilege to write some. I send you a secesh letter; I have seen the elephant![3] We have had some thing like hardships to stand for a few days. I send you some Southern paper & also some . . . cotton seed which I would like for you to plant,[4] but no more, But remain yours as ever,

Sam E

1. This is the Battle of Shiloh, named for Shiloh church, to the immediate left of which the 70th Ohio Infantry was camped. The Confederate Army of Mississippi attacked the camps of the Union Army of the Tennessee (commanded by Major General Ulysses S. Grant) on the morning of April 6, 1862. The 70th Ohio was in the heat of the fight, helping hold off the advance of a larger Confederate force for several hours in the early morning. The next day the 70th Ohio was part of the advance that enabled the recapture of the frontline of Union camps, including their own original camp. T. W. Connelly, *The History of the Seventieth Ohio Regiment: From Its Organization to Its Mustering Out* (Cincinnati: Peak Brothers, 1902), 22–24; Jay Luvaas, Stephen Bowman, and Leonard Fullenkamp, eds., *Guide to the Battle of Shiloh* (Lawrence: University Press of Kansas, 1996), 180.

The Battle of Shiloh opened up the lower South for Union invasion. Furthermore it portended the character of fighting and the magnitude of losses that would thereafter characterize Civil War battles. At the time, the battle of Shiloh, only two days long, was the bloodiest battle in the recorded history of the Western Hemisphere; by the war's end, however, six other battles would supersede it. McPherson. *Ordeal by Fire*, 2:229.

2. D. W. C. Loudon served as a quartermaster sergeant in the Mexican-American War. In 1861 he assisted in organizing the 70th Ohio Volunteer Infantry, in which he served first as lieutenant colonel and then as colonel until August 1864 when he was discharged on account of disability. Morrow, Biography Section, 26.

3. The term "seeing the elephant" means experiencing battle.

4. Sam, like many Northerners, was interested in cotton seeds out of a combination of curiosity and the North's desire for cheap cotton, due to the shortage caused by the interruption of trade with the South. Small plots of cotton were grown in south-central Ohio with modest success, but not enough to encourage continued cotton farming once the Mississippi was reopened to trade following the Union victory at Vicksburg in the summer of 1863. Eugene H. Roseboom, *The Civil War Era: 1850–1873*, vol.

of *History of the State of Ohio*, ed. Carl Wittke (Columbus, OH: Ohio State Archaeological and Historical Society, 1944), 83–84.

⇒ JANE EVANS TO SAM[1] / APRIL 28, 1862 ⇐

Dear Cousin,

I received your kind letter on the 26 inst and I was truly glad to here from you. I hope these few lines will find you enjoying good health. We are all well as common except Big Jane; she is just getting over the measles. She has not been able to do anything for about three weeks. Sam, you boys have seen a hard time for the first battle that you have had. You may see harder yet, but I hope you won't. Presley Lane died last Saturday week.[2] He was brought to Silos Huron on Wednesday and was buried at Fitch's meeting house the same day. Pap and Laban and I went to his burial.[3] He was buried in the honor of masonry. We heard the other day that they brought another man in the place of Pres. Lane. They tucked up this man down at Fitch's and found out that it was the wrong man.

Your folks are all well. May and Ibby, Peggy, and Amos and Burke were all out here last night & all had a fine time. You better believe we missed you. Ibby can tell as good a joke as ever. She told some pretty good ones last night on Burke; he could not say anything. George W. Early has another "soldier" [son] and Wisly Cunningham has one too, but it is a girl.

I got a letter from Frank Porter the other day. He is in Virginia. He said that they have been fighting where he is but he did not get hurt. Sam, I wish it was not so far where you are. I would come and see you. I never wanted to see anybody as bad in my life as I do you and John and, of course, I would like to see you all. Your folks are going to plant corn next Thursday. They all say that they miss John in helping to work and you also. I was down to Aberdeen the other day; I saw Miss Cal Campbell. She told me when I wrote to you to give her love and best respects to you. I told her that I would with the greatest pleasure. Grandmother sends her love to you and John and wishes you all the good luck that you can have. Sam, give my love to all and to John Evans in particular and keep a full share for yourself. You must excuse the writing, it is not very good. I guess I have told you all the news. I have not much to write this time. I will write more next time. Please write soon. You don't know what a pleasure it is for us to hear from you all. No more at present but I remain

Your cousin,

Jane Evans

1. This Jane is often referred to as "little Jane."

2. Presley Lane was shot in the leg at the Battle of Shiloh. See John's letter of April 10, 1862.

3. Here "Pap" is Jane's father Amos Evans, Andrew's brother. Laban and Jane are his son and daughter.

"We Can Endure"
May 1862–April 1863

⇥ SAM TO ANDREW ⇤
Tennessee / May 1, 1862

Dear Father,

As I have come to write you a few lines I thought I would do so. I have not heard from home for a long time. We started on march toward Corinth last Tuesday morning. We only marched about 5 miles the first day and camped. Thought we would get to stay a few days. But soon next morning we received orders to march. We took up our tents and traveled some 5 or 6 miles more and camped again. We cannot tell how long we will be camped here. Our Company only brought 3 tents; we have 3 days rations with us. The roads are so bad (in places) that it takes about two days to make a trip to the landing.[1] Officers have tightened the reins on privates till they are pretty [tight]. We are called out of line of battle at 4 O'clock A.M. and have [to] stand till sun rise. Every night we sleep on arms and must be on hands at every call to assembly. I suppose Secesh are near here, but I have seen none but prisoners. Some pass us every day. All kinds of reports are afloat in camp about the Enemy at Corinth. It is reported here that Corinth is evacuated. We know not as to the truth. I am of opinion that it is not so. They will not 'til they have to, for they have a large force as well as we and they can fight for I have seen them. . . . But I do not think they shoot as well as we did.

Some time since the battle the Col. had formed a company of "sharp shooters" by taking 5 men from each Co. I was taken first. The object of the Co. will be to pick Officers and Commanders when the line of battle formed. The sharp shooters are to advance by creeping in small squads near enough to make sure work. When not in battle we are to stay in our company [as] usual.

Several of our men are left at our old camp. The talk of Corinth is very bad on health "in some cases." James Galbraith was slightly wounded in the ball of the foot, while out on picket last Monday evening. John B. Campbell is still here waiting to know the result at Corinth.

We have not received our money. The payrolls are made to the first of this month and the Paymaster is here.[2] Well I will close as the mail will start soon. I will write as often as I have all the time. All the boys are well with whom you are acquainted but Hut Griff and Sam, but they are not dangerous. Write soon and give me all the news and tell all the rest of the folks to write whenever they feel like it. We love to hear from home. We write pretty often but they will not go for a long time.

Give my love and respects to all my relatives and friends and particular to them at home. Tell mother that I am all right.

Your son as ever,

Sam Evans

1. This is probably Pittsburg Landing on the Tennessee River, the site where Union forces were re-supplied and also the site of the Battle of Shiloh. Corinth, Mississippi, is just a few miles across the Tennessee–Mississippi border, southeast of Pittsburg Landing (see map).

2. Every other month soldiers were mustered for pay, but they did not actually receive the money at the time of the muster; it was simply a time to record information on which payments would be based. Pay was often tardy, sometimes more than six months, and was very meager ranging from thirteen to sixteen dollars a month for privates over the course of the war. Bell Irvin Wiley, *The Life of Billy Yank, The Common Soldier of the Union* (1978; repr., Baton Rouge: Louisiana State University, 1991), 48–49.

⇢ AMOS TO SAM ⇠
Aberdeen, Ohio / May 4, 1862

Dear Brother,

Yours of the 12th of Apr came to hand the 22nd. It is the only one I rec'd from you since you left. We are all well at present. The past week I was severely salinated so much so that it ulcerated my bowels & gave me scissors so I could hardly walk though lost no time. The neighbors are well as usual. I have just returned from P. J. Lane's burying at Fitch's. There is no mistake this time for he was opened.[1] He was buried with military & Masonic honours. We have just past a week of very fine weather & are nearly done breaking up [i.e., plowing]. We planted 20 acres on Amos Evan's place. I received the Union Neck Tie all right & Father his Hickory club &c. The war news looks very favorable (as we see all that is out in the Dailys).

There is nothing new here at present. So excuse haste & remember yours,

Amos A. Evans

P.S. Enclosed you will find a copy of Dixie for you & John

1. Jane's letter of April 28, 1862, relates the story of Presley Lane's attempted burial, where it was discovered that the army had sent home the body of a different man.

➤ SAM TO ANDREW ➤
Miss. / May 11, 1862

Dear Father,

John and I rec'd a joint letter from you last week. We were exceedingly glad to hear from home as it was the first that had found its way to us since we left Camp Chilae. Our mail has been very irregular since the battle at Pittsburgh [Battle of Shiloh]. Yesterday I received a letter from Amos and one from Mary. Tell them that I will answer them as soon as I get leisure. I also received a letter from Will Thursday that I intend to answer soon. I will give you a short description how our time is employed of late. Tuesday, April 29th, left Camp Chilae, camped about 5 miles toward Corinth, marched off the road a short distance, formed a line of battle and slept on our arms. Next morning, we started and marched 3 or 5 miles further where we camped 'til Sunday morning last. When we moved some 3 miles further at Camp No. 2, we built breast works. Friday last we moved to the camp that we now occupy, some 21/2 or 3 miles N.W. of Corinth. We have cut a new road all the way from Camp Chilae but 5 or 6 miles.

Everywhere we have been in Tennessee is a perfect wilderness. I have not seen more than 10 or 17 acres cleared in one place in Tenn. The soil is a red sandy clay, timber oak and hickory. The land here generally lies well. The weather here has been very wet. It has not rained for a week. This is a strange climate. The day is very hot. The backs of hands of a great many of our soldiers are sunburned and are, or have, peeled off. You can imagine that there is some little inconvenience on account of the weather. We have to carry a heavy load through the hot sun or freeze through the night. We (most of us) choose the former.

We have not yet seen Corinth. Pickets are firing at each other every day. Yesterday the alarm was raised. It proved to be false. We have thrown up breast works here too. Our time is almost all employed in some way or other. Pickets, regimental, guard, fatigue parties, etc.[1] We go to bed at 9:00 o'clock P.M. and are called out in line of battle at 3:00 o'clock A.M. so we sleep but little.

You asked me whether I think I killed any secesh, I will not say positively but give you some circumstantial evidence for you to form your own conclusion. First, we were ordered to fall back behind our camp, which we did, while I saw 3 "Brown backs" [rebels] come to one of our tents. One put his hand in the door and pulled it open than put his head in to look around. I was about 70 or 80 yds. off. I leveled my Endfield [sic] at 3 that were in range (including the first described). When the gun cracked, he let go of the tent. On Tuesday morning after the battle, I went to the place where I tried to shoot a man found one there with a hole throu his body near the spot I aimed at (no other person having shot at him.) The bullet struck him about 8 inches below arm pit.

Second . . . Our regiment was ordered back. I did not hear the order and kept firing on the Rebels after the regiment had gone back. Some bushwhackers had advanced very near me, as near as 50 yards. I had shot off my gun at some men [sic] a little further off and he shot very near me. I hurried to load, so did he. I spilled a little of my powder. I succeeded in beating him load. He put his head out from behind the tree, as he did it, I was ready to shoot. When my gun went off he tumbled. The first opportunity I had, I examined him. The temple artery was cut off. He bled very nice. These are the more noted cases. But some others I think felt my bullets. My wound was from a spent grape shot or rather it glanced off a tree by my side and made a considerable bruise. You want to know how I felt in battle, well I felt like shooting every fella I could see, fore I think my hair raised a little and I felt like I could shoot every secesh in the land and feel good over it. Whenever cannon balls and shells come whizzing by, when we were too far off to shoot with effect, I did not like it especially when it is near enough to smell. I jumped one cannon ball that came rolling by. A man was cut into by a ball and it knocked the blood in my face. Not boasting or anything of the kind, I think I am a better soldier than I thought I was. A great many of the men did not stand as well as they should have done. It is not strange why it was. They were surprised.

John and I are moderately well. The mail will start soon. I will close. Give love and respects to all the family. Reserve a full share yourself.

Your Son,
Sam Evans

1. Picket and guard duty are actually both types of duty that involved guarding the camp. Guard duty was done right around the camp while picket lines were out much further in front of the camp. It is not clear what Sam meant by regimental duty, although it is likely that he either meant regimental drill or that he intended to leave out the comma and refer to guard duty and regimental guard duty. Fatigue parties were responsible for cleaning and maintaining the campsite.

❧ GEORGE W. EARLY TO FRIENDS ❧
Ripley, Ohio / May 14, 1862

Dear Friends:

Being in Ripley this afternoon on my way home from Georgetown, and seeing Wm Bonman, who starts to night for Pittsburg Landing to resume his position in Fosters cavalry company. I will send the news as far as I know. I left home on Monday morning. The friends of all so far as I could learn were in common health. I just now saw Saml Hiett who left Pittsburg on Thursday morning and arrived at Ripley on Monday night. He is improving some, but looks pretty slim. He told me as much as he knew about you. although he had not seen you boys for some time. He says that some of the Aberdeen Boys came with him. All doing pretty well. Friends: you have all had a hard time. and we sympathise with you, and are willing to do all we can for you. If the cause was not good, you would all be at home. For you have suffered considerably. My opinion is that you will all soon return to your quiet homes. where you can enjoy peace and quietude once more. From the news in the papers, you are, or have been fighting. I hope if you have that you have killed all of them or enough to settle the thing, and all of you came off without a scratch. I have written several letters lately and told all the news. Consequently I will close this soon. All of you must write to me as often as you can and if you need any thing that can be sent easily, first tell me, and I will do my best to accommodate all of you. This letter is written to all of you that I am acquainted with, and all else who wish to know. I will send it to Lieut. Adams and he can read it to you. Mrs. Adams & children were well on Sunday. Hat was to see her Sunday evening. Write soon. From a true friend to his friends who are fighting for our country.

G.W. Early

Home / May 16, 1862

Dear Sam,

I deeply regret to be under the painful necessity of informing you that we had to undergo the task of following our beloved son, Abraham, to his final resting place.[1] He departed for the spirit land on Wednesday, the 14th, at 5 o'clock PM and was interred yesterday evening at one-half past 4 at "Fitches Chapel" with masonic honors in presence of a very large concourse of people. He rode on horseback to Wesley Kimble on Monday evening, stayed all night, and returned home Tuesday evening, walked up to town and talked with his friends as lively as usual. He returned down to his house, ate his supper and went to bed as usual. In the night he became restless and took some laudanum to enable him to rest. Wednesday I called in to see how he was about 10 AM and stayed a half hour with him. He was dull and flighty but said he was under the influence of laudanum and would be alright as soon as that passed off. I came home and he was taken worse at 2 PM and I suppose grew worse all afternoon. Cap Sharp sent Frank out to notify us. I started immediately but he was laid out and draped before I got there. He, nor any of his friends, had the least idea of his final dissolution being so close at hand, consequently none of us were there when he died. His friends in town did everything for him that we could have done. Among the prominent of them is L. W. Dennis & wife, who were untiring in their efforts, both, to minister to his wants while living, and in preparing for his interrment after his death. Those who were present say he prayed for some time before he died, and among the last words he spoke were, "I see the pillars of the Temple I am going to reside in." He is said to have died calmly and in his senses. His sudden and unexpected death has almost unnerved his wife. She will have to break up housekeeping. She will probably go to her father. No positive arrangements have been made. Our family all attended the funeral except Inda who was not sufficiently recovered to go. The Maysville, Ripley and Aberdeen Fraternities were in attendance, the ceremonies given by a gentleman from Maysville (whose name I did not learn), and were the finest I ever heard on any funeral occasion.[2]

Our health is about as usual, your Mother is quite weak. though she is going about, and tries to work. Mary is looking quite well, she was doury when you left home. The sore eyes from measles are nearly well. All your friends here are in usual health Inda's recovery has been very slow, though she is up and moving about now. She has a very large hearty boy. They call him Sam.

We are having a very dry spell, no rain since the 20th of April except a mere sprinkle. Vegetation is suffering severely for want of rain, some farmers have not commenced planting corn, others have commenced and quit for rain to come, we have all planted, and some is coming up but unless rain come soon it cannot do any good, it is cloudy now with a good prospect for rain soon. We have just finished our stone fence below the front gate with the exception of corn bin. we built it thicker and higher than it used to be. We will try to finish the big wall next week.

Will is helping Cannon to assess; creek nearly dry, no grinding has been done for three weeks. I advise him to sell the toll wheat, for if he grinds it he will create a new set of debts instead of collecting those you left for him to collect. There are plenty of applications for flour with a desire to pay for it after harvest. No go! Here these days, he has had nothing done to the race or dam yet. Sam Hiett is at home but I have not seen him yet. George had a talk with him yesterday, we got news much sooner by those returned soldiers than by the mail, which I think is not right. The mails should travel as fast as a passenger. I received yours of the 1st after I had finished John's on Sunday evening I added a slip acknowledging yours, I can't tell why you don't get letters for we start 2 or 3 a week regularly.

You speak of receiving one of mine addressed to Co. H. I may have the mark on the F low enough to make look like H but not otherwise, for I never forget the Co. F. Keep writing when you can, we have no letter this week.

Your father,
Andrew Evans

1. Abraham was William's twin brother. See Andrew's letter of March 9, 1862.
2. Maysville, Kentucky, was located just across the Ohio River from Aberdeen, Ohio, the closest town to the Evans home.

⇾ SAM TO ANDREW AND MARY (MOTHER) ⇾
Miss., within "bomb shot" of Corinth / May 24, 1862
Dear Father & Mother,

I undertake to write you a few lines. I do not know whether I can interest you or not. I may succeed in keeping your attention for a while. At any rate I hope you will please "take the will for the deed and all will be right." John received a letter from you, Mary and Ibbe yesterday. Yesterday I wrote to Amos and today write for John. All the forenoon I have been tending to John, washing and putting on clean clothes. Well, of course, you would rather know how he is than anything else I can write. Yesterday I wrote as near as I could his situation [this letter was not preserved]. I do not see much change in him today. His medicine is acting pretty freely. He has vomited considerably. I think it is a billious attack. All he vomits is bile or looks so. He is rather cheerful today, wants squirrel soup but it cannot be had. There is good beef soup. A sick man thinks what he has to eat is not good. I think the sick here have better than we had at Paducah. The Dr. thought John was taking Typhoid fever but today he thinks he will get along without it, no fever today at all. Very nice weather today, cool and pleasant, nice wind. I think when John is through taking what medicine he has on hand he will be better. The medicine acts as it is intended, which is favorable. I will do all I can in keeping up his spirits, waiting upon him and keeping him clean and he shall get as good eatables as can be had here. You need not fear that I will not do all in my power. I will say further for your satisfaction that Doc Heatow thinks he is not dangerous, though quite sick. The hospital tent is in a good place, is kept well aired and clean and has a sweet smell as can be for the number. There are 17 in now few of whom are not very sick. Jesse Howland is one of the inmates of the hospital and is quite sick with Typhoid fever, no others that you know. John Hiett has been sick in the hospital at Hamburg. Came back to the Reg't to day; he is almost well. All the rest of the Boys that were there from our Reg't are mending fast. I believe there is some improvement in the general health of the army here. Both of the Lieuts of Co F have been quite sick almost off duty. They are a lot better. I think besides this they are both Gentleman, have been to me so far. Dr. Phillips is convalescent and the talk is he is going home soon. He did not receive his pay for what he has done and I have understood that he cannot in consequence of some informality in his official papers to the paymaster. As to the correctness of this I cannot say, I give it as I got it. The Col did not take any pay because he could not get pay for all the time he was engaged in making up the Regiment.

This camp news, too. The paymaster is here paying off our brigade. If we remain here a few days we will be paid too. I wrote in Amos' letter that we expected to move on today. That order was not imperative and is countermanded. If you want [to] find "Knownothingness" in its purity just come into the army and you can find it from a Col down to a private. If on a march you ask, "Where are you going?" the answer is, "I don't know." The same way with subordinate officers, all is kept dark from us that can be kept. While I think of it, the prisoners take[n] from the 70th on Friday before the battle of Chiloh have returned to Gen Halleck's head quarters. (Except Hubbert and a corporal, they will not let officers loose on parole.) The privates are freed on parole and if they are exchanged they are at liberty to take up arms again.[1] They say that part of the time they eat "mule beef" and that the Rebels had not very plenty to eat. Rac Sutton is one that was prisoner. Wiles Co is unfortunate, lost 8 prisoners, 12 have deserted, some died of disease, some of wounds, and a few killed. Any quantity of "ordinary" men, fool's and— —asses. Stop! I will talk hard, it [is] so though.

The siege guns belonging to this division are stationed on a point a 1/ 4 of a mile from us on our left, six in No 5 32 pounders, and one 64 lb mortor. These are well supported by smaller cannon and infantry. Our pickets were attacked yesterday morning by superior numbers. They maintained their ground till a part of our brigade went to their assistance (3 or 4 Co's from the 8 Missouri) who pitched into them whooping and yelling like Indians. They made them skeedaddle. Went in and took possession of their camp. Took all the over coats, blankets, such other things as they wanted, sat down and eat the breakfast the secesh had prepared for themselves. Then gave them another chase. Returned to camp then with no loss having killed 8 secesh and wounding several. Took 2 prisoners. Today a company of the 70th brought in three prisoners they took while out on picket. So you see we are doing some good. We are on the extreme right except 1 Reg't, 53 Ohio. All has been quiet in front of us. The enemy is trying to flank our left and maybe the right. Gen Pope has a fine trap for Beauregard. Pope has a fine brest works in front with an open piece in it for the enemy to break into. Then Pope has his arranged to hammer that point. Let Mr. Beauregard try him. There is not a great deal of news that I know, that would be of much interest [to] you. I will now give you the market. Whisky $1.00 pr pint, butter 50 @ 1 lb, eggs from 30 to 60 cts per doz. Writing paper 2 to 3 sheets of 5 cts. Stamps 5 cts. Dried apples 25 cts per lb., peaches 40, cheese 25 or 15 cs @ pint. Other things in proportion. Well not withstanding these exorbitant prices, there are plenty of buyers. Not I for one. There is one thing that I did not tell Will or any one else to do. I forgot the listing of my property to the Assessor. If it is not too late and you can do it, will satisfy you for doing or Will can do it. You have the value of my tracks and pounds of iron steel and lumber. Oh, I forgot to tell you I was well as I can expect and am very well satisfied with what I have done in leaving home and going to war. You can see now that there are not more troops than we need. I have just received a letter from George and one from Burke. They have date of the 7 of May, also one from Aunt Diana. I am glad to hear you are all tolerably well and done planting corn. I fear you will be over tasked in reading this, consequently I stop. Give my respects to all relations and friends who make inquiry about me and Grandmother in particular.

Remember me kindly to all the family. Continue to write occasionally and I will do the same.

Good by father & mother. I subscribe myself,

Your undutiful Son,

Sam Evans

1. After the enormous capture of prisoners at Fort Donelson, the federal government succumbed to mounting Confederate pressure for an exchange cartel and negotiated an agreement with the Confederate Army whereby all prisoners were to be exchanged, with privates one for one and a specified number of privates for each rank of officer (i.e., four privates per lieutenant, sixty privates per commanding general). All excess prisoners were to be paroled, promising not to take up arms until they had been officially exchanged. After operating for about ten months, this system collapsed in early 1863 amid controversy over Confederate refusals to treat captured freedmen soldiers as prisoners of war. The Confederate captors regarded these soldiers instead as escaped or rebellious slaves. James M. McPherson, *Battle Cry of Freedom* (Ballantine Books, 1988), 800–801.

⇥ AMOS TO SAM ⇤
The Old Desk / May 25, 1862

Dear Brother,

I rec'd yours of the 16th yesterday. It relieved my troubled brain very much. I had almost concluded that you thought but little of me or that you had taken offence at something that I had said, I trust it has not been so. We are all well this morning & enjoy the stillness of a bright sabbath morning with the air perfumed with the sweet odor of Flowers & Roses just blown [*sic*, bloomed] & in their most beautiful state. Will has gone to church, Burke & I will go soon. Ma & Peggy are going to see George White. Father is perusing the Daily with an anxious heart. His heart has become softened & as "Paul said 'No' as King Agrippa said unto Paul he is almost persuaded to be a Christian." May God grant that he may be. His afflictions & Ma's have been severe but I believe they will work for them a far more exceeding weight of Glory.

You spoke of persons talking about you in a manner you dont like, please name some of those. I have not heard any such talk, it may have been on my deaf side. All that I have heard in that way was the many complaints about Smithing, Milling & numerous other inconveniences, which they feel to their sorrow, But there is no private soldier in the whole army, I venture to say, that commands greater respect or greater praise than yourself. So don't believe all you hear on the dark side of any subject, but weigh them both you & John need not be uneasy about these things for many of them are false—while there are some tales afloat that are quite unfounded & discredited.

I am sorry to hear of those Boys being sick & particularly those that are near & dear to me. Let them trust in God & do well. James Helm, Sam Martin & others have rec'd letters from you & seem proud of them. Helm was raised nearly out of his Boots. The Lodge has added some two or three members lately. Mary Campbell returned to her house on the 14th. She looks very well all of the folks down there would like to see you & John. They will have a strawberry supper soon. The managers have given me a free ticket for my kindness & labors. I must close with acts very briefly spoken of.

Walter and Andrew's funerals were preached by Rev. Pangburn last Sabbath. Matthew & he took dinner here Monday. Lane's funeral will be preached next Sunday. Doc's will be preached soon.

Father talks of writing to John today. He, with Pat and Gilmore (our rattlesnake Irishman) filled your mill dam this week in one day. It had washed all the dirt of the rocks to the bottom. I wish you could get the good water you wanted and I would like to bring it—but Our parents won't let me go from home far for fear I might go without leave. I will not leave them, for God knows I love & respect them. Give my love to all. Write when you feel like it & excuse this badly blotted sheet for my hands are worn out & stiff handling stone. We will send you paper if possible. Grand Ma sends her love to all the boys and particularly to Sam.

Good by,

Amos

Love God and obey him & I will do the same

Home / June 1, 1862

Dear Brother,

I will now commence another letter to you as the one I commenced got torn up I received your letter of the 19th it was eleven days old when I got it. It gives me great pleasure to get a letter from either of you but I am sorry to hear that John is sick for I am afraid that he will not be well taken care of. I wish he was at home so we could do for him. we can't do anything for you so far away. some of the letters that come from there have pretty bad news. I don't believe there is two letters alike that comes from there. Have you got any more clothes yet? I think if you have not you must need them pretty bad by this time. I am sory to hear that so many of your boys are sick. Sam Hiett is at home; he is getting better slowly. we heard that David Games and Simpson were going to start tomorrow morning to camp but it is not so they will not go. George White and Jim King have both been worse since they were brought from the Hospital at Cincinnati. Jane got a letter from John Mc yesterday it was dated the 22. He said John [Evans] was in the hospital and that he was a little better. Sam there is to be a large supper at Abberdeen Tuesday night, it is said to be for the benefit of the soldiers. I don't know how it will turn out yet. Lida has moved down to her father's since Abe's death.[1] His death was unexpected at that time. There was not one of us seen him die. Well he has gone to his bed of rest his sufferings are all over; he can now sleep in peace.

We had a nice shower here last night it made the things look bright and lively. Pap was up to see Sam Hiett this morning. Amos has gone to town to see if there is any letters there from Camp. I wish there might be some. The corn is not doing very well here this season. We will have a good deal of fruit if nothing happens to it till it gets ripe. Sam, try and not let the secesh get a hold of you if you can help it. Pap was at town yesterday and Sharp gave him a hand full of cotton seed that was sent from the patent office in packages.

All the folks are well as common around here as far as I know. Presly J. Lanes property is to be appraised the 10th day of this month Pap is one of the appraisors Ike is here. Burke said he wishes you were here to help him talk to him and to hug and squeeze Big Jane and Little Jane, Jane received a letter from you this evening; I heard it read. Grand mother is well and sends her love. And all the Abberdeen girls sends you their love also I give my respects all the Boys and my best love to you and John

Good Bye your Sister

Mary Evans

tell John I will write him soon

Sam these are my lines remember me as I remember John and thee

Burke

1. Lida was apparently a nickname for Eliza, widow of Abraham Evans, Will Evans's deceased twin.

⟫ GEORGE W. EARLY TO SAM ⟪

June 2, 1862

Brother Sam,

I hear that some of the boys are to return this eve to the 70 and I will send a few lines to you & John. Our health is only tolerably good. India has been quite feeble for some time, but is able to sit up and sew but not able to work much.

We call our boy for you and John "Samuel Benjamin Early."[1] He is a fine looking fellow. Granny and the rest of the folks up the hill are well as common. Pap's folks are tolerably well. The health is generally pretty good.

I have not heard who are going but guess James Waldron is one of them. there are several that might go. I expect I suppose you wish to know how the Good Templars are getting along.[2] Well, they are improving some. There have been two initiations since your departure and three propositions ready now, and accepted I think.

Cal looks about as well as she used to, but perhaps feels a little more lonesome.

The girls who used to attend regular still do the same. The order will not progress very much till all of the boys return. Elijah Proter starts tonight after his Brother Sam. And if you see him and can send John home do so. I have not seen Elijah but Harriet said he was going and she has to go and stay with Ellen while he is gone.

How many letters have you got from me? I have written four or five and never recd. but one.

Write as soon as you can. Excuse all mistakes for I am in a hurry. India is going to write to you soon, Sends her love to all of you.

Yours etc.

G. W. Early

1. Benjamin is John Evans's middle name.

2. The Templars were a temperance society with numerous lodges in Ohio. Byron Williams, *History of Clermont and Brown Counties, Ohio, from the earliest historical times down to the present* (Milford, Ohio: Hobart Pub. Co., 1913), Vol. 1. Historical, 398.

⇾ JANE TO SAM ⇽
June 2, 1862

Dear Cousin,

I received your kind letter yesterday that was written on 25th of May. I was truly glad to here from you that you was well. I was very sorry when I heared that John was sick. I hope that he will get well if he is well taken care of. We heared last Thursday that all of the Rebels had left Corinth, that was very good news, but I expect they will go some place and slip onto our boys and whip them if they can, but it seems like they don't gain very many victories. I hope they won't. I would be very glad if you would not have to be in another Battle. I hope that you will be spared so that you may come home and see us all once more. You say that you heard that Big Jane left our house. She has not, she is here yet. She went home about four weeks ago and stayed a week just after she had the measles. The measles did not hurt me much. I only was in bed to days. I would not went to bed but they told me I would get well sooner. You said that Cal C. never gave you her love before. If that was the first time you might be a talking. I guess I have heard her talk and you have to more than I have, I expect. Sam give my love and respects to John Evans and tell him that I would come and see him if it was not so far. Tell him to keep in good heart. I hope that we may live to see each other again. If we never meet no more on earth, I hope that we will meet in heaven. Big Jane and I was down to your father's yesterday. The folks are all well as common. I was at your house when I received your letter. Amos went down to see if he could hear from you boys. The folks was all very glad to hear from you and John. George Early's folks are well as usual; I was there this morning. Tom Simons and James Waldron and two or three others are going to start for the Regiment this evening. I will have a chance to send this letter to you. Our folks are all well as common. I hope that this may find you in good health. Grandmother sends her love and respects to you and would like very well to see you. She say that she is a going to write to you now soon.

Give my love to boys and receive a portion for yourself. Pap and mother and all send their love to you. I believe that I have told you all the news. Please write soon. No more at present but remain your affection.

Cousin,

Jane Evans

≫ WILL TO SAM ≪
Aberdeen, Ohio / June 6, 1862

Mr. Samuel Evans

Dear Brother:

I have just witnessed one of the most splendid affairs in the way of a supper I ever saw. We, Cal, Jenny and Mary Thompy, Mary Power, Virge, Lancy, Mollie Cs, Clara S & Charlie Dawson & myself did all the decorating & arranging. The town hall was covered almost with roses, pictures, & c. Overhead were robes of Cedar and roses suspended in ground-like style. Said to be the best ever in town. In each corner fronting the doors was Ice Cream strawberry & cream & cake table. In the front right hand corner was a candy, nut, orange & lemonade table—The speakers stand or platform was moved over on the opposite side curtained & robed with roses for the Maysville band—in it's place was a Queen's-wear toys bouquet & fancy table—I got the stenciling and painted a sign on canvas— Lucy and Jennie wreathed it with a border of Abivito & roses & suspended it in a conspicuous place. "For the benefit of the sick and wounded soldiers" was our motto & design, some things we bought and others were given to us. Candies & toys we bought at cost. Ice cream, we furnished all and got made for 60 cts gallon—.10 was the admittance. Two of the above-named girls were at each table—Frank, Charlie, Amos, John B. C. and myself, one at each door, our receipts for the two nights (June 3&4) were $110.18—the boys and girls galavanted each other around the room for some time enjoying themselves in the highest degree, the 2nd night ended in a dance. Cal said her "feller was not there". The band played Bells of the Mother Dale. I thought it was the purtiest thing I ever heard. Cal & Mary Carp listened a while then tears came trinkling down their cheeks. Cal said she looked up and saw our motto (For the benefit of sick and wounded soldiers) and she could not control her feelings. So ended our supper.

I am sorry to hear of John's illness. Poor fellow, I know he would like to be at home though I am certain you do all you have a chance to. I hope he may speedy recover, for tis hard enough to be a well soldier, truly.

I have sold your wheat, had in all 73 bush, for 90 cts; had to pay 4 cts for bus, for bailing, net price 86 cts. I listed your property, can't mind now how much but I put it low. I will ascertain if your tax is paid. If not I will pay it off, I will soon be able to square books with A. B. Have not sued anyone yet but if I can get a hold on Moore I'll walk him up.

W. H. E.

[illegible postscript]

⟩ ANDREW TO JOHN ⟨
Home / June 8, 1862

Dear John,

It is painful news to us to hear that you are sick so far from home. If it were in our power to render to you assistance in your afflictions, it would be freely given. When the distance is so great and mail facilities so poor, we cannot tell your condition till many days after it is past. We have been receiving news for several days that you were sick but in what degree, or what disease, we cannot learn. Jane received a letter from Sam (dated 25 May) on last Sunday stating you were sick. I received one on Friday last (dated 24) stating that he had written the particulars of your case as near as he could to Amos A. (which letter has not come to hand yet), so we are still in the dark. Only that Sam says in our letter that Dr. Heatow says that you are not dangerous, though very sick. George received a letter from Sam (dated 26 & 27 May) on friday last stating that you were some better at the time. I hope your convalesce will continue until you become stout. We have reason to hope that since Corrinth is evacuated you will have better chances to be nursed properly, and that if you recover sufficiently, you may be allowed to come home and regain your health. If there is anything we can do to affect an object so desirable, please inform us of the fact. We are perfectly satisfied that Sam will do anything for you that he can do, to either relieve your suffering or enable you to enjoy yourself as well as a sick soldier can in camp so far from home. John, we desire you to be exceedingly careful of yourself in your recovery for a small imprudent act may easily get a convalescent soldier on his back again.

Will has written to Sam and given the news of the day which I need not repeat as you will see or hear it. We have had several good rains within a week past and our crops are looking much better than when I wrote you last. Corn is coming up that has been in the ground since first May. We may have fair corn yet, wheat is injured by the drought. Oats good for nothing, fruit is much injured by the dry weather. Our small fruits are very fine, currants, gooseberries, strawberries, pie over such as we just had at dinner. Amos has just returned from church. He says David Games expects to start to Cincin. tomorrow and if the post surgeon think him fit for duty he will go on to his regiment. We will start these letters by him, if he returns he will mail them at the city. My respects to my friends,

Truly your Father,
Andrew Evans

❧ SAM TO ANDREW ❧
Tenn 19 miles from Grand Junction / June 12, 1862
Dear Father:

I received your welcome letter on the 9th by hand of James Waldron, also 4 quires of note paper, 3 packages of envelops including 1 of post paid, fine camp & c, also a couple of letters from you and George to John. I am sorry I have had no chance to send them with his portion of the paper & envelops to him. Our sick were sent back to the post hospital when we were starting on march. I saw no opportunity to forward to him, consequently I have to carry them. As we left Ch[illegible], Our teams come in, told me John was much better and that all the sick at the hospital would be sent home. If that is so he will be at hom[e] long before this reaches you.

We started for Grand Junction on Monday evening last and thence to Memphis. As we proceed the bridges have to be repaired. The roads are good except very dusty. You would naturally suppose that 1000 wagons [and] 12,000 or 13,000 men would make dust when roads were dry. How nice it mixes with sweat. The country we have been yet is poor, not better than "Swamp country", no good houses or improvements yet, but I think it looks some thing better as we proceed farther West, our march is nearly due West. People have planted some corn here in creek bottoms, it is waist high, rather spotted. We have only been marching eight to 10 miles per day. Yesterday we marched 8 miles from 3 till 8 PM. The health of this army seem[s] to be improving since we commenced march. Nearly all the houses seem to be inhabited. The men have returned, those that were away all have to take the oath where ever Gen Sherman goes. Sherman division is all that is marching this road that I know of. [I] Will finish another day, have not time now.

Lagrange, Tenn Saturday / June 14

Being on march some time we have not time to write and no opportunity to send them. The above name place is nicely situated on Memphis & Charleston R.R., pretty well built. Part of our division occupys a nice female college (that is formerly Female College) for their quarters, Lagrange contains 2 churches, court House, several stores, groceries and work shops. Business here is about gone up. Some little establishments are open and selling to Soldiers. U.S. money passes with some of the citizens, Southern Scrip with some, some will take nothing but Gold and silver. Most of the citizens are rather shy looking. The stars and stripes float over the Court House. Boys running for something to eat of the vegetable character, maybe the reason [is that] we passed a few very nice plantations, saw green cotton. It look a little like field peas planted on ridges 4 or five feet apart 1 way, 8 to ten inches the other. Wheat along the road is almost all cut, we would [think] it a very short crop, not more than 2 or 3 bus per acre.

Well I can't write, I feel tired and drowzy. We were up at 1/2 past 2 Oclock this morning in order to march very early. It is quite warm at Noon these days to carry knap sack, haversack, canteen and equipments, in order to avoid this was the reason for so early marching.[1] Water is scarce for so large an army to pass. I can do well on what we get. I have no doubt you think we live hard, Sleeping on the ground, crackers, fat pork and coffee (the latter we can't have allways on march) for eatables. Well you are not much mistaken but it looks a great deal worse than it is once one is into it. All is right, some of the boys are nearly always grumbling, but I like it very well, rather better than I thought I would, though I would not admire going much further South in hot weather. I am pretty lean but can stand fatigue [duty] if it does not require great strength. I feel moderately well but do not feel very stout. Still have heard nothing from John since we left Ch[illegible]. The Regt stands march well. Oh! I forgot to tell you my toes were a little soar. The boots I wore away are good yet. The same pants, vest, hat, socks and suspenders are still the best, I have about such as I wear at home. A great deal of the clothing is pretty ragged. The 70th will be paid for 2 months to night. The Paymaster is now nearly done paying the 72 O[hio] and then the 70 next on the roll. I would send what I get home if I could but, while on march no chance to do anything. there are no Secesh troop[s] any where near hear, if so, we can not find them. Cannot tell where they have gone. We see where they have been, all the cotton through here has been burned.

I thank you very kindly for all you have sent me although the "louse trap" is not needed for what they are generally. There is not much of interest to write, we don't know how long we will stay here or where we will be ordered. Sherman said we would have light [duty] to perform till we rested. He said, so I heard, that all the army here would be at home by the last of July. I don't believe it. If we live to get home safe and sound I will be perfectly satisfied and the object for which we came out should be justly and satisfactorily settled. Direct your letters as formerly. I shall continue to write as often as opportunity offers. It does me great good to get a letter from home. Give my love and respects to [the rest] of the family, Grandmother, George & India and the rest of man kind and Woman kind and believe me to be

Your affectionate son,

S. Evans

1. A haversack was a bag used to carry personal possessions and rations. They were typically worn with the strap over the soldier's right shoulder and the bag resting near his left hip. Web Garrison and Cheryl Garrison, *The Encyclopedia of Civil War Usage: An Illustrated Compendium of the Everyday Language of Soldiers and Civilians* (Nashville: Cumberland House, 2001), 107.

➤ AMOS TO SAM ◄
Home / June 15, 1862

Dear Brother Sam,

I again undertake what I feel quite incompetent to do in a manner that will give satisfaction. This a pleasant Eve after a warm dry day. Mary, Belle, Burke & I have just returned from Ebenezer.[1] We heard an interesting though short sermon by Bamsey. We are at present in moderate health. Ann has been very unwell but is now about as usual. Father was sick at the stomach yesterday, now all right. I had severe attack of the Lungs this week & yet feel very much bound in the chest when breathing. I am slowly mending. Grand Ma is well but she seems very lonesome &

poor [in health] much poorer than I ever saw her. All the rest as far as reported—all right. I rec'd yours of the 23rd on the 9th of June long after it was due yet it gave me the satisfaction to know you think of me as well as others—for my part I am ashamed I did not write oftener. Father & Will took my turn out of my hand some three or four times when I had not the chance to begin first. They sent several with David Games when he started. I suppose he sent them on with Shelton & Dragoo when he was discharged. His discharge was final. Simpson is (discharged) very much scorned & disgraced. Hiett is better; James R. King is mending very slowly. I have heard but little about the other boys. Father will write in a few days. I met Cal-C-last night. She stopped me and told me she had just rec'd a letter from you of June 6th & only read part. She told me John was still better but the camp was unhealthy & that you were repairing Locomotives just what I told the folks when I heard it was being done. Success to your trade & health to accompany you all in your great work. We have been expecting letters today but Will has not returned. So we still await them patiently. Do you get any extras at your trade? & how do you like the business & will you follow it. Where is Ammen? Fyffe & Co.? &c &c.[2]

Will rode all this week collecting for you—had moderate success some places. He has notified nearly all to walk up or he would call. Harvest has already commenced Some early wheat out. Ours will do in a week or 10 days. Corn is a little the worse of dry weather not over it the 2nd time yet. Pat left yesterday,[3] will work for Dyas a while.[4] Dyas has had his house upset & veranda in front. It looks sevengable [salvageable]. David Tarbell has a new office underway between stables & the tailor shop. These are the infernal improvements of the day. It does us much good to hear that John is getting well. We hope his health will still improve. You need not fear about our prayers for we supplicate the throne of grace daily in your behalf & of our country. Do not forget to aid us with your prayers. We trust you will not falter in your duty to God or your country. We do the best we can & hope for the rest. Lest I provoke you, I will not weary your patience with a long letter without life or interest. Write often, give my love & compliments to all the Boys & Except a Brotherly Share yourself. I will send you some stamps as soon as I can send them by private hand.

Yours in Brotherhood,

Amos

1. Throughout the letters Sam's sister Isabella is frequently referred to as Belle or Bell.

2. This is Jacob Ammen, a Brown County native who had volunteered as a private two days after the firing on Fort Sumter. Owing to his West Point education and his prior experience as a lieutenant in the regular army, he rose rapidly by both election and commission so that by the first summer of the war he was commanding colonel of the 24th Ohio Infantry. His service at Shiloh and in the Corinth campaign earned him promotion to brigadier general. Carl N. Thompson, *Historical Collections of Brown County, Ohio* (Piqua, Ohio: Hammer Graphics, 1969), 574–76.

3. Pat was probably one of the Evans's hired hands.

4. Dyas Gilbert was a farmer, thirty-one years old at the time, who lived in the same township as the Evans family. Josiah Morrow, *History of Brown County Ohio* (Chicago: W.H. Beers, 1883), Biography Section, 162–63.

❧ AMOS TO JOHN ❦
Our office / June 16, 1862

Dear Brother John,

It is a shame to think that I have not written to you since the 24th of May but the rest of them took a siege of writing nearly every day & I wanted a chance to send some news so it was put off from day to day until now . . . First to note the Good Templars took in 2 new members Rebeccah Carpenter & Miss Cobb (Geo Riders kin folks) the house was full.

Candidates David Tarbal & E. C. Devore are out for prosecuting attorneys. J. C. Waldron for Auditor &c &c. James S. Burke is out (in his new suit tonight) [illegible] Well I guess matrimony. This is his first set [*sic*, suit] since he has been here. Let him pitch in if he can.

Andrew Wood joined church at Bethelham last evening &c. We were at church to day & all the girls had to have a look at John in Mary's breast pin.[1] They would much rather see the original. At the sold[ier] supper a number of the girls longed for you & Sam. Miss Lucy D. sends her compliments. Also Miss Mary E. Humphrey & a number of others, too many to Single out. I had a grand time at my table. Mary Humphrey & Leanrd Sinder of Ripley were visitors at our Seat all of both nights. I put them through some considerable.

They had a big supper at Maysville to repair the church. The same week Thurs. & Friday & also one at Ripley for an alike purpose. It is said they did not compare well with ours. The boys write home some good ones about going into Corinth & the way they found things. Well it is time to go to roost & I want to put a deadener on the Itch. I tried some of the quack & bogus remedys & they nearly killed me without affecting the Itch one bit & I just told them it was no use. I was a going to use sulphur so I will dab it on . . .

Write often & oblige yours truly

Amos Evans

P.S. There is a girl close here told some folks she had received a letter from you once a week since you left Riply this will do pretty well for a sold.

1. The breast pin is probably a photo or sketch of John.

⇒ MARY EVANS (GRANDMOTHER) TO SAM ⇐
Aberdeen, Ohio / June 21, 1862

My Dear Grand Son:

I have neglected writing to you for so long so I thought to myself that I must get Jane to write you a letter for me to day. I am well as common and I hope that this few lines may find you enjoying good health. Burke got a letter from you the 18th he and Will and Amos was up here the other night, and Will read the letter for us. I am very glad to hear from you and that John is getting better. John is a good peace off to be sick. Sam, you don't know how well that I would like to see you. It seems like a good while since you went to war and I know that you would like to be at home for a while. You would rather be here in the shop than where you are, and go to see the girls when you want to. Your father is harvesting today. I seen Will and Amos a cradling and Burke a binding and your father a shocking. They have not got poor John to help them like they had last year. Old Pat has left your house. He is working for Dyas Gilbert, building a stone fence for him. Your Aunt Angeline was at Aberdeen today, she brought me a letter from your Uncle Abe's Elizabeth. They are all as well as common. Benjamin Evans that lived with the girls out there volunteered and went to war, and died since. Elizabeth said that Marian Ken's Cousin has come to stay with them this summer. Your Uncle Abe's Will has had the measles and after he had them a while he took the fevers. Elizabeth said that the measles affected his eyes so that he could never see good anymore. Big John has got another soldier [baby]. I suppose you have heard that Sarah wanted to call it for you and big John said that you was too far off to name it for you. Little Jane looked for a letter from some of your boys today but she did not get nary one. Sam, I will not be so long next time about answering your letter.

Give my love to John Evans, John McNilse, Doc. Phillips and the rest of the friends and receive a full share for yourself. No more at present but remain your affection grandmother

Mary Evans

Please write soon

Sam I don't expect you can read this. I did not write it very good. Give my love to the boys and receive a portion for yourself

Jane Evans[1]

1. Jane Evans wrote this from grandmother Mary Housh Evans's dictation. Grandmother Mary lived with Jane and Jane's mother, Angeline. The head of the house was Andrew's brother Amos.

⇢ WILL TO SAM ⇠
Aberdeen, Ohio / June 25, 1862

Dear Brother,

I have just received a letter from Bro. John, he is now at Cincinnati. He came there Sunday evening. He stoped at the Soldiers' home & awaits the arival of money which I expected this morning. He says he can come home without assistance—will come home Friday or Saturday. Bro, I would be glad to see you but for the present must relinquish hopes for the future, will have strong faith & await your coming. Nothing of importance has occurred since I wrote to you. Or since at least the date of some of your letters brought you by Wm. Case.

James McLawwill returned last night. David Maddox & Phillip Hawk arrived Monday evening are in modest health. John states in his letter that he had not herd from you since he left Montery. I sent him word that you thought perhaps you were going to Grand Junc.

We are done cutting early Wheat. The other we'll do in a few days. Bob Ridley has been pitching in himself—has no hand. Little Jane has helped in Backie [tobacco], making hills & setting. G. W. Early is at present distributing his Brownlows. I paid your semi-annual Tax, $6—& something —few cents. Have made some collections—Folks are slow in paying. Had I better not sue James Corrigan—guess he won't pay without. J. W. Moore still promises, but no money. Will sue him, or most any to get the money. I have an arrangement to trap him perhaps. Father is granting some with his side as Taxes. Write when you feel like it—we always feel like getting them.

Excuse haste—Remember me to all my friends receive my best wishes for your welfare & oblige

your Brother,

W. H. Evans

P.S. John has a furlough for 40 days.

⇒ ANDREW TO SAM ⇐
Home / July 3, 1862

Dear Sam,

I received yours of the 12 and 14 June on last night 1/2 past 10, which is the only one from you since yours of June 9th to Burke. We have passed an unusual interval without any news from you. John wrote us from Cincinnati on last Monday week, which was the first news we had from him since you wrote. He arrived in the City on Sunday the 22nd and at home on the 29th. He was able to walk a little with a cane and was about as poor a man as you saw (dead or alive). He is improving very sensably. His diarrhea is about dried up, his Urinary secretions are restored, his appetite fair and when we get the scales off his skin I think he will feel pretty well. The Perotoid glan of his right side is much swolen,[1] and from present appearances will superate before long.[2] It is giving him considerable pain and ear ache &c. Dr. Guthrey Jr. has visited him twice since he came home.[3] He advised us yesterday to promote superation for fear of internal injury.

John is gaining strength very well. He walked back to Inda's & back this morning and intends to go to his Grandmothers tomorrow if well enough. He has a furlough of 20 days from the 28th June, at the end of which time he will have to report in person if able, if not by certificate to the 4th St. Hospital in Cinti.

Our health is about as usual, your Mother is not stout at al. but keeps going, I am very moderate in health and strength. I slightly overworked myself in the beginning of harvest. I cradled and bound alternately, the first day, in order to keep two cradles going, it proved too hard for me, it stopped the action of my liver & kidneys for a few days which kept me rather uncomfortable for a few days. I am about as usual now except a little back ache. The residue of our family are well, so are all your friends and relations here abouts. The general health here is good, no epidemic or contagious disease prevailing here now. Inda is not very stout, but is gradually gaining, she has a healthy stout boy. Grandmother's health & strength is about as usual. We have had not news from the Buford people for some time. Sam Hiett is making a very slow recovery, though he is still on foot, George White will hardly ever be fit for service again. He can hardly sit up long enough to have his bed made, his hip is quite painful at times. Jimmy King is mending, he is able to sit up a little. Sawyers arm is mending very slowly, fractures of the bone are still coming out occasionally. It is believed now that he will be cured without amputating his arm. John Sibbald is not likely to return to his Regt. His health has farther declined since he came home with but little prospect on convalescence, "Sic transet & c".[4]

Our weather had been more favorable since I wrote you. Though still rather dry. We have a very favorable harvest season; no excessive hot weather, and many days very pleasant for harvest work, and no rain during our harvest to hinder successful operations on the wheat. Our wheat crop is a very fair one, the best in five years past. I think ours will go 20 bushels to the acre. There are many good crops in the neighborhood, some are thin on the ground, but the grain is invariably good, no rust or scab, some little smut in places but not bad.[5] Corn crops are much revived, and altho you could scarcely find in the neighborhood what you would call a pretty field of corn, we may have pretty fair crops. Owing to the drouth in May, corn came up very uneven, and not withstanding there are very many fields that are well set, they all look spotted and uneven, though it is strong and healthy.

Well, Sam, we are somewhat lonesome this harvest. We cut our early wheat on Saturday the 21st and Monday following and on last Saturday commenced on the big field. I had to go to Ripley on business that day, and thought I had four hands to run the two cradles and bind (Tad, Burke, Pat, & Will) but on coming home at night I learned that Burke had got his "—ss up" because Bill & Tad would not go to the shop and grind his scythe, (which by the way was in first rate order). He sat on the fence til Tad cradled once around, on starting the second round Tad asked him if he was not going to work. He said not without they would grind his scythe. Tad told him to go to work or leave, he chose the latter, put on his bib & goods & went to Maysvill, returned Monday about 10AM. I gave him his change, he packed his goods and skedadled.

Will stuck to us, he & Amos cradled and Pat bound, and Monday at noon Davis joined us, and we got along fine; finished the job yesterday at 3 PM. Jo gathered the sheaves and I shocked. Pat is building stone fence for Dyas. I chartered his services for harvest before he left or I don't know how we would have done. Pat is a good careful binder. Harvest hands are scarce & high priced, $1.25. With very few exceptions the wheat will be harvested by tonight, Tom will not quite finish, Amos will get done before night. Tad has a longer contract before him if I don't get another hand, 30 Acres of corn to plow, the wheat to stack & thrash, the meadow & oats to cut & put up besides many incidentals, must look rather formidable for our boy, though he will do as much of it as any one man can do. He is a perfect horse to work and no grumbling, but he can't do it all at once.

Well the "4th" is close at hand. I wish you a happy 4th of July. There [are] extensive preparations for a Big 4th at our fairgrounds (Camp Ripley). Very many are preparing to go. I don't know whether I shall go or not, but think perhaps I will. They are fixing for a one horse celebration by the "Invincible Templers" I. B. Campbell Jr & Co but it won't hold Cal, Mary Carpenter & Co of Aberdeen. They are set for Ripley. It will probably be a pretty large affair if the weather should be favorable. It is to be of the basket or Picnic style of celebration. Everybody & his wife and children are invited and expected to be there in company with the rest of mankind and "womankind."

We have some reason to suppose you are at Memphis, but have to guess at that. We have divers rumors among the wise, that Gen. Sherman's division is ordered to Richmond, & the 70th is coming home & such stuff, but we don't believe either. We think Sherman's Division has done hard work enough to entitle them to rest if there is any rest for the soldiers. I had rather you had a location farther North during the hot season of the year, but we are not allowed to choose where you may go, or what you may do, but must wait in prayerful patience for your return home with the laurels unsullied which you have already won, and those you may hereafter win. Our prayers follow you in all places you may be called, and hope it may please the giver of all good, to still extend his protecting hand over you to shield you from danger and deliver you to your friends in good health after the accursed rebellion shall be quashed. We are all, anxious to see you, and if circumstance would permit we hope you will come home and relieve the earnest anxieties of your affectionate parent,

Andrew Evans

1. The Perotid gland is a large salivary gland in the cheek, near the top of the jaw.
2. To superate means to form or discharge pus.

3. The person being discussed here is probably Dr. John W. Guthrie (born in 1841). Following the war Will Evans studied medicine with Dr. John W. Guthrie. Prior to the war Will had been studying under Dr. Denham S. Guthrie (born in 1827), probably the uncle of John Guthrie. The Evanses often misspell Guthrie, sometimes even as "Guttery." Williams, *History of Clermont and Brown Counties, Ohio,* 2:214; Morrow, Biography Section, 103, 165.

4. Andrew probably means *sic transit gloria mundi,* a Latin phrase meaning "thus passes away the glory of the world."

5. Scab, rust, and smut are three different parasitic fungi that damage grain plants.

≫ JANE TO SAM ≪
Aberdeen, Oh. / July 7, 1862

Dear Cousin,

I received your kind letter on the fifth and I was truly glad to hear from you. We are all well at present and I hope that these few lines may find you enjoying the same good health. It has been very warm here for a few days and I expect it is so where you are too. I don't see how you do stand it as well as you do. You have stood the times better than I ever thought you would when you went away. The times are very lonesome here. We hardly see any person stirring around. Some days when you was here I could see you comeing up to the shop most every day. You don't know how bad I want to see you I want to see you worse now then ever.

Since John come home, he come home Sunday week, I believe he is as poor as ever I saw anybody. I never looked to see him as poor as he is. John has a gethering [probably goiter] on his Jaw. I was down to see him yesterday, he looks better than he did when he came home. He has bin up to see us once and to Indias once. He could not get up the hill by himself. Uncle Andrew and pap help him up the hill. Big Jane and I was out to the Ridge to metting yesterday you better believe it was a pretty warm ride I saw one of the soldiers from the 70th regiment, Mr. Phil Hawk he looks pretty well I don't think he was very sick we heared that he was in the harvest field the next day after he come home.

Sam your folks are done harvesting the folks are all threw about here now. I got a letter from Jake Botner the other day you better believe he can curse the Rebels he is at Wartrace, Tennesee he says that they have 900 men able for duty he says that they give there regt. the praise down there. Jim Burke has left your house. Him and Tad had a little falling out and Will paid him of[f]. And your Pap was not at home. He did not care much. Jake Scott is a coming there today to work.

Big Jane is all right and fat as ever and has a beau every once and awhile. Grandmother sends her love and respects to you Sam I don't know whether you can read this or not I mad[e] a good many mistaks but it don't mak any difference. Give my love and best wishs to the boys and recieve a portion for yourself please write soon no more at present.

remain your cousin,

Jane

⇒ WILL TO SAM ⇐
Aberdeen, OH. / July 20, 1862

Mr. Samuel Evans

Dear brother I received your favor of the 9, 6 days from date Amos received yours of the 6 & 7 on same day yesterday, 19, Father opened your letter to Burke (he has left us—left in harvest as you probably have heard before this. We have not heard from him since) we were glad to hear from each that you were on the mend & hope you may have good times still in the pie trade.[1]

John is mending very slowly. The abscess in his ear and his Bowels still run profusely. The rest of our folks here are well Sam, I was at the mansion last night, was C's escort for and accompaniment for another gallant.[2] She said that she had received a letter from Henry Campbell with an address some what varied from former ones (Mrs. Samuel Evans) Cal is well and lively as ever. . . .

War at Home

Maysvill & Aberdeen together with all other burghs in this vicinity have been wild with excitement, for the last 3 or 4 days. Rebel Morgan suddenly took Cynthiana, George Town and another town on the road to Maysville. Lexington was surrounded but have no positive news, last news from Morgan was 18 miles from here had 2000 Calvary but had turned & tis now thought he will not visit Maysville. All moneys, meat, Flower grain & many other articles have been brought to this side or shipped to Cin., Men just rolled in from all parts to defend the town the Fery went about 12 O'c at night to Ripley was back by 4 AM. Had 84 men & artilery about 50 went from Aberdeen—the force ther now is a good one about 400 Calvary—can't say how much for the rest. 8 persons driven from Cynthia stayed with us last night. Some of them were in the

fight. There were two ladies with them. The Rebels stole most every thing
they could get their hands on & cruely murdered many. They left us this
morning hunting places for their families. Soon as this is done they say
they will go again and fight for their homes.[3]

Home affairs — We have all our wheat stacked hay cut & all but 20
cocks in the barn — hay is splendid — Dyas will thrash tomorrow (commence) and as soon as his is done will thrash ours. Corn looks poor —
wants rain the worst kind — gardens want rain as well as pastures & c.

Business — Progress slowly, left a few accounts with J. C. Waldron. To
hurry up. those stamps you speak of were given you by Amos & myself.
A sprained wrist is excuse offered for this scrible — can hardly write, love
to all,

yours truly

W. H. Evans

Home / July 20, 1862

[This note from John was enclosed with Will's letter.]

Dear Brother,

As Bill is writing to you I will enclose a small note Sam it will be impo-
sable for me to be able to go to the regt. by next muster day so if they will
marke me I can very easily set it straight before a court martial. I am
mending very slowly.

1. The letters mentioned here have not survived. The meaning of the allusion to
the pie trade is unknown. Sam may have been serving as an army baker.

2. "The mansion" probably refers to Andrew Evans's home.

3. In July 1862 Colonel (later General) John Hunt Morgan of the Confederate 2nd
Kentucky Cavalry led a raid into the heart of Kentucky, capturing numerous Union
soldiers, horses, and supplies. The details Will gives of this raid are almost completely
accurate, a notable exception being that Morgan had between 900 and 1,200 men with
him, not 2,000. Morgan in fact turned back south toward Tennessee and would not
reach Maysville or the Ohio River on this raid. Also note that the Georgetown Will
mentions is a town in north-central Kentucky, not the Georgetown in Brown County,
Ohio. James A. Ramage, *Rebel Raider: The Life of General John Hunt Morgan* (Lexington:
The University Press of Kentucky, 1986), 91, 94.

Memphis, Tenn. / July 22, 1862

Dear Father,

We came to Memphis yesterday about 12 o'clock. We started Friday morning from Moscow, distance of 40 miles. First day was rather a pleasant day for this climate. On our way Wm. John died, a member of our company. He had been sick since the march to Holly Springs, sick of lung fever. Second day, Saturday, was a very warm close day and the march so hard that not over 75 men were left in the Regt. at noon. I was informed that 5 or 6 men died out of our Brig. on our way Saturday, 2 of whom were of the 70, 2 of the 48 Ohio. They were overdone by heat or sun struck. It was all unnecessary to march so fast or at so hot a time in the day. We rested after Sunday, 9 miles from the City, and what I thought rather hard was very short rations. If we had not had the privilege of several cornfields which we stripped of all the roasting ears. I thought many of them would eat so much that they would be sick but not a one as I can hear was injured. This kind of soldiering tries a man's mettle. A great many of "Shirks" that never do any duty if they can prevent it, fell out of ranks and did not come up till all things were fixed up. They were very sick if asked to do any duty, but when dinner time came, they could eat as well as anybody. I do not hate to do my duty, but that of others is a bore, you know what I mean.

On Monday morning early we started for Memphis and when we arrived in town there was not the half of our Regt. present. We took a short rest and then marched to the lower end of town where we are now camped. on our arrival 5 of Co. A, 9 of Co. F, 3 of Co. D were present. Not more of any co. was present. I held out though I was very tired.

James Galbraith was here and brought some news from home, the first I hear for some weeks.[1] There was a mail here but nothing for me. The letter you sent by Thos. Simons containing Richardson's speech came to me yesterday but I do not know how. Thos. Simons is at Columbus, Ky. sick. I received yours of the 3rd this morning and was very glad to hear from home and to know that you were all so well. Your wheat crop is much better than I supposed from hear say. You may well say that Amos has his hands full. If he keeps his health he will do as much as any boy I know of. You perhaps would love to see me but be assured that you cannot want to see me more than I want to see the friends at home, yet, there is no use talking for I canot come for some time. There is nothing that troubles my mind — I take things as easy as possible. If I live I expect to stay 3 years, that is, if the managers of this affair do no better than they have been doing of late.

The news from Richmond is not flattering. McClellan will have to "Hawk" or do better than he has been doing of late, yet I have confidence in him that he will do the best he can under the circumstances. Things at this time seem to me to be in a "mess." There is not much business done in this place except of a military character. Yesterday there were more "tight" men than ever. I saw nearly all of the officers felt their liquor. Several of our officers were arrested for being in town without passes. They were let loose on promise to do so no more.

I received a letter from Geo. W. Early, Jane Evans, Amos and other too tedious to mention yesterday, all of which I will answer as soon as I can. All of Co. F are moderately well except Cris Dragoo. He is not near as well as when he returned. He will die if he stays here 2 weeks longer. I am very tired today, have the headache some and rheumatism considerably; otherwise, I feel very well. If I could get to rest a little while here but we will have to stand guard and throw up the breastworks. There are now 3 or 400 negros at work throwing up breastworks. All the negros in Sherman's division that came from slave states have to work on the walls.[2]

I must close by promising to write soon. Direct as before or to Memphis. Give my regard to all the folks at home and all inquiring friends.

I remain your affectionate son,

Sam Evans

1. James Galbraith was a twenty-year-old family friend from Aberdeen whose name appears several times in these letters.

2. This is Sam's first mention of blacks being employed by the Union Army. Sherman took advantage of the swelling population of black refugees in Memphis by employing them as cooks or teamsters, working on the construction of Fort Pickering, overseen by white soldiers. Sam himself was one of these men while serving in the capacity of assistant engineer in the construction of Fort Pickering. Ernest Walter Hooper, "Memphis, Tennessee: Federal Occupation and Reconstruction," Ph.D. diss. (Chapel Hill: University of North Carolina, 1957), 18; Morrow, Biography Section, 157.

⇜ SAM TO MARY (GRANDMOTHER) ⇝
Memphis, Tenn. / July 25, 1862

Dear Grandmother,

I received your very kind letter some time ago but had not the chance [to respond] till now.

Well, we are in Memphis and have been since Monday noon. We have had a very good time since. We came here and plenty to eat by buying it. The boys have not drawed their new clothes yet but I think they will to-morrow as they are here. Most of us are the raggedest set of boys you ever saw. I have had to patch a good deal to keep respectable and I think I can patch pretty well for a blacksmith. Wonder how the old is [*sic*] get-ting along without me. I don't reckon they miss me very bad. Any how I was a pretty bad boy at home and have not got much better yet. I use to trouble you a good deal but have not lately something over 5 months.

You would like to know what we are all doing. Well not much of any-thing. It is too hot here for white men to work. We have marched more than a hundred miles since we left Shiloh. Some time we had to march very hard and carry a big load. A good many of the boys gave out. Some were sun struck. Three of the 70 Regiment died by sun stroke. 3 of Co. F have died since we left Corinth. Oliver Gray Wilson M. Elles, Wm. Faughn none of our company are sick now. I am now about as well as I have been since I had the measels though not as well as when I left home.

I am now working on breastworks. We are making a fort here and we expect to stay here for a month or more. There are about 800 contraband negros here, General Sherman has put them to work on the fort instead of the Soldier boys. I have charge of 32 darkies, working on the fort. The name of the Fort is Pickering, my wages are raised to $25 per month. I have no work, only stay about and see that the negros work and show them where they must work.

John McDaniel is well. Decker is well. all our boys are well and in very good spirits. Now I don't know whether we will have to fight any more or not. If we do I am ready though I am not very anxious to fight. I would not mind killing a few secesh if they would not shoot at me but shooting at me would not make any difference if they did not hurt me. Tell Jane I will write to her before long. Tell big Jane [that] Decker is all right and is waiting patiently till the war is over.

I would like very well to see all of you and will come home some time if I live long enough. You thought I was joking about going to war or getting married. I would have got married if the girls would have had me. Wonder how Cal is? I have not heard from her for a long time. My love and respects to you all.

I remain your affectionate Grandson,
Sam Evans

✣ ANN TO SAM ✣
Home / July 26, 1862

Dear Brother,

I received your kind letter a few days ago and was very glad to hear from you. I received some flowers. They were all safe. You say you made one gallon of Jam. I think it would be good on bread.

We had a nice rain up here. Sam, I have been looking for you home for a long time, but you did not come. I would like to come down and see you if it was not so far from home. I would like to see the pretty flowers down there. Sam, come over and get some Dumplings they are so good. We have plenty of apples the trees are breaking down. It is very hot up here. Mr. John Dennis and Mr. Henry Guttery was here for dinner. The last letter we got from Will he was well as common.[1]

School is out. We heard Perse Ellis was going to teach school. I wish he would.

Sam, you will see me down there blackberrying, some of these days. We have only got enough of Berries to make one gal of jam and would like to have more. I want to know what you make your jam in. Did you put it in a pot and stir it with a stick? Well Sam, I think you will be a good cook by the time you come home, if you keep learning all the time. I must close

Good by Sam for this time

Ann D. Evans

1. This is the first reference to Will being away. He didn't officially enlist in the army, however, until August 12, 1862.

✣ MARY (SISTER) TO SAM ✣
Home / July 27, 1862

Dear Brother,

I recd your kind letter some time ago and I suppose you think I have forgotten to answer it. No never will I forget you while I live though it may be a great while before we see each other. But I hope there are better days a coming. Sam you need not offer any appology all I ask is to answer my letter, when ever you get a chance I will wait patiently. I would have answered your letter sooner but they have been mowing and thrashing here on Sundays. We have had so much company since John came home that I have not had much time to write letters. Amos wrote to you a few nights ago. John also wrote to you one day last week. John is mending slowly I think. If he was better every time that you heard from him he must have been pretty bad at first. He said he was a great deal worse after he went back to Monterey. Sam Hiett is at camp Denison his health is no better. Uncle Sam was here this morning a short time. I was glad to hear that you did not need any more cloths if you don't then they have lasted well but I am afraid they look pretty sorry by this time you say you have a nice needle book. I expect I know the girl that gave it to you. I am glad that you can patch your clothes when they need it. Sam when a man has more than one trade when he is in a pinch he can work at one if he can't at another. I think a man would make money if things sell so high down there.

Sam there was a great picnic down below Ed's yesterday. Mary Carpenter and Cal walked out Friday evening and Mary Cal, Foeby Tailor, Billy Guttery & I went down in the morning. Frank Sharp brought Fanny Campbell out and John B. Cam brought Clara Sharp. There was several here for dinner. Miss Liza Ann Grims was here be sides those I mensioned Doctor Billy and Ann took Mary and Cal home on the horses. Will walked to Aberdeen yesterday evening and has not come back yet.[1] Ben Noris got nine volunteers at the Picnic yesterday and he went to Aberdeen last [night] to a Military meeting. There was plenty of dancing at the picnic but I did not dance. John was down there a little while he is able to go about a little.

I have not heard from Lida and Luna for some time. I can not tell you whether they are well or not. Grandmother says her health is better than it has been for a good while. Mother is not very well today. All the rest of the folks all are well as far as I know except Indias little Samy, he has not been well for a day or so. Sam I wish you would stop over and give us a few good tunes on the Malodean. I have played on the sewing Machine a great deal since you left. It is the best one I have ever seen. It has not had one bit of repairing since you left or I have not broken another needle. Sam I wish you would come over and help us eat chicken we have plenty of them. Mother has a sore thumb. She thinks it is a felon.[2] George started to Feesburg this morning India did not go. It is to warm for her. I will leave the rest till some other time as I have a chance to send my letter to the post office. Father is going to town.

Your true Sister,
Mary Evans

1. This letter and the preceding one give contradictory accounts of Will's whereabouts just prior to his enlistment.

2. A felon is a painful, pus-producing infection at the end of a finger or toe.

⇒ ANDREW TO SAM ⇐
Home, Sun. Eve. / August 3, 1862

Dear Sam,

I believe it is just a month since I wrote to you (an unusual long time). There have been many letters written to you from here since that time. I received yours of the 22 July on the 1st Aug. which was the only one I received from you in a long time. Still I get to see or hear nearly all the letters you send to this part of the country.

I think you are enduring considerable hardships part of which I can see but little necessity for, such as, marching during the heat of the day, when there is no enemy to meet, or other hurried necessity for the concentration of troops at a certain post, hurried marches in hot weather, short rations and bad water, will soon reduce an army unnecessarily, in my opinion, but such is War. To be a good soldier one must obey the order of his officer, whether it be a reasonable or unreasonable order.

John is still at home improving slowly. He is increasing in weight much faster than in strength. He can't walk at ordinary speed without platting legs. He is not clear of his diarrhea yet. He often has to stool from 3 to 5 times in the course of the nght. He is also afflicted with "Diathesis" or profuse discharge of urine, as much as a gallon in one night but he is improving slowly notwithstanding.

He got a 20 days furlough at Cincinnati 28 June. In a few days after, we received an order from the War Department, that all absentees must report at Columbus in person if able, if not, to report by certificate of physician. On the 6 of July, he reported by certificate of Dr. Gutherey that he would not be fit for duty sooner than 30 days, afterwards another order issued requiring a similar certificate to be acknowledged before a civil justice he (the justice) to certify to the respectibility of the physician, etc., all of which formalities he again put through on the 1st of Aug. for 30 days time again. Since that the War Department has issued an order to actually abrogate all furloughs and leave of absence on all officers and soldiers on the 11th Aug. and if they are not in their proper regiments by the 18, they are to be considered deserters and their pay stoped. This may do justice in some cases, but I am satisfied that it will cause the unnecessary death of many a good soldier who might recover if allowed to rest at home for a few weeks. A good soldier will obey orders, kill or no kill![1]

Old David W. Early is said to have died last night will be buried this evening. Old Unkle John Hiett fell on Wednesday last and broke he thigh or rather the neck of the femur (incurable).

Our family are in usual health except your mother who has a felon on her thumb, with a smart bilious attack she is quite sick today sitting up but little. Amos has had diarrhea for a few days he is better today, your friends are generally well and the general health here is good.

We are through all our harvest work, we finished our hay on the 22nd and our Threshing on the 24 all in good order, our week cutting is all done & we are on deckhand work generally.

There are 2 Company organizations in this Country. One at Georgetown & one at Ripley they have some 30 or 40 men each. Georgetown Company Capt. William Hays 1st Lt. John W. King and 2nd Lt. David V. Pierson Ripley Capt. John Jolly (old Phils son) 1st Lt. F.H.B. Norris, 2nd. Geor DeBott. The above named officers have been duely appointed & commissioned by the Governor they are recruiting as fast as possible for the 89 Regt. Col. John G. Marshall. If the Companies are not full by the 15 they will be filled by drafting.[2] Jacob Scott & Harrison Housh have volunteered. Cyrus Lane has enlisted in Fosters Calvary. There will be a war meeting in Aberdeen tomorrow evening. They are canvasing the County for recruits, both to fill the old requirements in the field, and to make the new ones, and after a man has volunteered he is allowed to choose which service he will go into before he swears in. Amos will write to you in a week or less. The girls wrote within the past week. I shall not wait a month before I write again, we wish you to write as often as you can to some of us.

Your conclusions are correct in respect to our desire to see you and we have no reason to doubt your desire to see all of us, but as you say, "there's no use of talking for you can't come home for some time." We will have to stand it. I am fearful if John undertakes to live up to the last "order" we shall never see him again. He says he prefers death to disgrace I don't know what he will do yet.

Give my compliments to my acquaintances & friends in your army and be assured of the kind regard and best wishes of

Your affectionate father,

Andrew Evans

1. In the summer of 1861, Congress authorized state governments to raise volunteer regiments for three years' service. Regiments were locally organized, and whole companies and regiments often came from single townships or counties. Though officers were technically elected, locally prominent citizens were often given the appointments because of their recruiting work in raising the regiment or a company, political connections, or commonly, a combination of the two. The 89th Ohio, in which Will Evans, George Early, and Andrew's brother Amos enlisted, was raised in accordance with President Lincoln's July 1862 call for the states to raise 300,000 new soldiers to serve three-year terms in new regiments. McPherson, *Ordeal by Fire*: Vol. 2, *The Civil War* (New York: Alfred A. Knopf, 1982), 165; McPherson, *Battle Cry of Freedom*, 491.

2. On August 4, 1862, the federal government called for an additional 300,000 men to serve nine-month militia terms, and Congress enacted a law allowing the use of the draft in any state that did not fulfill its quota.

By early 1863, the North instituted its first national military draft. Men between ages twenty and forty-five were required to register for a draft lottery held in each congressional district to fill the remaining portion of that district's quota. Many unwilling potential draftees furnished substitutes or paid a three-hundred-dollar commutation fee. Many localities and states offered sizable bounties to encourage enlistment and avoid or minimize the scope of the draft. The bounty system boosted volunteering but also fostered significant corruption and profiteering. One of the most notable abuses was bounty jumping (desertion immediately after the receipt of a bounty). McPherson, *Battle Cry of Freedom*, 492, 600–607.

⇾ SAM TO ANDREW ⇽
Memphis, Tenn. / August 4, 1862

Dear Father,

I seat myself to bother you again, for a short time. I sent my money by the state Agent. Enclosed please find a receipt for 25 dollars, you will take it to Georgetown and present it to the Treasurer and draw my money. When you draw it keep it and Cr me with the amount and what I owe you. You need not go without you have some other business. You may send the receipt with some responsible person should there be any going out on business and let him draw. It will save you the trouble if you have no business there soon. I do not know how soon the money will be there but the Paymaster said it would not be very long till he would have it there.

You will also find a receipt for 35 dollars in favor of N. B. Thompson, enclosed when you draw mine draw his (N. B. Thompson) hand it to Dyas Gilbert and tell him to put in an interest. The reason that Nelse sent his with mine was that it would be as convenient and would save the trip of one man.

I guess you understand this as well as I can tell you by writing a sheet on the subject.

We are all well and have rather better times than when we were on March. William Wiles and Capt. Wiles wife arrived here yesterday evening. I am still acting as an assistant to the Engineer on the entrenchments. Last letters are coming in occasionally I have received a [letter] from each Amos, Will and John and will reply as soon as I have time. I am engaged from 6 in the morning, till seven in the evening. Sunday as well as any day. So far, I am well but not stout. Rheumatism still works on me pretty severely.

None of those boys marked deserter [got paid]. Capt. Nelson Capt. Brown were among the number that got marked and failed to draw [their pay].

This is all that I can write now please pardon me for not writing more.

Your soldier boy.

Sam Evans

➤ JOHN TO SAM ◆
Home / August [?], 1862

[By context, this is prior to John's letter of August 11, 1862.]

Well Sam I will give you some of the news in this part of the world. It is very hot here about this time and every thing is about dried up We have not had rain enough here to wet the ground for more than a month. Corn and all garden stuff is about gone up Father is threshing his wheat today it is splendid indeed he will have about 275 bush. Dyas is threshing it for him. It is the first crop he has threshed. Thomps Shelton & Tom Shelton are helping him run it. Littles machine started yesterday in slick away. Hands are very scarce here at present they are most all in "dixey". There is to be a Pick-nick in the woods just below Ed Martins Saturday. I don't know what the order of the day is as I have not been about much. I think it will be a fizzle. The intention is to dancing I think if the[y] can't get along with out that they had better blow out. The town girls talk of coming out. The girls up here are all fat and want to marry. Cal got a letter from your yesterday.

Bill wrote to you a few days ago, he has left a few accounts with the squire he told me to ask you if you warented [guaranteed] Rosenkrantz's hoe to suit him. If it don't will he take it back, he refused to pay for it on that ground. The health of the neighborhood is not very good at present but I believe the soldiers families are all well. Our folks are all as well as common. John Carpenter is at flat top mountain yet and is Hospt. Stewart [Steward] of the 12 he is in good health.

The girls say they will write soon, we write from two to three letters a week to you.

Your Brother,

J. B. E.

❯❯ JOHN TO SAM ❮❮
Home / August 11, 1862

Dear Brother,

I have written to you some four times since I left Cin and have rec'd one answer and that was to the one I wrote when I was in the City. We have recd several letters from you since you have been at Memphis. George got one Saturday sent by Hook which informed us of your new trade (of driving contrabands).[1] Are you a good hand to sling the knot I would like to see you at it. I suppose it is much easier on you than Rgt'l duty as you can get your rest of nights. I see by the papers that you are likely to be attacked soon but I suppose you are ready for them. If they do come I hope they will get worse than they did at shilo. They will be apt to find our Generals awake this time.[2] The Secesh day is drawing near they are fast nearing the last ditch. 600,000 more troops with the old ones will soon clean them out and our glorious old banner will once more wave triumphant over the land of the free and the home of the brave.

The boys will soon all be gone from this district. George Early, Aleck Hall, Bill, Bob Ridley, Bill Mc, Scyrus Lane, Jacob Scott, John Wood, James, Meart Flanghers's two boys, John Moore, Mahanah's two boys and others of your acquaintence have enlisted. Bill is not certain yet but will know tonight, I think he will go.[3]

The Governor has ordered that no more bounties be paid & that the quota will be filled by draft after the 15th of this month. So you see they are pitching in to keep from being drafted.

They had a big fight in town Saturday on the subject. Bill Carpenter maid some insulting remark to Pilot John Lowill on the subject. John up with a chair and knocked him down and then kicked and beat him till Doc says it will be hard to raise him. That is good they ought serve some more of them the same way. The people have got in the notion of putting down the Rebellion now & they are going to do it. Old Abe has brought that big foot of his down at last & the Southern Confederacy has to come with it.

I had maid all of my calculations for starting to the Reg't today though I am not any ways near fit for duty. I have now the Fistula in arm [?] which will likely disable me for 3 or 6 months longer.[4] It will cost me fifty dollars to get it cured as that is the least that Doc Paddock will treat it for (he is the man that cured Lafayette Parker) You will find inclosed a certificate from Doc Gutherie. He has been tending on me since I have been at home I could send the certificates of many others but I deem it unnecessary. You will please show it to the Col. & Surgeon and if possible get a discharge. Write as soon as you can and let me know what they think of it.

Sam I don't ask this to get out of the service because I am afraid or tired of it for I would rather be with you today if I had any assurance that I could stand it than to stay here at home. But desiring not to be a burden to the army nor & expence to the government when I can do no service, is simply the reason why.

I ask a discharge but if I obtain a discharge & regain my health before the war ends I will be with you again. Please say nothing about this [to] any one but the officers. If it is necessary for me to come down there please let me know all about it.

There is a report here that Capt. Wiles killed one of his men & was to be shot for it. I have disputed it. Let me know all about things in general when you write. Who is our Capt. now if we have any, we heard that De Bruin was.

There is not much news of importance here all business is swallowed up in the excitement of the times. The folks here are all well with the exception of Old Johny Hiett. He fell down and broke his leg but is getting well. Old David Early Died a few weeks ago. His sale will take place on the 28th of this month, father is one of the appraisers. George will clerk the sale if he don't go away before that time. Every body scolded because you went away & left the shop now they are on Bill for leaving the mill, but are not so glad to see him when he asks them for what they owe you. I have not been to town for some time consequently I can't tell you much about the one you would like to hear from best. I learn that

she is the assistant in the Aberdeen school. She says she can't get a certificate large enough for that position but I think that all a joke. Sam she
is the sharpest woman about here (that's so). The women up here are all
fat & best of all they are true patriots. If they had any assurance that you
would get what they sent you, you would live better than you do for I
know that they have the interest of the soldier at heart. I suppose you
heard that Jon Little & Noah Glanghers girl were married. He spoiled the
shape of her first though.[5] Tell John Mc that if he don't hurry up Frank
Porter will beat him for he is writing some mighty curious letters. The
two Janes are as fat as ever. I guess I have told you all that I can think of
so I will quit give my love to all and write as

Your Brother,

J. B. Evans

1. In this usage the term "contraband" means escaped slaves. The use of contraband for escaped slaves was coined by General Benjamin Butler at Fort Monroe, Virginia, in May 1861. Butler cleverly avoided the politically charged question of whether
the escapees were slave or free by calling them "contraband" — literally "enemy property that may be used against the Union." Robert F. Engs, *Freedom's First Generation:
Black Hampton, Virginia, 1861–1890* (New York: Fordham University Press, 2004), 15.

2. Grant and other Union generals were criticized for not being fully prepared for
the Confederate attack on the first day of the Battle of Shiloh.

3. This is a reference to John and Sam's brother Will, who in fact enlisted in the
89th Ohio Volunteer Infantry the next day.

4. A fistula is a tube-like passage connecting body cavities or organs that are not
normally connected. Fistulae can be congenital or can result from a wound or abscess
healing improperly.

5. This probably means the bride was pregnant before the wedding.

⇛ ANDREW TO SAM ⇜
Home / August 31, 1862

Dear Sam,

Brother Amos arrived here at noon today from Camp Denison on a
pass until Wednesday next.[1] George came up last Thursday and has to
return Tuesday next. Will has not been up, nor does he know whether he
will or not. They have the promise that each will have short leave of absence if time will allow it. Our oldest five children are gone from our
presence (except John who is but temporarily at home).[2] One of them to
his last resting place and the others we may never see again. I expect to

go with Amos A. to Georgetown this week and see if he will "Pass." His is one of the named cases of exemption but he will have to be examined before he will clear from draft.

Your customers, and Wills, will not find quite so indulgent a creditor in Tad [Amos] as they have been used to. Will put his business, and yours, in Tad's hands for settlement when he left. Tad duns all of them anytime or place he can see them and tells them the money must come or the wool will fly. He has got them considerably scared up and they are paying some money over. There is a time at which indulgence ceases to be a virtue and Tad thinks that time has arrived. He gives but little peace, no matter who they are. He will write to you shortly.

You will confer a favor on me by presenting my compliments to your Field & Company Officers and associates in arms with whom I am acquainted. Assure them of my high regard for their success in quelling this rebellion and their safe return to their dear ones that cluster around their homes, and be assured of the high regard of your

Affectionate father,

Andrew Evans

1. "Brother Amos" is Andrew's brother and father of "Little Jane." He was age forty-two at the time of enlistment.

2. The other four children to whom Andrew is referring are Sam, with the 70th OVI; William, with the 89th OVI; Abraham, deceased; and Indiana, married to George Early.

⇒ SAM TO ANDREW AND MARY (MOTHER) ⇐
Memphis, TN / Sept. 21st, 1862

Dear father and Mother,

I received yours of the 9th on the 16th and was very glad, as well as very much surprised at our neighborhood assuming a military aspect. You cannot well imagine my uneasyness about the welfare of all of you folk. When the news first arrived here that the Rebs had taken Maysville, all of our co. would have given almost anything to have been home to help defend our homes against invaders.[1] Various have been the rumors in regard to the Maysville affair. 1st that 1,500 cavalry under Smith had taken the town without firing a gun; the citizens having moved all their valuables to Aberdeen and Ripley and the ammunition and canons [sic] were moved to Ripley; that Aberdeen was prepared to surrender whenever the Rebs made an attack.

2nd rumor was that the above number of Rebs had taken Maysville without firing, and the citizens had come over to Aberdeen to make a defense together with about 1000 Ohio home guards, and several other reports differing but little from the former. And the last report says the town of Maysville was surrendered to cavalry [illegible] and that Wadsworth and some others have been arrested by our forces and sent to Columbus Ohio because they surrendered without an effort to so small a force. I would like to know who was so cowardly in our township as to be forced into the ranks by Bayonets. I have guessed, but I may be wrong [that] any man who would not come out upon such an occasion deserved to be published and branded as a coward (if he be able [able-bodied]). If the news is true that we have from Kentucky, you will not have to bear arms at home much longer and I will be indeed happy when you are safe at home. It matters not about me so [long as] you all are safe.

I have not taxed my time any more than was agreeable to me although I have to use a great deal of industry to get to write as often as I do. Be assured that it is a pleasure rather that a task to write to you, particularly all my correspondents who are punctual. I find that a number of the letters I have written have reached their destination. I wrote to John yesterday and enclosed a letter I thought you had read months ago. I take as much rest as I can, and as for grieving I am clear. I take evry thing as easy [as] possible, giving evry thing an appreciation. Mother, you may think me rather a recreant boy or that I have forgotten you, non, do not harbor the thought. Could you see me as I feel for you, you would not think thus. It [is] true that I have not written you a letter individualy but at the same time all letters that I have written home were intended for the family. If such has not been the application made, it was wrong and shall be corrected. There is not a day passes over but that I think of home and its circle. Even "Help" is not yet forgotten.[2] While you are all well and doing well, I am easy. Of course I would like to see all the family and take each by the hand and chat for a few minutes. But military rule in time of "war" must be submitted to. To see you all would give but temporary relief.

The health of the army here is very good. Some Flux not very bad, only a few cases have proved fatal, some Typhoid fever, considerable Ague and Fever, and that of light character. Some 4 of our Co have Ague. No[ne] are in the hospital at this time. James Drennin has been off duty for nearly two months with rheumatism in the spine. I feel pretty well again and am on the mend slowly. How the winter will settle on me is yet to be seen. I feel Rheumatism sensibly [because of] all this damp weather. To day our darky was gone up in town and I have been cook. The boys have been bragging of their grand dinner. We had for dinner soft bread, Pickled Pork, Desecated [sic] Potatoes, fried onions, Potatoes, sweet and Irish, besides good [illegible] water to drink. These are the first onions we have drawn since I have been out. There are plenty of good Apples and peaches, but they sell pretty high, only 3 or 4 for 5 cts.

All of Co. F. went reconoirtering [sic] on the Arkansas side [of the Mississippi River] and to bring in a lot of cotton belonging to a reble. The cotton fields look as white snow ready for picking but no one to pick it. We have picked a great many potatoe patches. There is but little news hear worth relating. We know of no Reble force near hear that we are affraid of, Guerilla posts of from 20 to 100 men in [sic, word missing]. The Fort is so near complete that we think it would be hard to get over with what men that are at our service placed at their posts, at least Gen Sherman thinks so. As soon as the fortifycations are complete, the instruction is to build a barracks. We may have the job of doing this if the Rebs do not drive us out. I learned a few days ago that our brigade would stay here as a garrison. Gen Denver (our Brigadier) has command of the troops inside the Fort. Gen Denver is one of the best fellows I ever saw. There is not a man (that I have heard of) that does not like him and would [sic] fight under him as hard as any now living. He is firm, strict, kind and brave and besides all of these he is one of the most jocous [sic, jocose, i.e., merry], with none of that hautiness that is so prevalent among "Red Rope". He goes among his men, talks with them, visits the hospital, notices whether the camp is well policed, but he is rather severe on Rebs. The news from Virginia is cheering. I think if Mc' is as above [like Denver], he will rout all the sesesh from the old Dominion. He is mad, old Abe is mad, the "Wool" (Gen Wool) has come with 75,000 fresh men, something will be done. I think I said in my last to you that ["]the darkest hour was just before day" an[d] so I think it will be. We can whip them here. All we want is to have a chance. I cannot entertain the idea of being whiped by the Rebles. We have the men, why not bring them out and do the thing up in a hurry. England will not stand off always although it is none of her business. The old maxim "many a man did well by minding his own business" would apply in her case.[3]

The Rebles are nearly all bearfooted [sic]. How can they do in winter if they do not get shoes from other sources. Negroes that have lately come in from Mississippi say the Rebles think they will have to give up, that [the Union] army is too large, and that they are getting short of clothing and provision and the chances are growing worse for that them as we advance. They also say the Reb's thought in the beginning we could not feed our army when we consumed what was on hands for the reason there would be no one left to raise it and they could raise plenty as the slaves could raise all they wanted. This has been true to some extent, so far as the slaves were concerned in producing for them. That is the reason I said take from them these great auxiliaries.[4] I hope the nort[h] will produce enough to keep our army from starvation for a while. We will yet be victorious. We have never yet seen what our revolution fathers saw to gain what we have enjoyed. We surely can do more than we have yet to maintain it.

What has become of Lafayette Parker? I have not heard of him for a long while. It will perhaps tax you longer to read this than you want to devote to such a mess of stuff. Give my respects to all who inquire after me. To you an mother and all the family, accept my love and best wishes.[5]

I am as ever your son,

Sam Evans

P.S. Tell Mary and Ibbe that I will answer their letters some time this week.

1. Sam is referring to the rumors spread and the panic caused in Maysville during Confederate General Edmund Kirby Smith's action in Kentucky. Smith had entered Kentucky as part of an invasion commanded by Braxton Bragg, which ultimately ended unsuccessfully with the Confederate defeat at Perryville on October 8, 1862. When a portion of Smith's army began moving toward Cincinnati, panic ensued in southern Ohio. In Cincinnati, martial law was declared, business was suspended, fortifications were hastily built, and armed volunteers appeared in droves. In counties on the Ohio River, like Brown County, however, volunteers were kept at home to defend any possible invasion further up the Ohio. The threat to southern Ohio ended with the arrival in northern Kentucky of slow-moving Union commander General Don Carlos Buell and his army. McPherson, *Ordeal by Fire*, 2:288–91; Eugene H. Roseboom, *The Civil War Era*, vol. 4 of *History of the State of Ohio*, ed. Carl Wittke (Columbus: Ohio Archaeological and Historical Society, 1944), 398–99.

2. Sam is probably referring to the hired hands on the Evans farm.

3. Sam is referring to widespread speculation that England was considering some form of intervention in support of the South. The Union victory at Antietam on September 17, 1862 ended that possibility. In this letter, Sam is not yet aware of that event.

4. Here Sam is very prescient about Union policy. Abraham Lincoln issued the Preliminary Emancipation Proclamation in part to deprive the South of its slave labor force. Ironically, the proclamation came just one day after Sam wrote this letter.

⇾ ANDREW TO SAM ⇽
Home / September 28, 1862

Dear Son,

I received yours of the 14 on the 24 and was (as usual) much pleased to hear from you. We have no reason to complain of your epistolary fidelity, you keep us well posted for which you have our kindest thanks. I might you oftner, but I assure you that my time has been all taken up for several weeks. I hardly take time to keep my news reading up, I work all I am able for every day, Our old cistirn let down, and we dug it out, a foot deeper than it was, got a fine hard blue rock for the bottom, walled it up and arched it nicely with stone, to lower side of porch door, six feet wide and fixed things rather general at that end of the house, and have the cistern well cemented, we think it will stay now. The ground has been much too dry to seed until last night. We had a very good rain and I think we shall commence sowing wheat tomorrow, We have the sand hauled in and leveled in the new cellar ready for flagging. The flag [stones] halled & c but it will have to stand until we are done seeding.

I got a letter from George & one from Will & one from Inda on Friday last. They were all well, the 89th is in Camp Shaler, Cambell Co. Ky., some three miles from Covington (their address is Co E 89 Regt Covington Ky). I am glad your boots are holding out so well. Your mother is preparing two pairs of good socks which we will forward to you if possible. We bought two nice silk pocket handkerchiefs expecting to send one to you by John, but he failing to recover sufficiently to go to his Regt we gave one to Will when he left, and will send the other to you if we can. We would be pleased to furnish you with many little things that would conduce to your comfort if you were where we could do so, but as things are at present, you will have to accept our good intentions in place of good deeds.

I think it almost a waste of time & paper to attempt to give "war rumors" in a letter. We can hear almost anything. We had a new one last night, that Augusta Ky, was burnt down by the rebels, and that they crossed the river and were marching on Higginsport & Ripley/the Militia were ordered to meet Companys & hold themselves ready for orders, but none have come yet, & I think maybe it is a War rumor. Those little raids & rumors are interfering most terribly with farmers' work, hands are very scarce, & to take all them, and keep them from their work for a few days now will cause terrible losses in seeding and cutting fodder & c. A great deal of corn is worth but little except for fodder, and if we fail to cut it in proper time it will be gone up too.

I received your Power of Atty. and will endeavor to faithfully execute your business according to instructions, I cannot expect to collect all your claims, some of them are very hard, but I shall try the [illegible] if all other plans should fail.

Our general health has not been quite so good as usual since I wrote last, the children have nearly all had scarlet rash but they did not lay up much, and are all well enough to go to school again.

Lee says tell Sam he went to school 2 or three days, and learned his A,B,C's and was a good boy at school, Ann & jo look rather puny but are able for their rations. The rest of us are about tolerable. Amos had a pretty steep tear of flux the fore part of last week, John went to Cincinnati last thursday to see what the authorities would make of him; he has not returned nor have we any letter from him. If he remains there many days he will write you from there. Your friend Bill West visited us last week, he passes a higher eulogy on you as a Soldier & man than you would ask any man to do. You are his first choice.

Accept the love and respects of us all, and of your immediate friends, and believe me

Your affectionate father,

Andrew Evans

Mary got a letter from John Mc on Friday last

My respects to your field and Co officers, and such of your associates as have my acquaintance

❧ AMOS TO SAM ❦
Aberdeen, OH / October 3, 1862
Confidential, but use your judgement[1]

Dear Brother Sam,

I write to you under circumstances that are indeed painful to all of the family & almost death like to a dear mother.

It is my painful duty to inform you that it is my unhappy lot to be (drafted) after offering in every way that could be honorable as a volunteer. I scorn the shame of being drafted though you will know it was not my fault. I have to bear by obeying my Parents. I shall bear it with Christian fortitude as Job bore all his affliction. It does not hurt me as it will the folks at home. God knows I love my own "Native Land" & am willing to sacrifice my life in her defence but I do not like to be forced to do what they refused to let me do voluntary. I have to start to Georgetown next Wednesday enrout to Portsmouth & further have to furnish myself.[2]

The folks are again about as well as usual. Nothing strange for news, only rumor. We have seeded 12 acres & cut 7 acres of fodder since any one wrote to you. We have been getting along very well since the raid. All the letters you wrote came in a pile to Pa. John & the girls, they will answer soon. John is still at Cincinnati awaiting to know his fate. Will & Geo were well up to the 28th last. You must excuse the style of this note & the haste, blotches, &c for I have to write several tonight. We may never meet again on Earth but be firm in your trust & we will meet in a more holy land.

My everlasting love remain with you while I remain

your Brother as ever,

Amos A.

N.B. Only 3 were drafted from this Tp. John Moore (Isaac['s] son) & one I did not hear.

Tad

1. Amos requested Sam's confidentiality because he was embarrassed at having been drafted.

2. See letter from Martin Crain, October 14, 1862, below.

⇒ D. B. KIMBLE TO SAM ⇐
October 11, 1862

Friend Sam,

I take the present opportunity of answering your kind letter which came to hand a few days ago. I read it with a great deal of pleasure. I was glad to hear from you. I had often thought of writing to you but had always neglected it. Far from forgetting you, I think of our short stay together in Paducah. It was a pretty lonely place as it was. If it had not been for you I should followed some drag off. Sam, have you forgotten the old washer women, the tuff [sic, tough] chicken or the apples she so kindly bestowed upon us. Now, Sam, you know I am no negro lover but I cannot help liking that old one a little for I believe she truly sympathised with the soldiers, or have you forgotten that little white house that stood back to the left some distance from where the calvary was camped. I think if you or I was there together we could enjoy our selfs for a short season. I sometimes think back & can hardly believe that we slept in a whore house!

Sam, I have not much news to write to you of interest as this is a dry time. I tell you there is not much news afloat and that that is there is no believing.

I believe that Maysville & Aberdeen is considered out of danger as the rebels are falling back. Sam, the campaign during the siege of Maysville & Aberdeen will make bright rage in the history of this war! I was there two days during the excitement & I believe I never saw people so confused in my life. We had nice rain on Friday last & farmers are generally very busy. Every thing is very discouraging to the farmer as things are so low that he has to sell, & every thing so high that he has to buy. Wheat is from 75 to 85 cts per bus, hogs from 1 to 2 cen per pound & other things in proportion.

Sam I expect you would like to hear some thing from the mansion. I can not give you any late news as I have not been down lately. I had the pleasure of taking diner there with your Brother John some weeks ago. They wish the war was over & I do too. I must stop.

Respects to all,
Your friend,
D. B. Kimble

⇒ SAM TO ANDREW AND MARY (MOTHER) ⇐
Memphis, Tenn / October 12, 1862

Dear parents,

I reced your favor of the 28th of last month on the 7th of this and I do assure it gave me great pleasure to hear from you. This is the earliest opportunity that I have had to answer owing to strong and heavy rains. Last Friday was one of the most disagreeable days that I have seen for a long time. The rain fell as fast as I ever saw it for the length of time (about 14 hours). During that time the weather was quite cool. The wind blew a perfect hurricane all the while and did not cease until yesterday. There was not a dry place in the whole camp except under our gun brackets, our goods were piled up and covered with our "guns".

I hope you will not overdue yourself at work. Take it moderately if you can. Your cistern must be very nice. I can see how it is very well [made]. I have not yet received a letter from George or Will since they left home although I have written to both. When I spoke of socks I did not want mother to go to the trouble of knitting me new but simply send me my old if they were good enough. I will stay here as I have before, do not discommode yourselves to do any thing for me while I have no worse times than I have seen. I come to protect you and your home and not take a morsel of you, but do not think what you have done or what you may do, is or will be underrated by me. You have been as you always was, kind to me. And while I am away from you, I hope I shall never be guilty of an act to lower me in your estimation but rather that [sic] do something worthy of my ancestors; as yet I think I have not. Tell lee to be a good boy at school and learn fast. I have not heard from John since you wrote. I feel somewhat flatterred on what my friend West said of me. I have no doubt but that he thought what he said. I do not feel deserving. My field and co officers accept kindly your compliments and in return tender theirs. Col Cockerell returned to this Reg't last Thursday night, looks quite well—also John Morrison. Elya Burboge came to Co F, also one new recruit by the name of Abrohours, all of whom look well. Since I commenced writing this I have heard that the 89th has gone to West Virginia. Sam Hiett wrote to Griff to this effect. . . .

We have been grading a drill ground outside of the Fort. It will be a very nice one too. I have gone into a nice business and given over my squad to Wm Mills. The Ordnance department was in need of hand. My name was given by someone to the Ordnance officer. The engineer gave me leave to be transferred. I was willing because the pay is the same, have a good house to work in. The weather is rather bad to work in now and will be worse soon. I have charge of the forging department. There are now in the department nearly 10,000 stand of arms to be cleaned and repaired. I cannot say how well I will hold out, so far the hands think I can make any thing. I did a job all hands said could not be done, mending a mainspring and making a good job. There are 12 partial sets of tools besides the forges. I think I will move my quarters to the shop, there being plenty of room.

The talk is still favor[able] to the 70th quartering here the coming winter. The health of the soldiers here is reasonably good. James Golbroth [*sic*] is yet in the hospital, convalescent. James Sibbald went in the hospital yesterday. Simons Willcase, Joe Badd are yet off duty. The remainder of the company is well. There is great aspiring for promotions since the Death of our Gallant Maj.[1] The Sutler started home with his remains.[2] Got as far as Cairo and could not be moved farther and was buried there. Capt Brawre of Co A is now acting Maj and will likely receive the appointment but he'll never be a McFerren. Who will [be] Capt of co A or F is not known to me. I hear that Joshua Simons is 1st Lient of a co at Aberdeen. Is that so? Is Sawyer Capt of some Co?

With this mail I send my mineature to Mary. It [is] not as good a one as I would liked to have sent but it may answer all purposes. I gave $1.50 for it. We have not yet been paid for the 2 months due. As soon as I get, I will send you all I can spare. There is nothing of importance to write you now for fear that I will weary your patience. I had better stop for present. Tell all who inquire often that I am moderately well and contented as a man can be in the same situation. Tender my highest regards to Granny and all on the Hill. You will receive for all our family my love and best wishes for your welfare.

Your big boy,

Sam Evans

P.S. Still continue as often as you please and I will as often as I can

Sam

1. On October 3, 1862, John W. McFerren of Adams County, major of the 70th Ohio Volunteer Infantry, died in the hospital at Fort Pickering. T. W. Connelly, *The History of the Seventieth Ohio Regiment: from its Organization to its Mustering Out* (Cincinnati: Peak Brothers, 1902), 44.

2. Sutlers were merchants who supplied goods to soldiers in camp. They earned a reputation for being dishonest and overpriced. Though sutlers were supposed to be licensed by the army, many of these merchants frequented Union camps without the approval of camp commanders.

⇒ HEADQUARTERS TO COMMAND POST ⇐
Camp Portsmouth / Oct. 14, 1862

Amos A. Evans, a drafted militia man of Brown County Ohio, is discharged on account of physical disability.

Martin Crain

Co. Comdg. Post

Memphis, TN / October 21, 1862

Dear father,

Again I seat myself to write you a few lines. On the 14th of this month I reced a letter from Amos informing me that he had been drafted. I do not like it, because there are 4 or 5 families who had not a representative in the war and yet none of these [have been drafted]. I would like to have seen the draft fall not like it did in the case above alluded to. Already three of your sons had volunteered, that I thought was our share. Amos would have gone before if it had not been for persuasion all of which I thought was right. I did not want him to go and told him so. Since it is so we will have to make the best we can of it. I do not think I be saying too much, today he is the best boy you have. That is he would suit you at home better than any of the others. He will not run if he sees the enemy but will be apt to stand his ground and obey his commander. You are left in rather a bad fix about work. I will send you all the money I can possibly spare. It may do you some good.

I learned that you have 12 acres of wheat sown and 4 acres of fodder cut before Amos left. I know it was hard for you to part from Amos, but I hope you will be able to bear it since fate has ordained it so. I would like to hear as soon as you get this what Reg't he has gone in, also give me his address that I may write to him. That is if you can do so; I have written to George and Will both and have received no answer. I don't know where they are. I heard some way or other that the 89th had gone to Western Virginia. What is the reason some one at home has not written? I would like very well to hear once a week at least if that is not more than my share. Dave Tarbell has shown his posterior very plain. I always had better opinion of him than that.[1]

There is not much news here worth relating. It is reported that guerrillas are gathering up over in Arkansas doing what little mischief they can in way of firing into boats as they pass. Some of our division went out yesterday on the hunt of them. I have not learned what success they have had. The 70 is on provost guard in town this week. All is very quiet up there now. I am working in the gun shop. I like it better than my former pursuit and get along very well. Thus far all the sick of the 70 are convalescent. I am moderately well again. I was rather sick with flux the first of last week but did not lay up. The weather through the day is again pleasant but the night are very cool and foggy. We have no stoves in our tents yet, but would like well to have one these nights. But I think we have no reason to complain; we are favored now. I am of opinion if the Rebels were served as they have been at Corinth and in Kentucky the war would soon end. Sherman has put the order into execution relative to firing into boats as they were passing up and down the [Mississippi] river. Twenty secesh families have already been sent out and 20 more have to go tomorrow.[2] I could write more but for fear you grow tired of this I will close. Remember me kindly to all of the family, to Grandmother and to all on the hill and accept my best wishes for your and Mother's welfare and happiness and believe

Me your devoted son

Saml Evans

1. See Andrew's letter of November 2, 1862.

2. As a wartime commander in Memphis during the summer and fall of 1862, General Sherman became incensed by attacks of Confederate guerillas on Union boats and instituted military reprisals. Sherman wrote to Grant that he would evict ten pro-Rebel families for every Union boat that came under guerilla fire. He also vowed to "devastate the country" until guerilla war could be stopped. Michael Fellman, *Citizen Sherman: A Life of William Tecumseh Sherman* (New York: Random House, 1995), 139–43.

⟫ SAM TO ANDREW ⟪
Memphis, Tenn / October 31, 1862

Dear father,

This has been the longest interval between writings since I came out but when you know the reason you may pardon me. The weather has been too cold to write in the tent. We had a snow here about a week ago that lay on the ground sufficient to track a rabbit for more than 24 hours; some laid on the north bluffs for 2 or 3 days. Then I have been at work in an armory and have been busy fixing up machines and had a great deal of job work to do. About half of the hands were sick; all the hands have been sick but one and myself. This made more work for the well hands. I may say I was a little sick for a few days but not off duty. I could state other reasons for not writing sooner.

I have received one letter from John and 1 or 2 from you and 1 from Amos contained in the same envelope as your last. I am happy to learn that Amos has returned home again to stay with you, also that John is at home. I think Will could not stand the hardships of camp life and will also be at ere the winter is over. As for myself I think I will stay. I came to stay when I left home; I did not much expect to return again and it yet seems that I never will see home again. I do not feel the least discouraged. I will return home if I live whenever I honorable can, and not until then.

I send you on this sheet a plot of Fort Pickering correctly laid off as I could do it with plotting instruments. Since I did it, nearly all of Co F have tried to get it from me but I have kept it from the officers for fear they would haul me up for it. There is not much news here. All is very quiet. Some changes in officers: Sgt Phillips has been promoted to capt of Co A . . . Erben of Co A to Sgt. Lone to Capt of Co F; Capt Brown to Maj, W. W. West to 2nd Lieut but to what Co I do not know. Sam Cochran is Sargt in John's place.[1] Thomas Grier in Sawyer's place. Several other promotions that I do not recollect. Thos Simons is discharged and will go home as soon as he is able. John Sibbald came to camp last night well but is sick today. Will Case, James Galbraith, and Turner Hooks are off duty. Griff Heitt has been sick for a while but I believe he is able for duty again. Lieut Drennin and Adams will both resign and go home under the arrangement if their resignation will be accepted. They both feel aggrieved. If Phillips had been captain of Co F they would have been satisfied and all of the privates, but few, are as it is.

The socks and handkerchief have not come to hand yet. I want a pair of boots of Ruggle make if there would be any chance to get them. Have me a pair made soon if you can and I will send the mony. A pair of good hip boots, 10s is the size of these I am wearing. The size may be taken from my fine boots. Use your judgement about having them made. Send me word soon about the prospect the earliest opportunity as I will not look for any others till you let me know.

I am well. I must close. Tell John and Amos I will write soon. Give my love and respects to all of the family and yourself a share

Yours &c

Saml Evans

1. Sam's brother John had been a sergeant in Sam's company.

⇻ ANDREW TO SAM ⇺
Home / November 2, 1862

Dear son,

After a lapse of two weeks I again resume my duty in writing to you. Several of our family have written to you in the interim. My rule for several months, has been to write you every sunday, and let the others of the family do the writing through the week. On saturday the 25th I had to go to Georgetown, a very cold, drisly day. Whilst there I concluded to go over to Feesburg and see Inda & the children. Before I got there it began to snow; in the morning found about 6 inches of snow. I left at 8 in the morning, arrived at home at half past 2 P.M. so much benumbed by cold that I could not write so you could have read it. John has written to you since that, we start at least two letters a week to you, if the mails fail to take them to you, we can't help it. We have but one from you in the last two weeks, our mails are very irregular. The Ohio River is nearly frose up. I received yours of the 21st yesterday, is the only one in 2 weeks. I am most happy to inform you that Amos' address is "Aberdeen Ohio". You have learned ere this that he was discharged and came home. There have been several letters written to you from home since he returned.

Our folks are well except Lee who has been sick for over a week. He is mending & I think will be well in a few days. Anjaline is quite sick with some symptoms of Typhoid Fever, Inda & her children are quite well. Sam is a very fine boy and quite a rowdy. Aunt Dian is sick with some troublesome disease of the bowels, accompanied with "prolapsus Ani". Tom Carpenter is at home on short "leave of absence". He has had the mumps. He expects to return today or tomorrow, his Regt is at Lexington K. [My] Bro Amos is in the hospital at Point Pleasant Va. deeply afflicted with Rheumatism & perhaps fistula in ani. Will & George are gone up the Kanhawa valley, they were both well when they wrote last.[1] Their address is Point Pleasant, Va. We have had no letters from them since they passed the "Red House" 30 miles up the Kan. V. Amos got a letter from John Carpenter, he is at the post hospital in Middletown Md. but expects to come to Galipolis O. soon. The general health here is tolerable good, our snow is all gone and the weather is beautiful, some few are gathering corn, but I think it too damp to put up in the husk safely.

We have not sown any more wheat since he returned, we are progressing tolerably well with our work, John has undertaken to put the mill in good running order. He thinks he will be able to run it. I hope he may; he has all the heavy machinery in good order, the tail race cleaned, and will commence to put in the residue of the arch tomorrow if the weather will permit. We put a new segment in the Master cog wheel and have things in the piling true and made fast (I say we, because I have to superintend, I think I know how it ought to be). Dave King does the wood work, Big Pat the mud work; Amos arched the race where the branch crosses, and put the good wall to keep the branch out of the tail race. We could not get Mitchell at that time; he is under promise to do the rest of the stone work and to commence tomorrow morning. John has repaired all the shutters, put in a new sash & glass and fixed for, and keeps things locked up. He will put a shutter on the glass window to defend it against s__t asses &c. He intends to finish and put up your cleaning aparatus. Dave says he can do the work, if I will make him do it right. I have consented to do so, I think the whole will be ready to run (except the cleaning works) during this week. The head race needs but little work. Dave will work for Doc Guthry this week, and then return and finish the mill work.

Dave Tarble has come out right side up. I am happy to inform you I am satisfied now that it was nothing but a dirty little political spite. His dirty political enemies intended to inflict on him, Cal Rankin, Sam Housh & others of the Political Abolition faith! When Tarble came to trial they failed entirely to make a case of him. We set them on their asses very nicely in the Ohio election this fall, the bogus Union, Republican party are not so hard to hold since the election. They have been saying rather snuringly all summer that the Democratic party would never be heard of anymore but I fancy there will be a few of them on hands when the "last horn blows". John B. booted our ticket voluntarily, he is through with republicanism![2]

You will not get your things (socks &c) as soon as we supposed you would when we started them. They were delayed at Ripley some time, but I think you will get them and be pleased with them when you get them. Wm Armstrong put your packet in [Regimental Quartermaster] IH Debruins box and put it in Capt Loves care, (at least I have been so informed.) If you have not got them, call on Debruin and see if his box has arrived.

The river is so low it is difficult to send anything by water. Amos says he will write you about the middle of this week, some of the girls will write also. I shall try to keep up the practice of writing you every sunday. Dont stint your own needs pecuniarly [sic] to send it to us; we will get along best we can. Take care of yourself before you think of aiding your friends at home. Your tendered love and compliments are gratefully received by your many friends, and in return are hereby tendered the compliments of the recipients.

Very truly your father
Andrew Evans

1. This refers to the valley of the Kanawha River, which runs from the Ohio River, through West Virginia, and into the mountains of southwestern Virginia. George B.

Davis, Leslie J. Perry, Joseph W. Kirkley, and Calvin D. Cowles, *The Official Military Atlas of the Civil War* (New York: Crown Publishers, 1978), plate 135A.

2. At this point many of Ohio's Democratic Party leaders still supported the war effort. The Evanses, who had been lifelong Democrats, were still voting against the Union (or Republican) Party, casting their ballots for War Democrats. Here, in rather abstruse phrasing, Andrew describes son John as abandoning "republicanism" (a reference to the "democratic republican" tradition of the old Jackson Democrats) and supporting the Union Party. This foreshadows the eventual political shift of the entire Evans family.

⇢ INDIANA EARLY TO SAM ⇠
Feesburg / November 5, 1862

Dear Brother,

I received your kind letter on Saturday, was extremely glad to hear from you. I do not mind getting a letter from you before, I know I should have written to you long ago. It was not because I had forgotten you, no; Sam, do not think so, I always think and pray for you all, almost every hour of the day, many, and many a tear has dropped for the loved ones in the army. I use to have George to weep with me, now he has gone too, and I have no one to comfort me as he did. He writes very often to me. The last letter I received from him was dated Oct 22nd; they were then camped one mile below Buffalow, on the Kanawho River, there was a good many of the regiment sick, and they sent them back to Point Pleasant. Uncle Amos was one [of] them. He had the Rheumatism and something like the Fistula, but not dangerous. George thought he would be discharged soon, or ought to be. George and Will were well, Will was not with them. He does not march with the Co. . . . George has gained 13 or 14 pounds, since he went into the Army. He has his purtyness taken and sent home, he makes a fine looking soldier. Father was down here last Saturday week. They were all well then but John; he was not any better. Father said he was getting the mill fixed up, intends to run it this winter. I should think it would be very bad for his health, to go to the damp mill. I fear he does not take sufficient care of himself to get along well. Amos had got home; he had no trouble in getting off. They said they did not like to let off, as useful a man as he was, but it was against the law to take him. Little Tom got off too. Di and Lina have moved to Georgetown. Lina is going to school, and Diann is going to keep a milliner shop I guess.

There is nothing going on here worth telling. There was 52 drafted in this Township, and 28 of them rejected. There are four or five Boys here from the 59, have been here two or three weeks. They say they ran off; they are all stout hearty men. I think somebody ought to attend to them. Now I must tell you about my nice little boys, little Sam is almost as good looking as his Uncle Sam, he can sit alone, and very near crawl; in fact his Mother thinks he is a very smart Boy. Morty has grown to be a good chunk of a lad; he knows where you all have gone; he says you are a going to give him your old grey cat when you come home; he talks about all of you every day. He thinks his Pa is coming/every body he hears whistle. Same, Pap said you had your likeness taken and sent it to Mary. I did not like it a bit, because he did not bring it down for me to see. He said I would hardly know you as a southern gentleman, but I think I would know you any where I would see you. I hope the war will soon be over then I will see the original. I must bring my letter to a close, it is getting late and I am tired. I wrote to George yesterday I write to him once and twice a week. We only have the mail twice a week. We only have the mail twice a week Tuesday and Saturday. I will mail this at Hamersville; we get the daily paper there. I hope you will excuse mistakes and bad writing, for I am in a hurry. Pa and Ma send their love to you. Accept my love and best wishes. Write soon,

From your true and loving Sister,
India Early

✦ ANDREW TO SAM ✦
Home / November 9, 1862

Dear Sam,

I received yours of the 31 on the 7, & am very much obliged, for your map of Fort Pickering, it is very satisfactory. There is one word (barquitte) in it that I confess I don't understand. I can neither find it in Webster, nor the military glossary. I don't say it is wrong, but don't know the meaning of it? Please explain it. Your plot and description is very easily understood, as good as I could ask. I am sorry to learn that you had not received the little bundle yet, I hope you have before this time. Armstrong put it in Debruins box, and put the box in care of Capt Love, which I thought very safe, and still think so. I will have you a pair of boots (Ripleys [?] best) made soon, and send them the first chance that looks reliable. I have not been down since your letter came, but Amos asked the old man yesterday about getting a turn for you. He said he was about 15 pairs of boots behind his orders, but that your order would be attended to "instanter" at any time I put in the order. I will attend to it in a few days.

John was operated on, on last Friday for, the cure of Fistula, Old Doc Wylie of Ripley did the work. He was here a few minutes ago to see John, he says John is doing very well. I think so too. The residue of our family are well. Angaline Amos' wife has been quite sick for about a week, she is mending a little. The rest of your friends and connections in the country are well. . . . I got another letter from [my brother] Amos friday. He is still at Point Pleasant Va. with Rheumatism and Fistula both. He writes me that he will be discharged soon as his papers can go the proper rounds. He thinks he will get home in three or 4 weeks, I hope he may. He is needed at home. We have had nothing from Will or George for some time, they were well at their last writing which I gave you in my last. From accounts in the papers they are about Gauley and have found no Rebels "worthy of their steel". You perhaps get the Commercial, as often as I do and are as well (or maybe better) posted in all army movements as I am. We have Company tonight, Fennon from Aberdeen, Lide Thompson, Becky & Fany Carpenter. Amos is playing the Melodeon & the girls singing. Well he can't play as well as you, but he has improved very much. He is playing "Never forget the dear ones", "Ballerina" & "Bonny E. Louisa". It makes me wish anew, that you were here to join in the choir. It would make me feel most happy. Oh for the end of this unnatural war! That our near & dear friends might return to us; our time on earth is but short, and full of miseries at best. O how it would increase out pleasures for you to be with us, vain thought for we have no right to expect such delight until the war ends, or your time expires.

Our weather is beautiful, tho pretty cold still dry the creek barely running. Three mile creek is almost dry, it has not run since August, and the holes are nearly dry. It has been a very bad season for wheat to come up; we can scarcely see the wheat that has been sown 4 or 6 weeks, we have the corn gathered that grew at Old Neddy's; we go about 450 bu off of that field. The new ground field is better; we have not commenced it yet. I don't believe I will have time to sue your customers before the 1st of Dec. We are striving hard to get our fall work done before winter sets in. I have to give part of my time to John's mill job; he is not able now to superintend, but I hope he will be soon. Pat has several rods of the head race cleaned, Mitchell pitched that last piece of arch and it let down to strait, after it was covered and Pat had to shovel the dirt off again. He must do it better than that if I have to stay by him all the time. I won't have it so.

Very truly your father

Andrew Evans

⇒ SAM TO ANDREW ⇐
Memphis, TN / November 20, 1862

Dear father,

Your favor of the 9th was received on the 17th. I am very thankful that you have been so punctual in corresponding. I ought to be more so but very often I cannot. You say you do not understand the word "Barquette". It means the same as burcade and is used for protecting a gap in breastworks thus for instance

[The original letter included a rough sketch here.]

The v is the barquette in the cut above and is on the outside of the work with a road between the ends of it and the main works; the horizontal line represents the main fort or wall. I made these things on the fort and while I was making the Engineer frequently visited me, that is what he called it and that is what it is written on the plot of "Fort". If it is not correct the Engineer is wrong. He often explain how he wanted me to do it. I am positively certain that I am not mistaken in what he called it. You are very welcome if what I have sent you is satisfactory in any way you will please keep it.

The box of Debruin's is not come nor Capt Love. The supposition is that he has been stopped at Cin'. Lieut. Brown has been sent after him (as I understand). I am sorry that Uncle Amos is so afflicted. I thought he had lived too close to Eastfork all his life to be of good cheer in the Army. We get the news every day (nearly) and keep as well posted for the time we have. You speak of "company" and of the girls singing and him playing the Melodean, well I would like to try a tune on the Melodean. Probably I could not play much now but think I feel a tune in my fingers. It has been a long time since I tried to play.

Do you recall at the last time I saw you. You were going to build a bridge on the turnpike in RattleSnake. You were about half way from the yard gate to the old sheep house (Oh! used to be) and I on the step at the

{ 80 } THEIR PATRIOTIC DUTY

well. I think I have forgotten nothing that was there when I left. Could go in to the shop and pick your tools and material from mine. While I think about it, do you know what is done with those small chisels that I left in the cupboard at the shop? There is part of two lots and I think there about 18 or 20 of them. I also left a keehole saw in the same desk. You appropriate them to your own use or any thing you want of mine. Is the washing machine done that was underway when I left? I have wandered from the subject. Those tunes you said Amos was playing are all nice. "Balerina" is a tune I think will never wear out and much pleases me as to harmony.

I have had every assurance since I joined the army that you all would be better pleased with me at home and it would be more pleasure for me to be at home than to be here. I did not join the army with a view to pleasure, rather "green". If any one has and he who has will be very likely, to be mistaken and find himself in the "wrong pew". When ever opportunity permits I shall be very happy to meet you all whether the war is over or not.

There are some very important movements in progress but I am not posted as to the movements all the division. Sherman's is under orders to hold themselves in readiness to march at a moments warning and to be ready in about 1 week. Most of the Officers think this brigade will not leave for a month or six weeks, and that they will not leave unless it is necessary for reinforcing some army down the river some distance. I should judge from the troops that are here (between 30 and 70,000) that the intention is to free this part of the South of Rebels. I cannot tell yet, whether I shall go when the Reg't goes or not. There is however a slight probability that I will not. There is a great deal of work here to do. The ordnance officer does not want me to go. The foreman does not want me to go, he is doing all he can to keep me. He told me yesterday (privately) that he would rather have me than any hand he had, that I was the only that did my work to suit him exactly. I am the spring maker for the shop. I have done but little else since I wrote you last. I do nothing but make new work in repairing. I do nearly all the repairing that is difficult on revolvers. I would like very well to stay if Sherman is willing. He ordered me detailed and his order can only take me out. I asked James Drennin to make out my "descriptive roll"; he said it was no use that when he went I would have to go too. It may be so, but Neely (the Ordnance Officer) says not. Direct your letters as formerly till further informed.

There have been some more promotions in the Army. Brigadier Gen Denver has been promoted to maj. Gen; Dr. Phillips late Capt of Co. A 70th . . . is Adjutant Gen on Denver's staff. That is good I say, he is a good officer and a brave one. I have not learned who will take Denver's place and what changes in the Brig will be.

I guess I have told you about all that is of importance. Will write to India soon. She wrote me that she and the children are well. Will also write to John. See what is the reason he has quit writing. Give my love to Mother brothers, sisters Pat and Peggy, to Grandmother and all on the Hill and retain yourself a share.

And believe me as ever your son

Sam

N.B. Ask Pat how he and Peggy get along if they are married.

Sam

※ SAM TO ANDREW ※
Memphis, TN / November 26, 1862

Dear father,

I reced your letter of the 15 today, also one from Jane. I have an opportunity to send you a few lines direct by Joseph Dadd who will leave for home tomorrow. He is discharged from service Honorably.

I will leave tomorrow morning with the rest of the boys. We are bound South but where I don't know. Sherman ordered all the men on detail back to their Reg't. My Boss says he is very sorry that I have to leave him. I send with the bearer a parcel of old letters, will you please keep them for me till I return.[1] If I should never come you can do as you will. I will send a sand book. Give it to Ann and tell her to remember me. I will put a parcel of little pebble from the "field of Shiloh", in the same pack. Give them to Ibbe to keep till I return. Inclosed please find five dollars to pay for my boots. Capt Love has not come yet nor has Debruin received his box. When it comes I will get my goods. We have not yet been paid. No more at present. My love to all.

Your affectionate Son,

Sam

1. This sentence explains, in part, why so many of Samuel's letters from the family were preserved. He sent old letters back home periodically.

❧ SAM TO ANDREW ❧
Headquarters Co. F 70
Near Oxford, Miss / December 6th, 1862

Dear father,

On the first of the month I wrote a short note but it could not go as we were informed before I mailed it all the letters that have been written since we started are yet in the division train.

We have received but one mail since we left Memphis and that on the 2nd or 3rd days march. I will enclose a note that I wrote on the first, as it contains what I could say of the march up to that time. 2nd started early marched to Myott on the Tallahatchee River, distance of 13 miles, stay there, 3rd/4th started out in the rain and mud, marched 10 miles through all the bad roads, build a bridge over the Tallahatchee. The Rebs evacuated the breastworks on Monday and are now 35 or 40 miles from here to the best of our knowledge. 5 day[s] [to get] here. All day 5th marched to where we are now today. We are waiting orders. I am of the opinion that the Rebs will feel our march very sensibly.

Well I will tell you a little about how we do it. If it is known how far we are going there is no plundering till within a few miles of the end of the march then hogs, geese, hens, duck, potatoes, beer, everything that is good to eat, had better not try "to bite" if they do they may get hurt. I can say that our Regt has behaved better than any Regt in this army or, at least it has the praise. As soon as we stop, some make fires, others carry fence rails for fires during the night. First on hands best served.

You could scarcely believe, the damage done to a country that so large an army marches through. All the fence is burned; mules and horses taken, fodder, and corn besides a great many other things that could not be properly called confiscated. I would call it stealing if at home. I can say that thus far I have not taken anything at all yet. We have plenty to eat besides all these things. I want the law on my side when I take anything. There are strict orders against this kind of disorderly conduct. It tends to demoralize an army. If men are allowed to follow this path they will many of them acquire habits that will remain with them for life. If I am fortunate enough to return to my home I do not wish to be any worse in morals than when I left home. Yet I am clear of the vice incidental to a Soldier's life. And intend to remain so, if possible.

We are out of "soap" and candles and can not draw any for some time yet. We do without soap and make rails answer for candles. I sleep in Adam's tent. Stick and I sleep together. My health so far has been very good. My toe is very sore. The nail is off, it having gathered underneath. Still I have been able to march in ranks and carry a big load, with considerable punishment. It is all right or will be. I think our destination is Jackson, Miss. I believe from accounts, the Rebs are gone thither.

My study consists [of] Geography and reading. My Geography is a military map; reading, McGuffeys 4th reader. I would carry a grammar if I could get Kirkhour and arithmetic if Rays. Oh! I will stop—for there is Webster's Unabridged and several others I could name. I guess you cannot read all I have tried to write. Perhaps I had better quit and write my [next] opportunity. I will write every opportunity and that will not be perhaps as often as I would like to. We are going from home now and where mail can not catch us often, but remember me, and I will strive to be worthy of you, father. I will try to conduct myself in such a manner as not to reflect shame upon the family of me. Remember me kindly to mother and all the family and all who feel an interest in Sam. And believe me ever

Your Son,

Sam

P.S. This is as good as I can do by fire light. Pardon mistakes and "Take the will for the Deed."

※ SAM TO ANDREW ※
Cholomoch [?],[1] Miss. / December 7, 1862

Dear father,

Tonight we learned that mail could be sent tomorrow morning. That being the case I thought I would write you a few lines. You may find it strange that I write on this paper. Well it is because my paper is put up in good order and cannot be gotten at conveniently. We have no candles consequently I write by the light of rails. Well, for some of the particulars of the march. You are aware ere this that I had to leave the shop though I did not much like to do so. I made no excuse but made ready, cleaned up my gun a little nicer than any in the Regt, packed up my knapsack ready for march. What I could not carry well I packed up and left at Memphis. Like all the rest of the Co., in care with the past quarter Master at that place and will be forwarded to us as soon as communication is open to us. Monday morning at 8 o'clock, came about 7 miles. My toes and feet got pretty sore but still I thought I must on and maybe they would get better. Thursday morning we started early, marched 17 miles. Am still carrying all of a soldiers "doeflicks", feet still worse; no rebs to be seen.

Friday marched 14 miles, carried knapsack, feet bled considerable. Camp in pigeon creek bottom till Sunday morning. After resting one day, Sunday, we marched about 6 miles where we now lay today. We have been waiting for orders. I feel quite well yet, over the march except my feet, which are very sore. I think I can stand as much pain as anybody. All the boys that came with us are well. There is nothing much of interest here to communicate as we have met no rebs yet. They are about 8 miles from here on the Tallahatchee River and it is said they are fortified. Since I commenced our calvary came in and say that Rebs have left but that may be all a hoax. Gen Grant's army is about 7 miles from this and about 9 miles south of Holly Springs. Gen Grant was here today to see Sherman. What the object was I did not learn. If the Rebs attack we will give them the best we have. We have a large army and one can fight. Sherman says 70th have to charge over the bridge of above named river. I think we can do that but that will be a tough place. It is our turn to march in front next and Co F time to go on picket next night. You need not send me anything more without some one is coming direct to us for we never get anything. Send my boots if you have reliable chance. I sent you five dollars with Dadd and all the old letters that I have not destroyed.

My love and best wishes to all the family

Your son

Sam Evans

P.S. write as often as you please and [I] will as often as I can.

1. It is difficult to decipher Sam's spelling of the town from which this letter was sent, but Sam was probably in Chulahoma, Mississippi, about thirty miles southeast of Memphis. George Davis et. al., *The Official Military Atlas of the Civil War*, plate 154.

⇒ SAM TO ANDREW ⇐
Holly Springs / January 4, 1863

Dear Father,

I have an opportunity to send you a few lines again. . . . I suppose you think me slow about writing. It is slow, these times. I have written to you 2 letters, to Amos, and 1 to Mary since I left Memphis, these being all the chances that I have had to send letters. I have had mail once since we left

Memphis. I received 9 letters the day we arrived here, the 28th, 3 from you dated Nov. 23rd, 30th, 1, Dec. 7th, 2 from Amos Nov. 19th and one 27th, and one from Mary, 21 of Nov. I was much pleased to read letters from home although they had been written a long while the contents of yours I can notice but briefly this time. The letters you spoke of John writing has never come. You think [in] the letter written on the 23rd that I have misconstrued your letter. I sent all your letters home, you can see for yourself. I may have overlooked your letter or misunderstood it "About the mill" or Wendell. You have made everything plain in your letters but what I spoke of. I honestly thought though I wrote and did it to know how it was. Not to "criticize." My wages in the shop was 40 cts per day extra. I want you to use anything of mine that you want. Amos asks whether Cud Carrigan acct. is $40.50 or $46.50 with a Cr. $1.25 paid by David King. He now owes $2.90. The Cr. was entered on a book that was mislaid and got in the weather. I found the book under the fence near the new cellar and was so much defaced that I could not find anything I could read, it was so rotted. There is a sheet of paper with the accts. of all transient customers made out somewhere among my papers. Sal Scott said he left money or means with Wiles to settle it (his acct.) and Wiles said he would do it. G. G. Game's acct. is not settled unless he settled it with you since I left. These are all the questions answered. I say see if it will be likely to get the money, if not there is no use of it. You or Amos may use your own discretion in this matter and I will be satisfied. I will write to Amos soon if I have an opportunity. I thought I would answer his questions in your [letter] for fear I [will] have no opportunity soon.

The Rail Road is now finished to Memphis; the cars came through yesterday and are going back tomorrow. We have plenty of provisions for some days before we reached this place. Our division went within 20 miles of Grenada, there camped till we heard of the raid at this place. Our provision all being destroyed here. We had nothing nearer than Memphis except what we could forage and that is about played out in this region. Breadstuff, sugar, coffee sugar sold have been very scarce not over 1/2 and sometimes as low as 1/4 rations. Meat has been rather scarce sometimes but nearly full allowance. The Beef is very tuff and not as fat as I like. Bacon very strong but we need not complain of meat. Corn, "Niger Peas" and Potatoes and sometimes hogs are what we get by foraging.[1] After the Rebles destroyed our stores at this place, we marched back. When we started, our destination was Moscow, Tenn. On arriving here the order was changed. Denver's Division stopped and McArthur's division went on to Moscow. The same evening that we stopped I was detailed to run a steam mill in town here which I have done till today. This mill furnishes more than this division in breadstuff. The grain is had by foraging. The reason I quit the mill was that I have been appointed Regimental Armorer. I am procuring the tools necessary, I am off of all other duty in the Co. and will receive 40 cts. per day extra, besides outside work which will likely made a good thing of it, in my opinion.

Our loss here in Government Stores is great at least $1,000,000. But there is nearly enough cotton here now to pay that back besides the forage of the country—we have more than got that $1,000,000 back with interest. Since they burnt our stores we have not been very reluctant to take anything we want. It is ordered that every family shall be left 60 days subsistance if we can find enough elsewhere, but if not take all. If either must perish for want of subsistance the Citizens instead of the Soldier. How many citizens are to live I do not Know. They are coming to the mill and offering 2 bus. of corn for 1/2 bu. of meal and say they have not had anything to eat of several days. They cannot but a bit of bread stuff. This looks a little hard but who is the cause of it. They let them feel it. This is a nice little place, or was once.

I cannot tell you any of the movements or what is going on. I have not seen newspapers for at least one month. Our trains came in from Memphis yesterday with provisions. Several of our Co. received things sent from home.

I hear Lieutenant F. W. Adams is going to Memphis; he is not well. He has applied for a discharge. His papers are under way and will in all probability go through. I may send this with him if he is going home. Our boys are well as usual. I have excellent health since I left Memphis. My feet are badly "stove" up. I can hardly walk though I have marched all the way. It has been raining for the last two days. The ground is very wet. Our Co. went on picket yesterday. It rained all the time they were out. We are camped near Grant's Head. It's 1/2 mile from town near the R.R.

My hands are cold; I can't write any more now. I hope you will still write as often as you can conveniently and I will as often as I have an opportunity. We are or have been in a very bad place to receive or send mail.

Give my love and respects to Mother and all the family to Grandmother and all on the hill and all who feel an interest in my welfare and keep for yourself a good share and believe me as ever.

Your big son,
Sam

p.s. How is Lee? Is he well and does he ever think of me? Tell [him] "Howdy." SE

1. Here Sam probably intended to write "Nigger Peas," another term for black-eyed peas.

✣ SAM TO ANDREW ✣

LaGrange, Tenn. / January 16, 1863

Dear Father,

Yours of the 4th came to hand on the 12th. I assure you that I felt at home when I received yours of the above date. It was the only one that came to the Regt. at that time. We have had some very severe weather since I wrote to John on last Sunday. Rain from Monday morning to Wednesday morning. The snow set in and and snowed till noon today. Snow is about 6 in. deep and is quite cold; we have but few tents and they are not good, everything received a complete wetting, with the rain and snow was a hard wind. There is the heaviest guard duty that has ever been since we came out, 200 of the Regt. is on picket every other day, and the remainder is on guard 8 hours every 24 hours. It is easy on me as I have no duty of any kind in the way of guard or fatigue. The Col made a requisition for some gun tools and a portable forge and an anvil and some other tools. The weather has been so bad since I got them that I could do nothing at gun fixing.

You speak of the 70 having been detailed or rather on detail duty. That is all a mistake. You may guess the 70th has been on duty. Guard and fatigue. I must make this note rather shorter than I would like to. My eyes are very sore from some cause or other. It is very painful to write but it is a duty and a high privilege that I esteem and embrace every opportunity. I do not like the way matters are working up north, I am fearful there will be a bad mess in this business of war yet. I would say there is but little hopes for an honorable ending of the war to us. If we are only used as soldiers ought to be, we will put down this rebellion; otherwise we cannot I am willing to still stake my life for its salvation.

Give my love and highest respects to George and Will and my friends in the 83.[1] My love and highest regards to all of the folks. I am very well except my eye. The health of the Regt. is good.

I subscribe myself as ever your son,

Sam

17th—my eyes are better this morning. Gen. Mcpherson leaves for Memphis this morning. Denver's division is all that is left there now. There are some troops at Moscow, yet our boys go on picket tomorrow morning.

Sam

1. Here Sam misspoke. George and Will were both in the 89th OVI.

⇾ SAM TO ANDREW ⇽
Lagrange, Tenn. / Jan. 20, 1863

Dear Father,

It is about time that I was writing you again. I believe I wrote you since I received a letter from you. Yours of the 4 is the last I have from home. There's but little news to tell you. It is still very bad weather it has rained for the last 2 days and nights. With the rain was a wind sufficient to upset our cabooses [huts] and tents. After all the exposure the boys of our Co. and Regt are in pretty good health. My eyes have improved very much, do not hurt at all now. My health is quite good. Yesterday morning there was a detail of 5 men from our Regt. to make coffins for soldiers who died in the Post Hospital at this place. There were not enough men who were willing to go. I had the privilege to go if I wanted. I thought it would be soldier like for me to go. We had 18 coffins to make. We went into a church and took out the seats. We finished the last at noon today. The Division Q[uarter] Master wants me to take charge of the shop and have the job of coffin making and wagon repairing. I am already on detail as armorer and Loudon says he cannot spare me.[1] I guess the job is better than the one offered. I will perhaps stay where I am. I have no news to give you about army movements in this region.

Denver's Division is the only one here. We may stay here for awhile. We are only 49 miles from Memphis by "Rail." Have enough to eat but would like to have some things of the clothing kind in a week or 2. Our Q.M. went to Memphis after the clothing we left there; if he gets that we will be right again. Where F. W. Adams is I don't know. He offered his resignation but it was not accepted. I understand he has been promoted to 1st Lieut. but would not have that. Said he was tired and sick.

I think quite a number of the troop would give all that is due them to get out of the service. There is nearly 7 months pay due all the old troops.[2]

In this army I am not quite so keen to get out as that. I never intend to desert this cause. If I could get off honorably on furlough or leave of absence, I would come home for short time. Last Sunday was 11 months since I left East forks about as long as any of the 70 have been from home. My best wishes be with you all. Continue to write and I will. Good bye,

Your Son,
Sam

1. Sam is referring to Colonel D. W. C. Loudon. For more information about Loudon, see note in John and Sam's letter of April 10, 1862.

2. For a brief discussion of payment problems in the Union Army see note in Sam's letter of May 1, 1862.

➤ AMOS TO SAM ◄
Aberdeen / Jan 25, 1863

Dear Brother,

I rec'd yours of the 18th inst. and the 19th. After looking long & anxiously I am now gratified. Father got one written the 4th from Holly Springs. He having the oldest right, [he] took the word out of my mouth and wrote some days ago—

I got one from Will of the 11th. They are as well as usual. They are camped on the Kanawha. He & George got the clothing, boots, etc that I sent to them. Little Bill was at home on a 20 day furlough. He went back last Thursday—he says that home is no place for him.

George Jimeson was here yesterday, he looks very bad. Adams has not got home yet[1] . . .

Our health is not very good. John has had a considerable backset. I honestly think he will never get stout, if he recovers at all. I have had a bad cold which came near laying me up. Bad colds are common with us, nothing else serious. Father weighs 186. He & I have been milling this week. We have things in good order. Stone Sharp & c. The big Snow is about gone and the roads are very muddy.

Well how do you like those things we sent you. Oh I wish you had them, they would relieve you very much. But you know we have done all we could & I Expect you will get them if Leave gets to the Regt.

We See in the Daily that Grant is gone to Vicksburg & we have to think that you are gone there too.[2] I trust that God may still protect & watch over you as he has done & that we may meet again to Enjoy peace & Liberty. Will expects to be at home soon on furlough to stay a few days. I wish you could come too. It is lonesome Everywhere that I have been for sometime but we try to keep from being lonesome. We have plenty of work & plenty of Books and Papers when we do not work. But Sam, I tell you one thing privately—Will Cunningham's family will break Aunt & Uncle Amos & make them as poor as themselves Soon if they keep doing as they are now. The whole family with Amos & Kate have been there all winter. They don't do anything, only Sponge & play a full hand at that. They don't bother us, nor cant.

Sam there is no[thing] new particularly here. There seems to be a general moving of troops toward the lower Mississippi—& the Army of the Potomac are ordered to cross the Rappahannock again, don't know how they will make it. Accept our love with that of grandmother. Write when you can.

Your affectionate brother,

Amos

The girls want to send you a few line in this[3]

1. This a reference to Lieutenant F. W. Adams. In Sam's letter of January 4, 1863, he mentions that Lt. Adams was going to return home, pending a discharge he had requested for medical reasons.

2. Amos's assumption was incorrect. Neither Sam, nor his regiment, had gone to Vicksburg.

3. Nothing from Sam's sisters has been preserved as part of this letter.

⇥ SAM TO ANDREW ⇤
Lagrange, Tenn. / January 28, 1863

Dear Father,

I received yours of the 19th today, also one from Amos. I thank you still for your punctillity [politeness] towards me and have endeavored to be so with you. If you have not received my letters the cause must be in the mail and not in me. I have written a number of letters you have not yet received. . . .

Did Thorton pay what he owed me? You ask "for whom I made the long knife in the drawer?" For a soldier that I thought would not pay for it, as he owed a bill before and did not pay it. You can let Dave have if he wants it. I believe it is a good knife. I am sorry that mother and John are not getting along better. We had a snow some 6 incs. the same time you had your big snow, and if you had more much than we, you had enough. More rain than suits our fancy.

I fear you feel too much interest in my welfare for your own good. I do not object to having the good will of all but don't allow me to give you trouble. I will endeavor for your sake to take good care of myself and not expose my self more than duty calls for. I cannot bear the idea of being cowardly, neither will I ever make an excuse to avoid being in battle. I have marched when I could scarcely walk. I am now well and have been ever since I left Memphis except my feet; they are nearly well. The health of our Regt. is very good only one man has died since we left Memphis and he was left at Memphis. Col. Loudon Started home yesterday on leave of absence of 20 days. I repaired his pistols before he left.

You spell "Vixburg" is that right?[1] I want to know. I think it is spelled Vicksburg. You have a better chance to know than I. It would be a great relief to me if I had Webster Unabridged for reference. All the spelling that I do is from recollection, as a guide that is not very convenient. . . .

James Drennin does not like the promotion over him. I think myself he was entitled to the position.[2] I think to some extent it was his actions that prevented him from being promoted. The first Lieut of Co. I was ordered to take command of Co. H as Wiles was not well. He refused and handed over his sword. He was court martialed. I do not know what it (the Courtmartial) did. There is sure foul play in the matter. Foster was promoted to the same that he was, that made 2 1st Lieuts in the same Co.

I am getting along very well in my new position. The boys think me quite a workman as some people did at home. John McDaniel and I have had a likeness taken for Grandmother, I will address it to Mrs. Mary Evans Son. Will you be so kind as to deliver it to her if it comes to hand. I thought she would be glad to have a picture of mine. She seems very interested in me.

The goods came to me all safe on Monday. The boots are first rate, a little too High in the instep, but they suit me better than any I have seen. The socks and handkerchief fit as nice as could be, suit me to a T. Thank you for all. I am comfortable as a soldier could well be. Give my love to all, to Will, and everybody generally, Mother in particular. Accept for yourself a share.

I am as Ever,
Sam

1. The letter in which Andrew first misspells Vicksburg has not been preserved. In later letters below, Andrew continues to spell "Vixburg."

2. As a response to the frequent incompetence among elected officers, in July 1861 the Union Army established an officer examination to ensure that officers met certain reasonable standards. Vacancies in existing regiments were usually filled from the regiment's ranks by promotion based on merit rather than election. The fact that most volunteer regiments' officers technically received their commissions from state governors, however, meant that this process could never be completely isolated from political concerns. McPherson, *Ordeal by Fire*, 171.

❧ ANDREW TO SAM ☙
Home / February 1, 1863

Dear Sam,

Again two weeks have passed since I wrote you a letter. I went to my table last Sunday to write you, and found Amos writing to you, thought it useless to write on the same day, and as Sunday has been my regular day for writing to you I have delayed until my day came round.

I received yours of the 20th on the 30th, John received one from you a day or two previous, (a good long one). I have been looking in vain, for the acknowledgement of the receipt of your goods, Cap. Love, W. W. West & others started for Memphis on the 3rd of Jan, & I had many assurances from Capt. Love, that you would get your things if he ever got to his Regt. I am truly sorry they have been kept from you so long, but they were out of our reach. I hope they will all turn-up right; you of course still need them. What is the matter with your eyes? You say in your last letter "my eyes are better" etc; you have never informed us of anything the matter with your eyes, we are at a loss to know what has been their condition.

The 89th O.V.I. has gone down to "Dixie," to what point, we are left to guess, to Vixburg I fear! They & 3 other Regts. passed down on last Wednesday. We had a letter from Will dated Jan. 19th which is the last. In it he spoke nothing of leaving, nor did we have any hint until we heard they had gone. It is reported at Aberdeen that [Sam's uncle] Amos was with them. For the truth, we will have to wait. The last time he wrote home, he was sick and dispirited, and feigned no hope of recovery. Perhaps the sight of his Regt. raised his spirits. We will certainly learn by letter from some of the boys, where they are gone, they may have been sent to Rosecrants but whether there or to Vixburg, they will soon get into a fight. I wish them the best of luck, and a speedy peace.

I cannot see anything very bright or flattering in our prospects for a speedy peace or to conquer the rebellion, the "vigorous prosecutionists" have subsided into safety of their own persons, and become contented with money making. Whilst the poor soldiers have to put up with all manner of hardships with small rations & no pay. If such stuff as Andrew Jackson could be at the head of affairs for a while, Washington's Shoulderstrap gentry would find something to do besides loafing away their time at hotels, comfortabley clad, fed & paid, while the soldier is in the opposite extreme. I can count the nine Major Generals to-day, who have no command, each of whom draw about double as much pay per month, as the soldier does in a year.

We will never close this war honorably under such a state of affairs, the Rebels know "its neck or nothing" with them, and they are exerting every nerve, while (with the exception of some of our western & Southwestern troops) nothing has been gained on our part. To make and unmake commanders of "the army of the Potomac," and hold Courts Marshall [sic] has been the principal business of the Pres., Sec. of War [Edwin M. Stanton] & Gen Halleck [General-in-Chief Henry Halleck] for the last 3 or 4 months. I must change the subject, or I will get mad.

Our big snow is gone, another ordinary one has come & gone. It has been raining all day, the creek is up. We have had but little cold weather, the roads are awful muddy, bad weather for outdoor work.

Our health is about ordinary. John's has been much worse since I wrote you, but he is better again, his bowels are in better condition for several days than they have been since he came home. If his cough could be controlled I should have more hopes of his recovery to health.

Your friends here are generally well. Davis' Infant died on last Monday, some of other children have been sick but are better. I have been obliged to make a miller of myself; it goes a little hard with me but I have to stand it. [Sam's brother] Amos helps me when through. We have given entire satisfaction so far. Flour all "Double Extra" clean. Wheat is a nice thing to make good flour of, that is what we grind nowadays.

Remember me kindly to my acquaintance's, both officers & soldiers, and receive for yourself the best wishes of your very many friends & relations here, and believe me

 your affectionate father,
 Andrew Evans

❧ ANN TO SAM ❧
Home / Feb. 1, 1863

Dear Brother Sam,

As father is writing to you I thought I would write you a few lines. I hope you have got your clothes by this time. It is raining now, it is very bad weather. Sam you must come up and get some of our Beef. We kild old crump. She was so fat we got 29 pounds of tallow out of her. Sam do you have to sleep on the ground. Sam I don't believe I would know you. Our schoolmaster was put out, tyre maddox. They did not like him much. He did not learn the scholars anything. Sam I wish you would come over and play the Melodeon for us. Sam I wish I could come down and see the boys. Nancy Evans' baby died last Monday at 10 Oclock. Sam it must took you a good while to make 18 coffin. Amos made nancy['s] baby['s] coffin. I must close.

Yours truely,

Ann D. Evans

excuse this bad written letter

❧ SAM TO ANDREW ❧
Lagrange, Tenn. / February 8, 1863

Dear Father,

I am at a loss to know what is the reason I do not receive any more letters. I received a letter from home on the 31st. Since then I have written several. Perhaps letters do not go home any better than they come.

Well I have but little in the way of news. There is some rather interesting from Vicksburg. The Queen of the West did a very nice little thing. She has proved herself very successful and daring. One would naturally think the Rebels would open their eyes at such a feat. Over one hundred guns fired at her and still she was not hurt.[1]

I am very sorry to learn that there are so many to put down the Rebellion. This is called "abolition war." For the sake of a little argument, call it an "abolition war." Were not the Rebels given nearly three months to show whether it should be? Yes! Who were the men who approved of the "Emancipation Proclamation."[2] Gen. McClellan, Gen. Halleck, Burnsides and other Democrats of what I would call the "Right Stripe." So far as I am concerned about the matter, it suits me in a good many points of view. My doctrine has been anything to weaken the enemy. This same negro has been the means of sustanance to the Rebels in the way of building fortification [and] furnishing supplies.

I am very fearful there [is] so much opposition to the war upon the Side of the Union that the lives of all the brave soldiers already lost, the enormous expence The Nation is already gone to, will be a sacrifice without bettering our condition. I verily believe if North had been a unit in the beginning of the war and all worked for the same end, (putting down the rebellion), the war would have been at an end. Such men as Vallandingham give the Rebels courage. I hope you will not think me too harsh. If I have my way, I would put such men as his where they would not do much harm to us. (I mean confine him to prison) till the war is ended. They may talk about Peace Democrat "Abolitionists" "Habeas Corpus" etc. & I hope that is all it will amount to.[3] I am more interested in making the Rebels "Conque" [sic, conk, meaning break down]. There is still hopes; great inducements that war should be vigorously prosecuted. May God grant that the hearts of all our men be in our undertaking. Well enough of this for the present.

All is quiet here. Our Regt. came off 3 days picket day before yesterday. During their picketing 22 Rebel prisoners, some deserters, came in. The cars are still running regular and seem to be doing considerable business in a military way.

The paymaster is now at Memphis with money to pay this division. Our officers were ordered to be ready for pay in a few days. We will perhaps be paid for 4 months this time. I had thought of sending my money home in a letter but the mail seems too uncertain to risk. If I have no reliable way to send it, I will send it as I did before ("By the state agent").

So far as I can learn the health of the army here is good for the exposure and hardships to be endured. There are no sick in our Regt. at present. I have been sick since I wrote last. But am now nearly well again. I had a "small case" of Lung fever. It is now the 4th day since I was taken. I have some cough it is much improved today; I am taking hoarhound candy pretty strong.[4] The weather is still very bad. Snow, rain, mud and wind and almost anything to be unpleasant. There have been 2 or 3 days of quite cold weather.

My articles from home suit me very well. $10.00 were offered me for my boots $2.00 for socks $1.50 for handkerchief. I said "nary" time would sell. Each and every article is the best that I have seen out here.

Capt. West is Regimental P.M. [Paymaster?] I think the Capt. told you that I was a better soldier than I am. He says he told you that a "Regt. of such men as I could whip 4 times their number." That is much better than I think I could do. Let me say, that Capt. West is "bravest of the brave." And one of the best men I ever saw. Our new Capt. is a first rate old fellow. The boys like him very well, he is very kind to us. I have been looking for a letter from Home for several days but I will be patient, they will come after a while. Write as often as you think you ought and I will be satisfied.

Remember me to al the family, to Will, Geo and my acquaintances in the 89. Accept for yourself a share.

While I remain as ever your

Son,

Sam

1. The *Queen of the West* was a Union ram, a steamer designed to destroy enemy boats by ramming into them. It was engaged numerous times during the first half of the war, including in the Union capture of Memphis, which was executed using only naval forces. The incident to which Sam is referring here is probably the *Queen of the West* running the defenses of Vicksburg, Mississippi, and defeating the CSS *City of Vicksburg* anchored there in early 1863. Virgil Carrington Jones, *The River War: March 1862–July 1863, The Civil War at Sea*, vol. 2 (New York: Holt, Rinehart, and Winston, 1961), 173; Garrison, *Encyclopedia*, 202.

2. This February 8 letter is the first mention of Lincoln's January 1 Emancipation Proclamation.

3. Former Dayton Congressman Clement Vallandigham spearheaded the antiwar movement within the Democratic Party. Known as "Copperheads," they argued that preserving the Union did not justify the loss of lives and abridgement of civil liberties, most notably President Lincoln's suspension of the right of habeas corpus. Vallandigham found strong support among many Ohioans, including Brown County residents with Southern roots. Though later letters show that the Evans family had not supported Lincoln in 1860, once the war started, the Evanses stood solidly behind military efforts to preserve the Union. The Evanses considered those who agreed with Vallandigham's pro-peace views disloyal or even treasonous and often derisively referred to them as "Vals" or "Valls." For more information about Vallandigham, see Frank L. Klement, *The Limits of Dissent: Clement L. Vallandigham & the Civil War* (New York: Fordham University Press, 1998).

4. Horehound candy is a cough remedy made from extract from the leaves of the horehound plant, a member of the mint family.

Home / Feb. 8, 1863

Dear Son,

I received yours of the 16th Jan on the 2nd Feb. some what out of time but it set matters right that appeared mysterious before its receipt. Mary Received a good letter from you yesterday, date 23 Jan. Our folks have not been writing you as much as formerly. Amos wrote to you two weeks ago today (in my place) and none of them since, except I & Ann on last Sunday. John is unable to write, and Amos has been engaged of nights frequently. The girls have been writing to Will, Georg & Inda and neglecting you, they will be on hand soon. We got letters from Will yesterday, he was at Canniton Ind. They were making up their fleet there. They had on hand 24,000 soldiers and he did not know how many more would be added or where they were going, he is of opinion that they would go up the Cumberland, but only his guess, he & George were well, Amos [Andrew's brother] is with them quite unwell, but was not put off at any of the Hospitals.

Will appears to entertain hopes of seeing you some where in Dixie, but such a meeting would be the nearest accident, for he don't know where you are, and if he did, he could not go to you. He wishes me to tender his love & compliments to you, he has been favored a good deal by being relieved from fatigue duty, and put at other duties that he is able to stand. They are armed with Springfield rifles with long bayonets and all the accoutrements. He is much pleased with them & thinks they will be very effective in battle if skillfully used.

We are about in usual health, my shoulders & neck are considerably bored with Rheumatism. Your mother is plagued with the same disease but we are both tinkering along with our business. The rest of the family are quite well except for John, who I fear will enjoy no more good health. His cough is very annoying day & night, and he has been spitting-up pus (matter) for several days. He is still able to walk about his room. Tom Carpenter is at home sick. The rest of your Relatives are well so far as I am informed.

We have had another big snow since I wrote you, about 12 inches deep, on hard bottom. Things are considerably frozen up, friday evening the Murcury went down to 0 and remained so until after 7 yesterday morning, since which time it has been gradually less cold, and to day is cloudy & thawing with some prospect of rain.

Ten days more, perhaps ere this reaches you, one year will have passed you left us. Within that time many a father, mother, brother, sister and orphaned children have been made to mourn the loss of near and dear ones, who have been brought to an untimely grave by the bloody hands of cunning rebel foes and by many diseases incident to camp life. God be thanked that you are among the survivors, and may He in His infinite wisdom, preserve and protect you from harm and enable you to return your friends at home is the earnest supplication of your parents. John has just been visited by his doctors who give him much encouragement. They both say there is strong reasons to believe he will get well. May it be so.

Your sisters have grown so much you would hardly know them if you were to meet them from home. Mary is tall, & Ibby thick, Ann has increased but little in weight though she is much taller. Jo is fat & heavier than Ann. Lee is much healthier than he was early in the winter, and is a pretty hard set.

I agree "entirely" with you about some of our fools up north, they are operating against the successful prosecution of the war, it would be a blessing to humanity to have a few of the head devils hung, they are more to be dreaded than the armed rebels in the field.

Will writes me that he had received and receipted for your West McKinley claim, and would send it home with his own money as soon as he gets an opportunity, he obeyed & the claim is saved. We have sued none yet are still getting your Book reduced.

My compliments to the soldier boys and
believe me Truly your father
Andrew Evans

>> JANE TO SAM <<
Aberdeen, Brown County, Oh. / February 9, 1863

Dear Cousin,

It is with pleasure that I now sit down to write you a few lines to let you know that we are all well at present. And I hope these few lines may find you enjoying the same good health. Cousin Sam this is the third or fourth letter that I have written to you since I have received any answer from you. I had began to think that you had forgotten me. Tad told me yesterday that you wanted to know what was the reason that I did not write to you. Cousin it is not my fault you did not get my letter from me for I wrote to you. They have bin missplaced some way or other. I never will forget my dear cousin Sam. I think of you every day but I can not see you. It will be one year the 18th day of this month since you was on old east fork! I hope it will not be another year before you will be at home with us all again. Cousin we have had enough snow and mud this winter. I expect you have had more mud than we have up here. Sam I pitty you when you have to march in the mud. A soldier's life is a hard life to live.

I wrote a long letter to Pap [Amos, Jane's father] last night. We have not got any letters from Pap [Amos] since he went down the river. Your Pap [Andrew] got a letter from Will last Saturday. He said that Pap [Amos] was not so well as he was when he left Point Pleasant. Will said that they was one hundred and fifty miles below Louisville. I expect that they will be down to see you before long. I expect that you would like to see one another first rate. I know that I would anyhow.

Sam we heard of another death yesterday. Old Aunt Nelly Grantham she died on Saturday and was buried yesterday. Her and Lafayette Parker moved in with Leige Newman to keep house for him since his wife died. There has bin a great many deaths around here lately more than they [there] has bin for some time. Miss Mary Carpenter was out to see us yesterday. She said that all of the folks was tolerable well. She said that her mother was not very well. Mary looks well and is as lovely as ever, She said that she would like mighty well to see you.

Grandmother sends her love and respects to you, John McDaniel and Nelse Tompson. Grandmother was mighty well pleased when your Pap told her today that you and John Mc has sent your pictures to her. She said that she would rather [see] all [of] you then your likeness. She says that she would be very glad to have them. I would like to see them pretty well myself.

All of your Paps folks is as well as common except John and he is getting a little better. I hope that John will get well. What pleasure it would be to John if he could get well and harty like he was when he first Volunteered but he never will be that stout again. Sam Give my love and best wishes to boys and receive a full share for your self. Mother and Big Jane and all the rest of the family send there love and respects to you. Cousin please write soon it has bin some time since I received a letter from you. No more at present but remain

Yours truly, Cousin,

Jane Evans

East Fork / Feb. 11, 1863

Dear Brother,

Father has given you the news up to Sunday. He rec'd yours of 28th on the Evening of the day he wrote.

John is perhaps about the same as he was. The rest of us are well. Father had the neuralgia for a day or two but is all right again.[1] He & I have been working in the shop & mill this week.

We have been grinding steady during daylight since yesterday morning & a little more—Some last night. The mill does splendidly. The wheat stone would be the better of cracking lightly.

We are still collecting slowly. We would sue some but it would make bad worse for our Const[able] is not as good as the worst creditor.

We heard this evening that they were fighting at Vicksburg but it is only a report. Our Dailys have not been rec'd this week—no one been down for them. Nothing lately from the 89th. Since the 7th were then at Candleton, Indiana, enroute to Dixie. There is not much exciting news from the Country.

Some Encouragment in the Church at the late Revivial at Fitches. The goodly No. of 22 were added to the Church. Meeting lasted 2 weeks.

By accident I will receive a volume of the Advocate as a gift as it is being sent (two copies) to G. W. Wiles by mistake. Wether it continues or not I cannot say. Our Markets—Wheat $1.20 @ 1.30. Corn 76. Tobacco raising from 10 to 15 cts. Cotton gone to Halifax. Coffe is played out, except Barley, Rye & Wheat, Some have used Corn meal.[2]

I am as Ever,
Amos A. Evans

1. Neuralgia is a recurrent sharp pain along the path of a nerve.
2. Sometimes these roasted grains were used as coffee substitutes.

➤ SAM TO ANDREW ◄
Lagrange, Tenn. / Feb. 15, 1863

Dear Father,

Yours of the 1st came to hand on the 9th. I wrote to you on the 8th but mailed it before I received yours. The mail goes out before we receive that due. Where our P[ost].M[aster]. goes for our mail he takes the exit. You say, "you have been looking in vain for acknowledgment of the receipt of my goods." They have come and are all right, suit me very much.

I have been acknowledging the receipt of them in every letter that I have sent home since they came.

Capt Love brought them and would not have anything for his trouble. You ask "what is the matter with my eyes?" nothing now, in a former letter I wrote what was the matter but the letter perhaps has never reached its destination. Inflammation was the matter caused by smokey tents and windy weather. They are now as well as ever.

I saw by the Ripley Bee that the 89 OVI had passed down by that part.[1] We have not learned its destination. I am not anxious that it should get into a fight but if they do I want them to do good work without loss. You speak rather disparagingly. I feel that we will conquer this rebellion. We can endure as long as the rebels, and are as brave, or at least ought to be. We have not yet seen the hardships that our Revolution fathers did to gain the country's freedom—that we must maintain at all hazards. It is true that the war on our side has not been managed as it should be. Look at the magnitude of the cause and of the machinery necessary to carry on such a war. Man's foresight is not sufficient to be blunderless; consequently will err sometimes.

Money-making is the theme of too many of our officers. As for the "Vigorous Prosecutionists," I never had much confidence in and have less now than ever. S. A. Douglas was the man I thought was the man to fill the chair and still think so.[2] But still Old Abe will bring out the thing yet if he can have a fair share with the support of the people. North has too many Major Generals and too much pay. One hundred dollars per month is enough for any man in the Army if the good of his country is what he is fighting for. And if any officer is not a good one, let him be reduced to that rank he is best qualified to fill (if that be a Private). The deeds of men should be the recommendation for the pay they should draw. Incompetent, inefficient officers should not receive the same pay as competent and efficient. The conclusion then, pay a man for what he does or for his sense whatever it profits the government.

There is nothing in the way of news here but that you have seen. The Commercial says Banks has taken Port Hudson with 150,000 prisoners. This may be like some of the other news. I think Vicksburg will have to fall some of these times. The boys are there who can if it can be taken. All is quiet here. Gen. Denver came back Friday last. This town is being fortified. It is a very good place to build a fort if not more than 3 to 1 came against us they had better stay away or some of them will get hurt. We have plenty to eat and wear and more to do than is convenient in this bad weather. 8 Co's of the 70 went on picket yesterday morning in the rain. It rained all day and night, ceased this morning. The wind is blowing very hard. Mud is plenty. We don't get much mail now. Several furloughs we sent to Grant to be signed. They were sent back all rejected. Dr. Phillips sent for one and was returned rejected. Grant will give no furloughs for some time, if ever. The commandant of the post gives some 20 days leave of absence. That would not do much good from here home. A man would get to stay at home about 10 or 12 days and it would cost him about 3 or 4 months wages to go and come.

B. F. Johnson was here last week after the body of William Ellis of Co. F who died at Moscow last year. Some of our Co. went and help[ed] take him up. He was found and is perhaps at home.

John W. Swisher of Co. F died in the hospital of this place about 2 weeks ago. I think he was a son of Jim Swisher. Our Co. are all well able for duty but very few of the Reg't are sick. W. M. Haynes reports for Rheumatism. He sends his respects to you. I been very successful in the gunsmith business. I made a lever hammer for one of the Colts Navy revolvers, the lever fulcrum consists of cogs underneath the barrel. You perhaps have seen one of these. I will receive $4.00 for it. The bill is on a good man. I make a great many spur wheels for each of which I get 25 cts. There is still talk of [regimental] pay, but no pay yet. I have as much money as I need and a little more if we are paid again soon. I will send you all I can spare. My comrades will beg me to lend them some. I do not like to refuse when I have money, and they have none. I must close as it is too cold to write very well, and you will perhaps be tired of this letter when you get through it.

Your acquaintances join with me in sending their best respect to you and your family, and believe me

Your affectionate Son,

Sam

1. In February 1863, the 89th OVI was somewhere in middle Tennessee, between Nashville and Carthage. Frederik Henry Dyer, *A Compendium of the War of the Rebellion* (New York: T. Yoseloff, 1959), 1536.

2. Stephen A. Douglas, senator from Illinois, was the Northern Democratic candidate in the 1860 elections. After the firing on Fort Sumter, Douglas expressed unequivocal support for the war, but died shortly thereafter. It is thus ironic that Sam still thinks Douglas should have been president. McPherson, *Battle Cry of Freedom*, 274.

Home / February 15, 1863

Dear Sam,

After sending the letter I wrote to you last Sunday to the P.O. I received yours of the 1st Feb. and was much pleased to find the acknowledgement of the receipt of your goods and was glad to know that they all fit, they made a slow trip, but are "better late, then never." Amos got 2 letters from you on Thursday last, one dated Jan. 23, [o]ther Feb. 3. They bring us information even if they are a little old. Amos wrote to you Thursday night last. We got a letter from Will on the 13th date 7th. They had just arrived at Nashville, Tenn. in good health. Amos was still with them, but would have to be left at Nashville for he was unable to march. They got to Fort Donalson in time to see a few of the last guns fired in the recent fight.[1] They walked over the battle ground and saw many dead rebels, from the "silver locks of age, to the beardless youth." About 135 in all. They expected to march immediately for Murphysborough. They consisted of about 30,000 troops, which will make a nice little reinforcement for the "Army of the Cumberland" and they may expect to fight when they join Rosecrans, for he is a "fitting Gent," he is! May success attend their enterprize. Will says give my love to Sam which you will surely accept. I have had nothing from George since the 1st weeks in Jan. He is said to be well & fat.

Old Aunt Nelly Grantham was buried last Sunday. She died suddenly of "heart disease." Old Abner Jury died last week. I did not learn of what disease. Mrs. Robert Lutow died on the 10th of "Puerperal fever".[2] She was a sister of Mary Murphy, and a very fine woman. Elliot Eubanks, was brought home dead Friday last. He was a member of the 7th O Cavalry stationed at Harrodsburg, Ky. and lost his life by fooling with a shell. He threw it into the fire to scare somebody, & it killed him and hurt some others. A clear warning loaded shells should not be tampered with.

I acknowledge the corr[ection] on the orthography of "Vicksburg." I have the means in reach, to enable me to spell all words correctly, but I seldom reach for any of them when I write. I go it by guessing and am free to admit that I guess wrong some times. You are a better speller than I, but in your letter writing you make many omissions of words & letters, that the reader had to supply by guess. If you doubt it, you can see when you come home, don't consider me complaining of the above fact. I only offer it as an offset to my bad spelling. I received the Amrotype likeness of "Parrot gun & Slick" (0, what names?) Two, rather fine looking soldiers, (for scrubs) and delivered as previously requested; receipt of which your Grandmother, tenders the aforesaid soldiers many thanks and good wishes.[3] I, on last Thursday, was the "Happy Family" in John Sibbalds hands, a well executed job, the faces look familiar, but the names did not. I saw W. L. Mockbee yesterday. He says the soldiers & officers of the 70th look cheerful & Happy and thinks it the best Regt. he saw in the field.

We are about as well as usual. Your mother & I are still bored with rheumatism, but not laid up. John is better than he was a week ago. The residue of your friends & relations are well so far as I know. You tickled Lee awfully, by addressing him a note. He said, "I knowed Sam would [send] me a letter." He has been plaguing me every day since to write him a letter to Sam. Your old Mill has already taken an enviable reputation for good flour. No odds how much dirt, filth, or smut they bring to the mill, they all get good flour. That is the way I like to hear them talk. . . . I should like you to see it running and have your approval on the job. We have plenty of water all last week, and hardly as much work as we could do in the day time. From appearances, we will have more to do this week. Let them come, we're in.

Accept our best wishes and believe me.

Your Father,

Andrew Evans

1. On February 3, 1863, a Union garrison in Dover, Tennessee, a town located on the Cumberland River close to Fort Donelson, held off a much larger force of rebels until late into the evening, at which point a Union gunboat arrived and forced the Confederates to retreat. Benjamin Franklin Cooling, *Fort Donelson's Legacy: War and Society in Kentucky and Tennessee, 1862–1863* (Knoxville: University of Tennessee Press, 1997), 195–201.

2. Puerperal fever is an illness associated with childbirth.

3. Apparently this refers to the picture of Sam that his grandmother had requested earlier.

⇒ SAM TO ANDREW ⇐

LaGrange, Tenn. / Feb. 21, 1863

Dear Father,

It is raining and blowing so hard that I cannot work in my shop. I conclude to write you some, and finish in the morning if anything of importance transpire.

Your letter of the 7th came to hand on the 18th. It brought that day, one year ago, to my memory. It seems but a few months since I left for "dixie." I have not yet regretted that I came. Still think that I did right in going when I did. If I had not, I should have felt a compunction of conscience that I could not bear.

Today I received one from Amos of the 11 and one from little Jane of the 9th. I wrote to Lafe Parker. He says he would like me to come up and fix his gun by the time young squirrels come on in the spring. It will be a mere accident if the boys in the 89th ever get to see us. We learn the fleet has arrived at Nashville. Your idea that they were to Rosecrans was correct. I think. I would as leave be at that place as here. I would rather be under Gen. Sherman than anybody in this part of the country. You spoke of the "Spring Field Rifle." It is the same caliber as the Enfield. They are the best gun in the Army. In all respects, I am very familiar with most of the guns in this part of the Army. The lock plate is 3/8 of an inch thick. I have one of those bayonets fit to my gun which I found on the field at Shiloh on Sunday. I had no bayonet then, it being a very nice one, I just "foch" it away and have it yet.[1]

Father, I thank you very kindly for the earnest supplication in my behalf. May God preserve you all and be with you and us and may He be with this army and lead it to victory. Stay the arm of Rebels South and [illegible] North is my earnest supplication. We have some poor discouraged men here—always growling at ration, clothing, at our leaders, our cause, and almost everything you could imagine. These are few but more than I would like to see in such a cause as our country. I cannot think of ever giving up our cause and do not think there is any reason to do so. We are progressing slowly, but the enemy is progressing slower. Have we not more of their territory than we had one year ago? Mo, Tenn., Ky, Va are almost rid of armed rebels. Ark. is nearer than one year ago. Va. is in a better condition than one year ago. Nearly all of the Miss. River was owned by the Rebs., or held by them. Not a boat was allowed to pass much below Cairo. We had no trade below that point.

In all wars the victorious army meet with some "reverses" of fortune. My Motto is hold out faithful to the end we will wear the crown. When I take a position I don't much like to "honk". I dont care very much fighting this weather but if the Rebs can I will venture to say we will try them a whit. I think I would know all the Family if I would see them in the "Heart of Dixie." I have made due allowance for growth. You have the advantage of me. You have seen me since I saw you. no matter all will be right some day. Tell John to cheer up and not allow the "blues" to take hold on him. I am of the opinion that they have killed more men than the sword. Never be discouraged, and think but little how both you feel.

I have been very sick since I came from home. I could have died if I had taken a notion to. Now I am entirely well of my old disease. (Bronchitus) (is this the way you spell it) and have been for 10 months. Cheer up John, dont drug yourself to death, take as little medicine as the nature of your case will admit. For a cough Hoarhound [*sic*, horehound] candy is better than nearly anything I have taken. . . .

I cannot see any honorable way of getting leave of Absince consequently I will not be home for a few weeks. My time is nearly out, actually 2 years and then I will come home I think. I am acused of being very "fond of soldiering", I do like it pretty well.

Sabbath morning — nothing new of importance. Col Cockerel informed us that Dave Dodd is 2nd Lieut. There ar several other promotions, none of whom you are acquainted. Oh! Yes, Doc Heaton is promoted to 1st Lieut so I have been informed. Capt. W W West is orderly of Co. F! All well at present and in good cheer. I will write to Will as soon as I hear certain where he is, if you learn tell me.

Remember me to all of my friends, accept my best wishes for you and family and believe me.

Your big soldier boy,

Sam

P.S. Pardon me for writing on this smutted sheet. The tent leaked so yesterday I could not keep it dry while writing. I will enclose $5.00 of Confederate money so you can see what sort of money they have.

1. This is a slang word for "fetch" used in the South.

❯❯ ANDREW TO SAM ❮❮
Home / Feb. 22, 1863

Dear Sam,

I again resume my weekly duty. Nothing has been received from you that has not been previously acknowledged, we have not heard from you, since your letter to Amos, (rather a long interval) I still write once a week, Amos about once in two weeks, and the girls about the same so, if our letters passed regularly to you, you would hear from home twice a week, we suppose the mail is in fault when a longer vacancy occurs between letters, as well with us as you, but we don't (like some), fall out with the President, and things in general, if we do happen to miss a few letters, for there are many difficulties in the way of the mail service that can only be corrected by restoring peace to our country, which has so far proved a difficult task, and to one at home looks like there were many dark stripes yet to be overcome.

I cannot keep clear of looking at the blue side sometimes. The South is vast in extent, in numbers, in wealth, resources, munitions of war, courage and Demoniac ingenuity. They have as good officers as we. They have got their men to believe they are fighting in a just cause, and defending their own homes against a lawless gang of wicked yankees, who are seeking to ravage and plunder, and that everything sacred will be desecrated unles they defend it. They are at home having all the advantages of spies to keep them informed of every move of our armies. With these advantages, and men thus excited, it will balance our success in number and perhaps amount to one of McNish's bull dog fights in Ireland, "where they fight till they eat each other up, all but the tails, and they jump at each other and growl." I am sorry that we have a few rebellious mischief makers in the Democratic party. They are a disgrace to the party and would do the government less harm if they were in arms. In the Rebel army, they will be spotted.

I have nothing to remark new in the way of health, about as usual. The weather has been rather pleasant until yesterday we had an east wind, last night it snowed a few inches deep, rained some, froze some, etc. which has made rather disagreeable weather. Our friends Owens, Pinkard & Barclay in Marysvill met a very serious loss some two weeks ago that I believe I have not informed you. Their Entire hardware store was consumed by fire, the work of an encendiary. Their loss is about $12,000. The vilian broke in to the house and took as much as he could carry and set fire inside and left to escape detection, but they did not get off so easy. They found tracks to & from the house in the snow, & on missing a stranger (who had been working about there a few days previous) Barclay went to Cinti and set the detective Police on the lookout. They took a man on suspicion on searching him they found goods on him bearing the private mark of the firm, and, Barclay identified him positively, and he was sent to the Maysvill jail, for trial.

We have had nothing from the 89th since I wrote to you. I got a letter from Inda on the 18th & she and the boys are verry well. She said she had one written to you that she would start by the next mail, she has not been to see us since she moved. John Sherring and Lile Hurrin have both sold out. Real & personal and will start to Illinois this week if nothing prevents. They both settled the accounts due you, we are collecting but slowly on account of pressure for time, but we still get some. G. G. Games received a verry positive notice and came right up. He claimed that he and Simpson paid 75 each for your Advocate, last year. I deducted it from their bills, did I do right?

Remember me kindly to my friends in camp and believe me as representing our family in tendering their love to you.

Affectionately, your father,

Andrew Evans

⟫ AMOS TO SAM ⟪
Home / Feb. 26, 1863

Dear Brother:

I rec'd 2 letters from you on the 12th and wrote you on the 11th, hense did not write sooner. We have reduced our letter writing to a system. Father writes to you & Will Every Sunday. I write Every 2 weeks. My other correspondents keep me in as much as I can get time to. For I make it a rule to go to church as often as I can consistently. If you desire me to write oftener, Say So & it will be fulfilled.

John is on the decline pretty fast. All of the Physicians Say he is beyond recovery, his left Lung is now gone or inactive & the other much injured. He is confined to his bead [sic] and has no appetite. You will please not write of him anything that will cause him to be restless or to[o] deeply concerned. I think he is a true Christian believer & has no fear of death, yet he has never said a word about his decline. He still talks of getting up and working & c. The rest of us are moderately well. I am laboring under depression in the Chest, trouble from breathing & c. Perhaps it is from the cold. The general health is good.

The worthy Lieut James H. Housh has returned from Illinois & has shot himself through the left arm, fracturing the Ulna & Radius. Dr. Guthrie tried to get the ball out but failed. It is very bad; He has been marked as a deserter for some time previous to his visit to the west & likely shot his arm to cover the guilt. The [illegible] got scared at the Rebels & again came to Ohio—went back today.

We have been informed that the fight is in operation at Vicksburg, the Morter boats are Shelling the Town & Fortifications. Nothing new from the East.

We got a letter from Will written the 15th from Camp [with]in 3 1/2 miles of Nashville Tenn. All were well, but needed rest after so long a trip. Inda is better than she has Ever ben. Father wishes me to Say he has not rec'd a letter from you Since the 1st.

Business. G. G. Games came up & paid after a square dun. Dyas assumes J. W. Moores claim. We cleaned his wheat & Dyas hauled it for him. Cud is satisfied, Pickezter paid up. Rosencrantz returned the hoe & refused to pay for the Mattock as it brok. What shall I do for the remainder? James Carrigans is not yet collected. I will prosecute the Const[able] & collect it off of him for his neglect.

We have had some very wet weather, quite a nice time for milling & I am happy to Say we have got the name of "Excelsior" or a[s] Botner used to Say the "World beater". Little Jane wrote to you today. Write when convenient & oblige my love to all.

Your brother as Ever,

Amos A. Evans

➤ SAM TO ANDREW ◄
LaGrange, Tenn. / March 1, 1863

Dear Father,

Yours of the 15th of Feb came to hand yesterday, also Ann & Lee's letters enclosed, & Mary's and Ibby's of the 18th. I am very much pleased with yours and would like you to continue. Most of your letters came through safely. I am of opinion Mary, Ibby, and Ann have improved in letter writing very considerable.

Rosencrans [sic] would be pretty hard to take with his present force. I accept Will's love and return to him mine. I have news from Nashville of the 17th. Will wrote to John Hiett inquiring whether I was with the Regt. or not, says he has not heard of me for some time.

Our Robert Fulton's wife was not a sister of Mary Murphy. She was a Dunn if I am not badly mistaken. I do not know who Ripley Bob's wife was.

You say I am a better speller than you I do not profess to be very good and here we have nothing but newspaper authority for our spelling and that is not very convenient or correct. I think it very likely that I make many omissions of words and letters. I do not "proof read" many of my letters, and do it in a hurry very often. I will see if that fault of mine can be obviated. It is rather a serious fault or neglect. The omissions might not be (filled) as I intended. Mary spells pretty well but she spells "schollar" one l is enough. I directed her attention to this word once before. Ask her how she spells scholar.

You have made a slight omission with regard to Lee "I knowed Sam would me a letter" as I may be mistaken. Lees letter is a pretty good one I want him to send me another sometime.

I am very well satisfied that the old mill is doing good work. If it will make good flour of dirty smutty wheat is more than it ever did before. I would like very well to see how it does the work, but for the present must defer. Make it pay if you can for you have been at a great trouble to repair it. What is the matter with John! that he can not write, is he too sick? Yesterday I wrote to Jane Evans, I will write to Will this week.

Co. F came off a 3 days picket this morning the weather was very rainy. The Company was guarding a bridge across Wolf River the River raised so they could not get to the Bridge. Some citizen undertook to cross the river with a Load of goods—meat, oil and cheese. His team Scared at something and ran off the levee, upset the wagon and spilled all his goods into the water, after he went a way the boys made a lograft and drew out the oil which they sold for $8.00, 7 sides of meat at 2.00 dols per side and some they sold to him. They recd in "green backs" $27. They drew one large cheese which was divided to the Co, several pieces of calico, cotton, shoes, pants, silk handkerchief and other things. None but our Co. know anything about what they got, they do not want it known here for awhile.

Last night our pickets were fired upon by some Guerrillas. Nobody was hurt and the rebs were gone. This morning there is not much force anywhere near here. We do not apprehend any danger.

We were mustered today for 2 months pay. Again the paymaster has not visited us as soon as we expected he would. I am proud of the Recommendation Mackbee gave the 70. He is a gentleman "every inch of him." I cannot say the same of our last visitor B. F. Johnson. I am still at the gun business and like it very well. Have not been Stalled yet. I can make the business pay me if I had no conscience in charging the price of repairing. Col Loudon came back a few days ago from Georgetown. He said he saw none of the Huntington folks but John

Buchanan. The Health of the Army is good, that of the 70 is the best of any here. The new Regts. are dying off much faster then the old, every man of Co. F is able for duty. We like our old Capt. first rate. Dave Dodd is promoted to 2nd Lieut. W. W. West is Ord Sergeant. Sam Cochran 2nd Thom E Grier 3 N.B. Thompson, E.L. Burhage, 5 Sergeants Corporals Stoudans follows Nelse Edgenton, Jep Shelton, Alex Rains Lawson, Dragoo, Wes Hart. Turner Hook is now reduced to the ranks. Report says the Queen of the West is captured. It may be so she has already done more damage to the Rebels than she is worth, if she is only destroyed so they can not turn it upon us.[1] It is reported that Vicksburg is being evacuated. I dont feel in a mode for writing much of interest.[2]

Mother asks for a lock of my hair. I will be pleased to send it, anything that I can do to gratify those at home. My head will be bald if I send to all who ask for a lock of my hair. My love to all.

I am as ever your Son,

Sam

1. Sam's information about the *Queen of the West* was correct. In February 1863 the ship ran hard aground under Confederate fire and was abandoned before it could be destroyed. Confederate forces manned the *Queen of the West* briefly. On April 14, 1863, the ship exploded from fires ignited in combat. Jones, *The River War*, 384–85; Garrison, *Encyclopedia*, 202.

2. Sam was incorrect about Vicksburg being evacuated.

⇨ AMOS TO SAM ⇦

Aberdeen, OH / March 12, 1863

Dear Brother,

I again take up my duty which is a pleasant one.

Father rec'd one from you of the 1st of March—on the 10th. We were as usual glad to hear from you. You seem to be enjoying yourself pretty well. I have done the same though my enjoyments have been confined to home this winter. John seems to be mending slowly he is very cheerful & can walk with his cane. He sits up about 1/2 of the time.

I took a load of flower [sic] to Acklin yesterday & when ready to start home Uncle Griffith came up Street & got in & came home with me.[1] He has been a cook & barber in the 10th O.C. [Ohio Cavalry] for 2 months, he does not belong to the Army but Eats & wears Uncle Sams Stores, he looks as well as Ever & is not grey headed. Well Sam I forgot to tell you how the rest of the folks are. They are well Except colds & etc. I got sick & then got The Blues because I did not get along right. I have a dry cough which has been very severe—Something is out of hang. I have been using Cod liver Oil & Whisky it does some good but does not cure or has not yet. I have been able to do light work as yet. We have a huge pile of Rock quired [quarried] out of the field above the Orchard & the New ground. We will build a fence along above the road with them beginning at the gate & continuing this way.

The weather is cold & the ground is frozen hard—

We have just got some Standard pears. They will bear in 2 years. We set a crab [tree] where the Flood broke yours, it growed from a bud last year. We will trim the Orchard soon. We have nothing from Will & George since Pap wrote. There is nothing new, only the Old Sow died. I am not in a very good moode for writing & I will quit fearing I weary your patience.

My love to all I am as Ever,

Amos

Esquire & I are Suppoenied to attend Court next Monday. The George-town Road is nearly impassable.

1. Samuel's Uncle Griffith was the youngest of Andrew's ten siblings. Morrow, Bi-ography Section, 155.

⇒ SAM TO ANDREW ⇐
Moscow, Tenn. / March 14, 1863

Dear Father,

I conclude to write you a few lines this evening. I replied to your two letters the last time I wrote. Your letter of March 1st is the last received. I wrote to Amos this week. We were paid today for 2 months. Paid till the 31st of October. I sent by Capt. H. L. Phillips $40.00 to be left with Den-nis & Bro or with T. S. Schliz. He did not know where he would leave it, he told me he would leave it at either the one place or the other. You will draw it and cr[edit] me with it. My extra duty money is forthcoming. It can not be drawn until the acct is sent to Washington. I keep over $16.00. I would have sent $5.00 more but did not collect enough in time. Cpt Phillips could not carry a letter for you or I would have send a letter with him. There is nothing new in this part of Dixie. The weather has been very nice for a few days though quite warm. The river still pretty high and falling a little. We are camped on a high point with in about 1/4 of a mile from where we camped, When here before, but in a much nicer place. The town was a very nice little village one year ago but now there are but few houses standing, and only 2 families are living here now. All the boys who had been in the army a year up to the 31st day of October drew the pay for clothing if they had not drawn their $42.00. If they had over drawn, it was taken out. The Government is owing me on clothing. I have drawn nothing on the new year (clothing). The pants we get now are worth but little. Shirts and drawers are pretty good. Shoes do while there are no good ones.

The health is still good here but I fear hot weather will change the nature of things somewhat. All of our company are able for duty but one (Wm R Hart) he is but slightly ailing. I am still as well as usual, am still working at the gun trade. I have a very easy time. Some of the boys have a hard time, a great deal of duty to do. I have none but repairing and can take my own time at that. Do what ever I can outside of my legitimate business, by that can make about my expenses, so that I will be able to save my government pay. I have no instructions to offer you about collecting. My best respects to all of the family and all the friends.

Good night,
Your [illegible] boy,
Sam
P.S. I will write Ann a note & enclose.

➤ ANN TO SAM ❼
Home / March 22, 1863

Dear Brother Sam,

I received your kind letter yesterday and was very glad to here from you. It is a very pretty day. It is muddy but the sun is shining bright and warm. We have made some garden. Mother has been spinning some this week she is spinning [illegible]. Grandmother is well. John is getting better.

Sam don't you get tired of fixing guns. Sam do you get any can[n]ed fruit. We opened a can of currants yesterday that were just as good as if they were just pick off of the bushes. You had better come over and get a piece of pie.

I will finish after dinner. Sam come over and eat dinner with us. You say you don't know who sent you that bottle of Bourbon. It was John Buchannan. He told Pap he did. I think he was [illegible]. Do you get eggs to eat? If you don't, come over some of these days forelong and get some. We have two hens sitting. I have nothing more.

Good by

your sister,

Ann Evans

Write when you please.

P.S. I send you a piece of my handy work in combining two hearts. ADE

<hr />

⇒ ANDREW TO SAM ⇐
Home / March 22, 1863

Dear Sam,

I have two of your letters unanswered. Yours of the 9th came to hand on the 18th & that of the 14th on the 21st (a tolerably quick trip from Dixie[)]. I started a "Bee" to you this morning, I will send any paper that you request, if in my power. I still take the Bee & Argus, they are of but little use more than for backhouse purposes. The one I sent you has some good interesting matter which perhaps you have not seen. There is a pretty good song in it that will answer for the boys for amusement when they are at leisure. I would send you the Commercial, but supposed you got it in camp frequently, fresher than I could get them to you; if you can think of anything in my reach, that you would like to have, just name it, and it shall be done, if possible. Your money will be taken care of, I have not been to Aberdeen recently, but learn H. L. Philips has arrived.

Money can't be loaned safely here, nobody will borrow who could make it secure, and I don't propose to loan on doubtful paper anymore. I received your claim on I. W. Moore yesterday. We have failed with Bill Carrigan; his tobacco was attached on delivery in Ripley, and we did not get anything, there is another chance, he is an heir to The Hietts Estate, which is in process of settlement, if he don't walk up sooner, I will try to catch him there, I assure you, we are doing you all the good we can, under our present pressure, Amos rode one day last week, but "didnt raise a red [cent]." You will have to look to Amos for our official report. I only write from memory, he keeps book of every transaction, we don't touch your book with pen, or pencil but keep a book of all accounts, on our own hook. I keep a book of all mill transactions. I am of opinion it will pay, if it don't use me up. We run from Friday til Saturday night without shutting the gate except to change stone. We ground 90 bushels of wheat Friday night no sleep at all, I feel pretty sore over it.

John is convallescent. He sits up most of the day now, and in good weather walks in to the kitchen and takes dinner with us, if he mends on, he will try to write you a letter in a week or so. He says everybody has quit writing to him because he can't write, the residue of our family are in usual health. I believe I am healthier than when you left, but am compelled to take more exercise than I am phisically able for. Your friends here are generally well. We are much pleased to hear of your continued good health and of the whole of the "Galant Old 70th." May it never be worse? Will & George were well the last heard from, I have reason to believe they are at Murfeesborough [sic] from a little remark you will see in the Bee about Capt Jolly of Co E. 89 Regt. We have no late news by letter from either of them. They disembarked 150 miles above Nashville on the Cumberland river is the last we have direct, it would be Contraband for a news paper to tell where they are, we will perhaps hear soon, for Will said he would write when he reached his destination.[1]

Since writing the foregoing, I received your money (40.00). Amos was at Aberdeen today and W. B. Dennis gave it to him. L. W. Dennis mooved to Chicago in Jan last. & W. B. Dennis is sole proprieter. Your money is safe if I don't spend it, I have been making common stock of all we have been collecting, it was very convenient. I think I can see through on our own means now, if we have our health, & will endeavor to be able to make a clean report to you when you come home, if I should live so long. I have contracted my flour and delivered part of it, it will bring us between 2 and $300.00 & we will try to get along with that until we raise something else to sell. We are practicing economy as well as we can & hope we may go through safely. I hope you may not be taken to a more dangerous place than you now ocupy. Amos will write you Thursday as usual, he is writing to Will now.

Good by for a week,
Andrew Evans

1. In this usage "contraband" meant illegal aid to the enemy.

Moscow, Tenn. / March 22, 1863

Dear Father,

I received yours of the 8th of March on the 17th also one from Amos on the 20th of March 12. I was much pleased to hear that the health was improving some, and hope it will continue until all are recovered. I notice from your letter, that there has been a considerable moving of neighbors in your vicinity I have heard that, Big John "thought["] it no use to plant a crop as the conscrip[t] [draft] would take a man away before he could tend it.[1] I would rather be in a battle than suffer the uneasyness John does for fear he will have to go into the army. I suppose he can't help it.

I also learn High's "back" is very troublesome about these times. I dont like it much, because I did not make the separator to run by belt, as does the smut machine. I was satisfied before I came away that a belt would be better.

I hope you will make enough off the mill to pay you for the trouble you have been at with a good percent on the expense (I mean over and above expense).

I learn you have taken a way some flour, from quotation you will do well on it. I suppose ere this you have had the pleasure of seeing Capt H L Philips of the 70 with whom I sent you 40.00 to be left at Acklins' or Dennis'. I should have sent a note with him to you, but he could not well take it. He and our Quartermaster went home on leave of Absence for 30 days I believe. There was talk of furloughing the Privates of this Regt a while but I believe it is all dried up. I am not able to say where we will be order[ed] to next but am well satisfied.

General Denver has resigned and Gen. Smith of the 13 O, or formerly Col of that Regt. is to take command. I have not learned the reason of his resignation. Gen. Denver is a very good man and well liked by his men. Since he had been with us there has been but once that his pluck could be tried, he did not falter then but stood to the works. I have thought he was rather loose with his command. The Guerillas have made a small raid on the Rail Road 3 miles above Grand Junction. All that I have learned about it is in the daily Bulletin of today which I send to you. If Grants order is put into execution there will [be] a great destruction for property.[2] All I wish is that the gang of Guerillas could be caught and made pay the penalty for such cowardly acts.

Will Haynes recd a letter from John Swisher of the 89th but a few days ago. They were there at Carthage Tenn, all the boys well the letter stated. I have written to Will and have not yet recd an answer. We had a meeting to day, Chp'l. Sullivan preached. I am still satisfied that a man should be a Christian as near as is in his power to be. If a man is a true Christian he can but be a brave man. Every soldier should be a brave man. Bravery is not recklessness. It does not mean that a man should walk up to the cannons mouth disarmed and peep into the muzzle while the enemy is standing with a lighted match at touchhole, but it does mean that we should be prepared to meet danger in the full consciousness of its presence, calmly, steadily, unfalteringly. A brave man is usually high-minded and really honorable man, not a duelist or murderer! He can afford to treat an insult with contempt rather than revenge. He can pity and forgive his enemy, though it may be his duty to stay him in defending his own life, or in protecting the honor and welfare of his country! He knows no fear, but the fear of God. The best of all books teaches us that "the fear of God is the beginning of wisdom." The man who fears God will reverence His authority. Led by this reverence, we will be brought to Christ, the Great Captain of our Salvation. With this view before me, I could not do otherwise than be a Christian as near as I can. I hope this will be the case with all my companions in arms and friends at home. A man with the assurance in his own breast that God has forgiven him is not afraid to die.

Now dear father and mother, I feel that this is a trying hour for us. Will you? (if it is God's will that we should not meet on earth again) meet me in Heaven. I am confident Brother Abe died a Christian. I pray God we may meet him in Heaven.

The health of our Army is still good, troops are in fine spirits and confident of success, if odds are not too great / They are very cleanly in their person, tolerably industrious. We have not yet heard of Vicksburg being taken though the papers talk that it will soon fall. I think myself that it will not be very long till it will be our possession but the idea that it will be the bloodiest battle of the war is rather doubtful. The Wooden Monitor that passed down by Vicksburg had a good effect, the old Indianola is likely out of our way. I don't like the loss in the first place, but in the latter I do.

My health is still as good as usual. The weather is too warm to work at Smithing with pleasure. The weather is as warm here now as it usually is at home in May. Vegetation seems a [illegible]. I have nothing more to write at present. Remember me kindly to mother and the rest of the family and believe me,

Your affectionate Son,

Sam

1. Big John is probably a relative on Andrew's side of the family.

2. On February 5, 1863, General Grant ordered General James B. McPherson to exclude all civilians from his lines, as Grant prepared for the second phase of his campaign against Vicksburg. Brooks Simpson, *Ulysses S. Grant* (Boston, Houghton Mifflin: 2000), 175; McPherson, *Ordeal by Fire*, 311.

⋙ JANE TO SAM ⋘
Aberdeen, Oh. / March 26, 1863

Dear Cousin,

Your very kind letter of the 15th came to hand on the 21st. I hope you will pardon me for not answering sooner. We was all very glad to here from you again, Cousin. Sam I love to read and write to you soldiers I don't no what I would do if I did not get any letters to read. I would think that I had not friends that cared anything about me. I am happy to think that you have not forgotten me. You are the only cousin that I have received a letter from for some time. I have 7 cousins in the Army, but none like you.

I wrote to Will and George about four weeks ago. I have not received any answer yet. I can not say whether they got them or not. I hope I will here from them soon. I have written three letters to Pap in the last five weeks. But we have never got any answers from him. We dont know what has become of him. He is not with the Regiment. We heared this week that Pap was discharged, but we dont know how true it is. But I am in hopes that he will be at home pretty soon. I tell Cousin I would like mighty well to see him. I got a letter from Jake Bottner last week. he is the same old Jake. You better believe he can curse the Rebels some. Jake says that he has bin in eight Battels. He says that he doesnt want to be in another if he could help it.

"You say that it is not worth your while to tell me that Cal is mad at you." Cousin Sam I know that there is no youse of you saying that Cal is mad at you. For I no that she is not. Cal was out to see us last Sunday week. She did not talk like she was mad at you then. I don't think that you wanted to marry very bad or you could a got Cal, but I hope that she will be in a good humor again [when] you get home. I think that I will get to go too that wedding yet, If nothing happens. I am a going to see Cal pretty soon. I hope she will be in a good humor with me if she is mad at you.

I and Big Jane was down at your fathers yesterday and spent the evening with them. They are all tolerably well. John is not much better. He looks mighty pale and bad. Grandmother sends her love and respects to you and John Mc. Cousin I saw the happy family yesterday at your fathers they are as nice looking pictures as I have seen for some time, I would like mighty well to see you come home but I expect it will be a long time, before that will come to pass.

Oh! Yes cousin, I will have to tell you what a joke. We heared on you the other day.—I heared that you had an old darky woman to cook for you and wash for you, and slept with her. I do not believe any such tales, but I thought I would tell you about it. There has bin some mighty bad Tales or anecdotes told on some of you boys here lately. I don't know how true they are. Big Jane sends her love and respects to you and John Mc. She says that she loves the soldiers and she cannot help it. I dont blame her, for I love them too. Cousin give my love and best wishes to the boys and receive a full share for your self. Please write soon, no more at present but

Remain your true Cousin,
Jane Evans

⇸ ANDREW TO SAM ⇷
Home / April 5, 1863

Dear Son,

Yours of the 23rd March came to hand on the 1st April, Amos received one from you since. We are pleased to hear that you still enjoy good health and spirits and that the old "70" is "head and tail up." I suppose the 70 is pretty well acclimated by this time and so well used to hardships that it has become a part of their rations and sleep. So long as you can continue cheerful, in good spirits and take all by the bright side, you will all enjoy fair health, but so sure as the Army gets hold of the dark side of all things, take the "blues," get homesick and complain of all things, then the upper lip ceases to be stiff, the sphincter muscle relaxed, then indeed you would cease to be a formidable body of soldiers and subject yourselves to the ravages of which would make you an easy prey to the enemy.

God grant that your health and spirits may continue, as you represent them!

Our health is good or at least not to be complained of except John. I can give you no better idea of his condition than to say to you that his lungs are deeply affected by tuberculosis or phthisis pulmonalis and is, in my opinion, in the 3rd or last stage of the disease.[1] It would be vain for me to undertake to tell you how long he may live, but I can say safely that he is weaker than Abe was the day before he died. He keeps cheerful and seldom speaks of his condition.

I still have some erysipelas on & around my nose, it is considerably anoying at times, but I have kept it in subjection with mild remedys so far, if these should fail to cure, the big remedy is at hand (Iodine) which will be applied with the above exceptions.[2] Your friends and relatives are well, the general health good. The season is rather backward, no peach blossoms out, wheat is looking well, pastures are backward, poor cattle plenty, poor pigs verry plenty, dollar corn don't agree with pigs, with the assistance the mill has given us in the feed line, we will go through safely without buying any feed.

Mary received a letter from Will yesterday, he and George ar[e] still well. Will is still acting Hospital Steward no word from Amos yet.[3] He is not with the Regt, nor has he Ever written home since he left Pt. Pleasant. We have no news worth naming. Tomorrow brings our Election day, Candidates are plenty. J. C. Waldren W. C, Buck & Massie Beasley for J. P., Wm. Fulton L. H. Martin, John L. Acklin & John W. Stewart for Trustees. D. Tarbell & P. W. Waldren for Clerk.[4] John Mitchell & W. B. Dennis for Treasurer. S. S. Canan I. C. Mitchell & W. G. Hiett for Assessor. B. B. Laurall John Ruggles. & Joseph S. Covert for Constable. Bob Bradford for Supervisor &c. &c. I will try to give you the result in my next. I will not vote for anyone unless he is of unquestionable Loyalty to his Government, and that he will abide the Conscription act without resistance. Any other kind, are neither my friends, nor friends of this Country, and should not be voted for. I will enclose the stamps, (you request Amos to send,) in this if I can procure them tomorrow Thursday is his day to write to you, which would delay their arrival several days.

I will mail to you my Bees of last week in order that you see a correspondence between Jas. S. Covert a "stay at home peace Democrat" and John W. Grierson "a go to war fighting man" of the 33 OVI, acquaintances of mine. John gives him blazes beautifully, and hits others of the same stripe. I say "lay on John" hit him again, God save all such soldiers as our friend, John. He talks right, as well as fights. Those who talked loudest about tyranny and resisting conscription, lying at home, etc. will perhaps find it convenient to hold their tongues, they are not very noisy and will find but few favors in their corner, the constituent parts of such (agreeably to my analysis) are one part coward and Southern sympathizer, 2 of all & 4 shitass. I am as much attached to true Democratic principles as I have ever been, but I don't use politics toward the army or suffer any political preferences toward soldiers of officers. If they do their duty, they are the men for me regardless of politics.

Truly your father,

Andrew Evans

1. Phthisis pulmonalis is another name for tuberculosis. Literally it means atrophy of the lungs. In modern medical parlance the course of tuberculosis is not classified in terms of stages.

2. Erysipelas is an acute infectious skin disease characterized by deep-red inflammation of the skin and caused by a streptococcus bacteria.

3. Hospital stewards were the only soldiers assigned to permanently assist surgeons and expected to have prior medical experience. Hospital stewards ranked above the first sergeant of a company and were the highest paid noncommissioned officers. Starting in 1864, candidates for this position, like Will, were examined by a board of medical officers. George Worthington Adams, *Doctors in Blue: The Medical History of the Union Army in the Civil War* (Baton Rouge: Louisiana State University Press, 1980), 67.

4. For information about J. C. and P. W. Waldron see note in Will's letter of March 4, 1862.

⇒ SAM TO ANDREW ⇐
Moscow, Tenn / April 12, 1863

Dear father,

Your kind favor of the 29th came to my hand on the 6th of Apr. I was as usual very glad to hear from you and to hear all were enjoying moderately good health. I would like to hear of Will getting the appointment of Hospital Steward. The position would suit him besides he would not stand out door duty long unless he has better health than he formerly had. It is rather a bad scald on the 7.O.C. I mean the Mt Sterling affair.[1] They were surely asleep or did not try to prevent their capture. In almost every instance where the federals have sustained consideral [sic] loss in any of the late battles a little caution with resistance would have insured success on our side. You may well say there are some as big Rebles in Ky. as Jeff Davis and that those who are gone to war for the Union are good fighting men. I think the same thing may be said with respect to many of the people of Ohio. Some Rebles at home while She can boast of as brave men as ever the sun shone are in the field. I hope that reble sympathisers there are at home are too few to amount to much.

There seems to be a change in the Reble base of operation. 6 months ago all eyes were turned toward Richmond. But now Charleston, Murfreysburo and Vicksburg seem [to] attract attention while Richmond is losing attraction. Rosecrans is one of the best generals we have, unless overpowered will never be beaten. Things are not progressing very rapidly. I do not see yet that we have lost any thing in position or prospect. Their victual Raid into Ky. did not prove very advantagious. If the federal army were in the condition of the Reble then we might begin to feel a little discouraged. As yet our prospects are quite conducive to victory from the movements of the Rebles. They are in trouble many places. Subsistance is scarce and prices enormous. Orders were received today from the War Department to muster all the men in our Regt to know how many conscripts will be required to fill up the regiment. I pity conscripts who go in old Regt., they will see but little peace. How glad I am that I came where I did but would go much sooner if I had the same thing to do over again. Our new General (Smith) is about the kind of man we need here. At least so far as we have learned him the right side up with regard to secesh.

We have had a perfect quiet for a few days. It is to be hoped they will give us no more trouble at this point but bring all their forces to a few places and then let us know what and where they are. If such was the Case the War would end. I am of opinion the end is more than one year hence any how though I may be mistaken. I still say we should strain the last nerve before we be conquered. I have no doubt we can conquer if our card is properly played. Father if you can stand the storm at home I feel that I can with a murmer. Let us be faithful and dilligent ever trusting Him who rules over the destiny of Nations.

I send John the Bulletin of today. There is little news in it but it may have something in it he would like to read. The furlough business is beginning in this part of the Army. 80 of the 53rd received 30 days furlough. I believe this reg't are taking steps to furlough the men. The married men well first be furloughed. This is not exactly according to the Law unless they are better soldiers than the Single. I have no objection to them going first. A married man has obligations that a single man has not therefore I do not care a cent for the time will be but short till we will all have a chance. The health is still good of our Reg't. I have been a little out of fix about the liver. I took a little blue that stirred up things a little. And now I feel a little better. My liver is somewhat stimulated you know what that feels like. I took this for fear I would be worse and liable to some kind of sickness. This is the first medicine taken since I got over measles.

I guess I have written enough for this time. My [company?] is called a way for a time consequently I close. My love to all the family, and yourself.

As ever your son

Sam

ps is my little gun in good order

1. Sam is referring to a minor skirmish at Mount Sterling, Kentucky, in March 1863. Sam is under the misimpression that the 7th Ohio Cavalry was defeated. In fact it had driven occupying Rebels from the town, although not before some of the town was burned. Captain R. C. Rankin, *History of the Seventh Ohio Volunteer Cavalry* (Ripley, Oh.: J.C. Newcomb), 3.

⇢ ANDREW TO SAM ⇠
Home / April 13th, 1863 [4 o'clock A.M.]

Dear Sam,

I missed writing yesterday in consequence of a press of Company. Sunday is a great day for people to visit the sick, and yesterday we had an unusual number of calls. I sit up the after-wach [?] Each night. I am not quite so well as usual this morning. I have headache, sore teeth & etc. John has become considerably weaker in a week past. He [never] sits up now, except to be propped up in bed while he eats his meals. He don't appear to suffer verry much, he is of course aware of his condition, though he seldom speaks of it, and don't seem to like the subject of his condition for conversation. He is calm and seldom complains, his cough is not near so troublesome as it has been, but his voice is failing, (becoming hollow). He rested better last night, and seems better this morning. How long it will last is more than he can tell.

Our family & friends here as well as usual. Inda & her boys arrived here on Saturday evening in good health, and will remain with us for some time. She has a fine pair of boys, Sam [India and George's son] is quite a rowdy. John's [Sam's cousin John Hiett] letter you speak of to the girls has not come to hand. I have nothing from you since I wrote you. I will therefore give you a short offhand epistle. Our spring is very backward, no peach blossoms yet, the grass & wheat has grown but little in a month, we have had quite a number of frosts, followed by cold dry weather. The blossom buds were brought forward a month ago, almost to the opening condition, and they are but little more forward now, we have about half our apple trees trimmed. I think we can finish in a day & a half, it is quite a job, being neglected so long. Amos is a good hand up a tree, we have but little plowing done yet but are going ahead as fast as one team can do it. Pat is building stone fence, Gilmore plowing & Amos & I trimming the orchard.

We have news from Will & George to the 5 April. They were well, and get to see Rebels frequently. They have had no battle yet, bout [but] some skirmishes. Will says, "Some may well say the Springfield rifles are good guns." "For when they are properly leveled, the Rebels make their obeisance in handsome stile before them." He & George speak verry highly of their commander (Gen Crooks). They think he is a regular built wideawake Gen, does a great deal of business with very little noys and few words. Gurrillas are verry plenty in that part of Tenn. but Crooks is always ready, and had paid them with interest, for every attempted raid they have made in his vicinity. We have no news from [Andrew's brother] Amos yet. His case is a verry singular one. His family are of opinion he is dead, for he has never written since he left Point Pleasant, Va. nor has he been heard from since the boys left Nashville. Butternutism is on the decline in the North, my present opinion is that by the time the Convention meets in June, "Val" will scarcely command a Corperals guard, and should he be nominated he will be beaten, that is my prophesy.[1] I have been appointed a delegate to the State Convention, but I will not go, if I were there I would not vote for him, and if he should get the nomination, I will vote & work against him. I want H. J. Jewett nominated for he is a whole sole War democrat and if he should get the nomination, will be Elected by a large majority.[2] I will vote for no man, knowingly, who thinks more of his political name than he does of his country, there are a few among us (I will not mention any names) who would go for "Val" now, but they will find the doctrine getting unpopular. They find fault with us the "green backs", the tax law and in fact every thing but the Cinti Enquirer. Well we have had such men, (if history be true) in all wars, they are called by hard names some times. I hope there are not enough to defeat our purpose, we are attending to them as well as we can. Good by for another week. Please give my compliments to my friends in your Army, and believe me as ever

Your affectionate father
Andrew Evans

1. The term "butternut" derived from a type of homespun cloth worn by some Confederate soldiers and other rural Southerners. It became synonymous with rebel sympathizers and antiwar Democrats, many of whom welcomed this name, which they felt identified them with common folk. James Rawley, *The Politics of Union: Northern Politics During the Civil War* (Lincoln: University of Nebraska Press, 1980), 121.

2. Hugh J. Jewett was the Ohio Democratic gubernatorial candidate in 1861. He lost to Unionist candidate David Tod. Jewett was not renominated in 1863. The Democrats instead chose Vallandigham. For more about Vallandigham and his nomination, see notes in Sam's letter of February 8, 1863, and Andrew's letter of June 11, 1863.

⇒ JANE TO SAM ⇐
Aberdeen, Oh. / April 14th, 1863

Dear Cousin,

I received your very kind letter some few days ago. We was all verry glad to here from you. Cousin I hope you will excuse me for not answering your letter sooner. We are all well at present and I hope that these few lines may find you enjoying the same. I got a letter from Jake Bottner to day. He is at Nashville. Well and harty. Jake says that he is tired of being in the service. I think that there are a great many more that will get tired before the war is over.

Cousin, I and Mother has bin out in the woods burning brush three days this week. We have been clearing a place to raise some tobacco this summer. I think we will be pretty good farmers after while. There will be more woman work out doors this summer that ever they did. Cousin I dont think that it is any disgrace for the woman to work out in the field do you? Cousin I think it is right for the woman to pitch in. While all the men is out fighting for our Country, I am on hands any time, I am in hopes that the war will be over some of these days if it dont verry soon.

I got a letter from Will last monday. They are at Carthage Tenn yet, all well, fat and harty. Cousin we have not heared any thing from Pap since I wrote to you before. Will says he does not know any thing about him.

He left him at Nashville, I think it is something curious that we can not here any thing about him. But I hope that he is alive and well.

Cousin your fathers folks are all tolerable well but John, he has been verry low, but he is getting little better again. I and Big Jane is a going down to see him tonight.

Sunday Apr. 12th. I have just come from your fathers, Big Jane and I. John is some better. He has bin bed fast for almost two weeks. John is the poorest man that I ever saw. India came in too see him yesterday evening. Nat Early brought her and the children in a carriage. She wont go home for some time. Inda and the children all look well.

Grandmother sends her love and best respects to you. Granny is trouble[d] verry much about Pap [Sam's Uncle Amos]. She talks about all of you Boys every day. Big Jane says that she wont fight with you about that [letter torn]. She says she would like to see you get whiped. Jane says that she hopes that you will get in a good humor. Big Jane says that she has got tired of kissing the girls there is no Boys here. Cousin I expect that she is atiring [?] to turn it off. She sends her love to you boys. Cousin give my love and best wishes to all the Boys and receive a full share for your self. Cousin write when you can and believe me to be

your true cousin,

Jane Evans

⇥ ANDREW TO SAM ⇤
Home / April 19, 1863

Dear Son,

Yours of the 5th of April came to hand on the evening of the 13th. Amos received one from you on Friday last. Johns [John Hiett] has not come yet, we are very glad to read of your continued good health and contentment and the general good health of your Company and Regt. Health is the most estimable of earthly blessings, and we are frequently too neglectful of the means to preserve it, until it is lost, you have certainly had due regard to the laws of health, or you would have been numbered among the soldiers that "were." I earnestly implore you to continue your watchfullness over your health, you are well posted on the laws of health; and are pretty well acclimated, and should you not disobey said laws, you will perhaps remain healthy. Will and George were well on the 9th (our last date from them.) They had just returned from a march of

36 miles "Rebel hunting." Rebels are plenty in that neighborhood but in too small squads to make a respectable fight. They are mostly guerrillas, thriving over the country.

Our health is about as usual except John. He is very certainly and steadily getting weaker, he has lost all his flesh, his cheerfulness and his hopes of recovery. He is not able to raise himself in bed. We do all we can to make him comfortable in his afflictions.

My nose, face, etc are annoying me considerably, though I am still on duty. I expect the Iodine will have to go on yet, I have been using milder remedys, but I guess they won't do. Your Mother has a little tear of rhuematism since I wrote you, but all is about well again. Amos is improving, the rest of our family are quite well. The Neighborhood is healthy, Robert Power of Aberdeen died last week. Old Peter Hunt also; Harrison Housh, Jr has come home, he claims to be in progress of discharge and also a paroled prisoner? He was taken at the battle of Somerset,[1] and marched to Chattannooga, all his clothes taken except a single dress, then paroled and turned loose 200 miles from home, he walked home and is remaining there, the above is his tale? If incorrect I am not responsible. Sam Housh has become corpulent, he is said to weigh 208 pounds and enjoys good health. John Housh is in Memphis in good health, you may see him.

We have nothing for news to interest you, we have in "Washington news" what purports to be reliable, that "Old Abe" has concluded to not put the Conscript laws in force. I don't like that, for the soldiers in the field are as free men, and generally speaking, better citizens than those who stay at home, and if he don't conscript a sufficient number, to enable those in the field to fill their ranks, and go forward to a successful and honorable conclusion of this war, I shall think him little less than a traitor. He is vested with full power to swell the Army to any desired number. We have only enough men in the field to hold our own, we are making no progress in agressive warfare. Our forces are held in check at every important point where we have an army, perhaps by an equal number of rebels, and if we are to have no more raised to assist those in the field, they had better take matters in their own hands. Soldiers can not be raised by volunteering now, and I think Lincoln is fooling his time away, and jeopardizing the lives of the soldiers, to attempt such measures. Let him fill all the ranks in the Union Army to its maximum number and enable them to close the thing out before winter.

Our peach blossoms are out, we have a few warm days, but much too dry for vegitation to flurish, we have about 2/3 of our corn ground broken up and if the weather should be favorable we will finish breaking up this week and be ready for planting the ground is in pretty fair condition this spring. We are fixing to plant 25 acres. The creek is too low to grind. I have got the new belt work all in to suit me but I have not water enough to try them on, they are sure to work well, or I am badly fooled, I would love to hand you a loaf of light bread in evidence of the kind of work we have been doing. I have an idea, that a soldier could force a little of it down, if he does like crackers better.

I will endeavor to do your will, with your money and any other matters on which you may instruct me (unless it would be sparking your woman, I should have to decline that!) anything else I am able for, and shall be "did."

Please give my compliments to Col's Cockerill and Loudon, Dr Phillips, Capt. Love, Drennin, Dod, West and any others of my acquaintance. And believe me

Your affectionate father
Andrew Evans

1. The "battle of Somerset" that Andrew is referring to was a skirmish at Dutton's Hill, Kentucky, near the town of Somerset. On January 30, 1863, a small Union force engaged Confederate raiders who had been operating in Kentucky and achieved a minor victory, causing the raiders to loose much of their booty. The Union troops, however, were criticized for failing to pursue the Confederates south across the Cumberland River. Cooling, *Fort Donelson's Legacy*, 245–46.

⇥ SAM TO ANDREW ⇤
Moscow, Tenn. / April 19, 1863

Dear father,

Your kind favor of the 5 came to hand on the 14 and as usual gave me great pleasure to hear from home. I thought from the news from home some time ago that John would be convalescent ere this but by the statement in your last it is uncertain. It is pleasing to know he is cheerful. We have the news of the township election by some mail of your letter. We hear you were elected instead Esqr Waldran. You did not say in your letter you were a candidate for any office but the ticket sent to Co F had your name printed on it. I would rather John Mitchell had been defeated by some good, competent man. It is reported here, that Dave Tarbell is inclined to "butternut proclivities." How true it is I do not know. You voted as every man ought who feels an interest in the safety of his Country. I never will vote for any more who has disloyal sentiments If I [k]now anything of character and course on this war.

I received the Bee you sent me and felt quite at home on reading it. The Stamps you sent come in good order, $1.00 as I asked. The corespondence between Covert and Grierson is interesting. John did not say more than he ought. I have a letter from Huntington that needs about the same kind of answer. I wrote an answer to be published but conclude it would be a better plan to warn him what will be the consequence if another such causes to come from him. He is not a friend of mine, but I no [page torn] as such.

Your analysis of the opposers of the "Conscript Act" is rather a natural one but I should arrange the constituent parts a little different. 1 part Coward & 1 S[outh] Sympathize. 2 Calf' [?] The combination of these parts now produce your last [shitass], is my analysis.[1] True democratic principles are safe where ever political lines may safely be drawn. My politics is the men who can and do most to put down this "Rebellion". As you, I do not make political preferences toward the army.

We are trying to stop the Rebellion in this part of Dixie. Smith is drawing the strings tighter on the secesh Citizens (The Bullitin and Argus Memphis) papers have been suspended for publishing contraband news. There is some great movement going on here. Day before yesterday half of the 70 (the left of the Regt) and the 99 Ind. went to Lagrange. Since there we have learned what the movement is. Gen Chalmers is South of here some place near Cold Water. Troops from Memphis and Corrinth, All the Calvary at and between these two points, and all the infantry that could be mounted went with the intention of bagging him (Chalmers). The day the order came a detachment from all the Regiment was sent out to gather all the horses that could be found in this vicinity for the purpose of mounting men. They have reached their destination. Gen Smith accompanied the expedition. The latest, they were at Holly Springs. The cars took them that far, from LaGrange. That being about as far as the Road was safe.

80 prisoners taken at Covington, Tenn came down by this place yesterday bound for the "North". We are gathering them when ever we can. Nothing of importance in this immediate neighborhood has transpired for some days. Some 5 days ago 3 furloughs were forwarded for approval.

They have not yet returnęd. I believe I stated in my letter the names to Mary. Our Co has decided on determining by lot who shall go in turn since the left half of our Regt went to Lagrange. The remainder have the same duty to do. The health of the 70 is exceedingly good. That of Co. F is exceedingly good. Every man is able for duty that is present, not a single man ever reported this morning.

Maj Brown is in command of the Rgt. Col Loudon is Commandant of the Post at Lagrange. I hear he is verry strict. The probability is my extra duty money will not be stopped. First class michanics will still receive their extra pay. Other extra duty is stopped by Law of Congress. According to the Regulations we mean Laborers are entitled to a ration and a half but that we dont get. Wet night was last. Much thunder and lightning. Wood[s] are perfectly green and have been for 10 days. Most fruit blossoms are gone. Clover is in blossom. There is no corn planted this season, no cotton, no wheat that I have seen. This part looks like starvation to the Citizens. Tell John I will write to him in a few days. No letters from the 89 latély. Give my best respects to Grand Mother and all who feel an interest in our welfare my Love to Mother John and all the family accept a share for yourself,

I remain Your son,

Sam

1. See Andrew's letter of April 5, 1863. Amos's letter of May 7, 1863, confirms that Andrew was elected (apparently to justice of the peace, if Waldron was his opponent) and explains that Andrew had not been a "formal candidate."

⇝ SAM TO ANDREW ⇜
Moscow, Tenn. / April 26, 1863

Dear father,

Yours of 19th come to hand yesterday. The quickest time a letter has ever made since we have been here. Yours of the 13 came to hand on 20, yesterday one from George of the 17, Will and he are well. The[y] had just returned from a Scout. Will received a hole through the tail of his overcoat. George said a ball passed very close to him. No injury done to either of them. He said they did but little good. George said nothing of Uncle Amos.

You say, "Butternutism on the decline in the North." I am very glad of that. When ever the Sentiments in the North are all loyal as they ought to be Sentiments South will (in my opinion) change for the better. If you who are loyal will talk to the "Sympathizers" as they should be, they will find but little consolation in traitorous programme. They should have no office, not even suffrage. A man who will not support his government in "word or deed" should not have any right garantied by that government. A mere political name should sink into utter insignificance when country is at stake. Most political parties are false, in their doctrine and teachings. The[y] are too much used for a kind machine to obtain office. The old Jackson or I I [sic] might go further back and include Jefferson (not Jefferson Davis) but old Thomas Jefferson and his follower's, politics suit me better. I am very doubtful if those old "Patriots" (for such they were) were alive whether they would endorse "Val", Waldran H Esq and others I could name. "The Union must and shall be preserved" Jackson. This is the sentiment that suits me, and upon this principle I am willing to stand the storm, if it should last long, We are looking for something to be done pretty soon, if reports are true.

Report informs us that the "Queen of the West" has been recaptured by our boys. There is now no doubt but Vicksburg is being evacuated and the force leaving is to operate against Rosecrans. Charleston attack was a fizzle, a grand one too, Admiral Dupont is not the man I thought he was.[1] Faragut is the man, not affraid of torpedoes.

Well I can tell you something about the expedition I spoke of in my last to you. The expidition has returned, they went as far as Penola Miss. Gen Chalmers heard of our boys coming and made their escape all but a few. Our boy[s] took over 1,000 horses and mules, some were taken from Chalmers, but most were taken from Citizens, Some 30 wagons, Some arms, did not get the No. Our troops came into Moscow Friday in the afternoon, Camped here for the night. The 5 Co's of the 70 left here, Started for Lagrange at 7 o'clock and arrived there 10 o'clock P.M., distance 10 miles a pretty good time. An Attack was expected at Lagrange. We stayed at LaGrange till 1 o'clock yesterday. We then started on a scout in the direction of Summerville. The day was very hot and we went on the fast line arriving at Moscow after travel of 15 miles. When we arrived the sun was just sinking behind the western hills. We found no guerillas took some horses. All of us were rather tired having made good time. The 70 is all here now. We would rather stay here than at Lagrange because we are better fixed here than we could fix ourselves up there. When we were there we would rather have stayed there. I dont care much myself.

Our health is still pretty good. W W West has been sick of flux, rather a light attack, he is now nearly well. He sends his best respects to you and John. All of Co. F except the above named are well and in fine spirits. Lawson Dragoo and John Hiett started home on furloes on Thursday. I should have written home by them, but They started at 10 A.M., at first they told me they would at 2 P.M., but John [Hiett] can tell you as much as I could, and write a whole day. I am very well and have taken very good care of myself. Warn against imprudence of every kind when ever I see it. The boys sometimes call me Doctor. If they feel bad I tell them so far as I know how to do. My doctoring is done without medicine, that is eat, drink, sleep, take exercise and all that tends to preserve health. It's much safer to keep health than to gain it when lost. I am very sorry to hear John is still growing worse. I was at one time in great hopes he would recover but it seems extremely doubtful. I wish he could keep his cheerfulness. It is much better for him if he could do so. I would like for him to get the letter I sent him. I will come home to see him if it is possible for me to do so. I learned Inda is at home now and will remain there for some time. I will enclose a Lock of my hair. Will you please give it to her. I have had no opportunity get my likeness to send her, but will as soon as I can. Nothin more for a while. My respect to all, to John B. give my love and best wishes, the same to Mother and yourself and believe me

Your big soldier boy,

Sam

1. Rear Admiral Samuel Francis Du Pont launched an unsuccessful attack on Charleston harbor on April 7, 1863. With his fleet severely damaged, Du Pont chose not to renew the attack the next day. Du Pont suffered wide criticism and was eventually relieved of command. E. Milby Burton, *The Siege of Charleston: 1861–1865* (Columbia: University of South Carolina Press, 1970), 136–45.

"The Duty Imposed Upon Us"
May 1863–November 1863

※ ANDREW TO SAM ※
Home / Sunday evening May 3rd, 1863

Dear Son,

Yours of the 26th came to hand yesterday, (the quickest time on record) which gave us pleasure to learn that you were "very well" and that the general health of your company is still good. I am sorry to learn the health of my friend W. W. West is not so good as usual, but hope by proper care he may soon be restored to health. His prudence will do a great deal towards restoring him to health.

Our health is about as usual. John is rather better than when I last wrote you (or at least he appears so). He had quite a bad spell Thursday morning last, since which time he has been steadily improving, he keeps cheerful, as any one could in his condition. Your friends & relatives here are generally well & the general health of the neighborhood is good. There have been some cases of Typhoid Pneumonia in the neighborhood but none fatal & all recovered that I know of.

We are done planting corn. We began on Monday and was hindered several times by showers of rain through the week, but we used all the suitable weather, and finished yesterday, all in good condition and in as nice mellow ground as you ever saw corn planted in. We planted 25 acres, most people are done planting. Thom has 6 or 7 acres to plant yet, but it is ready and will soon be done. The corn ground generally is in beautiful order. Wheat looks well, the prospect for fruit is very bright. We did considerable grinding last Thursday. The new Belt work roles so nicely, "its no use talking" no jerking like the ropes made, no noys except a buz! We have no trouble with the races or dam, we have kept the waste gate open when not running, if the water was not the least bit muddy. The result is both races are clean yet or nearly so. We have kept the mill locked the whole time day and night unless one of us was there. We have thereby let every man get his own, and no growling and we find things right where we put them, which is verry [?] in certain cases.

We have news that looks like things were being stirred up among the various armies, Hooker, Hunter, Banks, Grant & in fact about all our armies are on the move, except Rosecrants who is waiting to be mooved upon, and the last news looks like he will be accommodated soon. He is fortified as well as he wants to be & has every thing in readiness for the reception. Hooker is over the river with his army & will commence operations some where. Banks is on his way to Port Hudson & is doing good work as he mooves, Grant & Sherman are stirring and will do some good work if an opportunity serves. Upon the whole we are gaining on the Rebs, I know we are in the North, verry nicely and I think you are in the South. We have had but one reverce, that of Charleston, I think that will soon be paid with interest. The land forces are prepared to cooperate with the Navy at the next attack on Charleston.

I am glad that you Will & George have got to passing letters. You will get the news so much earlier than you can through your letters from home. We have several days later news from them than your letter gives but you have probably as early news as we have. They were well at our last news except Will had some Neuralgia in the face. He was on the mend.

Ole Matthew is holding his "hat show". It used to be bonnet show. Hat takes the lead now (Old hat! as well as new,) the ladies are wearing light summer hats for head dress this spring. They wear the "New hat" on the head! You of course could not guess any thing about the "Old![")[1] —they have had a bad day for the show, it has rained frequently during the day, the crowd is said to be smaller than usual.

Please give my compliments to my friends & believe me your affectionate

father,

Andrew Evans

George Jamison is here, he sends you his love & best respects, he visits John frequently.

1. This is another example of Andrew's several obscure attempts at humor.

⇒ SAM TO JOHN ⇐
Moscow, Tenn. / May 3, 1863

Dear Brother John

I will write you a few lines again and see with what success it meets this time. I wrote to you a long time ago but you have not yet seen it yet.

I am very Sorry that you have not had the privilege of reading it. I have just received a letter from Amos of the 23 it being the first for some days but Ere this you have had the privilege of seeing John Hiett who started home on furlough some days ago Lawson Dragoo went with him. John Midghall did not get his furlough at the same time but is now on his road to Ohio. I tried to get a furlough but was not successful. The weather here is beautiful, the Season is fully one month ahead of Ohio from what we learn. Young peaches are about as large as Musket balls. Yesterday I noticed some spontaneous stalks of corn a high as my knee.

The health of the army here is very good. I think it never was better than at present. Only 2 men have died of the 70 for more than 4 months. All of your acquaintances in Co F are well but Sibbald he is convalescent. I would be pleased to have you enjoy as good health as I do. I am not as heavy as when I left home but I am as heavy as I want to be down in Dixie's Land. Bronchitis has affected me but very slightly. I think I am perfectly well of it now. Measles cured me I guess. My teeth are going, I have lost 3 since I left home. This I hate but must be satisfied. Gold plugs wont stand hard "Tacks" very well.

Capt. Zimmerman has handed in his resignation. I do not know what his reasons are for it. Perhaps he is tired of the service. Co G has no Captain. Carter was dismissed from the Service by sentence of Court martial. Capts Naylor and Wiles have offered their resignations. Capt Wilson resigned some 5 months ago. Q. M. deBruin talks of resigning his post. Smiths division is to make up a contraband Regt & officered by men of the division.[1] There are to be 4 white officers to each Co. The Capt, 1st and 2nd Lieut, and orderly Sergeant. One Co I understand is to be officered from the 70th. Capt Bouton (of Bouton Battery) will be Col of the Regt. I dont know who any of the rest of the officer[s] will be.[2]

By todays mail we forward Resolution adopted by the 70th expressive of their views in the present struggle to save the Nation.[3] They will be published in the Cincinnati Paper, Brown and Adams Co. papers, I will close for this time. Give my love to all the family and accept for your self a bountiful share of love and best wishes for your welfare. I remain as ever

> your affectionate brother,
> Sam

1. This is a usage of "contraband" meaning escaped slaves. For an explanation of this term see note in John's letter of August 11, 1862. Under the terms of the Second

Confiscation Act of 1862 and Lincoln's Emancipation Proclamation of January 1, 1863, the Union military was empowered to enlist escaped and freed slaves.

2. In this letter we have the first indication of Sam's potential involvement with blacks as soldiers.

3. Sam quickly emerged as a leader in efforts to get his regiment to endorse the Emancipation Proclamation and served as the chairman of a committee that drafted several resolutions the regiment adopted with little change. One resolution, which is probably the one referred to here, read: "Resolved, That we believe it should be the policy of the Government to employ the blacks in whatever manner they can be made most serviceable to the United States Army, whether it be to handle the spade or to shoulder the musket." Colonel Robert Cowden, *A Brief Sketch of the Organization and Services of the Fifty-Ninth Regiment of the United States Colored Infantry, and Biographical Sketches* (Dayton, Ohio: United Brethren Publishing House, 1883), 177.

☞ AMOS TO SAM ☜
Aberdeen / May 7, 1863

Dear Brother,

My time is again at hand to write to you. Yours of Apr. 23rd arrived May 1st. I am much pleased to hear from you & to be corrected. I know that I cannot write correctly for want of a more thorough knowledge of grammar. You can correct yourself, but I do not know what is correct. Do you think I could get a correct understanding of grammar by reading Kirkham carefully? Can I become a master of it without a teacher? I did not get to inform myself on anything except milling & general news during the past winter. I am willing to drop my side, hoping you will remain my advisor.

John had quite a backset today but is some better, it is not for us to know how long he will survive, Brother Wm. Ramsey visited him to day, prayed for him & cheered him up very much. John was not but very slightly acquainted with him but formed quite an attachment for him. Ramsey came at my request. He is our present minister & is highly esteemed by all who know him. The folks generally are well. Grandmother has a very severe cough and looks very bad. Our Mary has a tooth-ache. Peggy has a felon on her thumb, nothing serious.

John Hiett has been to see us—he looks well. "Midghall" came home friday night. Spon's boy & James. Frame told me he brought a letter & some money from you. If so he did not mention it himself. They may have been mistaken, but I do not like to ask him, he would certainly mention it—if so. I like the looks of the news at the present time as you will too. I will Enclose some Scraps to you. Sawyer & Father were both elected. Father was not a [formal] candidate.

This is a cold damp day, it has been raining for Several days though very moderate with Some intermissions. I ground 21.46 lbs of flour out of a part of the late wheat tuesday night & hauled it away today. The last I ground & took down has the name of the best flour Ever Sold in Aberdeen. Flour has fallen a little but ours brings the same old price. Your mill has a reputation that would be hard to break down. We have been selling corn meal at $1.00 per bu for Sometime with a demand Equal to the Supply. the mill will net a nice profit or rather pay well for tending.

Father gave you the news of the Bonnet or rather hat Show. It was as good as usual with few Exceptions.

There is little new to write. Crops look well generally—corn is coming up fast. Oh, Wm. Shelton raised a large barn on the Creek near where Carry quit[s] the Pike on the left as you go up.[1] Fulton is building a frame house for his Engineer at the far End of the Bridge. I will not weary your patience longer. I will close with my best wishes for yourself & all,

I am as ever,

Amos

1. This is the first mention of William Shelton, who later became Sam's father-in-law.

⇥ SAM TO ANDREW ⇤
Moscow, Tenn. / May 10, 1863

Dear Father,

Your kind letter of the 3rd of May came to hand on the 9th which gave much pleasure. I also recd. one from Mary same day. As you are my regular corespondent, I have fixed a day to write to you and always write on that day if in Camp. The news about the Virginia is very contradictory nothing can be relied on the news by papers is that Hooker's army has fallen back to the old Camp. But a few minutes ago by telegraph the news is that Stoneman Cavalry has hoisted the stars and stripes over the Court State house in Richmond, and that Hooker has received 30,000 reinforcements and has recrossed the Rapahannock.[1] Whether this is true I am not able to say but I hope it is so time will show. Stoneman has taken Richmond I hope he will destroy the town and all the Rebel property in it, that is if there is danger in holding their place. The news from below is very wholesome to me and I am rather disposed to credit a consider-able portion of it. Paper states that all is quiet at Murpheysboro.

I have nothing of very late date from Will or George the latest is they were well. You perhaps have heard of the last step if [*sic*, I've] taken. In my letter to Amos I gave my reasons for doing so.[2] I do not think that it was rash in me to do so. My own conscience is clear on the subject. The position I am offered or rather recommended for was not solicited on my part, but was solicited by several to take it. Col. Loudon said he could officer a Regiment from the Nonc[ommissioned] officers better than the 70th is now. Whether we are the choice [the best] of the No[rth] or the refused, you may judge. Give me your opinion about the matter in which I am engaged. I would rather have consulted you on the subject but time would not admit of it. I thought $100 per month was as much as I could make here. I thought I could do as much good there as here.

The 70th is still enjoying good health, And I hope that I shall never be under the painful necessity of writing anything else. I am still well. Direct your letters the same way you have been till I inform you, to otherwise. We are recruiting our Co. now have 31 men enrolled. 3 days work. we have not drilled any yet, but expect to tomorrow. The way we recruit [is to] mount a squad of about 50 men, ride out into the country where the darkies are, take all the negros (able bodied), all their mules (able bodied) and any gun that can be found in the hands of Citizens.[3]

I will write you once a week as usual. I will write to all who write to me but can't write always when I would like to. Will now write to Ann and enclose with yours. My compliments to all the family.

Yours etc.

Sam

1. General George Stoneman was, at this point, commander of the cavalry of the Army of the Potomac. In April and May of 1863, Stoneman's cavalry crossed the Rappa-hannock and raided the Virginia countryside, destroying transportation lines and com-mandeering supplies. The report here however is erroneous; at no point did Stoneman's cavalry move on Richmond. Stephen Z. Starr, *Fort Sumter to Gettysburg*, vol. 1 of *The Union Cavalry in the Civil War* (Baton Rouge: Louisiana State University Press, 1979), 351–61.

2. This letter did not survive, but apparently it indicated Sam's acceptance of a lieu-tenancy in a newly formed black regiment.

3. This method of "recruiting" black troops was common practice in Union-occu-pied territories and raises the question of whether the blacks were genuine "volunteers."

Aberdeen, Oh. / May 14, 1863

Dear Brother Sam,

It has been just one year since the death of our Brother [Abraham]. This day brings us to witness and to feel again that death reigns triumphant. Our dear Grandmother died at 1/2 past 11 o'clock today. She was afflicted with a cough and cold for several days. Wednesday, she was taken with quick breathing and a fast loss of the vital powers. Her sickness was no form of disease. Life gave way under old age and trouble. She said she did not suffer any pain, life passed away and she now sleeps in peace. She will be interred by [next to] Grandfather at 2 P.M. tomorrow. I went this evening for her burial clothes and her coffin made. She was constantly grieving about you and Uncle Amos. She esteemed and loved you more dearly than any among her grandchildren. She cried to John to see her but it could not possibly be so.

Before she died she asked them to send for Dr. Moore. She only wanted to see him but he could not get to see her alive. The funeral will undoubtedly be a very touching one. Her name is endeared by all who know her.

John remains about the same except his strength is failing slowly. Mother is rather unwell. She is fatigued and troubled. We are all much wearied by losing sleep. Our neighbors are about as usual.

We all fully Endorse proceedings.[1] [We] leave you to Consult your own conscience for advice. I am in for making the Contrabands fight & drafting the free Negros & Butternuts & forcing them to do the labor for the Soldiers. Butternuts are among us but they have to lay low. Many of them get treated as they deserve & I shall arrest any man I see of that Class. Several of our [letter torn] are getting the most severe [torn] from Soldiers. Hi-Jacks Jones [torn] I could mention. You know [torn] oposed the draft as well as I [torn] No man shall wear a butternut & [bear?] forth his sentiments in this neighborhood. A butternut & rebel horse thief was taken at Aberdeen Wednesday. He is now Safe. Sam I do not feel like writing. Will [you] please Excuse this time. Respects to all.

I am as Ever,

Amos

1. This is a cryptic expression of support for Sam's decision to command black troops.

Moscow, Tenn. / May 17, 1863

Dear Father,

I am again seated to perform my weekly duty. I believe there has not been a week since we came to Lagrange that I have not written to you or John. I have reced no letters from home since I last wrote—I expect one today. I have been [illegible] for the last week very well, and quite happy comparatively Speaking. I of course do not feel so much at liberty as if at home. It seems that home would not be [a] much better place than [the] ranks while this horrible state of Affairs exists. When ever I have an opportunity to come home will do so, but it seems that it will take over one year to get through furloughin, if that be the case the time of the last will be nearly out.

I believe I have told you that the 70 is not here but at Grand Junction 13 miles above here. They are detached for awhile for garison duty. We cannot now tell you how long they will be there, I was up there last week recruiting, they were well. Gen. Smith received orders to raise a Regiment of Negros within his division. He has issued his order in conformity to the order of Gen. Herlbuts [Hurlbut], to each Regt. of his command. With orders that suitable men should be Selected Command, I understand all the Cos are under way. Our Co. has now about 70 men. We have been drilling them some; they learn the school of a soldier much readier than I anticipated.

A Gen. Thomas was here day before yesterday and made a speech with refference to the contraband question.[1] He said the aim of the President was to make the Negro Self sustaining and when they organized into Regiments [they] were to be clothed and armed and should receive the protection of the Government, if taken prisoners should be treated as prisoners War. My doctrine is that a Negro is no better than a white man and will do as well to receive Rebel bullets and would be likely to save the life of some white men. There is another thing that seems right in the premices. There are more Negros inside of our lines than we can use otherwise to advantage. It seems to be the policy of the President to take all the Slaves from their masters as a means of harassing their facilities for propogating Subsistence, thus cause them to Sue for peace. Then what can be done with them. I believe that most of our Generals approve the plan, I am not much inclined to think they will fight as some of our

White Regts, but men who will stand up to the work, may succeed in making of some benefit to the Government.

The news from Vicksburg is still favorable but the stronghold is not yet fallen, it seems that Grant has been around trimming off the knots and limbs preparatory to entering on the trunk. I think Grant will take it. The news from Richmond is conflicting but Stoneman's raid has been pretty gallant and successful.

I have nothing late from Murphreysburough. I received a letter from the 89th last week they were generally in good health. Will had been sick but was convaliscent at the time the letter left. George was well, Tell India that I have had my picture taken for her but it is not a good one and I will try for a better one before I send her one.[2] Many of the artists who follow the army are very inferior. They are men who want to make money, and escape the Conscription. If any of my acquaintances are conscripted I would like to know who they are, I saw Dr. Kenedy and talked with him, he is with the 53 O, he sends his respects to you. Did he ever pay you, for the cane you Mounted for him?

I will have to come to close. Remember me to all the folks. My best respects to you and family.

I am as ever,

Sam

1. This refers to U.S. Adjutant General Lorenzo Thomas, who was sent to the Mississippi Valley to enlist ex-slaves as soldiers. By the end of the war, Thomas had raised 76,000 troops, 41 percent of all Union black soldiers. McPherson, *Ordeal by Fire*, 350.

2. The Civil War created a vast new market for photographers, and up to a thousand may have operated in or around Union camps. Many soldiers wished to send home portraits to loved ones, sometimes for the purpose of leaving a keepsake in case they should die in battle. Because of the difficulty and length of the photographic processes of the era and the possibility of sudden moves, most photographs taken for individual soldiers were ambrotypes, a lower-quality kind of photograph that was easier to produce. Keith F. Davis, "'A Terrible Distinctness': Photography of the Civil War" in *Photography in Nineteenth Century America*, ed. Martha A. Sandweiss (Fort Worth, Texas: Amon Carter Museum, 1991), 130–79, 142–46.

ANDREW TO SAM
Home / May 18, 1863

Dear Son,

I again missed writing to you on my usual day, (cause press of Company all day,) but having no chance to send to the P.O. no time is lost.

Yours of the 10th came to hand yesterday, we were pleased to hear of your continued good health & the good health of your Regt,—Our health is about as usual, your Mother & I, are considerably worn by care and loss of rest owing to Johns illness, there is no improvement in his condition, he sits up none at all. Even in the bed, he has to be cared for, as a child. He seldom speaks above a whisper. My kind old Mother died on the 14th just one year after Abm. She died calmly and with a short illness, no form of disease but a general cessation of the functions to do the part they had so kindly done for 87 years 9 Month and 4 days. I believe her spirit is among the blessed on high, a good woman has gone!

Mr. John Hiett has paid me $7.00 for you which is duely credited.

We have nothing of interest for news, [no] more than you get in the papers, & I suppose you get that about as soon as we do, sometimes sooner; If the authorities at Washington have gained anything in the shift of Commanders of the army of the Potomac, I am not able to see it. I was so anxious as anyone, for old Hooker to whip Lee's army, but I never believed for a moment, that he was any better commander than G. B. Mclellan. Hooker's stock is not as high now when the first news came that he was playing thunder generally. Some of our abolition hot heads said "Hooker is the first abolitionist that has had a chance at the Rebels, that he would annihilate Lee's Army, and be in Richmond in a week from the time he struck the first blow." How do things look now, Lee is in his position, & so is Hooker as they were before the battle only that both have lost largely in soldiers and officers, Lee's loss is perhaps greater than ours.[1]

You ask for my opinion about your new position; which I will impart very reluctantly I had much rather you had not asked for my opinion, or even informed me, that you were making yourself so willing, to accept a degraded position, (I would rather clean out S__t houses at ten cents pr day, than to take your position with its pay,) you have made enviable reputation, as a "good & worthy soldier" we are proud to say, that we hear nothing else of you from any quarter, Alas what a step! Would to God you had kept us uninformed on that subject. We deeply regret that it is taken, but you say, your conscience is clear. Be it so, never mind us. We will soon be out of the way. We had expected to see you some day, ere you took the "step." We are in doubt now—In as much as you asked for my opinion I shall expect you to Excuse me for the sentiment. It is frankly & truly given, I am sorry you asked it, and Expect you to be in an ill humor with me for giving it but I shall still try to keep you posted on matters at home.

We have had several days of clear cool weather, quite cool at night but no frost yet, fruit prospect is still bright, wheat looks very well, corn came up very well, we have late news from Will & George, they were neither very well on the 10th. We just commenced building a wall on the back side of the house to keep the wash of the hill from running in the yard. We have no news from Valandinghams trial.[2] Hope they will do him justice, if it hangs him, John F. Moore of the 10, Ky., C, has been exchanged and gone back to his duty.[3] John Hiett will start for Memphis on Wednesday next, he has had a pleasant time & is quite well.

My compliments to my friends in the 70th and believe me your affectionate father,

Andrew Evans

Home / May 17, 1863

Dear Brother Sam,

I received your kind letter to day in [illegible] and was very glad to here from you. It is a nice day, quiet hot. Ibby and Peggy and Tad went to meeting to day. John is no better to day. Sam come over this evening and see mothers garden, Sam don't you ever think of coming home. I would come down if it was not so far off, but I don't know the way. Sam, Cousin Will Evans came here yesterday and went away this morning.

I have been going to school some. I have bad news to tell you, our dear old Grandmother is dead, she died thursday about noon, buried friday at ten o clock, she died of old age.

India got a letter from George to day, he was not very well, Will well as common. You say you have command over the negros again. I would not like to have Command over them. I must close.

Good by,

Ann Delia Evans

1. Andrew is referring to the Battle of Chancellorsville on May 2–4, 1863, in which Lee's army defeated the Union forces under General Joseph Hooker, even though Hooker had twice the number of troops. Lee's victory marked the high point of Confederate military fortunes and set the stage for Confederate disaster at Gettysburg two months later. James M. McPherson, *Ordeal by Fire*, Vol. 2, *The Civil War* (New York: Alfred A. Knopf, 1982), 322–23.

2. See note about General Burnside's Order Number 38 and Vallandigham's trial in Andrew's letter of May 22, 1863.

3. For a brief explanation of the system of prisoner parole and exchange, see note in Sam's letter of May 24, 1862.

Huntington Township, Brown Co. / May 19, 1863

Dear Cousin,

Your kind letter of the 4th came to hand on the 12th inst. We was all very glad to here from you, and that you was well, Cousin Sam I ought to have answered your letter sooner, Cousin but I have not had the heart to do anything since poor old grandmother has left us, Cousin you don't know how hard it was for me to part with her. She was not bed fast but two days before she died. Well she had a bad cold for two weeks and a cough too but she had got good deal better. Mother wanted to send for the doctor for her cough she said that she did not want to take any strong medicine for it would make her weak she said. Mother made her all sorts of teas that she thought was good for her. She was most well. She said that she felt as well as ever she did, only she was weak.

Last Tuesday evening about half past two o'clock she was taken with a chill and it lasted her an hour, and after the chill went off her She did not complain of anything. We would ask her how she was and she would say that she was better. I went down after your Pap he came up with me. He said that he did not know of any thing that could be done for her, he said that She was too weak to take anything, She died Thursday half past 11 o'clock.

Cousin Sam this is a lonesome house indeed—if they ever was one. Cousin, I can't come in the room but what I have to look for my poor old grandmother. We could always see her sitting in the corner. But now it is vacant. Everything looks lonesome without her. Granny told me two weeks ago or more before she died that she was not a going to live very long. I did not think that she was going to drop off so soon. I read your letter to her when I got it. She said that I must give her love to you whence I answered your letter.

Cousin I have never written a letter to you yet, but what granny always to [sic] told me to give her love and respects to you. She said when I read the letter, that she would never live to see her Sam any more. She said that she would give anything in this world if she could only get to see you.

I will not finish this letter this evening. I will write the rest in the morning, I am going down too sit up with your Brother John to night. John has bin very bad all day to day.

Wednesday morning May the 20th, 63 Cousin this is a verry pretty morning. We are all well at present, and I hope that these few lines may find you enjoying the Same. I have just come from your Fathers. John is no better he is very weak, poor John he can not last much longer I think. He can not hardly bear to be moved any way. The rest of the folks are all as well as common. John told your mother night before last that he was not a going to live verry long and he said that he wanted to see you once more before he died, Cousin you ought to come to see him if you could any way at all.

Cousin give my love to the boys and receive a full share for yourself. Mother, Big Jane and all the rest of the family send ther love to you. Cousin, write when you can. I remain

your affectionate Cousin,

Jane

⇒ ANDREW TO SAM ⇐
Home / May 22, 1863

Dear Son:

I have received no letter from you since I wrote you last . . . We had a letter from Will & Geo—each during the past week. Will was well, George not well but expected to be soon. They were still at Carthage, Tenn. and are fortified in their position . . .

The weather is hot and dry, Crops are suffering for want of rain, wheat is heading but cannot thrive without rain, corn is generally well up, but won't grow much for want of rain, wheat, oats, flax, & grass of every kind is suffering severely; we have had no rain for some weeks, East fork is almost stopped running we have not commenced tending corn but expect to tomorrow. Cut worms are injuring our field considerably a few more dry weeks will shorten the fruit crop, well we have to stand it. Our folks are in usual health. John is about as he was a week ago, or at least he appears so, he has given up hopes of a recovery and chosen his last resting place (at Ebenezer) and made some other requests pertaining to his assetts after his death. Expresses himself ready for the great summons and is happy. Inda's Sam has been rather unwell for a few days but is up and stirring about. The friends & neighbors are generally well and the general health is quite fair.

Vallandingham is said to be sent to Rosecrants to be delivered to Bragg and not to return until after the war. It is also said that Burnside's order 38 arrested William Norris & John Lafaber, and they were immediately taken to Cincinti.[1] They may learn yet. That it is best to obey that order, it is no trouble to obey, if we mind our own business, & let other peoples alone the order is obeyed etc. It is no trouble for me to retain my old political feelings without going against the interests of my country. I attend no meetings political of any name. I accept no appointment of any of them, nor will I have any agency in nominating a candidate of, or for any of the parties, but when the candidates are before the people, I will choose among them, keeping an eye on the assessments of the candidates. I can't vote for an Abolitionist, nor for a Reb. Simpathiser.

We hear that you have enlisted in the Nigger service for the term of 5 years, if such is the fact, your Stomach has become quite strong compared with its condition whilst you were at home, if such is not the fact we are misinformed, you give some evidence of the fact in Mary's letter for you speak of recruiting "Contraband". It must be a fancy business, compared to that of staying with common white men "Sic transit Gloria, etc." If we are erroneously informed in any of the above statements, please correct them in your next after you receive this in order that we may be posted.[2]

Truely your father,
Andrew Evans

1. General Ambrose Burnside, commander of the Department of the Ohio at this time, issued order no. 38 in accordance with the dictates of Lincoln and General-in-Chief Halleck. The order provided for military trials for any behavior that could be considered disloyal or sympathetic to the Confederacy. Under the order, Vallandigham was tried and sentenced to imprisonment. President Lincoln commuted the sentence to banishment behind Confederate lines, reasoning that Vallandigham would be less of a political threat there than in an Ohio penitentiary. Willliam Marvel, *Burnside* (Chapel Hill: University of North Carolina Press, 1991), 231–32, 235–37.

2. Note that Andrew has already expressed his displeasure in his letter of May 18, 1863, but it is apparent that Sam has not yet responded.

⇒ SAM TO ANDREW ⇐
LaGrange, Tenn. / May 24, 1863

Dear Father,

Again I am seated to write to you although under somewhat different circumstances than here to fore. I have just reced a letter from Amos containing the mournful intelligence of the death of my good old Grandmother, I feel that the relatives of the deceased have sustained a severe

Loss, and the neighborhood a kind and generous parent. Although she attained a great age I know of no one who was will to part from her. I have every reason to believe she held me in high esteem but it would be very difficult to have a higher regard for any one than I had of her. There is one consolation we can meet again where there is no war, no sorrow, no afflictions, no parting! But all is peace and pleasure. God has call another of his children home away from this world of trouble! How short the time before we shall all be called from earth away. "No one knows of the day nor the hour," then let us be prepared to met the "dred Monster" death Whenever he may come, and not await the awful sentence, "Yee [sic] know your duty, but you did it not: Depart ye in to ever lasting darkness." It is not my purpose to write more on this subject But would request of all of you to think of death "the final doom of Man" and be prepared to meet him with a smile, or a welcome. Be as happy under the bereavement as God's Will permits.

I have been quite busy for a few days. I have been in command of our Co for the last eight days and will be for 2 or 3 days yet. The other boys are out recruiting. The Co is now about full. Clothing has come for the Negros. Most of the Camp equipage. The officers tents are here — two officers tents to each Co. Wall tents 10 square with a fly to cover it, they hold each 2 men without much crowding. Capt & Orderly Sergeant take one and 1st 2nd Lieut the other. The Regt number about 50 men. Some of the Co.'s only have about 10 men in, 3 are about full. I will report a full Co tomorrow.[1]

There is a prospect of an engagement at this place a considerable force is marching in this direction. Some of our force is gone out to meet them. Gen. Smith says he will give them the best he can if they come on. We (the Negro Regiment) are building a fortification, but I am not at liberty to describe it to you or where it is at this particular time. Gen Smith is out where we are at work 3 or 4 times every day and talked very freely with us, he says he will put us inside of it, to hold it and defend the cotton belonging to Gov't and that he wanted to see it the best diciplined Reg't in the service in one year and the best drilled.

The health of the 70 is very good. John McDaniel is here in camp tonight he is well. John Hiett and Lawson Dragoo, came back to the Regt yesterday, both are well. My health is very good yet. I hope it will continue. I would like to be at home a while but do not see much prospect of it. I learn that John would like to see me. I would him too. I would like to have the privilege to go home and get my uniform.

Give my love to all the folks at home accept a share myself [*sic*].

And believe me, your undutiful Son,

Sam

1. The standard size of a regiment, composed of ten companies, was one thousand men. Sam probably misspoke when he said his new regiment had fifty men, with three companies almost full. McPherson, *Battle Cry of Freedom* (New York: Ballantine Books, 1988), 326.

➤ AMOS TO SAMUEL ◄
Home / May 27, 1863

Dear Brother,

John breathed his last this morning at 8 o' clock, he died without a struggle. He called us all into see him & spoke but few words. In the morning of the 19th he told us for the first time he did not think he would live long, or that he might die at any moment or live Several days. I could not be absent scarcely a moment with out him calling for me, his last moments were as bright as his first "I am ready to die at any time," said he, "and want to be buried in the new graveyard in front of Ebenezer Church & get W. W. Ramsey to preach my funeral." His desires will be complied with at 11 O'clock A.M. tomorrow.

He frequently Spoke of you until 3 o' clock this morning, his looks are natural although he is poorer than any man I Ever Saw. He died a faithful Christian & his soul is free from trouble, his Sufferings were borne with patience, & a Crown of Glory is his reward. I cannot write or give utterance to my feelings, None but those that have watched & prayed & helped to bear the burden of the Suffering Sick can know them, his long last look was centered on me. Sabbath last he said he was Sorry to leave me So lonely but God had called for him. Oh! bless him, today he is happier than I.

I wrote to you that Grandma died on the 14th. All looks desolate & lonely. I Set 2 Evergreens in the front yard in memory of Doc [Abraham] & John knowing he must die, if I am gone when you get home (if you Ever do) you will see them & think of Me. I cannot write more.

Your Brother in Christ,

Amos A. Evans

Home / May 31, 1863

Dear Son,

I am under the painful necessity of informing you of the death of your dear brother, John. He departed this life at 8 o' clock on the morning of the 27th (Wednesday last). He had shown but little symptoms of declining so soon until within a very short time previous to his departure. He rested not quite so well during the previous night, but on being washed, and taking his usual stimulus, Bell [Isabella] asked him if he would have his breakfast, he answered yes, and told her what to get. She did it quickly but when she brought it to him he could not eat, said he would eat after a little, when he would get the phlegm coughed out of his throat. At 1/2 past seven he told Jo and Ann to go to school or they would be too late. I went to work in the yard and at 1/4 to eight, he told Inda to call me. I went in instantly and found him dying. He asked me to raise him up and see if he could breathe easier. I did so at once. He said "lay me down, it won't do. He then told us to send for Amos, which we did (he was in the field). He came in a few minutes but only in time to see him breathe his last. He spoke no more, but died in perfect calm. Rationally, he had talked freely of his departure for several days previous, expressed himself ready at any minute to meet his God. He expressed a reluctance to leave Amos, said he would be so lonesome. He often spoke of you, Will and George, said he wanted to see you all.

Our worthy old friend Thomas Simpson was buried at Ebernezer on the day John died, his illness was short . . . We are not getting the usual No. from Will & George, Will is on detach duty, as Hospital Steward in Stokes Cavalry.[1] He don't know how long he will be kept in that service, We are tolerably well. Inda's boys are neither well, tho are not confined, your friends are generally well. We have had a few nice showers of rain since Friday, which were very welcome visitors vegetation has revived finely, more rain would do a great deal of good, our fruit prospect is still verry flatering.

Our news from Vicksburg is still Encouraging I think we may safely say Grant will take it, he was well along with the work at our last news, he is still Unconditional Surrender Grant, May God preserve & protect him and his army. He is a working General as well as a fighting one? He and his army may have to take Richmond yet, he & old "Rosy" are all or nearly that gained anything in the last 6 months. Burnside is curing Butternutsim considerable in his department I wish him success in so desireable an undertaking. What few we have in Huntington are "laying low" the best of their way, we have no new's [sic] from Old Billy Norris, but his political enemies in Ripley are petitioning Burnside to release him, I believe they think, they have got their foot in it & are trying to lift it out the Easyest way.

Accept our best wishes.

Your father,

Andrew Evans

1. At this point Will was apparently with the 1st Middle Tennessee Cavalry commanded by Colonel W. B. Stokes. In Tennessee there was a strong Unionist element, and enough of these men volunteered to form over a dozen Tennessee Union Cavalry regiments, as well as several artillery batteries and infantry regiments. Frederik Henry Dyer, *A Compendium of the War of the Rebellion* (New York: T. Yoseloff, 1959), 1636–47.

⤞ SAM TO ANDREW ⤛
Camped near Lagrange / June 1, 1863

Dear Father,

Your kind favor of the 10 & 18th came to hand on the 28 and as usual were welcome. I am very sorry to hear that John is getting no better. I am sorry indeed that you have to be so confined. I would be very happy to relieve you if I could. I have tried in evry way that I could to get home to see John but have been thwarted in evry effort.

Grand Mother is gone! Would that I could have seen her ere she died. I know she loved me, and I did her. I believe she has gone to that land where suffering is no more. Her Spirit dwells with those of the redeemed. She was a kind parent and good woman, and a pious woman.

I am like you about Joe Hooker. Do not see any improvement over Mc[Clellan] and some others who have held the Same place. I am and have been very anxious that all of our Gens. should be successful in their efforts to save the country no matter who he was or where he is from.

You say you wish I had kept you uninformed about my new step. Well, father that would be almost impossible and besides I do not mean to hide from you what I do; Such things as you have the right to know.

"So willing to accept a degraded position." The fact is, you have never marched so far with a heavy load and Sore feet as I, and have never noticed so plainly the privileges of Commissioned officers. I beg leave to differ from you as to it being a "degraded position." I would much rather have my position that the "one" you Say You would rather have. All right as will be.

I would like to See you and think very likely that I will see you as soon where I am now as where I was. Do not be discouraged Father & Mother.

If I have done wrong it is not your fault but mine and will be held accountable to God. You Say you "expect I will be mad" But, I am not the least out of Humor at you. Although you have rated me very low. I think you are mistaken, I am glad you have not discarded me altogether, and will continue writing. I will not trouble you[r] patience more on this point at present but hope at the same time you will forgive me if I have done wrong.

Well, I am now about 1 mile from Grand Junction camped in the woods. Yesterday I was up at the Junction. The boys are all well. I saw John Hiett and Lawson Dragoo, they come back on the 24, Midgall has not yet come. There is quite stir about Vicksburg. Troops are passing down by here, we suppose to Vicksburg.

I was on a scout Last week with 22 of the 46th Ohio. We were mounted. No one was hurt. We took several guns and pistols and two prisoners. I reced a letter from Will a few days ago. George had been sick but was much better. Will was well nothing of importance was going on there. Tell Inda I sent her my picture on the 29th. I directed to Aberdeen in your care. My best wishes to all the family.

I remain your Son,

Sam

➤ ANDREW TO SAM ◄
Home at the old blue table / June 7, 1863

Dear Son,

Yours of the 24th May did not reach me until the 3rd June, we have none from you since. I am glad at all times to read of your good health, hope you may never be otherwise, health is the greatest of all earthly blessings we Enjoy, & I am sorry to inform you that we are not so blessed just now. Your good Mother is quite unwell, I am of opinion it was caused by loss of rest during John's illness. Part of her affliction is Rheumatism & part, general debility. She is still going about, and I hope will be better soon. Morty & Sam (Inda's boys) are both sick, Morty has some kind of slow fever, he is able to be up part of the time, Sam is teething I think causes his derangment. The residue of us are in usual health, Amos is not stout as he was last season, his lungs or pleura is out of fix slightly.

We are yet suffering for rain, we have had none since I wrote you. Late sowed wheat will be "gone up" if rain don't fall here very soon, the Early [wheat] was headed [up] before the dry weather hurt it, and may make tolerable crops without rain. Oats are nearly gone. I need not enumerate for all things growing are suffering. Corn is by no means past redemption, Oats is, so is flax, potatoes might be redeemed with rain, Gardens are suffering terably, Fruit is being injured seriously though suitable rains would save us an abundance. We are still building some stone fence we have [done] the East side of the orchard so the pigs will not root under it any more. The general health of the country is fair. No epidemic or contagious disease prevailing here now. Money matters are Easy but cannot be loaned to anybody that would Ever pay it, it might be loaned to Stafford or Bill Cunningham but I dont like such loans after trying them.

You perhaps feel ruffled at me for the blunt manner in which I answered your inquiry with respect to your new position. I felt just what I said at the time. I was pleased that you would get better pay, which I have no doubt you deserve, but I was of opinion that you increase the chances to loose your life. And still think so.

I am as willing for the Negro to fight as anybody is, and would rather have them shot than white men, nay more. I would have the race extinguished than to loose a single Co. of the white soldiers, but I had rather let their friends lead them than to do it myself. I wish you the best of luck, but cannot feel as comfortable under the circumstances as if you were in command of white men. What could four white men do with 100 armed negros if they should become mutinous? I hope they will not, but I have no confidence in Negroes.

Truly your Father,
Andrew Evans

⇾ SAM TO ANDREW ⇽
Camp near LaGrange, Tenn. / June 7, 1863

Dear Father,

Your very welcome letter of the 24th came to hand on the 4th of June, one from Amos on the 5th, which brought the mournful intelligence of the death of a beloved brother. It has been more than 12 months since I saw him but little did I dream at our parting that it would be the last on earth. Again has an impressive warning come to teach us that death is sure and life is uncertain.

Two years ago no one thought that I could have survived more hardships than my deceased brother. Would that I could have seen him before he died. I tried every way to get home but could not without deserting and that I would not do. I know you nor he, would like to see me desert the army. You are all too well acquainted with the deceased for me to write a eulogy. Amos says, he died without a murmur, believing he was called to a better world.

Bereaved parents, you have parted from a noble son and devoted Christian; brothers and sisters we have lost a kind brother. Be this our consolation, he rests with the people of God never to suffer more, and, if we but travel the road of righteousness, we will all be permitted to meet to part no more.

I attribute his death to the unjust and unholy rebellion on the part of the enemies of our country. Exposure I think caused his disease. It is wrong to harbor revenge in our bosom but it sticks in me. Some Secesh shall suffer for that if I am last in the attempt.

I cannot think why he wished to be interred at Ebenezer. I would have thought he would have chosen the old ground. There is where I would like to rest my last rest. If I should fall or die out here, you may do as you please about having me brought home and I will be satisfied with whatever you do.

You spoke of Norris and Lafabre being taken to Cincinnati. If you learn what has been done with them I wish you would tell me. Your politics suit me exactly and if at home would be governed as you are.

Well, I will reply to Some of your inquiries about the Negro service. I have enlisted in a negro Regt. but for the term I don't know how long. Our Company is full and will be mustered today.

Smiths Division has moved toward Memphis, the 70 went yesterday I would tell where they are gone but it would be contraband news and the authorities are very strict just now on that subject.

I am still in good health. I reced a letter from George on the 5, he was much better. Will had gone to the Tenn Cav to act Hp Stewart, was well. Nothing of interest going on there. All is quiet here at present.

Direct your letters to me

Lagrange Tenn

Care Capt. Bouton

Give my respects to all the family and accept a share for yourself

and believe me

your son,

Sam

Lagrange, Tenn. / June 9, 1863

Dear Brother Amos,

Amos, your very welcome letter of the 27th came duly to hand. I wrote to father on Sunday last, and will try to write you now. I have just finished a letter to George.

The news of the death of brother John was sad and affecting though not unexpected. But it is consoling to know that he died in the faith of a true believer of Christ. He has suffered long, and patiently waited the summons calling him home to dwell with the redeemer above. Let us, since it is God's will to call our beloved brother from this world of sin and sorrow to a world where neither can enter, be content if we have done our duty in comforting and administering to his wants and conduct ourselves in a way that death will not be dreaded, and after death be permitted to meet those who have gone to the throne of our Father. I cannot express my feelings, my deep emotion, or the sympathy for bereaved parents. God be merciful and be their comfort and stay in their hours of affliction. Sad sore afflicitons seem too thick and heavy on every side. In the short space of one week two dear friends have departed. Oh, that I could have seen them. I give you great praise in attending your brother so closely. I am confident everyone of the family did their whole duty, did all they could in every way. I have been sick at home and have seen others and know something about the attention sick receive at home. Fortunate is the sick who meets with such attention. Your affliction is heavy but bear up under it with Christian fortitude. God's will and not ours be done. I cannot write more on this subject at present.

Father is very much dissatisfied at my last step, for which I am very sorry. I think he does not take the proper view of it. No matter for that, it makes it none the less disgusting to him but it seems that I am deeper implicated and "degraded" myself (as he has it) more than anyone else in the situation. So far as a sense of duty is concerned, I feel perfectly easy, but I cannot be as well satisfied as if I had his approval in the case. When I was a Private in the 70th, I (according to what I hear) was a pretty good soldier. Was there doing my duty or what I thought was. Now duty calls me, I thought to take a place where I could do more good, or rather make a class of human beings who were an expense to the Government of an advantage besides individually doing the same as where I was. Again, my place is easier than a privates, have better quarters and more privileges. The last signifies nothing. As it is, I will do my duty as well as

I can. In the meantime, I will be pleased if father would be better satisfied. I am sure no one thinks any the less of him because I am where I am. It is not his fault, nor any fault in the way I was raised. My political faith is the same as when I left, and circumstances the same now as before the war, I would advocate the same doctrine. In a logical point of view, what is the conclusion we arrive at? That a Negro is no better than a white man and has just as good a right to fight for his freedom and the government. Somebody must direct these men. Shall I require, as a necessity, someone to do what I would not myself condescend to do? No, I could not do that. It would be very unjust. Enough of this.

My respects to all the family,

As ever your brother,

Sam

Direct your letter to Sam Evans

LaGrange, Tenn.

Care Capt. Bouton

⇨ ANDREW TO SAM ⇦
Home / June 11, 1863

Dear Son,

I am again ready to discharge a pleasant duty which I have not failed to do once a week since Oct. last. I received yours of the 1st on the 10th and was pleased to learn that you still had good health and were in good spirits. I hope your health and spirits may be of the best possible character, and that you may be protected by the divine hand, and thereby be restored to your home & friends there to remain in peace & prosperity until the gray hairs of old age shall admonish you that your stay on earth has been long & useful to man, and pleasing to God, and may the Divine hand rest lightly on you, when he calls you hence. May the green sods and evergreens stand lightly over your remains and may your spirit be with the Redeemed in Heaven till time shall be no more.

I am happy to inform you that our health is better than when I last wrote you. Your kind Mother got much worse after I had enclosed my letter, but she is now much better, and is on foot again though much weakened. My own health is not very good, but I am still able to see to my business but cannot stand much work, Inda's boys are better than they were a week ago, if they mend on, she will probably go home the last of this week. The residue of our folks are well. Dyas Gilberts little son (Casius) will die soon. He has Congestion of the brain and spinal column generally, he has had convulsions for the last 36 hours, and his head is drawn back almost to his shoulders. With the above exceptions your friends & relatives here, are as well as usual. I am called upon to solemnise the marriage of Mr. George Sibbald & Mrs. Mary Ann Dryden (widowed daughter of old Jesse Ellis) this Evening at 4 o'clock at old Jessies, if anything interesting should transpire I will post you.

Sam; I am fearful I cannot fill this page without swearing. The pretended democracy of the State of Ohio, have nominated that Tory & Culprit C. L. Vallandingham for Governor of the great state of Ohio (I wonder they did not take Jeff Davis).[1] I look upon it as a disgrace to the State and a Slander to the name, Democrat. They are nothing more, nor less, than a set of foul-mouthed cowardly Tories. I don't wish to deceive you with the idea, that I have any fears of him being Elected. I have too high an opinion of the Patriotism and good sence of the people of Ohio to tolerate the idea, but it is like the case of the Dutchmans spur. "Its sick a [illegible] on a feller" to have an Enemy to his government who is in banishment, by a just sentence set before a free people for their suffrages, is what I complain of, well, the Ohio Soldiers can all vote this year, and they won't vote for a traitor sure, they would rather stop his wind! And I am with them heart & hand. We will get up a better man on Wednesday next. I am a delegate to the Union State Convention but I cannot go, I would like to be there but cannot.

We have word that Smiths division is gone to Vicksburg, is that so? If so are you with them? Who will garrison the places on the road you have been taking care of. We have no news of the fall of Vicksburg yet, but we are confidently looking for it every day. It, & Port Hudson must fall and I will be glad how soon, the Big ones have aimed all the time, at having the best officers & soldiers in the "Army of the Potomac—but they have missed it badly, the Western men have done nearly all that is done, and I believe that Grants Army is a better Army and a better officer[ed] army than the Army of the Potomac.—

Early Candlelighting: At the end of the above sentence I was interrupted by a notice that my horse was sick. Amos & Ann went to Sunday school & Church at Ebeneezer, Amos rode the young black horse, apparently in good health. When he arrived there he found [it] sweating profusely and sick with Lock Jaw. He sent for me immediately. I rode there quite fast & found him dead . . .

[last page is missing]

1. The Democratic Party of Ohio defiantly awarded its 1863 gubernatorial nomination to exiled antiwar leader Clement Vallandigham. In so doing, the Ohio Democratic Party made the gubernatorial election a referendum on continuation of the war. Eugene H. Roseboom, "Southern Ohio and the Union in 1863," *Mississippi Valley Historical Review* (June 1952): 29–44, 32.

⇢ SAM TO ANDREW ⇠
Lagrange, Tenn. / June 14, 1863

Dear Father,

I have not recd. a letter from you since I wrote to you. The reason I cannot tell. I suppose the changing of troops on the road and elsewhere has something to do toward retarding the mail.

Smith's division has gone to Vicksburg. Two days after the troops left here I was informed that Smith's division would stay at Memphis but that was all a hoax. They are gone to Vicksburg, The 70th boys left with the rest of the Division. I wish they had stayed here. There will in all probability be warm works at Vicksburg and the fresh troops will very likely be called in first if there should be an action. Gen. Smith is the best man we have been under for this place. Guerrillas made but few raids on him but he frequently raided them. This proved to be the best method to keep them off the R Road. Maj Gen Oglesby is in command here now, he may be a good man, I know but little about him, he has a good Reputation.

Well now I will tell you a little about the 1st Alabama Colored Infantry.[1] The Regt. is not yet full. 6 Co.'s are full and mustered in, The Co. to which I belong is mustered in and, place designated. Co. B the Left flanking Co. They learn more readily than I Anticipated. The Strings are drawn very tight. I have never Seen a white Regt. Governed by as rigid dicipline. I have nothing to do with them that would Shock the pride of any Honest man. Nothing but that which we were subject to in the White Regt. The association with them I have seen a few times Since I have been in the South Some of the most fancy women riding in Cariages by the side of a Negro. I understand this is the Case all over the South. I am pretty well satisfied that Negros can be made to fight.

We have no news from Grant's army of importance. Grant seems to be holding fast. His terms of surrender are easy (an unconditional). I hear nothing more of fighting Joe Hooker are [or] the Army of the Potomac. There is nothing of interest that I know of in this region. The R Road from Grand Junction to Jackson, Tenn. has been evacuated, and the troops moved on the road that leads from the Junction direct to Corinth. The road is much shorter and will take less number of troops to guard it, besides it moves our lines further South.

My health is still good. I feel better than I did this time one year ago. The health of the troops is generally better this season than last. The weather is very pleasant here, often the weather is hotter at home the same time in the year.

Give my best respects to all the family and inquiring friends.

I am as ever Your Son,

Sam Evans

P.S. Please, Direct your letters for me to Lagrange, Tenn. Care of Capt. E. Bouton

1. Sam was apparently confused as to the designation of his regiment. The name it actually received was the 1st West Tennessee Infantry of African Descent. The Alabama unit was brigaded with Sam's unit.

➣ AMOS TO SAM ≼
Aberdeen, Oh. / June 17, 1863

Dear Brother,

Samuel, yours of the 9th is at hand this evening. Father received one from you Wednesday. We appreciate letters from our friends more than ever since the loss of some of our near and dear friends, who were always ready to relieve our wandering minds by kind words and tender affections. We have one consolation that gives peace in the dying hour. We will meet in heaven. I never experienced what true and devoted Christian feelings were until parting with one with whom I spent days and nights, weeks and months, watching and praying, and knowing that our souls were bound with ties than can never be broken. His last breath breathed my name. Sam, his last looks would melt your heart and cause your soul to weep. And so often he would ask about you. Oh! could he have but seen you was all he could have desired. That he did not get. Brother Ramsey said as he was preaching. All he could ask was to die like he, with all of his natural and rational feelings and senses.

I cannot question your faith, neither could anyone John's. He talked freely to father and Mary on the subject but could not talk to mother and me without bursting into tears. He held me in too great esteem. I fear he suffered wherein he should not have done. The night before he died he begged for mother not to let me do anymore hard work and said if I did I would go the way that he and Doc did. Why he thought so I do not know. Father, mother, sisters and brothers all promised to meet him in heaven—with you and all. Amen.

I think father is not so much dissatisfied as at first about your change of position, though he would rather it were not so. The people think no less of you, or him, for so doing. What does your position pay & etc . . . The Rebels made a raid into Maysville doing considerable damage as you will See by Daily Sent to you—The Most of them have been taken, Jo Frank is also a prisoner. Father & I were making a Coffin . . . when we got the news & before we got through the Rebels were frightened away, hense I was not there. All of the Militia are ordered out—30,000 volunteer immediately from this State, they are rapidly rolling in. All the militia will be forced to muster on & after the 4th of July, P. W. Waldron has got a 2 gun battery. Southerland is arrested.

Our rifleman wounded 7 Rebels from this Side of the river . . .

Our harvest will be on hand by Monday. The weather is very dry & warm. Corn looks better than it did last year but would be the better of rain.

I cannot think of anything at present but will write often,

Yours as ever,

Amos

[Illegible Postscript]

⇒ SAM TO ANDREW ⇐

Camp Lagrange, Tn. / June 22, 1863

Dear Father,

I again write to you my usual day is Sunday but owing to press of duty on that day had to defer till tonight I have received but 3 letters since the 70 went away, 1 from you 1 from Amos 1 from Mary. Mary's of the list is the only since my address has been changed. I suppose you have written since I order my letter directed to me at Lagrane [sic]. None of us have been to get today's mail, I look for some letters. Drennin told me he would remail my letter if any went to the 70 for me. I would like quite well to see them before they go down so far in dixie.

The news is very exciting both here and in the East I notice in the commercial that the Rebs have made another "raid" in Maysville and taken considerable property. S.S. Minor seems to be the greatest looser, Descar, John Anderson, O. Andrew have all lost considerable. I hope they will not get into Ohio I am very much afraid Joe Hooker will not be fast enough for Lee, no one but George B. [McClellan] is able for him in the Eastern Army. He is my choice among the Gens and ever has been I felt while he was in com'd that Lee had an equal to contend with but since he was superseded I have been very doubtful about any of the other commanders being his equal. It looks very much like Lee could go to Philadelphia or any of the cities in that portion of our territory. The late call of President may if promptly acted upon stop him. If the authorities had raised the number of men required to be conscripted there would have been a sufficient number of men armed, drilled & equipped, ready for almost any emergency.

I hear the 70 is at Hairs Bluff. The Black Regt. here is nearly full only lack about 20 men of having the maximum number and that we will get tomorrow if no bad luck. We have nearly enough guns and are drilling as fast as we can. I thought it would be rather hard to keep Negroes from deserting, but yet, we have lost few. They are learning to drill much faster than I expected.

My health still continues very good I was vacinated last Sunday week ago but it did not take very strong.[1] There is no contagious disease here except mumps. I think I have had them on one side if not on both, about a dozen of the White officers in this Regt. have sore eyes. Thus far I have escaped and think by proper conduct will at least that "Kind" [of symptom]. When you write to me address:

Saml Evans

Lagrang Tenn

Care Capt Bouton

Remember me kindly to mother and all the family also to all inquiring friends and believe me

your Son,

Sam

1. The vaccination Sam refers to was probably against smallpox.

> ANDREW TO SAM ·

Home / June 27, 1863

Dear Son,

I received yours of the 7th on the 17th which was a welcome visitor being a little behind time. We were without letters from Will & George from some time until Friday last. I got one from George the 89th is at Murfeesborough, except Will he is still with Stokes Calvary at Carthage. We are in usual health, your Mother is nearly as well as usual. Inda's Sam is about well. Morty has intermittent fever and is sweating. Your Aunt Betty Evans died at her residence near Buford on last monday week, but the news did not reach us until yesterday Evening. The health of your friends so far as I know are well. The Rev. I. P. Bloomhuff is said to be dangerously sick, and but little hopes of a recovery.

We have no news other than what you see in the papers that would interest you. Wm. Norris case, was perhaps the making of a political spite, by some of his neighbors, The charge was, "Being a Confederate Officer, found, within the Union lines." He was retained in Prison some time, and no one could be found to attempt to sustain the charge, and the citizens of Ripley, opposed to him in politics, petitioned Burnside for his release offering assurance that Norris was not only Loyal, but that he had assisted in recruiting men for the Federal service and that he had two sons in such service. Norris insisted on a trial, but Burnside discharged without, he is at home working at his trade. The information was erroneous, with respect to Lafabre's arrest.

I had the pleasure of a shake of the hand of my old friend, Gen. J. Amen, in Ripley yesterday.[1] He is on short leave of absence, at home, and is looking very well. He says there are but two ways of settling our difficulties, one is to get whipped and the other is to whip the enemy well. He prefers the latter. He, (like I), think that voting for "Val" would do but little towards affecting our object. We have a ticket for the lovers of the Union. In my opinion the ablest men that have ever been offered in the State of Ohio at one time. John Brough is an old Hickory Democrat but loves his country. Charles Anderson of Dayton (brother of Maj. who defended Sumpter) is of the same stripe, both bright in talents and two of the best stump speakers in Ohio.[2] Let us give them 100,000 of a majority over the Val ticket this fall. What do you say? The Coppers will make a strong effort but I think will be considerably short. I have sent you but few Bees, the reason is that is nothing in there, if I get one that has anything of interest in it I will send it to you. Amos started a Commercial to you containing the raid on Maysville, I presume you see that paper much Earlier than we can send it to you. Give me the No. & title of your Regt., Commanding officer, letter of your Co, name & grade of Co Officers &c.

Our wheat crops will be fair, there is more complaints of smut than I have Ever heard, but we make none, I walked through one field a long crooked route & found but two heads. There are many fields in the township that are said to be 1/3 smut, Dr. Moore & Sutton each have such a one, Our crop will be as good as last year from present appearances, we expect to commence cutting tomorrow with a very small company, whether it will increase or diminish we cannot tell yet. Sam; I enclose herein, the Photograph of one of your old acquaintances who you have not seen lately, it is nothing Extra, but may answer your purpose.[3] Inda has not received your picture yet, we don't why. I will still write once a week and desire you to do the same. I dont write so much to Will, but some of the family write him frequently. Our love to you, Believe me as Ever your

Father

Andrew Evans

1. This is Brigadier General Jacob Ammen. See note in Amos's letter of June 15, 1862.

2. Major Robert Anderson was Union commander at Sumter when the fort fell, in April 1861, beginning the Civil War.

3. This is another of Andrew's attempts at humor. The photograph is likely one of Sam's "girlfriend," Cal.

➤ ANDREW TO SAM ◆
Home / June 28, 1863

Dear son:

Yours of the 14th came to hand on the 24, letters are traveling much slower than they did some time back, yours are generally 10 days old when they arrived at their destination. Your picture has not arrived yet, whether it will in future is yet to be tested. I have neglected to attend to Lees request, several weeks ago I cut his hair, when done, he gathered a bunch of his hair to send to "Sam". The girls fixed it for him & he gave it to me to put in your letter & I forgot it, but will send it in this.

We have had rather a hospital at our house this week. I done nothing to call work last week from indisposition, I did not lay up but had the "slows". Your mother is not well yet. Amos & Pat [hired hand] were off duty most of the time. Amos with sore throat & debility & Pat with "[illeg-ible]". Lee & both Inda's children have Scarlet Fever several of the other children have symptons of it & Lee took it last Monday and is (we think) on the mend slightly. Morty & Sam took it about the middle of the week and have not passed the height of the disease, it shows on all of them so far, to be in its simple form (not malignant). I hope they may all get along well, they are taking a good-deal of attention, their throats are quite sore the Eruption had been verry annoying on Lee but is receeding, it is just commencing on Morty & Sam, they are not totally confined & I hope by my next to be able to announce their recovery. The general health of the country is fair, there has been but little sickness tho' many deaths this season. There has been a heavy rain on the head of East Fork and there is plenty of mud and water running to grind, though we had but a moderate shower here, we had considerable of light rain last week, and wether verry cool, so much so that wheat did not ripen, we turned off to a plow-ing corn again—we did not cut more than 2 or 3 acres during the week. We will try it on tomorrow if permitted. Wheat crops are good except injury by smoot [sic].

We have just received the painful news of the death of our friend N. B. Thompson at Vicksburg by drowning, Nelse was a good fellow. We have the good news to send you that there is organized, under the Militia here of this one section of Artillery for a 2 gun battery. The organization is accepted by the Governor. Election of officers ordered & consumated & return P. W. Waldren & A. W. Wood are elected. The Caison [sic] & am-munition are Expected this week, the company consists of the bone & sinew of the town & part of the country such as Jim Helen, Jo Chrisman, Bill Marvin, George Rider, Andy Wood, Pete Waldren, and Enough more to make 40 or more men. When they get the tools, Rebel raids on Mays-ville will be more scarce. Your old friend Sam Espey & others have orga-nized a similar one at Ripley so you can see we are getting ready to help our friends in the field. John Mitchell, Thos I Galbraith & William Rug-gles have a permit to raise a Company of voluntary militia and are all recruiting, If all hands would join in good Earnest, the rebellion would soon close out.

The army news is much mixed, Hooker has let the Rebels into Mary-land & Pennsylvania whether he can get them out is yet to be tried. Grant is doing his work steadily & surely. We cannot learn what old rosy is doing, but are assured that he is not idle. If Grant & Banks could be turned loose & start east I think they would clean things up as they go. Our Blockade is doing its work beautifully.

Political matters are not running very high but we find some in our township who will vote for the Exiled Traitor for Governor, I can't. John Brough is good enough for me, the Val-men make large calculations on the soldiers vote, I think that is a vain hope. Why would a soldier vote for a man who voted to withhold supplies & pay from the soldiers. I think they would rather vote a rope to hang him than to Elevate him to the Gubernatorial chair.

Ann Delia is showing plain simptons [sic] of Scarlet Fever this Evening. Good by for another week, be assured of the high regard of your father,

Andrew Evans

⤜ SAM TO ANDREW ⤛
Lagrange, Tenn. / June 28, 1863

Dear Father,

Your favor of the 31st May came to hand on the 25 of June having been fowarded from Snider's bluffs where the 70 now is. Yours and Amos' dated June 19th and 21st came today all of which are very welcome visitorers, I almost left out one, yours of the 14th is received I hardly know how to answer all of them at once. I thank you kindly for your good wishes in my behalf and in return may you be blessed with all that makes life pleasant and when you shall have been summoned to join those who have gone before may have a peaceful hour in which to depart from Earth and fly to Heaven.

It is so, that Smith's division is gone to Vicksburg, it has been been gone about 3 weeks since the 70 left. N. B. Thompson has all the particulars I have [which] I gave in Mary's letter.[1] The 70 is at Sniders Blulls [Bluffs] Miss. I am sorry you lost your fine horse, it was Bob was it not?

It is cheering to hear your crops are so good. The vegetables I appreciate very highly and would like to help you eat some of them. I do not allow myself to long after anything of the kind, but try to be content with whatever we can get and whatever happens. In yours of the 21st I found enclosed "the Photograph of my old acquaintance" as you were pleased to call it. I think it is a good picture of the original and is just the kind of Likeness that pleases me. I was not expecting anything of the kind but I esteem it.

It seems that our friends are dying off very fast, every letter from home for some time announces the death of some relative or friend. It seems to me all my misfortunes come at once and after that all seems to go on pleasant for a time I am glad that our old Friend Norris is free again I am not a politician at present but will do all I have the opportunity to do for Brough and Anderson if we get to vote. I will go for them and induce others to do the same. I say go in for Brough and Anderson it is a "Militare necessity." I have not received the Commercial Amos sent yet. I saw the Raid particulars of which I mention in a letter home some days ago. I only wanted to see a Bee occasionally when any thing of interest was in it.

As you ask for the No of this Regt. By whom commanded I will do so. It was till lately I could do so: First West Tenn. Infantry, of African descent Commanded by Col. Edward Bouton, formerly of Co. G, 1st Ill[i-nois] Light artillery. Lieut. Col. Robert E. Phillips, formerly 53rd Ohio Our Co. is B officered as follows Capt. Henry Johnson, formerly 2nd Lieut of Co. H 70 Ohio, Maurice M. Covan 1st Lieut formerly Sergt. of Co. A 70 Ohio, Sam Evans 2nd [Lieutenant] formerly Private Co. F 70.0. I will enclose you the appointments of the officers of this Regt. . . . I wish India would get my picture it is not so good as I have had taken but however it will do. I would like you to send me some more letter stamps. That amount you can send most conveniently not more than 50, but that amount if convenient ($1.50), charge me with the same. We can only get stamps here occasionally. I have some letters from Ann but have not time to answer them now, tell her that I will write as soon as I can. My health has improved some since I wrote to Mary and I think I am on the mend. Don't understand me that I have been much sick but that I was not as well as I have been for months.

Remember me kindly to all the family and accept my best wishes for their and your welfare and believe me as ever.

Sam

p.s. Direct your letters to Sam Evans

Co. B. 1st West Tenn. Infantry Of African descent

Care Col. E. Bouton, Lagrange Tenn

I think I will be sure to get them if thus directed.

I have 4 more letters to write yet to day.

1. Sam apparently had not yet learned of N. B. Thompson's death, which Andrew mentions in his letter also written on June 28, 1863.

Home / July 5, 1863

Dear Son,

I am again [at] my weekly duty. I received yours of the 22 June on the 2nd July, we have had but one letter per week for some weeks. We have not written twice a week as regularly as we did some time back, but I never miss. The girls & Amos do some times, but not often Amos missed last week and pleads press of business, he cracked all day evry day and was too tired to write at night. He expects to finish cutting wheat tomorrow, he has no help yet, or at least not Enough to bind what he cut. He has to help bind and shock, the girls have been helping the last two days. Pat is still off duty but mending. Amos has had rather a hard time he was not well from Scarlet fever when he began, but he has stood up to the work & is better than when he began. Pat has the same disease besides Ague fever![1]

Our health is moderate—I am better than I was when I last wrote, Mother is also, the children are not well yet, Ann & Lee are nearly well of Scarlet fever, Morty is mending little Sam is over the worst, he has been quite sick, the worst of any but Lee. Mary is just taking it today, Ibby & Jo stand clear yet, the general health here is good as usual.

We sure had fine rains quite sufficient for agricultural purposes. We run the mill 18 hours on last Monday & night, ground out clean, both of customers & our own work, the old mill still does its whole duty. Our flour sells for 50 cents per barrel more than Fulton or Worstells in Aberdeen. I am quite happy to inform you that the mill has a very Enviable reputation for manufacturing Extra flour. I have sold about $350 worth in Aberdeen with nary murmer besides the custom work, give[s] entire satisfaction. We grind the wheat and dirt separate now, is the reason of our success. We have been very careful in grinding, we grind tolerably close but no complaints about not rising at all.

You were very correct in your fears that Jo Hooker would not be fast enough for Lee & I coinside with you that G. B. Mc is the man, and I fear the only one that is fully Lee's equal. Mc brought him out of Maryland in a hurry, but Jo has showed his ass and got out. The new commander, Mead, is handling Lee very well if our news be true. I hope he may do the work. We may have telegraph news that Dix has taken Richmond, that Mead has almost annihilated Longstreet's Corps of Lee's army and that he had the others split in two, and that old Rosy was thrashing Brag in quite satisfactory style, but how much of it [to] dare to believe is the thing that time must tell.[2] That Grant will whip Pemberton I have no doubt, Banks' condition is not satisfactory, But Rosy will thrash Bragg, if he has any show, for he fights to whip! We have rumors of important cabinet changes whether true or not we can't tell yet, Rumor says McClellan is to superseed Halleck, and old Pickayune Butler to supercede Stanton, those changes would be an improvement on the present.[3]

Well; our Military Elections went off yesterday. The Township is divided into 3 military Dists. I cant give you the boundaries, it is not well done. No. 1 takes the S.E, Corner of the township No 2 the S.W. and No. 3 (ours) is a string from Legan's Gap, to Luck Run. In No. 1 John W. Stewart is Capt Harve Luters 1st & Dave Lawnwill 2nd Leiut In No 2 William Riggs Capt. T I Galbraith 1st & Jo Lodan 2nd Leiut (the best officered Co. in the township) In no 3 Morris Lane Cap, G. W. Wiles 1st L.B. Moore 2nd The Militia organization will soon be completed in this state, I think John Mitchell will fizzel out in getting up his Co, the Artillery Co. will stand up they have 50 men Enrolled now.

Why you dont get your letters is more than I can tell, for I write evry sunday evening. Your minature for Inda has not arrived, most likely miscarried or hooked. I started our photograph to you 2 weeks ago to day, & one to George the same week. I have not started one to Will for they loose about 1/2 of their mails at Carthage.

Be assured of our best wishes & [illegible] love

Your father,

Andrew Evans

1. For a definition of ague, see note on Sam's letter of March 16, 1862.

2. Here is another example of incomplete, and often erroneous, information received on the home front. In this instance, only the news of Meade's success against Lee is close to actual events.

3. This is Major General Benjamin Butler, who coined the term "contraband." He probably received this nickname because of his service as Union commander of New Orleans. These rumored changes in the war department never occurred.

❧ ANDREW TO SAM ❧
Home / July 12, 1863

Dear Son:

Please find enclosed fifty letter stamps as per your request. Yours of the 28 June came to hand July 6. I thank you very kindly for the contents and the "enclosed" document, which is just the thing I desired. Since I wrote you we have received important and gratifying news from our armies. Vicksburg has fallen! Lees army whipped [at Gettysburg] and

Bragg's routed and demoralized.[1] God bless the officers and soldiers who have effected those desirable objects. Our prospects are brightening. Old R. E. Lee has at last found the man who is his equal (if not his superior) and if our latest news is correct, Lees invasion of Pennsylvania will be a sorrowful one to him and to the Southern Confederacy, for there appears to be a fair prospect for the total demolition of Lee's entire army.[2]

John Morgan (of Guerilla notoriety) has put himself & army of from 6 to 8000 in the sory place for their welfare (I think) he has invaded the free state of Indiana!—from which I fancy he nor his army will never return alive, the Hooziers will give them Tom Corwins "welcome".[3] The first move was to prevent them from getting to Ky. We have no deffinite news only of the rapid move of troops & gun boats, Burnside is on hand in person. Morgan got to the river some 30 miles below Louisville, and planted a battery and waited the arrival of Steam boats, when they came he brought 2 fines one to, by his guns, ferried his army & artilery over and burned one of the boats and let the other go. The news was tele-graffed to [Indiana] Gov Morton who issued his proclamation for all the Militia South of the National roads to assemble at once armed & equipped, at our last news there were 50,000 in arms and ready for the conflict. The Ohio river fleet of gun boats will keep him from crossing back to Kentucky while Burnside & Co. close him out.

I started you a "Bee" last monday, not a very valuable one, but will serve to give you some Military & other news from home. The last Bee has a political war between some "Butternut" & Will. I could not give up that paper. I drew a verbatim copy of the correspondence & Enclosed it in Amos letter to you a few days since, thinking that Wills reply would suit you, he dont "sugar-cote" the pills for his correspondent.

I am happy to inform you that Will is growing with popular favor in his army. He has choice of several good positions offered him—the one he is temporarily in or steward of the Post Hospital at Nashville and oth-ers, but he will accept none of them while there is a good prospect for him in his own Regt. He has been acting surgeon for over two weeks and been entirely successful. He says he has been visited twice by the Sur-geon-in-Chief who examined all his patients, and offered no change of treatment. He says he would rather be with his friends and old associates in his own Regt.

We have nothing new from George since Amos wrote you, he was still sick at our last news. We are rather better than we were a week ago, Lee is improving but is considerably swolen yet. Morty & Sam are very puny yet mend very slowly, the after part of Scarlet fever is worse than the disease itself. Ann had it so lightly that she had no after part—Mary got it over it verry easily & is about well. Your Mother is afflicted with Muscular Rheumatism about the chest for a few days but is not laid up. The general health is fair. The weather has been verry warm & corn is growing verry rapidly & is generally in good condition. Potatoes suffered so much before the rain, that many will take the second growth. We have entirely too much work for our forces, if we live another season we will aim at farming much less. Amos will try to do all of it, & I can't help him much & hired hands don't pay these days.

You have the love and good wishes of the family and of your father,

Andrew Evans

1. Confederate General Braxton Bragg retreated across middle Tennessee to Chattanooga in July to avoid a battle with Union General William Rosecrans's much larger force. Bragg remained at Chattanooga awaiting Rosecrans's advance, which would come in the form of the Battle of Chickamauga in September 1863. Judith Lee Hallock, *Braxton Bragg and Confederate Defeat* (Tuscaloosa: University of Alabama Press, 1991), 2:21–22.

2. Andrew is referring to General George Gordon Meade, who profoundly disappointed President Lincoln by failing to destroy Lee's army after the Union victory at Gettysburg.

3. Andrew is probably referring to Ohio politician and longtime Whig leader Thomas Corwin, who had previously served as the U.S. Representative and Senator, Ohio governor, and Secretary of Treasury under President Fillmore. After an extended absence from politics, Corwin was barely able to win the Republican nomination for Congress in 1858. In another of Andrew's abstruse attempts at humor, he is suggesting that Morgan's raiders would be greeted with as hostile a reception in Indiana as Corwin had received in Ohio. Eugene H. Roseboom, *The Civil War Era*, vol. 4 of *History of the State of Ohio*, ed. Carl Wittke (Columbus: Ohio Archaeological and Historical Society, 1944), 256–57, 337–38.

⇥ SAM TO ANDREW ⇤
Lagrange, Tenn. / July 12, 1863

Dear Father,

Again my regular writing day has rolled around again. I have received [nothing] from home. Since I wrote to you, I received a letter from little Jane 2 days ago that had gone to Vicksburg and returned. Also a letter from G. W. Early written on the 20th of last month he was then at Murphreysborough. You of course have later news from him than that. I have heard nothing from Will for several weeks the last I heard he was well, I look for a letter from home to day.

Well I will talk a little while about matters of war etc. The long expected fall of Vicksburg has come at last. Gen. Grant has made a good thing of it. The beauty of it was the day on which it was done, the 4th of July has now a double Significance. I am well pleased with every thing but paroling the Privates, It would be much better in my opinion to feed than fight them. Although they are unarmed, they, or, at least many of them, will go into the army again. The officers will not be very apt to go back soon, I think it will be but a short time till the Miss River will be clear of Rebels unless it be small gangs, The Rebels seem to think Port Hudson is invulnerable, So they said about Vicksburg. Let Grant undermind it and blow it up and what will they think? Port Hudson will fall as certain a Grant [line missing] Mission.

Give Grant his and Rosecrans' army and he can whip the "dog matter" out of Lee. Well, this reminds me that Lee has got into the "wrong pew" since he attempted an invasion. It is to be hoped Gen. Meade will be equal to the emergencies. If what we hear be true he has cut Lee's army considerable. Well I must stop a while, the mail has just come. Well here's one from you dated July 5th, I will proceed to answer it. It is pleasant to hear that your health is improving I am glad you have ground out all the grain in the mill and that your success has been so complete. We have reason to think that no political measures will be used against Meade as he is not a native of America therefor is not elligble to the Presidency.[1] Rose is making Bragg "get" but Bragg will not fight him on fair show, Must have more men and the advantage of the position. You were very correct in your assersion that Grant would whip Pemberton. I would not be much surprised if Pemberton & Co would have the privelege of going up north for some days.[2]

Well, how do you like the Surrender of Vicksburg? Is it not glorious? Banks army was not in good fix the latest I heard but Reinforcements were not far from him. Where they were from was not at the writing prudent to tell. Those changes will not like[ly] be made now. I am not much acquainted with Butler's capacities for sect of War. The other change would be a very good one, I would like to see Mc take the army of the Potomac and give Lee a trial where he is now. Could not more efficient officers be found for the Militia than many of those who are appointed?

Some of the officers I think would do very well and some of them ar[e] emminently disqualified for the position. I know considerable about incompetent Commanders of Co. & Regt. John Mitchell in my opinion does not want to do much for the war he has been Gassing ever since the war broke out. Tried to get up several home guard Co's. Perhaps to hide his disloyalty (there is no harm in thinking if you have grounds)

I have received you[r] photograph a notice of which I gave in a former letter. Some things go through safely while others are lost. I have sent the 2nd picture to India whether it will have any better luck you can inform me. If it does not get through I will try till one does.

I still hear from the 70th. They are well, still at Snider's Bluff. Well I guess the Black Regt. is doing very well, still doing a great deal of guard duty about town and other places adjacent, all is still quiet here. Some guerillas about in small Squads no other force near here that we know of. There will be a guerrilla hung at this place for shooting one of our soldiers. He deserted at or near Corinth more than a year ago and has been guerillaing ever since.

The weather is very hot. Some diseases privailing to consideral extent, Flux and Billious Intermittent Fever.

I have again got able for duty, but have not got very fat yet. Have a notion not to fatten up very fat till fall. The weather is to hot. I will writ to Ann and send it with yours. This letter is written on government Paper. How do you like it, not quite as good a[s] Congressmen write on.

Love to all the family,

As ever your Son,

Sam

1. Though born in Spain, George Meade moved to Pennsylvania when he was just one and a half years old. Nonetheless, being born on foreign soil, he was, as Sam correctly stated, ineligible to run for president. Sam believes, therefore, that Meade will not be a victim of the political infighting that affected the careers of other ambitious Union generals. Freeman Cleaves, *Meade of Gettysburg* (Dayton, Ohio: Morganside Bookshop, 1980), 3–5.

2. Sam is suggesting here that Confederate General John C. Pemberton might have been taken to a Union prisoner-of-war camp; he was not.

ANDREW TO SAM
Home / July 19, 1863

Dear Son,

Yours of the 6 July arrived at 2 O'clock today containing one to Ann with some little fixins all in good condition. "Morgan's Guerillas" have hindered our mails for a week, we have had no mail since last Sunday until today, we have written our usual amount of letters but they have of course laid in the office at Aberdeen, you will perhaps get them some time. You may rely on me writing to you evry sunday unless providentially hindered. The risidue of the family write frequently but not tied to any regular day, Amos & India will write you some time this week; Amos recd one from you in the last mail previous to today. We got a letter each from Will & George today. Will is still well, George is mending thinks he will do for duty soon, he is still in the convallescent camp at Murfeesborough. Will is still in Carthage acting steward in the Cavalry Brigade 1st M Tenn Cav—

I enclosed 50 letter stamps last sunday to you but am fearful they remain in Aberdeen yet, though I think the mail went out Monday & Tuesday, if so it would perhaps pass on, but no Cinti mail arrived after saturday night. The O[hio] Militia were called on Wednesday last to repel Morgan, on the same day he passed through Brown county going East, some 300 of them came through Hammersville, Georgetown, Russelville, the main body Entered about Williamsburg and passed via Mt. Orab, Arnheim, Lincastle, Eckersley & Winchester, Adams County thence via N Liberty, Tranquility, Locust Grove & Duck town Adams Co, & thince to Piketon Pike Co. thence to Jackson Vinton Co., and were intercepted at Rodney 7 miles beyond Jackson, where if our news be true, they will suffer annihilation. They are said to be surrounded there by a very heavy Union force who are receiving reinforcements very rapidly. Our forces expect an unconditional surrender without a fight. It was a pretty bold & successful move of Morgan. He crossed the River into Indiana 30 miles below Louisville, Ky. and passed through Indiana and half way through Ohio without meeting any resistance. The Militia never would have hasled him, but when he came on our State, Burnside telegraphed the troops in East Ky., West Va. and East Ohio to concentrate immediately in Eastern Ohio and to intercept Morgan at all hazard, "that's what the matter".[1]

There is, and has been, Ever since he crossed the river, a cavalry force equal to his own pursuing him in the rear, but he being a head has choice of horses, and keeps 2 or three hours ahead of his pursuers, he has done but little harm except in plundering horses, money, Goods etc. His rate of travel was about 60 miles in 24 hours, hence the organizations of troops were too far behind him to do any good. He, you will notice, keeps back from the river, so our gunboats cannot reach him. Our Ohio river gunboats are all up in that country from Portsmouth to Galipolis. I hope they may close him out, Vicksburg & Port Hudson are ours, and Lees Army badly thrashed & rumor says Charleston taken, looks like they were closing the thing out!

We have our wheat staked in good order, we got it done by going into it ourselves, we have a very nice crop of about 400 bushels more or less. We have our oats and hay to cut, we Expect to go in tomorrow and finish as soon as we can. We are fully up to, and ahead of many of our neighbors in our harvest work. I hope you may be at home in time to grind to our wheat crop.

P. W. Waldron is 1st Lieut of the Aberdeen Battery. A 2 gun Battery is classed "a section of Artilery" by our laws and is not entitled to a Captain. Pete [P. W. Waldron] is Commander and A. W. Wood 2nd Lieut. Our health is much better than when I last wrote you. Lee is nearly well, Inda's boys are out of danger & mending smartly, I think Bell & Jo will escape. The general health is good, weather verry pleasant tho rather dry for corn. Doc Guthry, Bill Fulton, Big John and perhaps all the McDaniel family, J. C. Waldren and others will vote for their friend Traitor Val! I will give you more of it when I have more soon. Truly

& affectionately your father,

Andrew Evans

1. Confederate General John Hunt Morgan, given the duty of harassing Grant's line of supplies, crossed the Ohio River into Brandenburg, Indiana, on July 8, 1863, with 2,400 men and at least as many horses. From there, this guerilla force rode eastward through Southern Indiana and Ohio plundering numerous farms and retail stores along the way. Morgan sent one detachment southward by Georgetown (in Brown County) with the intent to make the impression that they were trying to recross the Ohio River. Instead they again met up with the main force, and after a failed attempt to cross the Ohio at Buffington Island, what remained of the force continued east hoping to cross the Ohio into West Virginia. Finally General Morgan and what remained of his men were captured just short of the West Virginia border on July 18. James A. Ramage, *Rebel Raider: The Life of John Hunt Morgan* (Lexington: University Press of Kentucky, 1986), 161. Byron Williams, *History of Clermont and Brown Counties, Ohio* (Milford, Ohio: Hobart Pub. Co., 1913), Vol 1., Historical, 428–31.

⇒ AMOS TO SAM ⇐
Aberdeen, Oh. / July 23, 1863

Dear Brother,

Your very kind letter of the 4th came to hand on the 13th. If I have not forgotten I have kept my regular time since Harvest.

Your pay & position is good if the darkies prove as good as they did on the Coast of Georgia.[1] I would not fear you position any more than commanding Whites. As to the Daily's it seems very near useless to send more for scarcely any of them reach their destination, either to you or elsewhere. P. W. Waldron was instrumental in recruiting, getting guns for battery, etc though guns have not come yet—don't know his rank in [the] Co—

Cal is all right again. She is one of [the] right kind of women.

I shall "remember" you to jesse as soon as I see him. He will likely teach School for us this winter. Do I understand you, you had to take your "Col" by a charge he being drunk at Grand Junction? I am glad to hear your boys Stand to you when ordered, this is the best evidence that they like their commander.

Father rec'd a letter from you Tuesday, Inda one from George, he is not fit yet for duty. Well I Suppose you are pleased with the way things are going Except Morgan going through your own State. He will not be likely to make any more raids though he is not yet taken. Basil Duke his right [illegible] & Morgans' brother are taken, together with more than 40 other Commissioned officers & about 3,000 prisoners—1,500 of the first that were taken are officially reported. 140 were killed & drowned in attempting to cross the river but the gun Boat made them Skeedaddle back.[2] 35 were killed at another place. The remainder are completely Surrounded. They are Scattered & Squandered & are being picked up Every day. They attempted to get to the interior of the State but the militia kept them back—Morgan is now near Pomeroy—but cannot stay long.

The Draft has caused Several Riots. Those of Ny. City—Boston & Portsmouth, N.H were quelled by Grape & Canister, they being the most formidables. Papers Say Canister prevailed & all is quiet again. Butternuts think since the Morgan raid that Old Jeff is no better than Lincoln. Val has given his letter of aceptance for Gov. He is now at Niagra falls—Sneaking home like a Sheep killing dog. Well the fall of Vicksburg & Port Hudson is glorious isn't it & Meade gave a Severe thrashing & is still in pursuit harrassing his [Lee's] rear.

Sherman has driven Johnston across the Pearl river with heavy loss, [illegible] & Old Rose has driven Bragg into Ga—This is cheering—Charleston must fall under her present attack. Gilmore will dig it down like Grant did Vicksburg.

Well Sam I ought to have been after Morgan but Father prevailed against me. I cannot get to do as I would like. We have our meadow cut, fin this morning Jo & I hauled Some of it in Since noon Squire & the children mow it away. We will cut oats Saturday—Corn will be good if it gets a good rain Soon—We are about as well as when father wrote Sunday Evening. My health is very good, I have not Exposed my Self to night air or night travelling Since last winter Sleep with windows open, wear flannel all the time & take plenty of Exercise. Inda will Enclose 1/2 sheet & give you news I neglected. Except a brothers love & remember the old homestead—

Amos

1. Amos may be referring to the pacification campaigns in the Sea Islands of South Carolina and Georgia by the 54th Massachusetts Infantry and the 1st South Carolina Volunteers, two of the first black regiments. On July 18, 1863, the 54th Massachusetts mounted a courageous, though ultimately unsuccessful, assault on Fort Wagner on the South Carolina coast at Charleston. This valiant effort did much to dispel widespread doubt about the combat capability of black soldiers. Dudley Taylor Cornish, *The Sable Arm: Negro Troops in the Union Army, 1861–1865* (New York: W. W. Norton and Company, 1965), 152–56.

2. Basil Duke and John Morgan's brother Richard helped lead Morgan's raids, but they were captured with many of Morgan's men on July 19, 1863, before John Morgan and the remainder of his force were captured on July 26, 1863. Eugene H. Roseboom and Francis P. Weisenburger, *History of Ohio* (Columbus: The Ohio State Archaeological and Historical Society, 1953), 194.

≫ ANDREW TO SAM ≪
Home / July 26, 1863

Dear Son,

Yours of the 19th came to hand this morning only a week old. Our Mails were obstructed for over a week while the Morgan fever was high, but since that time our mails have been regular, we are pleased to hear from you once a week at least and oftener when convenient, we are glad to hear that you are restored to ordinary health again, you must be very careful of yourself, if flux prevails to any extent in your camp, for that disease will put a man through on the first time if he don't check it in time. We are in ordinary health except little Sam who is quite sore from the Effects of Scarlet fever. Your relatives here are generally well, your Aunt Sarah Hiett was sick last week but was mending at our last news, the general health is good. The wether has been favorable for taking care of harvest crops. We have our hay put away & part of the oats in shock—we had a good rain yesterday that was fine for corn.

I hardly need give you the Morgan news by letter for you see it in the papers sooner than we can send it to you, he & some 700 or more his men still in Ohio, they were in Guernsey County the last we heard from them, and were doing more mischief than they did in our part of the state, I would not be surprised to hear his Escape, for he is slippery, and is quite tired of Ohio and will resort to any means, (no odds how desperate) to get out of here, the folks in the upper of the State agree that he cannot Escape; but they are making a slow out of catching him, they are still taking some of his men, we have official news of the arrival of near 3000 of his men arriving at Cinti during the last week as prisoners, among them over 40 Commissioned officers of various grades. I, like you, wish one may be captured or killed before they leave Ohio, but I am fearful that they will work up the river further than our gunboats can go, and Effect some kind of a crossing into Virginia. The forces are so much reduced that they are not very formidable, but I want them reduced to zero before they get out.

Your picture for Inda has not come yet, she dont wish you to send her any now, for it is an expence on you for nothing, if neither of them comes, she will get a picture of your[s] copied. We have news from Will to the 10 July, he was well at that time and still at Carthage. Our news from George is to the 16th, he was in the field hospital at Murpeesboro with Diarrhca rather of the flux character, they are both away from their regiments, and complain of getting no letters, or but few, we start as many to them as to you, but not with the same regularity. Inda generally writes to George twice a week, never less than once, some of the family generally start one pr week to him and sometimes more, He said in his last that he had not recd a letter from here since the 15 June, until that day. We start from one to two per week to Will, but the guerillas often capture the mail to Carthage & he is then deprived of news from home. We try to discharge our duty faithfully towards you all, and if our letters fail to reach you we are certainly not to blame, we allways address as directed.

I agree with you about the surrender of Vicksburg but console myself by admitting that Grant knew better than we, what was the best thing he could do for his Government. His course [to parole confederate prisoners] was certainly a great saving of human life, besides a very heavy expense of hauling & transportation of sick and wounded. The surrender of Port Hudson was unconditional and they are also paroled. They must either parole, or feed & take care of the prisoners by the terms of the "Cartell" for the care & Exchange of prisoners. Our Government is awful slow in Enforcing the draft, & thereby prolonging the war, and hazzarding the lives of the brave boys who voluntarily left the comforts of their homes and endearments of kindred ties, to face the cannons' mouth on the bloody field, and for what? Self aggrandizement? No; but that generations yet unborn, may Enjoy a peaceful and free government, attempted to be destroyed by a wily & roothless foe! May God in his Infinite wisdom bestow his choicest blessing on each of our countrys protectors in the divers voluntair corps of our Union Boys.

Truly your father,
Andrew Evans

⇒ SAM TO ANDREW ⇐
LaGrange, Tenn. / July 27, 1863

Dear Father,

Yesterday as I was preparing to write I was put on duty in place of another man who was sick, consequently I had to defer writing till today.

How do you like the Looks of things down in Dixie? Do you think Grant did right in paroling all that army? I do not myself. I am of opinion Lee's invasion did not pay him very well. Morgan the beast of northern Kentucky has gone further than I had any idea he could. I noticed by paper accounts that some of his scouts went to the River opposite Maysville and were shelled back by our gunboats, by that I would suppose he was in Aberdeen but have recd no letters from home since that. He was in Gerogetown and West Union. I would like very well to hear of Morgan and all his men being killed or captured particularly the former. I notice there has been another raid in Maysville. I endeavor to keep posted on all that is going. I am just in receipt of Resolutions passed by the Good Templar Lodge in Aberdeen upon the death of Brother John. They are pretty good and quite appropriate in the case.

I am very glad to hear you are improving in health. The health of this place is not as good as it has been but, is perhaps as good as could be expected. The weather is extremely hot, I think the health is considerable better than it was this time one year ago—My own health is not as good as it was a few months ago, but I guess nothing very serious sometime a little sick and others not "very well myself". I do not suppose I could stand the Service of "Uncle Sam" many years—But I am well satisfied and think but little of Slight "ails."

I will stay as long as I am able to do the least good, I am as I was when I came out. This Rebellion must and shall [be] subdued if men and money or any other means will do it. There never was a war that was so much at stake as in the present. The question to be solved is this; can a government founded on the basis of civil and Religious Liberty be maintained? I answer yes. There never was a war in which the whole world were so deeply interested in. I, for one, can feel the importance of conquering the Rebels. My motto is follow up our advantages quickly and keep the Rebs. in a state of confusion.

I must close for the present.

My love to all

and believe me as ever,

Sam

⇢ AMOS TO SAM ⇠
Home / Aug. 6, 1863

Dear Brother,

Again it is my lot to convey to you by the pen the mournful intelligence of the death of one of our dear and near relatives. Little Samuel died at 11 o'clock today after a short illness, which is perhaps the effect of scarlet fever.[1] He died of dropsy in the head or water on the brain.

The little suffer[er] is now at rest. He knew no Sin, he died in innocense & has gone to dwell where all is peace and his is everlasting. The sorrows of this earth can never trouble him. Would to God I had died as pure. When dying he burst out as if to cry but changed into a hearty laugh and died calmly and smilingly. The scene was very affecting, too much for Inda. I telegraphed to George at Inda[']s request but he had gone to Louisville, Ky. and I had to change the dispatch. We have had no answer yet. I think he must be on his way to Ohio as he said he Expected to be Sent to the City—Cin soon. Will is well he took 2 prisoners while on Scout a short time ago. The rest of our folks are only moderate health. Father and Lee are complaining smartly but are going about. Inda recd a picture of yours to day. News is not abundant at this time. We have very wet weather at present. Have not threshed yet, will Monday, nothing preventing.

Morgan and 60 of his officers are now in the Ohio Penitentiary with their heads and beard shaved, faring as other criminals. He never was in Aberdeen and many other places as you have been informed. I have not time to write now so you will please excuse haste.

I hope your health will be improved ere this reaches you please keep us correctly informed as to your condition. George has chronic Diarhea.

You have our most earnest desires.

Your brother as ever,

Amos A. Evans

N.B. Please excuse me for not addressing you as Lieut. S.E. & c as it was unthoughted [*sic*]. Yours A

1. This was Samuel's nephew (Indiana's son) and namesake, first mentioned in Andrew's letter of May 16, 1862, and G. W. Early's letter of June 2, 1862.

❧ ANDREW TO SAM ❧
Home / August 9, 1863

Esteemed Son,

Yours of the 27 July came to hand on the 5 Aug., and found our house in mourning again, Our dear little pet Samuel (Inda's babe) had just departed for the Spirit land, his disease fell upon his brain in a compound form "Hydrocephelous and congestion" he died at 11 O'Clock on the 5 and was intered at Ebenezer on the 6th. We can't bring him back, but we can go to him. "Suffer little children" etc. Inda is very heartbroken, and will go home this week if possible. I am in better health than when I wrote you last, I have had considerable trouble with my kidneys, but they are much better, Your Mother is plagued with rheumatism considerably it is hurting her ankles today, but is continually shifting, the residue of our family are in usual health, your friends generally well, your Aunt Sarah Hiett is mending. I am sorry to read of your poor health, it is bad enough to be sick at home where one can be cared for by kind friends, but to be sick in a distant country and away from home & friends is certainly doubly bad, if your health is declining, why not come home? We would be pleased to minister to your wants in any and Every way that is in our power, we are anxious to know what is the matter with you, you have failed to tell us, we are anxious for your welfare and would be pleased to have the facts (so far as you know) of your disease & condition. Please inform us in your next? and if possible get leave and come home before you get unable to do so. We had one letter from Will last week, he was still at Carthage & not verry well. I got one letter from George also, he was in Hospital at Louisville Ky, we telegraphed him the day his child died but got no answer, he has chronic diarrhea. Will will be steward of his own Regt as soon as he can get there.

I honestly differ from you about Grants paroling Pembertons army, if our news is correct they will never be got together again as an army and again, if he had held them we must [illegible] fed them. I think the sooner we can make them eat up all the provision they have, the sooner we will be through, besides the awful Expense of transporting them North.

In case of John Morgan Et. al, it is different. We caught him and his associate thieves close to good boarding thereby saving transportation. They will be securely held as hostages for the good conduct of the Rebels. Your information with respect to part of his gang being in Aberdeen was wholy incorrect, they were not even at Decatur: Georgetown, Russelville, & Echmanvile was the route of the most southerly branch of his gang, they took a trough of ten miles wide many places, the main army in the center & flanking & pilaging Companies extending out on each side, The Ky. Election is over, and the "Union ticket" Elected by overwhelming majorities. Good.

You are correct in what is at stake in this war, but that don't signify that a man because he has been a faithful soldier, must, or ought to stay in Camp until he die or is rendered incurable before he comes home, it would be better for men to go home and recover their health while they are able.

The draft will soon fill the ranks of the old Regts. We have heresay news that the draft has been made in our district but we know not who are drafted, so soon as we get the thing official I will post you.

Your last suggestion "following up advantages gained and keep the Rebs in confusion" has been very much, if not shamefully, neglected on the part of our armies. Mead certainly should have annihilated the half (at least) of Lee's army whilst they were crossing the Potomac but such has been our luck, from the start. I am not disposed to be a fault finder, but would be much pleased to see some improvements in our South Eastern armies.

Truly your father,

Andrew Evans

Inda has received your 2nd pictures

LaGrange, Tenn. / August 11, 1863

Dear Father,

Your kind favor of 26 came to hand some nine days ago, but as I was on picket Sunday rather out of turn and did not get relieved in time yesterday, to write before the mail went out. Consequently I have waited till this morning. I have received very few letters within the last 10 days I do not know what is the reason. I know of no raids by the Rebs that would stop our letters. You were "agreeably disapointed" about the escape of old Morgan. I learn by papers that Morgan is now boarding at the largest Hotel in the state [the state prison] and that he is now wearing our uniform that all the gests do who board that Hotel. His raid was very extensive, but did not result so to him or his men.

Things seem to be on a stand not much moving. I suppose all are taking a rest. We are not exactly resting. I am on duty every two days and others are on about the same. This is not much in good weather but in wet rainy times it is oftener than I want to be on duty. Last Sunday I was on Picket at an old citizens house. A man of very strong Southern principles, otherwise a very clever man. By the way he has an abundance of fine peaches and was very free with them, he also gave me my dinner. He seems very much discouraged about the restoration of the Union and that We had call an Armistice and then call a convention of all the states, he thinks that the dificulties could be settled on the terms of the Constitution. I think very differently. My opinion has been, for more than one year, that peace is to be had only, by conquering the Rebs. I see nothing to be discouraged at yet, I say now what I said at first.

There is nothing of importance going on here all is quiet. There is much sickness but this the sickly part of the year, I am very thankful, that I am not among the number of sick, I have recovered my former health. My weight is 158 lbs. not quite my usual weight. Nearly every one in camp has had Aches and fever, so far I have escaped, have not even had the slightest symptoms of it. I hope that I never will as long as I stay here. I have no news from George or Will of late. I hear of the 70 about once a week the boys of your acquaintance are well except Dr. Cooper, he has been very sick but is now convalescent. The 70 is at Bear Creek on the big Black and are again in Shermans Corps. Gen Smith was not in command of his division, he was sick.

The 70 behaved very gallantly at the battle of Jackson. I believe none of your acquaintances were killed or wounded.

Give my best respects to all and my love to all the family.
Believe me as ever, yours affectionately,
Sam

⇀ ANDREW TO SAM ↽
Home / Aug. 16, 1863

Son,

I wrote you again without anything to reply to. I have nothing from you for two weeks, this is the second one since from you. Mary recd. one from you yesterday, which is the only news from you for so long, we were getting the "blues". I took Inda & Morty home last Thursday. They were tolerably well when I left them. Mr. Earlys folks are well. Our family are well as usual, your friends here are generally well. We have had a great deal of rain, corn crops will be verry good in this neighborhood, some districts are still suffering for rain, but we have had enough to insure good corn. Our wheat was not much injured. Ours thrashed out 22 bu pr acre making 416 for our crop, but little injured by smut, not near as bad as we expected.

Sam you must not expect a verry good letter, for we have company here who bother me so often that my ideas are wandering. One of your good old friends is here, looking pretty well, and as cheerful as possible. We are in receipt of nothing from Will. I had a letter from George yesterday, he is Louisville Ky, and still has chronic diaerhea, he expects to come to Ohio soon, to Cinti or Camp Denison—he had heard nothing of the death of his child when he wrote.

We have nothing in the way of news that you cannot see in the papers, except our Election matters and Conscription matters! I have been Conscripted! Don't be scared, I have been put on the Union ticket as a candidate for [state] Representative, quite unbeknown to me. I was not a candidate for any office, nor do I desire any, but since it is done, and the friends of the Union argue that my name will give strength to the Brough ticket, I have decided to let it rip, but I would not be suited to have the office for I want to stay at home as much as possible. The Val's have not made their ticket yet, Newt. Devore is their Candidate for the Senate, Old General Loudon is ours on the Brough ticket.[1] Deck Mitchell for Clerk, Charley Campbell for Probate Judge, Alf Loudon, Treasurer etc.

I can't guess how the Election will go, but if all the Ohio Soldiers vote the Union ticket, it will carry, even in this County. Jack Applegate is home on furlough & is one of the hard Democrats and he is stumping the County for the Union ticket.

I shall not make any speeches, nor attend political meetings of any party, but if Elected, I shall try to do my duty to my country and its defenders. John Acklin has declared for the Val ticket and is a candidate for Clerk of Court before that convention. I am of opinion the Val ticket will loose heavily in this township, I know many good old fassioned democrats, who will go the Brough ticket might [illegible] G W Wiles, Bra-Lourne Davis, I. F. B. Fulton, W B Dennis, W. B. McQuilking Samuel Canary P. W. Waldren, W. C. Buck & many others too tedious to mention. There is a heavy majority to overcome in this County, perhaps too much, to overcome in one season.

Have you not written to me or has your letter been mis carried. I still write once a week [illegible] We would be pleased to hear from you once a week, but if your letters are miscarried it is no fault of yours.

You have the compliments and love of the family, and the highest regard of your Father,

Andrew Evans

1. General James Loudon was the father of Colonel D. W. C. Loudon. For more information on Colonel Loudon, see note in John and Sam's letter of April 10, 1862. Josiah Morrow, *History of Brown County Ohio* (Chicago: W. H. Beers & Co., 1883), Biography Section, 26.

☞ SAM TO ANDREW ☜
Lagrange, Tenn. / Aug. 16, 1863

Dear Father,

I am again seated to talk a few minutes with you. I have had but one letter from you or any of the folks at home for nearly 2 weeks. Two or three weeks ago I received a letter from Little Jane. I do not know what can be the matter. Today I received a letter from John McDaniel it stated the Regt was generally in good health. John Gattes of Co F 70 & a citizen of Aberdeen died very Sudenly at Snyders Bluff a short time ago. But did not state what was ailing. Wm Mills died. F. M. Richards had started home on furlough.

Mc said the 70 had a merry camp and but little to do. Such is not the case with us here. We go on duty every other day. Some times oftener. All the troops have heavy guard duty to do here, there not being enough for so extensive a line. It does not seem to hurt me any.

Last night 40 guerrillas undertook to Slip inside our picket lines at the Picket post of which I had command, but they did not succeed. I had 19 of a reserve. The Rebs Sent forward 4 men advance to feel for our pickets. The Picketts fired on them (the Rebs) but did not seem to do much damage. Both parties exchanged shots. I, as soon as possible, took up the reserve to the place of action. By the time the main body of the Rebs came up. I then sent out one man through a thicket to see how many rebs were on hand. All remained quiet till my spy came back. We let into them pretty heavy for a few minutes and they fled leaving two on the ground, 1 killed and one seriously wounded, 1 dead horse and 3 loose horses. Do not know whether any officers of the number were hurt or not. One of my men was hurt. We were in a thicket and they in a place plain to view except darkness of the night. After they fled we were reinforced by a company of infantry but were too late to do any good or see the fun. These are a part of the same men that have been lurking about here for a few days. As soon as our Cavalry comes back off of a Scout, these gents will be very likely to find it convenient to leave.

There is a great deal Sickness here. So far I have escaped. I have done more duty then any officer in this Regt, because I have not been sick. I am inclined to believe some men "Play off" Sick, to avoid duty, I may be wrong. It has been remaining for a few days, but still the week has been very hot and seething. I have had no news from George or Will since your last. Have you heard any thing of Uncle Amos whereabouts?

The corn crop here, will be a very good one for this place. The cotton here will be very light here, No news particular to write I feel Sleepy having Slept none last night Consequently you may excuse errors and a Short note. Today I read an Advocate sent by Amos on the 29 of July. Remember me to all the family.

I am as ever your affectionate
Son,
Sam

⇒ SAM TO ANDREW ⇐
Lagrange, Tenn. / August 23, 1863

Dear Father,

Yours of the 9th came to hand on the 17th, Amos' of the 6th came to hand the same day. Yours of the 2nd came to hand on the 21st, the reason of this Last delay I do not know. I thought It was Lost but some delay of the Post Masters perhaps was the cause.

I was very sorry to hear of the death of Little Sam. I was fearful from what Amos wrote upon the margin of the Advocate he sent me that his recovery was doubtful. As you say, "we cannot bring him back, but, we can go to him."

For your Satisfaction I will say that I have always given you as near as could the state of my health. I thought for some time back, that my health was failing not from any particular disease but a kind of general debility. Still I was not sick enough to be off duty. I do not know that I have lost any time since I have been with this Regiment. Evry time my regular day for duty come round I was on hand and for nearly 1 week I have been the only white man in our Co. able for duty. My health has improved very considerable so that I feel very well except some symtoms of Neuralgia, this is not very pleasant but I can stand it[1]. I do not know that it is so much worse to be sick away from home if one will only keep a stiff upper lip! I have only been bed fast once since I came away from home and that was when I had the measels. Since that time my health has been as good as it generally was at home.

The news from Ky. election is glorious I hope the news from Ohio will be so too. It would be a compromise with traitors to elect Val. Our state surely has enough loyal people left at home to vote "nae" to everlasting oblivion. He and some of his followers are as insulent as Jeff Davis.

Well now I will tell you a little about the Black Battallion [sic, regiment]. I believe we have fighting stock. They are dying rather faster than I want them to. There are about 300 sick. This is reducing the strength considerable. I am of opinion we need all the strength we have here, duty is very heavy. Officers and all coming on duty every other day. . . . Measles is what is the matter with the darkies.

We have not been paid since the last of Feb. I would like some of Uncle Sam's moneys Bags to come this way, we could relieve him of some of his burden. There is being some change in the troops here I cannot say whether we will leave or not. This Regt. is not in a condition to go into a heavy fight, never having been drilled in Battalion drill. In fact I am not very certain that Regimental officers can drill much, though I might be mistaken.

Well I have written about all that can interest you and perhaps more consequently I had better close for the present. I have heard nothing from the 70 since I wrote last.

Give my best respects to all the family and believe me as ever
Your son,
Sam Evans

1. For a definition of neuralgia, see note in Amos's letter of February 11, 1863.

ANDREW TO SAM
Home / Aug. 24, 1863

Dear Sam,

Yours of Aug. 11 came to hand on the 20, which made a gap of two weeks between your letters to me. Mary received one from you in the interim. We were pleased to learn that your health was restored again for we are always uncomfortable when we have news of your bad health, until we hear of your restoration to health again, I see by the papers that it is very sickly both at Vicksburg and New Orleans. Typhoid fever at the former in which 7/10 of the cases are fatal: Yellow fever at N.O., fatality not named, such diseases are worse than Rebel bullets on our armies in extreme Southern locations. I read a letter from the 89th yesterday, they are in the healthiest location they have been in since they entered the service; they are on top of Cumberland Mountain in the woods, where they have a great abundance of the best of water and invigorating air.

I got a long and good letter from Will date 9 & 10 Aug. he is very well, and started on the 10th to his Reg, he was ordered by Gen. Rosecrants to "report to the 89" without unecessary delay, he started same day and Expects the appointment of H[ospital] Steward as soon as he arrives, for he had previously received a letter from Dr. Green (Surgeon) that he would ask Gen. Rose. to order him to his Regt for that purpose, for the vacancy was there, and that he (Will) must and should have the appointment, for he was Entitled to it in the first place, and had been cheated out of it and that since that time, he had proved that he was both competent & worthy of the position. He says that the Post Surgeon voluntarily gave him a splendid recommendation when he was preparing to leave the post of Carthage.

I got a letter from George on the 20th he was still at Louisville, but expected to move to Ohio in a day or two. His health was improving slowly, I have one from Inda, she & Morty were well, though lonely and despondent, Our health at home is about "midling", I have been out of hang for a few weeks, my liver kidneys & bowells have been wrong for a while & "not very well myself." I have been on light duty most of the time, and am mending now. Your Mother is better of Rheumatism & is on duty. The rest of the family are well, your neighbors & friends here are generally well, and the health of the neighborhood is very fair: the wether is very warm during the day & rather cool at night. Lieut. Jas Drennin has arrived at home in good health. Amos saw & talked with him yesterday, I have not seen him yet, Amos says Jim was giving the Val men fits. Yesterday was their primary Election day, and Jim got loose and said what he pleased to them & they had to take it, he told them that he was somewhat used to fighting Rebels, and that he could do it as well here, as in the South, and that if any of them were agrieved, to just "Pitch in" and he would show some of them how they treated Rebels in the South, but they "didn't come in." So Ended yesterday's battle.

We have nothing in the local news line worthy of your attention, and you see the general news about as soon as I do. There is but little war news of interest now, the Armies are about on a stand-still Except Gilmore at Charleston, he is keeping things in rather a stirred up fix about the ass hole of Rebeldom, I think he is preparing injections, that he will soon administer, and purge off the enjoyment of many a rebel Stomach & bowels, May success attend his Enterprise! Our draft has not gone off yet, why, I cannot tell, our authorities are certainly tardy in their operations, they ought to have been in the field by the 20th July. To have followed up the advantages we had then gained, but that is our luck, or management, to whip them & wait for them to get in as good fix as ever before we go any further. This is only applicable to the Eastern Armys, the Rebs have been well pushed in the Southwest, and we can see the advantages resulting therefrom.

Truly your Father,
Andrew Evans

SAM TO ANDREW

Lagrange, Tenn. / Aug. 31, 1863

Dear Father,

I am again seated to write you a few lines. Yours of the 16th came to hand on the 25, Amos of the 20 on the 27. I also received a letter from my old friend Parker. You say you have not rec'd my letter. Why they do not come regularly I do not know. I have bee mailing as many letters as heretofore. You spoke of one of my good old friends being at our house that he was looking very cheerful. I could not think who it was.

You say you were "conscripted," I suppose you will go or furnish a substitute. I have not learned who your opponent is. I would be much pleased to see you elected [illegible] You say you will not make any political speeches. That is right. You would do well to state you position in public in reference to the war. That is the question paramount to all others. I still feel very confident of success if the people at home will support us; keep cowards from attacking us in the rear while we are trying to wind up this infernal Rebellion. Can you tell what is the matter with Acklin [Democratic candidate for Clerk of Court]? He was allways opposed [to the] Democracy, [but] now . . . he takes the position as strong. I see no "Democracy" in the "Val" party. They have not the good of the majority in view but the ruin of the Nation. You speak of P. W. Waldron (although I do not like him "every" way) is a much better man than his . . . [opponent]. He has been conducting himself since the war commence . . . We would hold an election here if we could find enough Ohio men together. There are but about 18 Ohioans here in this Regt . . .

Today is Muster day for Pay and for several day I will be busy working. There is nothing strong here in the way of war news. Duty in the way of guard is still pretty heavy. There is a strong shift in the weather now [illegible]. Last week the weather has been very cool. I never new it cooler in Ohio at this season. There have been several frosts already and last night seemed quite severe, could sleep under four blankets and then be cooler then I ever was at home with the usual amount of covering in the coldest weather.

The old troops have gone away and new come in their stead. The health of our Regt. is much improved. The men are cheerful and watchful on duty. A Negro makes a good guard at night as I have seen and I see they will fight if secesh bother them. It is rather dangerous to fool about them at night when they are on Picket. I hear Gen Thomas is in this part of the country. I am again tolerably well—I am not very fat but think I am doing fine. It is again a very hard matter to get a leave of Absence.

My love and respects to all the family

Yours,

Sam

P.S. excuse this scribbling I did it in a hurry.

Aberdeen / Sept. 2, 1863

Dear Brother,

Yours of the 19th Aug came to hand on the 26th, it gives us the Satisfaction to know you are getting better, And yours to father Says you still improve.

Sorry to hear of So many of your Negro & fellow Soldiers are Sick, but hope you will be able to be relieved of double duty soon.

Mother has about recovered from flux but is Still rather feeble. Mary has a bad felon on her finger which disables her much, Father has a boil in the inner corner of his eye which is now beginning to mend. All the rest are well. My health is very good & I weight 160 in my Shirt Sleeves. My great toe is very sore.

There is not much news up here at present. Things are moving Some what after the old fashion. Political Excitement is pretty high. Opsite partisans frequently meet each other with fire arms at a present & greeting the Ear with many a heavy Curse.

The war news all seems favorable to our cause.

The receipts of wheat in you mill add up to 13.15 bu this [?]. Even if the Season is favorable this Season we will make it pay. The weather has been dry for Some time. We had a hard frost Sunday morning.

Our Markets are as follows Wheat 80 @ 85, Corn 75 @ 80, Potatoes 60 cts, Sweet [potatoes] $4.00, Onions $1.00, Chicken 12.00 per doz, Ducks $2.50 doz. Sold all of our marketing at the above rates, Butter 20 cts p[er] lb. Eggs 5c per doz.

Query! did Joseph Fulton Settle his acct before you left.

Collecting is a dull business now, Even on good men. I will push it pretty soon & see if I cannot Suceed. Our cider mill has not arrived yet, don't know why it is delayed. Apples, Water Melons, & [illegible] are abundant this year. Peaches are plety but not of good quality. We have but few.

We are putting the old buggy in running order for a Market wagon, father painted it to day.

There is but little to write worthy of your attention hense I will close after giving you the Militia Election, Col Will Riggs, Lieut Col Thos Stephenson, Maj D. S. Guttery, Adgt. J. W. Guttery.

Accept our most ardent desires.

Your Brother,

Amos A. Evans

Lagrange, Tenn. / Sept. 6, 1863

Dear Father,

Your kind favor of the 24th came to hand a few days ago. Also one from Amos same day but I shall have to offer as an apology for not writing sooner want of an opportunity. This is your day to have a letter as you write once a week so do I, with duty I have not failed for many weeks at Least within a day or two. The delay you speak or rather "gap" was not my fault because I wrote. If you never got the letter, it is the fault of some body else. I am very happy to know that your health is improving and that the health generally is improving. It is good news to me that Will is about to get in the "pasish" [position] Hosp'tl St. It is a very good position and one that will pay a man something. The wages is $30 pr month. It is the Best office in the Army except some Commissioned office. I am glad to hear Lt. James Drennin has arrived home. I think he wanted to come home before. He is a great Anti-Val Man. Perhaps he would fight Rebles harder at home than he would if he was facing a considerable [number] who were shooting at him.

The health of this place is still very unhealthy but I am of opinion the health is improving slightly. As for my own it is very good considering the vast amount of exposure I have to go through. I cannot see that I have recd any permanent injuries from soldiering. Rest is all I need.

We have been very busy making Pay Rolls for a few days past. There is a great deal of work on one of these and there is still being more added, you can take a pay roll and tell all the Particulars of a Co as to strength, health, and the former condition of a Co. It would take a very shrewed man to Swindll the government because all the Reports must agree. Our pay master is here and will, I understand, pay us tomorrow.

We have nothing of special interest to write. There are no military movement[s] of importance near here. There are still a few Guerrillas in this vicinity. They have not made their appearence here yet. They perhaps know that we are always on the Lookout and that we have a larger force than they wish to come in contact with . . . I hear the draft will not be enforced in Ohio. That I do not like much, but it may all be right. I would rather they would volunteer. [General] Gilmore is still going into the Rebles. It will be a glorious thing when that place [Charleston, SC] is reduced. There should not "be one stone Left upon another" unless it be of some military importance to us in [the] future. Trade is growing better, there is some talk of allowing free trade, allowing citizens to purchase goods in quantity to Suit theirs. That I do not go in for, but if the authorities say so I shall come under at this Particular time. It is very hard for a Citizen to Pass in through our Lines, even these who reside very near our lines. That suits me exactly.

Think it Probable that I wil come home Sometime this Fall or winter, 20 days Leave of Absence i[s] the Largest We can get and that is pretty hard to do. I must close, Give my best respects to all accept a share for Yourself.

I am as ever your Son,

Sam

[Note to Ann attached to bottom of Sam's letter to Andrew]
Lagrange, Tenn. / September 6, 1863

Dear Sister [Ann],

Your note came to hand in one time. I am always glad to hear from your or any of the family. You spoke of seeing a lady with a red ribbon on her shoulder with Val's name on it. I will say she is no Lady only a thing perhaps in the form of a lady. She is a traitor and does not deserve the countenance of any one. She only did that for Bravadoe and should be treated with contempt. You can spite such persons by not noticing them. Butternuts will "play" some of these days as did the "Blue Light" in olden times.[1] I have plenty to eat now. Plenty of vegetables but they cost very high. No more at present.

Good Bye Your Brother,

Sam

1. "Blue light" was used as a nickname for traitors. The term may have originated during the War of 1812. Webb Garrison, with Cheryl Garrison, *The Encyclopedia of Civil War Usage: An Illustrated Compendium of the Everyday Language of Soldiers and Civilians* (Nashville: Cumberland House, 2001), 30.

⋙ SAM TO ANDREW ⋘
LaGrange, Tenn. / Sept. 13, 1863

Dear Father,

Since writing to you I have Recd two letters from you, yours of the 30th of Aug on the 9, of the 6th on the 13th. I recd several today from other sources. In fact I had quite a good time reading and felt quite at home while thus engaged. I am very glad to know that our folks are in better health. I was fearful mother would not get along well with flux.

I admire your "Patriotism." I think it the best of your way to avoid all political controversy unless the Nation or your honor are at stake. Brough is charged with being an abolitionist by some of our Huntington "Traitors" (as I call them for short). I will give you my principals again and I am not particular who knows them.

What we are fighting for is the great questions before my mind to be settled, and the men who are willing to support us while we settle this great work are the men who we take to be our friends. Shall this once almighty, prosperous country perish or shall it endure? Shall this heritage of blessings descend unimpaired to our posterity, or shall it be ignominiously thrown away? Shall the territory of the United States, once so happy, be broken up into miserable fragments, sure to engage in border wars, and all lying at the mercy of foreign powers, or shall we preserve its noble integrity? Admit the right of the seceding States to break up the Union at pleasure, nay of each and evry State to do so, and allow them to enforce that right by a successful war; deny the right of the General Government to control its members, and how long will it be before the new confederacies created by the first disruption shall be resolved into still smaller fragments and the continent become a vast theater of civil war, military license, anarchy and despotism? Better settle it at whatever cost and settle it forever. Let us meet it like men. Let us show ourselves equal to the duty imposed upon us, and faithful to the trust to which we are called. The cause in which we are engaged is the cause of the constitution and law, of civilization and freedom of man and God. Let us engage in it with a fortitude, a courage, a zeal, a resolution and hope worthy of the fathers from whom we are descended, of the country we defend, and of the privileges we inherit. Let the venerable forms of our Pilgrim Fathers, the majestic images of our revolutionary sires and of the sages that gave us this glorious Union [continue to endure].

The hardships and perils of our brothers in the field, the fresh green graves of the dear ones who have fallen, evry memory of the past, evry hope of [the] future; evry thought and evry feeling that can nerve the arm, or fire the heart, or elevate and purify the soul of a patriot should arouse, and cheer, and inspire us to do, and, if need be, to die for our country. The saddest feature of war is the loss of humans. In this view, war is most horrible, but human rights are worth more than human life, such is the conflict now raging. Let us compose and arm ourselves for the conflict, the sacrifice. Let us look defeat, disaster and even death steadily and calmly in the face and grasping the pill[ar]s of Gods eternal truth and justice, and holding up our country and all its interests before His throne, let us entreat Him to turn us from our transgressions, that iniquity may not be our Ruin. May His mercy arm us with strength to live and labor, to suffer and die for our native country and for the Kingdom of Christ. I could write on till you would perhaps tire reading but prudence dictates to stop a while, change the subject.

We still continue to receive cheering news from our army. Rosecrans has again made the rebs "git." [General] Gillmore and [Admiral] Dahlgren have been at work. Report says Beauregard has ordered the evacuation of Charleston but that I think is a little too fast.[1]

I am glad to hear John Mc has been allowed to come home. He is a good boy. I never thought he would vote for "Vall". I learn that the agents for the State election are at Memphis with the Books and paper necessary to give all Ohio men to vote in the ensuing election. I am confident Val will not get many votes though he may get a few, very few.[2] I suppose the chances for me to come home are very doubtful, from an order read on "dress parade" which ordered that no more "leaves of absences" would be granted except in "cases of urgent necessity." Such seldom occur. I may have a chance.

We are expecting to have a fight soon. We feel confident if we have a fair show we will "flax" the force that is marching against us. We still have plenty of duty but I think it is a little lighter than when I last wrote. Health of the Soldiers is slightly improving. My own health is very fair though I am not very fat. My weight is about 150 to 155 lbs. I feel much stouter than 150 pounds.

I reced a letter from Little Jane today. She talks like their folks were all "Val" men. What is the reason of that? [They] need not talk to me about Vallandingham for I think Brough is the man.[3] . . .

As ever yours affectionately,

Sam

1. Sam was correct about Beauregard not evacuating Charleston, though some of his positions in the vicinity of Charleston Harbor had been weakened or abandoned because of the intense attacks he faced from Gillmore's troops and Dahlgren's fleet. E. Milby Burton, *The Siege of Charleston: 1861–1865* (Columbia: University of South Carolina Press, 1970), 188–97.

2. Ohio had passed laws allowing soldiers to cast absentee votes, a major boost to Republican-Union candidates. Several other Northern states had no such laws, and great efforts were made to furlough soldiers, especially those likely to vote Republican. Sam was correct: Union gubernatorial candidate John Brough received 94 percent of

the soldier vote. Although Vallandigham would have lost the election even without the absentee-soldier vote, those votes helped to give Republicans additional victories in legislative and local races, including that of Andrew Evans, as will be seen below. McPherson, *Battle Cry of Freedom*, 687–88.

3. After Andrew's brother, Amos, was lost at war, his daughter (Little) Jane, Sam's first cousin, shifted from support of the Union to the type of antiwar sentiments espoused by the "Vals." There is an exchange of letters between Jane and Sam in 1864 bringing this fact to a head.

SAM TO ANDREW
Corinth, Miss. / Sept. 19, 1863

Dear Father,

I have received nothing from you since I wrote to you, but having changed my place of residence Since, I thought it necessary to write to Let you know how I like the place, how I am, and some other matters.

I wrote to Amos the evening we recd. the orders to march. We were ready to march agreeably to orders, but did not get a Locomotive to draw us to the place till 3 O'clock P.M. We arrived safely to this place about 8 P.M. same day. It was too late to find our Camp consequently we had to roost on the ground without blankets. The night was quite cool and I did not sleep much in consequence of it. I only felt bad for about one day. Yesterday, at noon, we went into barracks. They are very good too. The water is pretty good, at least I like the taste of it. This is strongly fortified, I have been to see some of the works which gave Vandhorn and Price thunder. It all looks very much like the papers stated. There are still plenty of seige piece[s] left here and more works being made, the brest work[s] here are not yet complete. Besides fortifications there are several Government buildings, such as depots, Commissary buildings, Machine shops, etc. I have not yet been out to the Old Reble Works but expect to in a short time. There are a goodly No of troops here. We expect to stay here the coming Winter.

Sept 21, 1863 / I have delayed finishing this letter longer than I anticipated, when I commenced it, but the reason is apparent when you consider the duty which we have to do . . .

I do not Like the place much, yet it is a dry old place. I think, I guess we have enough to eat and more work than we would Like too do if I could well avoid it. Still I will do whatever I can to help end this war. Several of our officers are sick. That makes our duty heavier on those that are well. There is another Colored Regt. here larger than ours, but it has never done the duty that ours has. They are well drilled. The[re] is a battery here manned by darkies. I have not seen Gen. Carr, our Commander, he is said to be a very fine man. I believe I wrote to you telling you that you need not Look for me, that "Leaves of Abscense" had played out by orders of General Hulbuet [Hurlbut] I do not expect to get home very soon . . . Our Orderly Sergt. has gone home on Sick furlough, left 8th of this month with orders not to return till he was able for duty . . .

When you write direct to Corinth in stead of LaGrange. I will now Close. I have the Co. to drill as I am in Command, I will write again in a day or two. Remember me kindly to all the family. And believe me as ever.

Your son,

Sam

→ SAM TO ANDREW ←
Corinth, Miss. / Sept. 27, 1863

Dear Father,

Your kind favor of the 13 came to hand yesterday which gave me much pleasure, accompanying it was one from Amos dated 16th. They were the first I have received since We moved to Corinth . . . I am very glad to hear all are getting better. I am glad George has got home and that he is getting better. I suppose he thinks he has been [away] from home a long time, but not quite as Long as I have, I do not expect to get home for some time. Those "Leaves of Absence" have dried up except in cases of extreme necessity. I am not good at playing off. I tried to get a furlough before John died but did not succeed. It is quite a dificult matter for an officer in this Corps to get a "leave." I Suppose the reason to be, this Corps (Hulbert's) [Hurlbut's] is under marching orders . . . It is the opinion of quite a no' of officers here that we will not be ordered away yet, I would be willing to remain here the coming winter, although this is a very mean place, seemingly to me . . . The pickets are frequently killed on post. Not long since, 2 of the Union Soldiers were found dead hanging. Some days after, 7 Rebles were found hanging on the same tree, two of whom were hanging by the same ropes.

I notice that there have been arrangements made to exchange all prisoners but [not] Colored and the officers who command them. I am of

Andrew Evans, From *The History of Brown County*, by Josiah
Morrow (Chicago: W. H. Beers, 1883).

Samuel Evans, From *The History of Brown County*, by Josiah
Morrow (Chicago: W. H. Beers, 1883).

Evans Mill barrel stamp. J Evans refers to Samuel's grandfather John Evans, Jr., the original owner from whom Sam purchased the mill. Both courtesy of Ann Guise. Photos by Robert N. Engs.

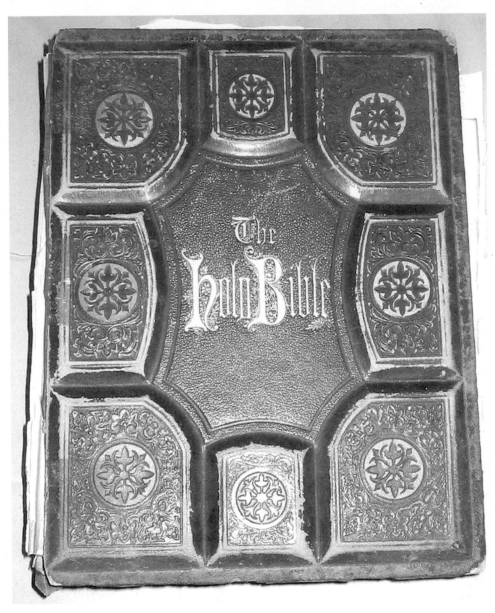

Evans family bible. Courtesy of Ann Guise. Photo by Robert N. Engs.

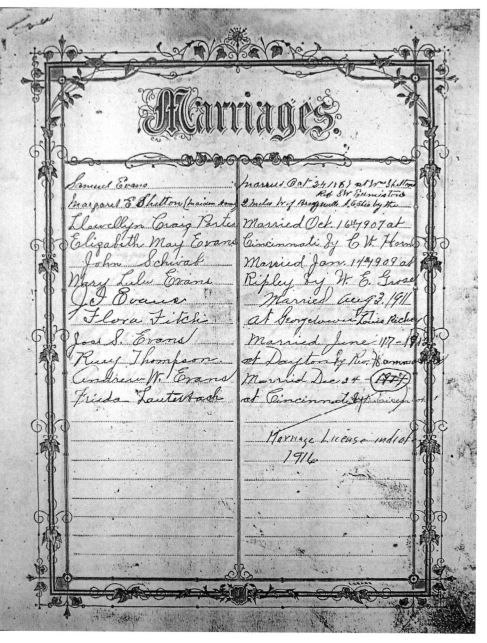

"Marriages" page from Evans family bible. Courtesy of Ann Guise.
Photos by Robert N. Engs.

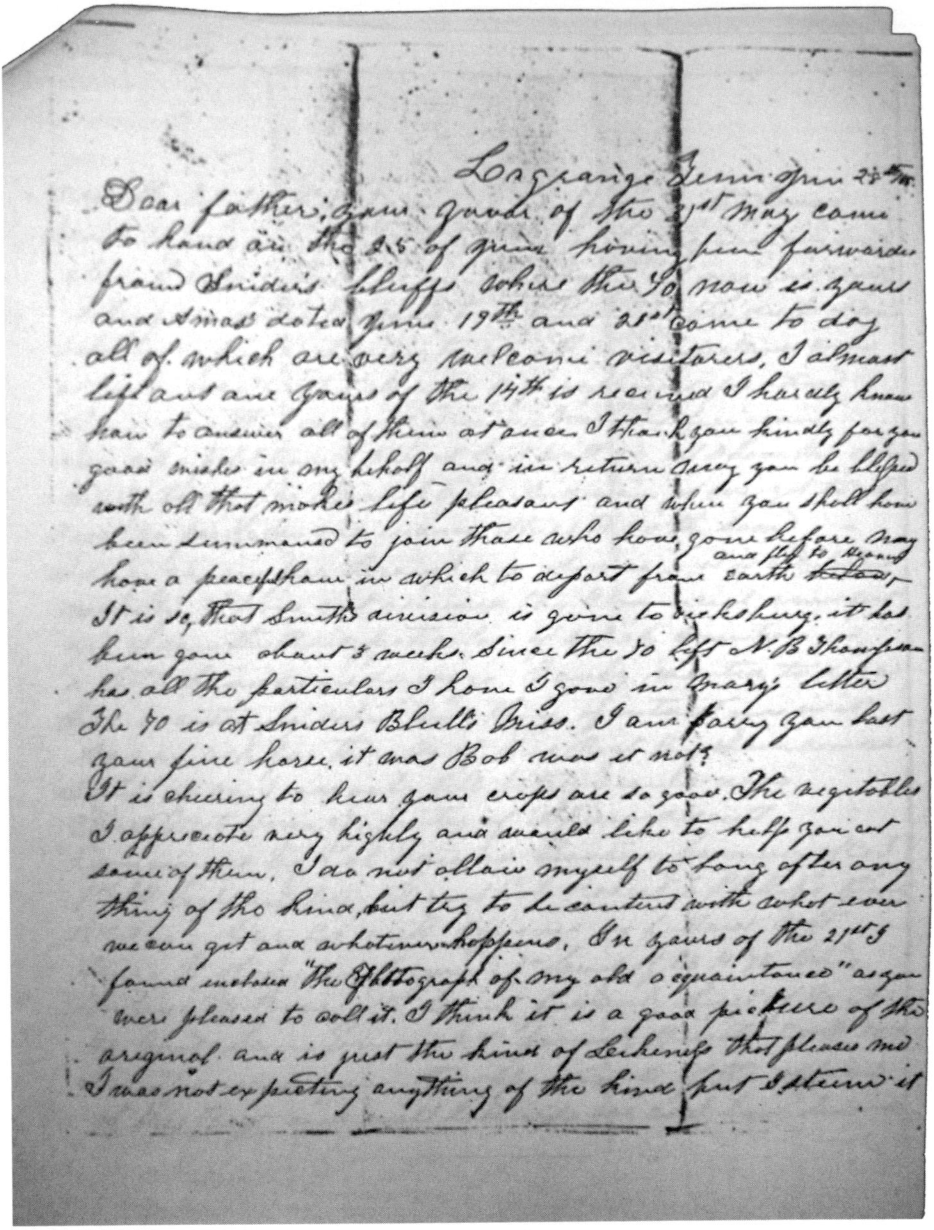
Lagrange Tenn June 28th
Dear father: Yours of the 31st May came
to hand on the 25 of June having been forwarded
from Sniders bluffs where the 70 now is. Yours
and Amas dated June 19th and 21st came to day
all of which are very welcome visitors. I almost
left out one Yours of the 14th is received I hardly know
how to answer all of them at once. I thank you kindly for your
good wishes in my behalf and in return may you be blessed
with all that makes life pleasant and when you shall have
been summoned to join those who have gone before may [you]
hope a peaceful haven in which to depart from earth and flee to ...
It is so, that Smiths division is gone to Vicksburg. it has
been gone about 3 weeks. Since the 70 left N. B. Thompson
has all the particulars I have I gave in Marys letter
The 70 is at Sniders Bluffs Miss. I am sorry you lost
your fine horse. it was Bob was it not?
It is cheering to hear your crops are so good. The vegetables
I appreciate very highly and would like to help you eat
some of them. I do not allow myself to long after any
thing of the kind, but try to be content with what ever
we can get and whatever happens. In yours of the 21st I
found enclosed "The Photograph of my old acquaintance" as you
were pleased to call it. I think it is a good picture of the
original and is just the kind of likeness that pleases me
I was not expecting anything of the kind but I esteem it

First page of Samuel Evans letter to Andrew Evans, June 28, 1863. Courtesy of Joseph Evans, Jr. and the Ohio Historical Society.

the Letter I wish India would get my picture it
is not as good as I have had taken but however it will do
I would like you to send me some more letter stamps
that amount you can send most conveniently not more
then 50 but that amount if convenient ($1.50) charge
me with the same we can only get stamps here occasion
I have some letters from Ame but have not
time to answer them now tell her that I will write
as soon as I can. My health has improved some
since I wrote to Marge and I think I am on the mend
dont understand me that I have been much sick
but that I was not as well as I have been for months
Remember me kindly to all the family and accept
my best wishes for their and your welfare and
    Andrew Evans & believe me as ever. Sam

P.S. Direct your letters to   — Sam Evans
                    •   Co. B. 1st West Tenn. Iffa
                                   of African descent
          Care Col E Bouton & Lagrange Tenn
I think I will be sure to get them if thus directed
I have 5 more letters to write yet to day

Last page of Samuel Evans letter of June 28, 1863.

3–014.

ACT OF FEBRUARY 6, 1907.

DECLARATION FOR PENSION.

THE PENSION CERTIFICATE SHOULD NOT BE FORWARDED WITH THE APPLICATION.

State of _Ohio_

County of _Brown_ } ss.

On this _2nd_ day of _March_ A. D. one thousand nine hundred and _Seven_ personally appeared before me _a Notary Public_ within and for the county and State aforesaid, _Samuel Evans_ who, being duly sworn according to law, declares that he is _72_ years of age, and a resident of _RR #2 Ripley_ county of _Brown_, State of _Ohio_; and that he is the identical person who was ENROLLED at _Ripley Ohio_ under the name of _Samuel Evans_ on the _18th_ day of _February_, 1862, as a _Private_, in _Co. I 70. O.V.I._

(Here state rank, and company and regiment in the Army, or vessel if in the Navy.)

in the service of the United States, in the _Civil_ war, and was HONORABLY DISCHARGED (State name of war, Civil or Mexican.) at _Memphis Tennessee_, on the _31st_ day of _January_ 1866. That he also served _as 2nd Lieut_ in _59th U.S.C. Inf. from June 6th 1863_

(Here give a complete statement of all other services, if any.)

until the 21 day October 1863 as 1st Lieut Co A 59th U.S.C. Inf until discharged at Memphis Tenn Jan. 31st 1866

That he was not employed in the military or naval service of the United States otherwise than as stated above. That his personal description at enlistment was as follows: Height, _6_ feet _1_ inches; complexion, _Dark_; color of eyes, _hazel_; color of hair, _Brown_; that his occupation was _Blacksmith_; that he was born _April 18th_, 1834, at

That his several places of residence since leaving the service have been as follows: _near the place of Birth 5 miles North of Aberdeen, O._

(State date of each change, as nearly as possible.)

That he is _____ a pensioner. That he has _____ heretofore applied for pension _No of_ _Certificate 352,982_.

(If a pensioner, the certificate number only need be given. If not, give the number of the former application, if one was made.)

That he makes this declaration for the purpose of being placed on the pension roll of the United States under the provisions of the act of February 6, 1907.

That his post-office address is _RR #2 Ripley_, county of _Brown_, State of _Ohio_.

Samuel Evans
(Claimant's signature in full.)

Attest: (1) _Samuel Laurie_
(2) _John Schwob_

Also personally appeared _Samuel Laurie_, residing in _RR #2 Ripley_ and _John Schwab_, residing in _RR #2 Ripley, O._, persons whom I certify to be respectable and entitled to credit, and who, being by me duly sworn, say that they were present and saw _Samuel Evans_, the claimant, sign his name (or make his mark) to the foregoing declaration; that they have every reason to believe, from the appearance of the claimant and their acquaintance with him of _14_ years and _20_ years, respectively, that he is the identical person he represents himself to be, and that they have no interest in the prosecution of this claim.

Validity accepted
S. A. Cuddy,
Chief, Law Division.

Samuel Laurie
John Schwob
(Signature of witnesses.)

SUBSCRIBED and sworn to before me this _2nd_ day of _March_ A. D. 1907, and I hereby certify that the contents of the above declaration, etc., were fully made known and explained to the applicant and witnesses before swearing, including the words_____, erased; and the words _as_, added; and that I have no interest, direct or indirect, in the prosecution of this claim.

[L. S.]

S. G. Evans
(Signature)
Notary Public in and for Brown Co. O.
(Official character.)

U. MAR 6 1907 OFFICE

Samuel Evans's declaration for pension, March 2, 1907. Records of the Veterans Administration, National Archives.

opinion if the government employ black men to fight, they ought to have some protection. If the rebels will not exchange for them, the government should retaliate if any of the officers or men are mistreated. This war would have been ended long ago if the principle of no prisoners had been adopted by the Rebles. They still threaten to hoist the "Black Flag." If they do; we should too.[1]

Rosecrans has been fighting again. I fear he has been over powered, but if reinforcements will only come in time he will thrash Bragg and Co. so nice. It is the place of the Rebles to crush Rosecrans if possible and that will give new confidence in their army.

Amos says the Union candidates will have about 30 of a majority in our township without any soldier vote. He said some one rode up to your gate and holloed [shouted] for Val. I do not know what I would do but I think if I were at home and one should thus insult me, I would shoot him down. If those fellows are allowed to continue thus insulting people, they [might] try something by violence. It is no matter what a man's former politics were, is he "right" now, should be the test. Those peace Dem[ocrats] have given the Rebles encouragement. Instead of ending the war they have been the means of Prolonging it, Thus causing the death of many a good soldier. That is another reason I hate these fellows so intensely.

Well I must close I am well and hope these few Lines May find you all enjoying the same blessing. Remember me kindly to all the family and
Believe me as ever your affectionate
Son,
Sam

1. Sam is referring to the Confederate policy of treating captured black Union soldiers as escaped or rebellious slaves, thereby justifying their immediate execution. For more about prisoners-of-war exchange, see note in Sam's letter of May 24, 1862.

✥ ANDREW TO SAM ✥
Home / Oct. 4, 1863

Dear Son,

Yours of the 19 & 21st came to hand on the 30th. Our mails are verry irregular owing to low water. Our household is again mantled in gloom at the news of the death of our beloved son, William H. We received news yesterday evening that he was killed in the Battle of Chickamauga. It is but hearsay news, but we are fearful it is true. We have had no letter from him since the 3rd Sept. We have news from official source that the 89th has but 125 men for duty inside the fortifications at Chatanooga. We also have news that the Col., Lt. Col., 4 Captns., 4 Lieuts. and all their men were captured. We have no lists of the killed published yet except a few officers. We are painfully afraid it is true. He has not written to us and it is two weeks since the battle was fought. Our news came through L. B. Moore. He got it from somebody else. Amos is gone today to chase the news to its source if possible. I will not close this until he returns so that you may have the latest news.

John Grierson & Isaac Dryden are said to be killed. Dryden, I suppose, is dead. He was dangerously wounded which fact was telegraphed to his father. He started after him and before he had time to get there, news of his death was telegraphed to Maysville. They fought a terrible battle against large odds, and with terible losses on both sides. The Rebels admit a loss of 12,000 and claim ours to be much larger. We have no official news of our loss, nor do we expect it soon. We have long antici-pated a hapy meeting of our soldier sons in our family circle. Are we to be derpived of that privilege? God alone can answer. The uncertainties and vicisitudes of war, as well as the uncertainly of life, with us all, go to admonish us that we may meet in Heaven, but may not on Earth.

Our family are in usual health, I have some rheumatism in my right hand that stiffens it considerable but it is still fit for light duty. We are in a terrible throng of fall work just now, fodder cutting, seading, potato digging, Apple gathering, race cleaning & c, we have but little time for doing mischief, we have two Acres of wheat sowed and intend to sow 16 more, we are nearly done cutting fodder, but have a large amount of apples & potatoes to gather yet, we have the race to clean from the bridge to the dam. We have done nothing at the race for two weeks or more, we have had to go to the mill once, we got good flour but not equal to "Evans' best," come over about Christmas and take dinner with us, and we will show you as nice bread as you have seen in all Dixie. We had a light rain yesterday, and now have verry cool wether, fire feels verry pleasant.

Well, Amos has returned from his search and reports that there is no grounds for the report that Will is killed, but there is good grounds to believe that there is no truth in the report.[1] C. F. Campbell Esq. has re-ceived a letter from Co. E of the 89th from a man that he knows is per-sonally acquainted with Will and he makes no mention of his death or other incapacity; therefore, we have ground to hope that he is still living.

God grant that it may be so. We find in the Commercial, the name of a William Evans and a Samuel Evans among the wounded but they are of Indiana Regiments. We are of [the] opinion the story is a fabrication of some person who desired to circulate news. We have nothing in the way of news worthy of your attention. The Vallandighamses are showing their asses whenever they can, but their cause is certainly dying, and on Tuesday [next] week we will give the thing its death blow and send it to its last resting place.

Truly your father,
Andrew Evans

1. In the bloody and chaotic two-day battle (September 19–20, 1863) of Chickamauga, the Union forces were defeated, falling back into Chattanooga, Tennessee. During that battle, the 89th Ohio held a key hill that enabled General Rosecrans to retreat, but the regiment was flanked and surrounded. The Confederates captured most of the regiment, but Will was not among those captured or killed. McPherson, *Ordeal by Fire*, 2:335–38; Williams, 1:427.

⇛ SAM TO ANDREW ⇚
Corinth, Miss. / October 4, 1863

Dear Father,

I seat myself to write you a few hasty lines. It is now 9 o'clock P.M. I have been busy all day isuing new Enfield Rifles to the men and turning over the old (Austrian). Besides this, I have been making preparation to start at 6 tomorrow morning for the Tuscumbia bridge. Five cos, the left wing, are going down to guard the bridge for one week. It is about 23 miles West of this place on the railroad. Guerrillas have lately been cutting the railroad in that region to stop the troops from coming up in here to reinforce Rosecrans and to cut of[f] supplies. As yet they have only succeeded in stopping the cars 12 hours. Yesterday several Regts. went from this place to reinforce the forces at LaGrange. Report came that there was a large force of rebles coming against that place, but it all proved to be a hoax, I think.

I have still had my health pretty well. I think I am "run down at the heel" a little as consequence of hard duty but nothing else. An officer cannot get Leave of Absence without the surgeon [who] will certify that a change of climate is necessary to save life. I do not suppose anyone would do that. I am sure I will I not ask it of them yet and perhaps never. I cannot tell you whether we will stay here the present winter or not. The probability is at present that we will is so. When this campaign is over I will come home if, "if," I can obtain consent from proper authority, not otherwise. Sherman Corps arrived except Smith's Division. I think it will go to Batoon Roughe.

I am waiting very patiently to hear the result of the Ohio election. I find myself getting very mad whenever I think of the opposition to the Union and those who have endeavored to defend their Country and all that is dear to a Patriot. To avoid getting very mad and "tearing up the ground," I turn to something else. I am sure if any one would insult me by any of his disunion slang, I would kill him if I had anything to do it with. I have about resolved that no traitor shall crow over me, unless I am placed in a situation that I will be compelled to. The health of the Army is improving finely. I do not think Rosecrans was much whipped if any at all. I hope ere long will [come] the good news of Rose flaxing the "dog water" out of Braggs entire Army or all that oppose him.

Goodnight,

Yours in haste,

Sam

✦ MARY (SISTER) TO SAM ✦
Home / October 7, 1863

Dear Brother,

I will now commence my duty that I have neglected for two months or more but I hope that you will not think hard of me for my finger was so that I could not write for several weeks or do any thing else. It is about well now, quite tender yet. I received your letter of Aug 7th on the 15th, things in it are most to old to answer. Pap recd one letter from you, one from George, and one from Will, the first we had had from him since the battle. He was in the Field hospital near Chattanooga. He says, to his knowledge none fataly but most severely of Co. E Seargt Thomas Hafer of Ripley near the ankle of the right leg, the ball loging in the Tibia. Cor-p[oral] Alfred McNulty of our Township in the middle of the lower third of the left thigh breaking the bone and is very dangerous . . . The rest were captured . . . Some few that he mentioned came out safe but not many of your acquaintances. He got a slight taste of grape on the right wrist but not to hinder him from duty . . . Amos is writing to Will to night. He wrote to India last night to let her know how and where Will was. We have been quite weary since the battle untill we got a letter from him. We also heard that you got shot out on picket duty, but we did not believe it. Sam we can hear all kinds of news just after a battle from every body and some that was not there.

Father and I are going to Ripley tomorrow. Father will take four barrels of apples to Mr. Armstrong. We will sell several barrels I suppose: we have some 16 or 17 trees to gather yet. We gathered Rambo's [a variety of apple] since dinner today, come over and get a load for your own use. Pap and Mother was at Aberdeen to day and brought out Dyas Gilberts cider mill. They are quite a handy Machine, we can keep fresh cider to drink all the time this winter.

Sam all the Girls around here are Valls. I guess only a few. Little Jane is a strong one and her, Big Jane, Hannah and Harriet Swisher are going to a Val meeting some place. I expect they will make a fine show, all dressed a like. I have got out of practice writing letters. This is the first one that I have written since my finger got sore, you will please pardon mistakes. Amos will write soon. My love to you believe me

As ever your Sister,
Mary Evans

⇻ ANN TO SAM ⇺
Home / October 9, 1863

Dear Brother Sam,

As I had nothing much to do I thought I would write to you. It is getting cold here. Sam, I wish you would get to come home. Pat has come home again. The Vals had a meeting at Fulton's Mill. They could not come in with the Union girls. (We work for Brough). I think the Vals had better keep dark. I must close.

Ann D. Evans

⇻ ANDREW TO SAM ⇺
Home / October 11, 1863

Dear Son,

Yours of the 27th Sept. came to hand on the 7th Oct. It found us enjoying good health & we were pleased to learn that you were "in the same fix." The general health here is fair, no epidemic prevailing in the County that I am aware except "Val fever," which will have reached the turning point before this reaches you. On [the] day after tomorrow, the kill-or-cure dose will be administered, and you will learn the result in due time. I can give you nothing new with respect to the election prospect, unless there are gross deceptions being practiced. The union vote has been steadily gaining, a portion of them may be deceiving us but we will wa[t]ch them closely at the election. We have some fears of a troublesome election. Fists, clubs, knives and pistols will be there in abundance and one misstep may lead things badly astray, perhaps to blood shed. They anticipate a verry quiet election in Ripley. The Union majority being so verry larger, and the men there say that no interruption will be tollerated against any man for civilly voting as he pleases. Here things are different, we shall be in the neighborhood of a tie vote, and the party, (or rather the fag ends [remnants] of the party) who used to rule in our township, are growing somewhat savage at their numbers being so depleted. They have to behave themselves or meet the consequences, is our terms.

We have but little additional news from "Rosy." We are receiving Casualties, but you will see them much sooner than we can send them to you. It was an awful battle, and but little gained, all that was gained was on our side for Chattanooga was the prize fought for, & "Rosey" holds it, therefore the Rebel loss is an irreparable loss with no gain to compensate. Jo Hooker passed through Ohio some ten days since with an Army Corps verry quietly on his way to "Rosey."[1] He should be reinforced quickly, for the whole available Rebel force will be hurled against him just as soon as they can be concentrated, and we certainly cannot afford to have his army destroyed. The authorities should Enable him to move forward against all obstacles the Rebels can place in his way. The best saltpeter beds in the South are in E, Tenn., and the Rebs are cut loose from them, hence, their anxiety to retake & hold that portion of the State. I am of opinion that Mead ought to push his work vigorously just now, if he could take Richmond now, East Va. would be clear in less than a month. That once clear, North Carolina is ready to declare for the old Union. We would then soon be enabled to let the Rebs find the "last ditch." Away out in the South End of Floriday, or perhaps in a climate more hot.

Our weather is pleasant. Some sharp frosts in the mornings, but the weather is fine for business. We are making the best use we can of it, but, still more than we are able to keep up with tho' we keep trying. We are not done gathering apples yet, the crop is heavier than we anticipated.

Our orchard will pay us more this year than any land we have under cultivation. Some trees go as high as 4 of 5 barrels. . . .

Accept the love & compliments of the family.

Affectionately your father,

Andrew Evans

1. In one of the most impressive logistical feats of the war, twenty thousand troops from the Army of the Potomac, under the command of Joe Hooker, were moved by rail through the Ohio Valley on their way to Chattanooga. McPherson, *Ordeal by Fire*, 2:337.

⇒ ANDREW TO SAM ⇐
Home / October 18, 1863

Dear son,

I again enter on my weekly duty, I am quite unwell, but the glorious news stimulate my nerves to action. Yours of the 4th came to hand on the 14th which gave assurances of your fair health. We are sorry to learn that you suffer too much duty put upon you and thereby are being worked down, you are neither physically nor constitutionally able for verry much Extra duty, and I don't like the principle of "whipping the willing horse". We have news that appears to be reliable, that you have been shot in the neck! inflicting a flesh wound, is it so? If so why did you keep the fact from your parents? It is certainly our right to know the facts of the case, your letters are verry satisfactory to us, but you certainly should not conceal your true condition from us.

Our election news is glorious; the whole Union ticket is gloriously elected in Brown and Adams counties. In Adams they have shown the proper honor to her brave sons of the 70 OVI. Capt John T. Wilson, late of the 70, is elected Senator, our good friend, W. W. West, is Representative,[1] and our young friend, John D. Taylor, is sheriff of county. Good for Adams!

In Brown, we have elected the soldiers friends; "Narry Reb." Our Treasurer is now in the service. I do not remember what his grade of office is. He is on Gen. Ammens staff. Two or three others of our county officers elected are discharged soldiers. Old Gen. Jas. Loudon is our Senator and your humble and unexpecting father Representative in Brown. The old Courthouse is called upon to give up its Rebel sympathizers, send them out, that the places they have been disgracing may be filled by honest loyal men, who will hold the welfare of our brave boys in the field above any other consideration.

I did not want the office to which I am elected. I was only notified two days previous to the nomination that my name would be used. I protested against it but was unanimously nominated. Then (for the sake of the cause), I did not feel at liberty to decline, though I had no idea of being neglected, but since it is done I confess I feel the proper pride that I have been instrumental, in part, of making Brown a loyal county, and if the position I am placed in will enable me to do our gallant soldiers any more good, or the Rebels, either north or south any more harm, than I could in any private capacity at home, I cheerfully make the necessary sacrifice.

Our victory in the state, and particularly in Brown, has caused the boys to pay for a good deal of tar and powder. They have had happy times with illuminations, torch light processions and sending the news forth from the cannons. Report says some of them got a little "high." I can't say, I was not there . . .

Yesterday was George's day to start to his Regt. [89th OVI]. All the boys of the 70th will start back on Wednesday next. I have been sick for the last 4 days, but have kept up and feel much better today. I think I shall be all right in a day or two, your mother is also not so well as usual. I think our work is the excuse in both cases. The residue of our family are verry well, Mary is gone to Ripley for a week or more, she is gone to get Dian to help her make Amos &me, each, a Coat. She will not write to you until she returns.

We have our fruit secured, seeding done & the race nearly cleaned, potatoes to dig yet & some fencing & we will be ready for the corn as soon as it will do, Corn is heavy & down and must be gathered as soon as possible.

Accept the love of the family and the highest regard of your
father,
Andrew Evans

1. W. W. West served as captain of Company F (Sam's company) in the 70th Ohio.

⇢ MAJOR T. T. TAYLOR[1] TO ANDREW ⇠
Head Quarters 47th Ohio Infty
Camp on Cherokee, Franklin Co. Ala. / October 24, 1863
My Dear Sir:
I had the satisfaction to receive your entertaining letter at Corinth, Miss. a few days ago. It conveyed the first information of the whereabouts

of your Son Samuel and I congratulated myself with the thought that I should see another Brown Co. boy, but the next morning orders came to move on and I among others, had to march without the pleasure of an interview.

Accept my condolence in your hom[e] of affliction. The bereavement is painful in empathy [illegible], yet it is but the common lot of mankind; such a death is robbed of its terrors, the sacrifice of life in such a noble cause is the highest evidence a man can offer of the purity of his motiv[e]s and the loyalty of his heart. It is glorious thus to die and though the body is convulsed with pain, the countenance will beam with smiles and the last flash of the eyes sparkle with the fires of patriotism. I have hear men mortally wounded singing our national songs and exhorting their companions to stand by their country. Grief pales and softens at the reflection that such was the death of a friend. I'll mention a case of a death in Camp. A member of Co. K. 37th O[hio] was about to die. The Chaplain waited on him and asked his last wish: He replied "tell my brother to vote for John Brough & the Union ticket" and in a few moments expired. These were his last words. His brother was a Vallandigham man.

Well I presume I may congratulate you upon your election. I saw in a Commercial of the 16th inst that Brown Co. gave 191 maj. for Brough & one township to hear from. That township I presume was Eagle, Jackson or Byrd, neither [sic] of those could change the result. We wer at [illegible] on the day of the election; our regiment has 160 men on detached duty, many of those men are from Brown, I cannot state whether they voted. We the regiment, we polled two hundred votes, five of which were for Vallandigham. The Val. ticket in Brown did not get a vote, the Union ticket received twenty-two. The boys from Brown had concluded not to vote the County ticket but when I gave your name as a candidate for Rep. I told them we must vote and so all who were present and competent to enjoy the franchise voted for you. Our brigade gav 790 majority for Brough. I nev saw a more impartial election in my life, not an officer had anything to do with it except to vote. The enlisted men wer left perfectly free to vote as they pleased and tickets of both parties were circulated.

I am rejoiced to learn that our County has established her loyalty by so decided a vote and has administered Such a Sterne rebuke to treason. How it would have rejoiced those Conspirators had they been able to have forced our County to repudiate her sons who are now fighting this glorious war. Many a day I longed to be with you, meet them face to face, and to hurl their treasonable speeches back upon them.

The rebels are now harassing us considerably by attacking our pickets, trains, & c. Indeed day before yesterday about three thousand of them dashed almost into the Camp of the first division and gav us a little fight. The first formed and by superior strength drove them back steadily four or five miles, thinking they had then retired, our forces returned to Camp but hardly had they reached it ere the rebels wer back and the same performance had to be repeated. They fought stubbornly and skillfully. Showed excellent drill and superior discipline. The 30th Ia. [Iowa] formed and double quicked forward from Camp and were called to halt, the Major replied they wer going to the front. The rebels wer duped almost like our men & when the Col of Ia. ordered his men to fire, the force at which the aim was directed hollowed [shouted] to fire, they were federals. The Ia. Col ordered "recom arms" and, as he did so, the rebels, among whom they then were, fired. The Col. of the 30th was killed, the Adjutant wounded in four places & many others were Killed & wounded. We lost about forty in the fight & I presume the rebels nearly the Same number. Our regiment was on picket that day. None of our division participated in the engagement. I think from the actions of the rebels they hav not sufficient force to attack us for the purpose of bringing on a regular engagement but only to annoy us & impede our advance. Their force is all mounted & their movements made with great celerity.

We are repairing the Memphis & Charleston railroad which is along her[e] badly destroyed.

This is the finest land I hav seen since I left Memphis. It is known as the Valley of the Tennessee. The improvements are of a Superior Character and the people intelligent. The soil is red with Clay subsoil, well drained-raised on an average fifty bushels corn & 100 lbs cotton to the acre, was worth before the war forty to fifty dollars per acre, owing to distance from railroad. It had been under cultivation since 1834 and that without any [illegible]. At this time it carries a pretty good soil. The Valley I am told extends from Bear Creek to Decature & impressive in fertility as you ascend.

Remember me Kindly to your wife & family & believe me

Truly your friend,

T. T. Taylor

I don't Know where we are going, you may direct [illegible] via Memphis.

1. This letter from Andrew's friend Major T. T. Taylor, of the 47th Ohio Volunteer Infantry, indicates that Andrew likely had several wartime correspondents, not just family members, but this is the only one that has survived in this collection.

Home / October 25, 1863

Dear Sam,

Again I write you without anything to answer, Yours of the 4th, is the last from you. I referred to it last sunday.

I was somewhat mistaken last sunday, when I said to you that "I would be all right in a day or two,["] I had to call on a Doctor the next day, and am of no account yet, tho I have kept up I am quite unable to work, tho I am improving, my disease is of the Typhoid Character tho in a mild form & is certainly subsiding. Your Mother has some Rheumatism but is still working and is better than on last Sunday, The residue of our family ar verry well, we have not heard from Mary since she left, I shall go & see her tomorrow if I am able. J. C. Waldren is dangerously sick of Typhoid-Pneumonia, some say there is but little hope for his recovery, I have not seen him.

We received a long letter from Will, the past week, dated 4th to 10th containing 2 1/2 sheets cap, & well filled in fine hand he was verry well, but not verry well fed at the writing. 2 Crackers pr day. He has Entire Charge of his Regt in the Surgeon department, their Asst Surgeon being Captured & the Chief has charge of a Division. Will has but 8 patients, all doing well. I cannot undertake to rewrite his description of the Battle, it is too long. He appears to be glad that he escaped. He was dressing a wound on the field when his wrist was cut by a grape, he says the wounded are generally doing verry well.

Well, the Rebs will find something to do there soon. The whole thing is put into Grant's department and "Plenary powers" given him, he is there in person and as soon as enough of his vetran troops arrive, Bragg had better go "yon way". Lee & Mead appear to be running foot races, playing Hide & Seek etc., but little good is to be Expected from that quarter, "its too close to Washington." Alass!!!

Our weather is fine, some light rains & some verry sharp frosts, We have our apples & potatoes secured, the mill race cleaned, & are pretty well even with the season, The wheat sown has come up beautifully. Many are not done sowing yet, and some are just beginning. Tobacco crops are up though many of them were injured in the patches by Early frosts. The crop will be a heavy one, tho, but little of it will be best quality. Irish potato Crops were fair & the price is good, from 60 to 80 at town, Our apples go at $2 pr bbl. we have sold some 20 barrels but have not delivered 1/2 of them yet, oweing to me being off-duty, I take them on the Spring wagon, it don't bruise the fruit any.

Amos, Davis, Gilmon, Peggy & Ibby went to Aberdeen on Monday night last to a jubilation. They had Torch lights, town illumination, speeches, songs, hung, shot, & burned Val and returned home at 11 P.M., some of the party kept things going all night, if report is true . . .

Our Union boys are making heavy preparations for a general Jubilee at Georgetown on next Tuesday night. I can't go. They had [better] give their money to some poor soldier's family to keep them comfortable than to spend it for fire works, powder, etc. We have a letter from George of the 15 & Inda of the 17, George started for his Regt on the 16, he was well, Inda & Morty were verry well, we have but little to manufacture news from hence you must look to the papers for news.

Broughs majority in Ohio will be about 100,000 it is about 62,000 by the house vote, the Soldiers will do the rest of it. The Vals have about 100 average majority on the house vote in this Co., but they have come down, they know soldiers vote.[1]

Truly your father,
Andrew Evans

1. Andrew's estimates here are quite accurate, with Brough winning a 61,752 majority of the home vote and later receiving a nearly 40,000-vote majority from soldiers in the field, who went for Brough almost seventeen to one. This victory over Vallandigham and the peace party, aided in part by Union victories in July at Gettysburg, Pennsylvania, and Vicksburg, Mississippi, was hailed by Republican and Union partisans nationwide. On election night, President Lincoln purportedly sent sitting Union Party Governor David Tod a telegram, in which he wrote that Ohio "saved the Union" by defeating Vallandigham. Frank L. Klement, *The Limits of Dissent: Clement L. Vallandigham & the Civil War* (New York: Fordham University Press, 1998), 252; Roseboom, "Southern Ohio and the Union in 1863," 33–34.

⇝ AMOS TO SAM ⇜
Aberdeen, Oh. / Oct. 28, 1863

Dear Brother,

. . . We were all very glad to hear from you but Sorry to hear you are in so poor a place & have so much risk to run, We trust all to him who rules Supreme. He alone has power to Save. Father is slowly mending but not well. The rest of us are about as usual. Mary is Still at Ripley, She will return friday. Belle & I will go down afternoon tomorrow as Mary Carpenter & Saml Espy will get married at night . . . Rev. John Bloom & Lou Simpson will marry on Thursday night. Sam Porter & Euphemia Games will hitch soon. . . . There is room for Soldiers to marry as Ohio has filled her quota without a draft.[1] There is nothing of interest going on here now. Everything is dull . . . The Buttenuts undertook to put our present School mistress out of [work] because she would not let their children holler for Val. The directors met & she claimed her rights & maintained them. She is a good teacher & is loyal to the Core, since the fuss her school is much increased . . .

I am making my own dwarf & Standard pears—& have the best. Also the best & most complete collection of Peaches in the County. Also have collected many Curiosities—have a large No of fine varieties of Plum, Apricots, Nectarines, Cherries & c. Come & See them and Judge for yourself. One of my plum buds growed a 4 ft. body one inch through All this season & a fine handsome too. I will set one or 2 hundred trees this fall. Corn is drying very fast, will do to gather if husked & Sorted. We will gather ours soon. No more in doc for this time. Please excuse haste & Write as often as convenient.

Yours as Ever,

Amos

1. This relation between the draft and marriage illustrates the draft's impact on basic aspects of Northern life. For more insights on this subject see Joan E. Cashin, ed., *The War Was You and Me: Civilians in the American Civil War* (Princeton, N.J.: Princeton University Press, 2002). Also see Paul A. Cimbala and Randall M. Miller, eds., *Union Soldiers and the Northern Home Front: Wartime Experiences, Postwar Adjustments* (New York: Fordham University Press, 2002).

⤜ ANDREW TO SAM ⤛
Home / November 1, 1863

Dear Son:

This is the second letter since I received one from you, yours of the 9th? Oct is the last. Amos received one last week written at Tuscumbia bridge. We are getting fearful that you are sick, or otherwise rendered unable to write, and that you are keeping us uninformed with respect to your true condition. We are not aware of any serious obstacle in the way of the mails between here and Corinth, via Memphis. I received a letter yesterday dated Oct 24 from Maj. T. T. Taylor of the 47, this written at Camp Cherokee, in Franklin County Allabama. It came via Memphis, he passed through Corinth a few days previous to writing. He says he received a letter from me, while in Corinth which informed him where you were, he congratulated himself that he would se[e] you and have a good time, but recd. Marching orders and had to leave.

I continue to write you evry Sunday. Whether they reach you or not is more than I can say. Some of the family generally write in the middle of the week. We direct them plainly to your address and put them in the P.O. If they fail to reach you, the fault is not ours, I have not failed to start a letter to you once a week for more than a year, Amos & the girls miss sometime, but send you a great many letters. We have nothing from Will or George since I wrote you. My health is much better than it was a week ago. I feel well enough though not quite stout enough for business. Your mother still has occasional Rheumatism. The residue of the family are verry well. The health of the neighborhood is fair. J C Waldren has been trying to "Peg out" [?] ever since the election, but it is thought by many that he will not make it. Old Jacky Lawwill says, there is nothing the matter except the result of the Election, and that there is no danger of him dying. I cant say.

We have but little, or no additional Election news. It is supposed that the Soldiers vote will elect the whole Union ticket in this County, but we may be mistaken. The Poll Books will not be opened for 30 days after this election, that will be on the 12th of this month. I will try to inform you as soon thereafter, as I can get the result. I am certain that I will leave Amos enough to do if I should be elected, and go to discharge the duties, but such are the vicisitudes of life, and we must bow submissively.

We had considerable rain on friday. Yesterday morning we started the mill & ground several grists of wheat, but by noon water was too scarce for good work, and there is considerable of work standing over for the next rain. The machinery had worked well, we did not have to drive a key or a wedge, the trunk is in bad condition from decay, it has not lasted well, & then wood is so weak that it will [be] difficult to make it answer the purpose, & I dont know where the next one will come from.

Thoss [sic, Those?] weddings have gone off. Bloomhuf & Lee Simpson, Sam Espy and Mary Carpenter were all married on thursday night last. Sam Porter & Phemia Games will marry soon.

Lafe Parker paid us a visit last night and staid until Church time this morning. He is about as well as usual.

I am out of material to make an interesting letter, therefore
I tender you you [sic] the love & best wishes of the family an
Particularly of your father,
Andrew Evans

Tuesday Morning Nov 3 / I failed to get this letter out yesterday. Mary Recd one from you dated 22 Oct. I congratulate you on your promotion. I am 2 or 3 letters out, I can't tell why, for I have no doubt you write as usual. I am sure I do, Mary will write in a few days. No news, dull damp weather, pretty sore on invalids, I shall go to town if the weather will justify it today. Keep writing & we will get some of your letters.

Truely,
Andrew Evans

⇒ SAM TO ANDREW ⇐
Corinth, Miss. / November 2, 1863

Dear Father,

Yours of the 18th came to hand 2 day[s] ago, it having been 13 day[s] on the road. I should have answere[d] it yesterday, but, was on duty and to day I have not yet been relieved and it is now 2 o'clock P.M. I was sorry to hear of your ill health, Duty is still very very heavy. There is a Loose Screw some where. I am now doing 3 men's duty and have been for some time. Many officers have not been on duty once while I have been [on] a doz. The officers of this Regt go on as often as I do while others get "sick" about 1/2 the time. You are much mistaken about me not being able to stand much duty, at Least My experience is different. I have been stand-ing a great deal, and to day I feel quite well and have Lost 1/2 of my sleep for a considerable Length of time.

You ask about me being Shot, I was shot slightly. I thought I had told you all about it. I[t] was a slight flesh [wound] and soon healed up. The scar shows very plain. I think I have told you the truth always. I tell you always what I think is necessary and then stop. A little wound does not amount to a hill of beans.

I like the election news from home very well. There is a big move on hands here. I do not know all of it but could not tell under the circumstances.

These Lines are closed, no citizens have been allowed to come in or any to go out. Shermans army has gone on. I hear from good authority that they Left with only 10 days rations and will March to Chattanooga in side of that time.[1] We would not be much as tarnished [astonished] to have a brush with the rebles soon. Preparations being made to evacuate the R.R. from this place to Memphis and open the Road from Columbus, Ky. to this place. The Route being shorter and more direct, supplies could arrive before they could be brought to Memphis. I have not the time to write any more but will try to write something more interesting next time.

Remember me to all the family. I have the honor to Subscribe myself as ever,

Sam

1. Sherman was indeed marching east to Chattanooga, to join with forces of Generals Hooker and Thomas (commanding the Army of the Cumberland, previously commanded by General Rosecrans). Grant was preparing to lead them in an assault against Confederate positions on the outskirts of Chattanooga. Sherman actually arrived in Chattanooga on November 15. McPherson, *Ordeal by Fire*, 2:339.

It was during the subsequent battles around Chattanooga (see note on Andrew's letter of November 29, 1863) that the Army of the Cumberland, in which Will served, met up with General Sherman, commanding the Army of the Tennessee. When Grant was promoted to general-in-chief in the spring of 1864, Sherman was appointed to succeed Grant as commander of all armies between the Appalachians and the Mississippi. Most of his former command in the Army of the Tennessee joined the Army of the Cumberland and the Army of the Ohio in Sherman's famous campaign in Georgia, including the battles around Atlanta and the notorious March to the Sea.

⇒ ANN TO SAM ⇐
Home / Nov. 8, 1863

Dear Brother Sam,

I have not wrote to you for some time, I thought I would write to you. It has been a nice day, Cold though. Do you have to sleep on the ground. I think you have a cold time.

John Carpenter was home the 2nd of november. Sam Come home Christmas on a furlough and stay a while. Get some apples to eat and cider to drink. We got a letter from Will. He was well. George had not got to the Regt yet. We have sold a good many apples. We have more to sell yet. The Val men do not say any more, they have gone up—but you think so they do not Hollow [shout] for Val (Hurrah for Brough).

Your sister,

Ann

Corinth, Miss. / Nov. 15, 1863

Dear Father,

Your kind favor of the 25 came to hand yesterday, the first from you for two weeks. I recd a letter from Amos a few days ago, I answered it last Wednesday. Letters have been coming to us rather unregular for about one month perhaps it is on account of so much army movements in this quarter. Letters have commenced coming in again. It may be that some of our Letters going out have been garbled [*sic*, grabbed?] thinking that they contained money as the Paymaster has been in this region and Paying the Troops. "Such is the Suspicion at Least."

I am Sorry that your health is not good. I hope you will soon recover from your illness. Rheumatism is very disagreeable and hard to get rid of. I have not been troubled with any yet this Season if we have to lay out in the rain and mud I think it Likely that it may visit me.

It is very satisfactory to know that our State Election has been in favor of the Union, but I do not think the bonfires, "burning, shooting and hanging Val" will do him or other rebles much harm. It would please me much better to see [it] done in reality. Apply the Strings and Powder to the men themselves not to their images. We have some of the Live Stock down here. If any one is very keen to shoot or hang Rebles, Let them come down and he can have a chance to try it on. I presume there is less danger in losing ones Life up there than here. I Like to see rejoicing but do not Like to see it go too far.

The War horses reins seem to be lightning up evry where as if there would be something done. I fortun[ately] favor our cause, you will see before Christmas glorious work done. Some of the Rebles are in the last pit. I predict at least Braggs army and "Bo'gards" at Charleston get a flogging during the next 5 or 6 weeks. Grant has quite a large com[man]d.

Gen Grant says that Sherman is worth $5000 per day to the government more than any other in the Army. That is a Large Recommendation from a High place. This is said to come from Grant Himself, why it is so I cannot say. It may be the part he is about to play, the positions and so on he is taking. There is one thing certain, there is no man Living [illegible] than Maj Gen W. T. Sherman as a Diciplinarian. No man in the Army is a head of him. I know him personally, have talked with, worked for, him and Seen him fight. While I worked in the Shop at Memphis he frequently came in to the shop and talked with us. I had the honor to repair a pair of Revolvers, shot gun, and polish his Sword, and while I was doing it he was frequently Looking on.

Well news is a little scarce. Duty is a little lighter now but still it is as heavy as I care about. Guerrillas are still Lurking about. One of my men was captured on picket a few nights ago but he made his escape. Guerrillas are shooting all the Union Soldiers they can catch, and we still use them as prisoners of War. If I am alone, and get a chance at him he will not get away. Gen Stevenson commanding here has caused the lines to be closed and none but Refugees [probably means escaping slaves] can come in. No citizen is allowed to go out, no goods of any kind is permitted to go through the lines, any one attempting to take goods or eatables out [of] these Lines must be arrested and confined, his goods taken from [him] and appropriated to the government. The Gen says things will remain [so] untill guerrillas let the R Road alone [and] quit troubling our [patrolled] Lines. I heartily approve the doctrine. This is rather hard on women and children but if citizens will try, they can prevent guerrilluing, also prevent the capture of our Soldiers.

My health is pretty good. My cold is getting some better. My Lungs were quite Sore for a few days and my throat felt Little Like Bronchitis but that has entirely Left. Enclosed find a "photo". It is I think a Little darker than I am but a Light colored one could not be expected, [given] the Regiment I am in. However, you will judge when you see me.

My Love to all the family as ever your Son,

Sam

⇨ ANDREW TO SAM ⇤
Home / Nov. 15, 1863

Dear Sam,

Yours of the 2nd came to hand on the 10th in which we learn that your health is still good. We are all well. Your mother, Lee & I, have just returned from a 4 days visit, we went to Feesburg on Thursday, staid with Inda until Saturday morning . . .

I am in poor mood for writing. I drove from Russllville in a cold drisling rain, and the result is a stiff numb hand, that refuses to go the way I want it to, I am truely sorry that you are still doing so much Extra duty, you certainly will not stand that kind of duty verry long, I would be pleased at all times to hear of you doing your whole duty, but I do not want you to more than you are able to stand and thereby break your self down.

George was in Louisville at last accounts, he reported at Headquarters 2 days before his time was out, they considered him unfit for active field duty, and set him to writing at Headquarters in which capacity he is still kept. He says he likes the business verry well and his health is improving and he thinks he will soon be sent to his Regiment, he says he lives very well and gets proper rest . . .

The Great Conspiracy, both in the U.S. & Canada, has been detected & frustrated—it was a deep laid scheme to release all the Rebel prisoners in Ohio and on Johnson's Island, and to burn Buffalo & other Cities.[1] The prince of Traitors (Val), I believe is at the head of the whole affair. He ought to be hung, shot, & his ass kicked.

Sam please Excuse this thing, I cannot write to-night.

Accept our love and believe me

As Ever your father,

Andrew Evans

1. Johnson's Island was a forty-acre prison camp in the Sandusky Bay of Lake Erie. Its proximity to the Canadian border led to several plans by Confederate agents in Canada to free the prisoners and to even more rumors about such plans. This conspiracy was foiled with the help of British intelligence and a show of Union military force at Sandusky. There is no evidence that Vallandigham was involved in this conspiracy. Charles Frohman, *Rebels on Lake Erie* (Columbus: The Ohio Historical Society, 1965), 1–4, 40–42.

⇒ SAM TO ANDREW ⇐
Corinth, Miss. / Nov. 22, 1863

Dear Father,

Yours of the 8th is at hand also one from Amos of the 13th all of which were welcome guests. I am sorry my letters fail to reach you. I am sure I direct plainly. You Speak of my coming home to eat some of your good apples. That I would like to do but think it is a little doubtful about coming as early as Christmas. It is highly probable that I will obtain Leave to visit home between Campaigns. If I was to be sick for 2 or 3 months and get a certificate that a change of climate was necessary to life or permanent disability I could go home, but I would rather remain than to be sick. Duty is not so heavy as heretofore. It has been reasonable, once evry three days for picket.

I am truly glad to know that our Union ticket [was] elected. Conscripting is going on here in this department. The army suckers have to walk up here now there is no buying off or hiring substitute, the only excuse will be "inability." There are a great No. of "Deaf," "Blind," "Lame," and such like. Even some Neutral, some Foreign Citizens Refugees have to stand their chance. Evry Man that Passes examination must be a soldier. All Business Houses, "Shelterings" of evry kind are closed. All Sutlers who are not Regularly Commissioned from the President came under the order.[1] All Sutlers clerks. Some Sutlers have many Clerks. Some of them left home to keep from Soldiering. Now they are just where we want them. I say good for Sherman, a wise order that must be obeyed, Hurrah!

The Lines are still closed against Citizens, nothing in the way of subsistance or Clothing is permitted to go through these lines. Gen Stephenson [sic] says when citizens quit their Guerrilla warfare they can have the Privilege of coming in and not until then. The Gen is boss of this place. When he says no "the thing [is] up". Says he does not like to see women and children suffer and [if] Rebles will act honorably they Shall not so far as he is able to prevent it. We are getting along very smoothly. The Paymaster is here and will pay us again in a few days. The First accident happen[ed] to two of our men a few minutes ago that had ever happened since it had been a Regt. A man let his gun go off accidently and shot two through and through. Both will die to night I think.

My health is fare. It will perhaps remain so if I can take care of myself as I have always done since I came out. The health of the army is generally go[od]. I feel as though sleep would not hurt me, So I will beg leave to close. Remember me to all the family and friend[s] who feel an interest in My welfare & accept my best

respects as ever,

Sam

1. From Sam's comments, apparently, some Northern men had been dodging the draft by entering Union camps as unlicensed sutlers (army-camp peddlers). See note about sutlers in Sam's letter of October 12, 1862.

⇒ ANDREW TO SAM ⇐
Home / November 22, 1863

Dear Son,

Again I have no letter to answer. Amos received one from you last week which brought the gratifying news of your continued good health, that is to us, a great gratification. Yet we are still fearful that so much extra duty as you perform will ultimately break down even the stoutest of men. Is there no remedy for the Evil? Are your associate officers sick, Lazy, or good at Excuses? Is the commanding officer so careless of our fundamental principles ("Equal Rights") as to impose double duty on the willing? Whilst the careless or unwilling get off with half duty or less? Your reputation as a faithful officer and soldier, would certainly receive no Stain by you making the proper complaint before you are broken down. Have the Evil corrected, while you are able for duty.

You need not stay away from home on account of the request to your mother, she has had your socks ready some time before the request came to hand. If it is convenient for you to come home before I have to go away, I would be much pleased. I will have to leave Either the 31st Dec., or 1st Jan at farthest. I should be plagued to hear of you being at home, and [I] not be able to see you, for I am of opinion that I want to see you as bad as any of the family do.

If you cannot come before I start, please notify me in time to come & see you, I presume I can get a leave of absence long Enough to visit home if "I be a good boy." I cannot give you the precise majority in the County. The vote has not been published. My opinion is that from 150 to 200 is about the way the Soldiers vote made things stand. I am, therefore, the Soldiers Representative and will be pleased to represent them faithfully.

We are receiving some war news of interest. Longstreet has undertaken to drive Burnside out of East Tenn, but if our news is correct Burnside don't drive well, and was fully confident of his ability to hold his position and to administer a proper thrashing to his antagonist. If Grant, & Co. will take advantage of Longstreet's absence and thrash Bragg all over, they will have done a good job for their country. We have news of Sherman's arrival with his Corps at Chattanooga, I think Sherman, Hooker, & Thomas, can put them through. If so, and Burnside thrashes Longstreet, we will have gained an important point, for Mead is furnishing Lee enough to do without sending of any more of his troops. Mead is maneuvering all the time & keeping Lee's army in a fighting condition and I would not be surprised to hear that a great battle has been fought there. Mead has certainly out-Generaled Lee in getting a favorable position, and my opinion is that he intends to use it soon.

Our health is fair, no complaint worthy of notice, Miss Clara Sharp died of Diptheria on Wednesday last after a long confinement, she has been sick since the 25th Sept.

We have letters from Will & George last week. Will is still in fair health, and at his post in Chatanooga. George is writing at Headquarters in Louisville, Ky.

Mr. William P. Wiles & Miss Hannah Martin were married on last tuesday morning. Success to them.

Good by for an other week. Accept the love of the family,

and believe me,

Andrew Evans

⇢ ANDREW TO SAM ⇠

Home / Nov. 29, 1863

Dear Son,

Yours of the 15 Nov. came to hand on the 25th which brings us the wealcome news of your continued good health, such news is verry gratifying to us at all times. We found enclosed your Photo, for which you have our kind thanks, we are verry proud of it, tho we would be much better pleased to see the original than the picture. Just send, or bring the original over about Christmas, so I can have look at it before I have to leave, which will be about the last day of the year. Don't wait for the "Socks" they are on hand, ready at any time.

We, us & Co. are as well as usual, your friends generally are well, the general health is verry fair, the weather has been temperate and rather drisly. Friday night we had a good rain which gave us plenty of water for grinding and we used it, up to 11 O'clock last night to good advantage, we had just overhauled and put the wheat side of the mill in good condition, such as cracking the burrs, hanging & tightening up the coarse machinry, repairing the steps gudgeons &c. of both upright shafts, leveling packing bush and jacking. The "[ma]Chine" all runs to suit us and does splendid work, with but little labor to the Miller, our hand can tend with more Ease than two could under the old arrangement. Amos ground at the rate of 8 bushels pr hour, while on wheat yesterday & last night, and made the verry best quality of flour. I want[ed] to overhall the corn mill before I have. It don't run near so smoothly as it should do. It grinds well, but makes too much noise & jar to suit us. The trundlehead will have to be mooved.

Our Army news, is glorious! glorious!! Grant has done just the thing I supposed he would do when Longstreet went away to destroy Burnside & take East Tennessee (which he has failed to do at our last news), but Grant & Co. made his absence pay and gave Bragg a beautiful thrashing. I am sorry his want of provision and forage will not allow him to follow up the advantage he's gained until he runs them into the "last ditch".[1] He could soon do it of he had supplies with him Burnside (at our last news) was holding Longstreet flat, Keeping his communications open, Saving his own men, and killing a good many Rebs. If Longstreet cannot Escape into Virginia, he is a used up Reb. Grant has him decently cut off from Braggs army. I would be surprised if Burnside would "go a peace with him" when he leaves East Tenn. Nothing new from Mead & Lee, they are still working at their old trade trying to outgeneral without a fight.

Our weather has changed considerably in the night time, last night, it cooled off. The ground is considerably frozen, snow has fallen slowly several times to day. It is now 7 PM quite cold with spitting snow. We had the pleasure of a visit by Mr. Tom M. Espy & lady, they came up yesterday evening, staid all night & until afternoon to day. They appear to be quite hapy, I hope they are.

Amos recd a letter from Will last night date 20 Nov. He said he was verry well and Expected to go into the fight verry soon. We are anxious about his wellfare, and shall be until we hear from him. No thing from George since I wrote you.

Accept the best wishes of the family and be assured of our anxiety to see and talk with you whenever your duty will permit.

Your Father,

Andrew Evans

1. Andrew is referring to victories around Chattanooga in November 1863 by Grant and the Union Army over Bragg's outnumbered Confederate force. Bragg had sent General Longstreet's men away in a failed attempt to drive General Burnside from Knoxville. There followed the great Union victories at Lookout Mountain and Missionary Ridge, forcing the Confederate retreat away from Chattanooga. McPherson, *Ordeal by Fire*, 2:338–42.

"Forced into a Responsible Position"

December 1863–November 1864

⟩ ANDREW TO SAM ⟨
Home / December 6, 1863

Dear Son,

Yours of the 22nd of Nov. arrived on the 1st [Dec], better time than usual. We are pleased to know your health continues "fair" and that your duties are getting less. You have already done Enough Extra duty to Entitle you to a leave of absence during this winter, but those who do the most Extra duty, are the most valuable to the service, and of course the authorities are the most reluctant to part from such, hence those who are of the least use to the army get more privileges than better men. We do not desire you to do any act that would injure your reputation as a faithful soldier & officer, but we do believe that you are as much Entitled to leave to visit your friends, as many who have been home once, or more, but as you often say "such is war".

Our health is fair. Amos is complaining of a sore & Enlarged liver, of a few days standing, he is still at work. Your mother is occasionally plagued with Rheumatism, with these exceptions, we are verry well. We have nothing from Will since the battle of Chatanooga, his last that we have recd, was written on the Eve of that great battle, he had his "kit packed" and ready to start. We see by the papers that the 89th was in the fight but no casualties published yet, of our acquaintance. We are again looking with great anxiety for a letter from him.

We have a letter from George but a few days old, he is at Louisville yet mending slowly but not well Enough for field duty. We have a fresh letter from Inda, she and Morty are verry well, she says George has been paid, and that she has received the money. The general health here is verry good, and the weather beautiful, no rain or snow for more than a week.

Army news, has been verry interesting for a while. Grant has shown the rebels that he can fight as well in the center of Rebeldom, as he can on the Miss: he has won a complete & glorious victory over Bragg & his Cutthroat Associates. The last news from Knoxville says, Burnside had

{ 220 } THEIR PATRIOTIC DUTY

thrashed Longstreet and that L. St. was retreating, & B Side following. Sherman was holding the road to Braggs army & Foster would hold the rout[e] into Va. and prevent his retreat in that direction. If all these things are true, Longstreet is caught in his own trap, for he is between three of our army Corps, with his means for supplies cut off, and the three Corps within the sound of a cannon of Each other, I hope Sherman will catch him, for I have as much confidence in his skill, Energy, ingenuity and fearlessness, as any man in [the] army, he is certainly second to no officer in the army. Grant ought to have a great load, with such wheel horses as he has.

We are having most beautiful weather for a week past, rather cold a week ago but gradually the cold has subsided. We have our Beef, hogs etc all stowed away in salt. We butchered our hogs last wednsday. We had 8 little cherubs to spare weighing 1604 lbs which brought us $108.27 at 6 3/4 c[ents]. We have 10 acres of good corn to gather yet which we will enter on tomorrow if no providential hindrance.

Will Tomlinson died on sunday night of the wounds he received in the affray I spoke of in my last. Mitchell, his [illegible] will recover. My competitor did not choose to contest my Election, for he has given me no notice and the time is out, in which he can give notice, all the other officers in the County have been notified in time of said contest.

They hang their hopes on setting the soldiers vote aside as unconstitutional. "Let Er Rip."

Accept our compliments,

Andrew Evans

❧ ANN TO SAMUEL ❦
Home / December 6th, 1863

Dear Brother,

I have not written to you for some time. I thought I would write to you. I got a good long letter from Will a few days ago. He was well then. We got a letter from India. She was well, Morty also. We have killed our hogs. Sam, you had better come home christmas and get some apples to eat, some of everything you want if we have it. We heard the Rebels were in Maysville. Sent out for all the men that could come. We thought they were on us, but they did not come. Old John Morgan has got out. He dug out.[1] He ought to be hung if they get him again. George was at Louisville the last we heard from him. He sent Pap his Ferrotype, he is bloated a good deal.[2] I think your photograph is nice. Sam, do you have to work hard now? Sam, you will soon be an old man, won't you? Pap is writing to George tonight.

I have nothing more to write.

Good night

Your affectionate sister

A. D. Evans

1. Ann is talking about Confederate General John Hunt Morgan's escape from prison.

2. A ferrotype is a type of photograph.

➤ AMOS TO SAM ◄

Dec 10, 1863

Dear Brother

I had the pleasure of receiving yours of the 28th Nov. yesterday. I am very thankful to know you are well. Though I cannot Say as much, Last monday I had a light hemorage of the lungs. Tuesday took flux, both together very nearly took me down, I kep on foot & Succeded in Stopping both but do not feel very stiff yet.

The rest of our family are as well as usual. We rec'd a letter from Will yesterday, he is Still one of the living. He says the last great battle was one of the grandest Scenes he Ever looked upon, He is troubled with disentery though not Serious. George is improving, Inda & Morty are well, Dy Cook has been Sick, Lina is teaching, She & Dy Cook want to visit us Christmas, business is very brisk. Pork & Corn are (the) present Employ. Wheat is active at $1.00 to $1.60. We fin[ished] gathering Corn to day, the New ground yielded 600 bu—60 bu per acre, we have 1000 bu corn yet. We will have made a handsome pile of money this year when we convert our crop into cash—(for two hands). The mill will pay when there is water to run it. We get customers from Manchester to Ripley, frequently. We are pretty nearly ready to meet bad weather if it Should come. There is nothing here worthy of quoting as news, Our Subscription to the Daily ran out & our renewal has not yet come an[d] hense no news for 2 days. I fear we will not have any School this winter as the directors failed to find a teacher. Some one may yet turn up.

Last Sabbath was Quarterly meeting at Bradysville. Next we will have big meeting at Ebeneezer. Rev. W. W. Ramsey is one of the most talented young men I ever Saw, he is improving Every day. Father & Mother are very fond of his Company. I Shall close as there is nothing of interest to write, you have our best wishes for your future Success,

Your brother as ever,

Amos

⇒ GEORGE W. EARLY TO ANDREW EVANS ⇐
Brown General Hospital
Louisville, Ky / December 11, 1863

Dear Father,

Yours of the 6th inst was recd. by me yesterday, carefully read and the tone of it was quite good. I rec. one from India at the same time and answered it last night. She & Morty now very well. I have not heard from Will since the battle, but I got a letter from one of the boys in Co. A, and he said that Will was at the division Hospital on duty, so my conclusion is that he was not in the battle.

Sorry to learn of F.M. Creekbaum's ill health, also of Lieut D Bolts, for they were two of my best friends in the Co. Both intelligent and truthful so far as I know. Sam's duty is heavy yet, if he has picket duty in three days, I think. Old U.S. [Grant] did thrash the very devil out of Ole Corporal Bragg and his cubs. "All quiet on the Potomac" has become too common, for all look for it before they see it. That army is very unfortunate. The rank and file are good, but there is something wrong, too close to Washington I guess. It has won some laurels, and I hope may soon win more.

I fully agree with you in regard to the men who are trying to set aside the soldiers' voting law. I knew, or thought they would just [be] mean enough. How do the common people who voted for the infernal Copperheads think? Do they too think that the soldier should not vote or is it only those who ran and got beaten?

I used to have, what I thought, some good friends in Ohio, who were professors of the Union, but lo and behold they were only wolves in sheeps clothing, for I can never hear from them. Gone, gone, to the devil, I suppose. Too bad.

Thank God that enough still cling fast to the government of our Fathers, to keep the old flag above the land of rebellion. Enough yet stand fast by the boys in the field who are the guardians of American Liberty to encourage them to press onward, and upward, until the last vestige of this ungodly rebellion shall only be on record as among the things that "were." Then peace, that sweet messenger, will be proclaimed to all, and the veteran soldiers will return to that loved home and to the loved ones and only dream of past wars and receive the honors due them. May such a day soon be proclaimed is my ardent wish. Then such as C. A. W. & Co., who oppose the soldiers, will cry for the mountains to fall on them and hide them from the defenders of the Union.[1]

My health is about the same, and I am still writing in the office. The name of the Hospital is changed to "Brown" General Hospital and you will please direct to the Same, My respects to all the friends. Accept for yourself and the family,

Yours as ever,

G. W. Early

1. This refers to Chilton Allen White, the Democratic congressman who represented the Evans's district from 1861 to 1865. "White, Chilton Allen" *Biographical Directory of the United States Congress, 1774–2005* (Washington D.C.: U.S. Government Printing Office, 2005), 2147.

❧ SAM TO ANDREW ❦
Corinth, Miss. / Dec. 12, 1863

Dear Father,

Yours of the 29th ult[imately] came to hand Last evening which brought me The cheering news of your good health. That you would be pleased to see me, I have no reason to doubt. I must say it is extremely doubtful whether you will for a few months. It takes a better excuse than I can find or a "bigger lie" than I am willing to forward to Head Quarters for Leave of Absence. Notwithstanding all that, I would be much pleased to visit home about Christmas and will make an effort To do so. I love to hear of the old Mills continuing to do good work, I think if the mill was in good order I could grind corn yet.

The news from our army is very encouraging. Grant did the work up much sooner than was anticipated by many. The rebs acknowledge quite a heavy loss about 4 or 5000 killed, wounded, and missing. Most of the missing they think deserted. The News from Meads army is "glorious" (in a horn). He has recrossed the Rapidan without being captured. Another Gen will soon try his skill if they will hold on, Grant will be up in that vicinity by an by with his victories. All of Grants Subordinates seem to me to march to landmarks laid out by him. They are better workmen perhaps than those in The Eastern Army. When Grant Frames a building they work closely to the scribe. Perhaps the old saying "That Too Many Cooks Spoil The broth" would be applicable to the Eastern army. I have just finished reading The Presidents Message, rather a glancing or hurried reading, I like it pretty well, it is written, plain and easily understood. I do not like his plan of reconstruction in every respect.[1] There are too many Rebles at home here, in my opinion, To be allowed to go to work and elect Their Representatives and carry on business in a body distinct free from The presence of Federal Troops. I think time has not yet come to reconstruct. Congress organize[d] with less difficulty than I thought. I saw the present speaker of the House Colfax, he is a pretty Sharp looking fellow.[2]

There has been some little fussing in this vicinity. I wrote in my last letter to you [that] we expected a fight here, but [it] did not come. Rebs are getting a "little" tired of Corinth. Instead [of] coming here, they moved in the direction of Pocahou and Lagrange, perhaps with a view of Tearing up and burning RR Bridges cutting off communication from This place. They did not succeed well and almost failed in stopping The cars at all, though the road was cut in several places, Rails and logs piled on the track and fired. Some small Bridges were cut. All was repaired in a few days. The road is now in good running trim. . . .

Nothing more in the way of war news in This vicinity. Weather very rainy and warm, mud plenty and waters high, Streams here are very deep and narrow. Any small stream will Swim a horse although we can nearly jump across.

I have letters from George & Inda same date as yours. Both were well at the writing of their letters. Will has not written to me in some time not since I wrote to him. I received a letter from my old friend Robert B. Gilbert he was well. We had not heard from each other since the battle of Shiloh or shortly after. Well I suppose you will be gone from home soon. I would like to hear from you occasionally. When you write tell me how to direct a Letter. I will continue my home correspondence and will [write] as many other letters as the exigencies of the time demand. I am still well plenty to do, duty is more equally distributed than some weeks ago. Nothing more in the way of news. I send enclosed a likeness of all the officers of this Regt who had their Photos at the time this [was] taken. They are numbered on the face of the card, on The back a corresponding

No with name and rank also to what Co They belong. Keep it, if I ever Live through This war and return home I shall want it, otherwise you can do as you please with it. Most of them are good representatives of the originals.

Remember Me To all the Family

I remain as ever,

Sam

1. On December 8, 1863, President Lincoln issued a proclamation dictating the terms by which he hoped to reconstruct the Southern states. In it he offered pardon and amnesty to all Southerners who took an oath of allegiance to the United States and its laws and proclamations, excepting Confederate officials and high-ranking military officers. If 10 percent of any Southern state's amount of voters from the 1860 election took the oath of allegiance, these loyal citizens would be allowed to constitute a new state government, which would be recognized by the president. James M. McPherson, *Battle Cry of Freedom* (New York: Ballantine Books, 1988), 698–99.

2. Indiana Republican Congressman Schuyler Colfax later served as vice president during President Grant's first term.

⇥ SAM TO ANN ⇤
Corinth, Miss. / Dec. 21, 1863

Dear Ann,

Intended to write to you yesterday but was prevented by heavy [duty] on picket, so I write tonight. I would be pleased to be at home 15 days, including Christmas and New Years, and would give a hundred dollar "green back" if it would only take me there. I have to expose myself at night and of bad weather but do not work otherwise very hard. What makes you think I will soon be old? It has not been [a] long time I came from home. I will be an old man in about 70 years more if I live that long. Maybe you mean an "old Bachelor". That is correct if you do. I don't care if I am. Too many are married now for their own good. I could mention some men who are married and bringing up families that will be a nuisance to the country and a trouble to themselves. Such families are like cattle, as soon as they are dead and gone they are forgotten. They have left no mark behind them. Their lives are as an "empty void", Simply lived to eat and drink and grasped for nothing higher. Do not live for that alone but live for something useful, and when you are gone from this world, future generations will know that you Lived and present generations will feel that you are a loss.

Be a good girl, obedient to your parents, love God and serve Him and you will be happy.

Your brother, Sam

→ AMOS TO SAM ←
Home / Dec. 31, 1863

Dear Brother,

I recd yours of the 17th on the 28, Ann Delia recd one yesterday. I should have written last week but we had a faint hope you would be at home Christmas. But we were disappointed. I will see about your Quarterage, Though I think there is none charge against you Since you left. Thompson Maddox said, the books showed your delinquency 75 cts was all that he knew of. I do not know whether James rec'd any money you Sent or not, I will see the facts. I will send the Advocate of the 30th Dec with this letter. Our health is moderate Joseph is not wel. Most of us have colds & coughs.

Father Started for Columbus this morning on the Magnolia accompanied by Capt West of the 70th. Father hated very much to leave home yet felt that it was his duty to do all he could for his country. We heard from Will yesterday, he & the boys were all well. No thing from George or Inda Since father wrote. I have almost enough to do for one of my years, yet I will Endeavor to act my part, be my lot what it may. I have the mill & farm both resting on my Shoulders and all financial affairs concerning all. I sold our flour to day for $3.00 per hundred, Sacks furnished to be delivered when we please. We sold to McQuilkin & Mrs. Gates. I have a building 20 by 16 or vice versa, to build for the Sheep. I don't know how I will get along Smithing though I will try to do it.

Thomas Evans, Will Wallace & Dy Cook, Tilla & Leina Evans have been here on a visit since last Friday. They went home yesterday.

Amanda Gilbert is at Uncle Samuel Hietts. She will visit us Soon. Uncle had a great chopping & frolic to day, they have a fine rain to help them to night.

We have no teacher [sic, school] this winter for want of a teacher, There are a series of festivals at Ripley this week And a Great Sanitary fair at Cincinnati which will far Surpass all Expectation.[1] it is the greatest Ever yet known & likely larger than any other Ever will be.

We rec'd a Complimentary letter acknowledging the receipt of all that we Sent & thanking us for Exertion in raising & delivering Money. The

Daily publishes all concerning it. Nearly every body went from this County.

There is no news of much interest & I have to write to Will yet to night. Hense you will please excuse the present, Our love to all.

Your Brother as Ever,

Amos A. Evans

1. The U.S. Sanitary Commission began as a voluntary organization to aid in soldier relief efforts. The War Department officially recognized the commission in June 1861. The commission's works included successful lobbying for improved organization of the ambulance corps; providing soldiers with additional food, clothing, and medical supplies; sending nurses and doctors to help staff army hospitals; setting up stops where convalescent and furloughed soldiers could sleep; and instructing soldiers in camp on proper sanitary procedures to help prevent disease. Though run by males, female volunteers did most of the commission's work. Frequently they held "Sanitary Fairs" as fund-raising efforts to support the commission. McPherson, *Ordeal by Fire: Volume 2, The Civil War* (New York: Alfred A. Knopf, 1982), 385.

⇒ ANDREW TO SAM ⇐
House of Reps., Columbus, Oh. / January 5, 1864

Dear Son,

I supposed whilst I was at home that I could write to my friends as often as I please, after getting here, but I have not found it so yet, without neglecting the duties assigned me. I have but a taste yet of legislation, though we have been very busy so far, whether we have done very good, is yet to be determined by the people. We organized very smoothly and have a good set of officers who diligently and faithfully discharge their duties. We have 23 copperheads in the house who are doing all the dirty work in their power in order to procrastinate business, and put responsibilities on the Union members. We will hold them to the work and let the consequences be what they may. They die hard, but they must come under. We are about to adjourn to Thursday morning in order to give the use of the Hall to the State Board of Agriculture tomorrow. Legislation is a slow business, too much talent, and further, that "large bodies move slowly." I like the business no better than I expected and had much rather be at home attending to my own business.

My health is very good. I have a very pleasant room in the "American" with James Loudon, Wm. W. West and Amos Dawson for roommates.[1] All first rate gentlemen. Our boarding is very good and I have nothing to complain of but my absence from home and family. I am not used to that yet and am fearful I shall not [become so]. Otherwise, I am enjoying myself tolerably well. This is a beautiful city, a great deal of copper tin in it.

We have several inches of snow on the ground and pretty cold weather. I have visited none of the public institutions yet, except the State House. It is a splendid edifice, perhaps not excelled in the Union. In as much as wages are low and boarding high, I shall seek only such enjoyments as cost nothing or nearly so. I desire to visit (during my stay here) all the Benevolent institutions of this place and the penitentiary. I will write you again in course of a week as I have nothing for news now. I will close by assuring you of the high regard of,

Your father,
Andrew Evans

1. For more about state Senator James Loudon, see note in Andrew's letter of August 16, 1863. For more about state Representative W. W. West, see note in Andrew's letter of October 18, 1863.

❧ ANDREW TO SAM ❧
HR Columbus, Oh. / Jan. 12, 1864

Dear Son;

I have been at the Capital City Eleven days, and have not received one word from home, or from any friend from any other quarter, I am fearful I shall get the blues, if I don't hear from home soon. My health was very good during the 1st week, but since that time it has not been so good. The change of water, air or diet, or perhaps all combined, has considerably disturbed the peace of my bowells. I have been on duty all the time but not feeling as comfortable as I would wish, perhaps I will become acclimated soon and get along better, I hope so at least. I would not give the Blacksmith shop, and the comforts of home connected therewith, for the honor of the legislative hall. I feel no elevation from my position, and feel no diffidence, or fear that I will not do right, yet I cannot drive home from my sight, . . . I also feel that no flattering inducements can draw me from the path of virtue.

The Inauguration of Gov. Brough passed off yesterday, it was truely a grand, and imposing scene. I can offer no idea of the numbers present, they would have to be estimated by the Acre, both Military & civil. The address is one of the best and ablest documents that Ever emanated from any of our great statesman, Either Ancient, or modern. With such a Governor and such a Legislature as I think we have, we cannot get far astray, May the ruler of the Universe, aid and guide us in the true path, and so guide us through the turmoils of the times, that our actions may result in the general good of the whole people.

We have but little in the way of news that would interest you, the wether has been exceedingly cold since we arrived here, it is slightly moderating now. The ice is about nine inches thick on the Scioto river, verry large amounts of the article are already put away for summer use.[1]

This is a splendid City for excellent music, we can hear the best of music Every night, without leaving our rooms. I have visited none of the places of amusements yet, nor do I know when I shall, we are in session and I must close.

Father,

Andrew Evans

1. This refers to the process of collecting ice from frozen rivers in the winter and saving it for refrigeration purposes in the summer.

⇥ SAM TO ANDREW ⇤
Corinth, Miss. / Jan. 17, 1864

Dear Father,

Yours of the 27th of Last Month and the 5th of this Month have just been received I am very glad to know that you can at least write once in a while to me. It is cheering to hear that matters at home are passing off Smoothly. You speak as though, "you would rather be at home than where you are," that may all be so but we cannot always be at home. I am Satisfied in my mind that our family will not Suffer in your absence. They have plenty to eat and wear and as for more, we need not be particular. I am not sure many men could Leave their families for a few months at a better advantage than yourself, notwithstanding your presence may be needed at home. Perhaps your abstainance from heavy Labor may recruit [renew?] your health.

Well, Last Night had powerful "Scare" here. Evry thing was turned "topsa turva" in about 4 minutes.

About 8 o'clock Last Night we received orders to be ready to march at a moment's warning consignment. Preparations were being made for a march. About the time every thing was well torn up, The 2nd order came Stating that the 1st order [was] wrong, that we must be ready to "fall in" at a moment's and not to "March." That we were going to be attacked. All the while it was raining like fury.

Morning came, we fell in. No Rebs have yet been seen to "Scare" much. We will perhaps move from here some time during the coming week in the direction of Memphis. It is the opinion of some that we will remain there. But I do not console myself with any such "Stuff," I only guess at things. I think we will move in to Arkansas or down along the Miss coast and perhaps none of us have guessed. I think that this place will be evacuated, this R Road so far as Grand Junction and the Road from the Junction opened to Columbus, Ky. I give this not as authentic, but is a kind of "Rumored fact." Several of the old Regts. whose time is almost expired have "reenlisted" the 7th Kansas (jayhockers) Cav have all Reenlisted, most of the 3rd Mich Cav have also.

The weather is extremely rigorous. New Years day was cold, 20 below "o". It [is] very much like[ly] exposure to the kind of weather we have for a month would "Shorten a man's" days But it does not seem to affect me.

My health is very good, and it [sic] the service requires it of me at this time be cause I have sole control of Co. A now, Capt. James C. Foster has tendered his resignation and I have receipted for all of the Co. Property. 2nd Lt. Calvin A Campbell is Sick. I have no orderly Sergt. Why Capt. Foster Resigned I will tell in some future Letter and then I do not know how interesting it will be to you. So with "these few remarks I leave the floor for a more able Speaker".[1]

Give My Respects to Capt. West and accept My Respects and Best Wishes for Your Welfare

As ever,

Sam

1. Sam is teasing his father about his position as a legislator.

ISABELLA EVANS[1] TO SAM
Home / Jan. 31, 1864

Dear Brother,

I seat myself to write you a few lines as I have not written you a letter for a long time. It is raining this evening, very muddy. I think it will snow pretty soon. Mary is writing to Father Amos is writing to Will. You said you got no letters from home. I don't know what is the reason, some of us write to you every week and if you don't get them it is not our fault.

Mary rec a letter from Will last week he was well, he was getting along fine. Amos has been grinding flour last week. I have been helping to sweep the mill for him. Old Dr. Wylie Died last Sunday night of bilious colic, he died very sudden, was not sick long.[2]

Cousin Amanda Gilbert came down to see us, stayed two or three days with us. Sam if you don't come home pretty soon and get married all the folks will get ahead of you. There was one great wedding went off to day, Samuel Hawks and Lucy Lentenny, they were a pretty couple. I think I shall start to school in the morning if nothing happens. It is such a bad road to our school house I don't how I will like the young butternut. I can learn anyhow. I wish you could come home and teach a good school for us, if you don't come home for two years and a half I won't know you. If you can get a chance you had better come home sooner.

Some of our potatoes froze in that cold air weather but none of your apples were hurt. If you just come over you can have as much good cider and apples as you want and anything else. We have plenty of good cabbages and potatoes if you like them as well as you used to. Sam I weigh 137 pounds you will not know [me] if you stay away to long. Ann looks just like she used to not grown much. Joe is big and fat works like an old man. Lee is the greatest mischief you ever saw.

Father came home last sunday morning, started back on tuesday morning, was not very well when he went back. We have not heard from him yet. All the rest of the folks are well as common. Mother is scarcely ever well of the rheumatism. I have written enough foolishness. I remain as ever your true Sister.

With truth,
Isabella E. Evans

1. Isabella was fourteen years old at the time of this letter.
2. A bilious colic is severe pain in the abdomen, caused by bile or liver problems.

⇾ AMOS TO SAM ⇽
Home / February 4, 1864

Dear Brother,

Yours of Jan. 11th came to hand on the 23rd. & owing to a throng in the mill I did not get up with my correspondence. I generally write from

6 to 12 letters per week as time may permit. I hope you will excuse me this time as I had to mill day & night often. I am very glad to hear of your good health. Ours is good, all were well. Father was at home 2 days & went back sick. We recd a letter from him written last Sabbath, he was better but not entirely well—Also a note from Inda [and] one each from George and Will—they are all well but George & he is better. The cold weather has subsided & it is now moderate and changeable.

I am alone without help & have a rough time of it, but while I have health I can stand it well. The river is now open & trade is brisk, Wheat is worth $1.25 pr. bu, Corn 75 to 80. I have ground about 200 bu of our wheat so far. The mill continues to keep her reputation up as the best in the Country. And [sic] old Gent from Cincinnati came to me a few days ago to buy our flour for his own bread. Persons from Riply come here to mill occasionally.

How do you like the 500,000 call [for more troops] of March 10, don't it suit? And do you like the Service you are now in? Do you think of reinlisting? How are your finances? Please acquaint me with money matters &c, though private it is prudent for us to know. Should you be so unlucky as to lose your life, There is not one [who] knows anything of your affairs. Answer these questions if you think proper—Will Sends nearly all of his money home & at least once in 3 months sends a list of what he has—including moneys &c. He has sent home about $300.00.

William Botner was here Since reinlisting & left $200.00, he has now $400.00 here for safe keeping. Numbers of the boys are reinlisting, this is a hard lick on the Rebels to see old troops still ready to face them.

I don't think the folks could do without me or I would have gone long ago. I keep up all our own repairs, I am a pretty fare botch. I made an axeltree for our Spring wagon & Drove it today. We will try to Ripley to-morrow, I had to put Brass boxes in the Smutter for bearings. There has not been a Cog broken since you left. I watch & mend before anything breaks.

We still have plenty of Apples to sell & keep. We are getting 75 cts per bu now. There is but little news here now. Some of the girls have had curious ailments from the Effect of the too frequent use of the "Root".

Our Revivals are having a good Effect generally. Capt. Sharp is already Class leader in Aberdeen—fast promotion though very worthy. Meeting at Fitches 2 weeks from next Sabbath, it is expected to hold 2 weeks. Mr. Games Said he had never rec'd any money from you since you left.

I Saw all the girls in town Sat. night. Cal Says "She fears Sam is mad at her" What for Eh! [I] Don't believe it yet.

I have concluded to stay here next summer & go to school thereafter for three or more years if possible. Then get a good farm & go to living if it can be done. This is anticipation

Lafayette & Sam Hiett give send [sic] their Respects. All join in sending their love to you. I will send an Advocate with this.

I am as Ever your Brother,

Amos A. Evans

⤞ SAM TO ANDREW ⤝
Memphis, Tenn. / February 10, 1864

Dear Father,

Your kind letter of the 1st of Feb [was received] on the 8th and was heartily read on the 9th. I recd a letter from friend West. Today one from home, all were well. I was sorry to know that you[r] health was not good, but hope it will improve, I am very glad the Legislature sustains the President in his efforts to put down this infamous Rebellion. By that we are assured that State stands by her brave "Sons" in the field, who I am happy to say have no Superiors either as to disciplin or Bravery.

There are men in our own township but "Little" better than the worst enemy in the field, and while the old soldiers are at home I have [hope] they will meet with their just desserts. I should Like to be at home while the boys are there but cannot be abscent [sic] from here. It Seems to me that [I] will not be able to get home till the war is over "unless I should be sick". I would rather stay the remainder of my time than to be sick, although a man may get a certificate from a Surgeon that a change of climate is necessary to Save Life when but little is the matter if he will court it and make of himself a "Sick [man]—" That is more than I have been able to do yet. It is not honest.

You can board cheaper than we can here and perhaps you can have nearly as good to eat as we can. I think we are living now well enough for soldiers. There is but little news to communicate. We are plagued a Little with old Forest, he is reported to be within 6 miles of here with considerable force.[1] Nothing serious is anticipated from him. We have force enough to whip two or three such armies as his and not be badly "strained." He may succeed in capturing some pickets and devil them in one way or another, but if he will come up and fight like a man, he can have all he can make off of us, if We are Nigger as some call us.

There are more Smugglers about these lines than any place I have ever been. I have almost concluded that every woman who passes these lines, carries contraband goods and that perhaps in "regions" you would least misstrust them. I have been under the painfull necessity of examining the bosoms and hoops of quite a No Since I have been on picket, Women say "we are very mean" but we ask them no add[itional item]s, and by the examinations have been able to send several women to the "Irvin[g] Block" (Military Prison).

I found a woman a few days ago that was Loded with "Quinine". She wore a hoop skirt, the hoops were between broad tape about 1 1/2 inches wide and suspended by broad tape nearly the same width and at each cross of hoop and suspenters was a Small bag or pocket filled with Quinine. There were 5 hoops and 12 suspenders consequently there were 60 sacks all full of medicine—a sack one by two inches will hold a very large dose of the Stuff. When I asked the woman what made her skirt so heavy she told nothing, I then touched the hoops and gave them a little stroke which convinced me that there was some thing wrong. I found the Quinine and sent her under guard to the general who after investigating the case a little had her in Prison. She offer[ed] to give me 500, in Green backs if I would let her pass and not send here to "Hd Qrs" That money would have been very casily made but I thought perhaps that medicine might save the life of a Rebel who would take mine if he could and the surest way would be to save her while I could. Well enough of this. It is getting late and I will be on Picket tomorrow. I am thankful for the Compliments and good wishes of Gen Loudon, West & Dawson & ["]Co" and in return please to extend to them mine. Write when you can and I will do the same. Excuse this bad letter, I will try to do better in the future. I am well. The health of officers and Men of the Regt is generall good.

I am as ever your affectionate Son,

Sam

1. Memphis slave trader Nathan Bedford Forrest, the only lieutenant general on either side to rise from the rank of private, was a skilled cavalry commander, regarded as one of the Civil War's most dangerous generals by contemporaries on both sides. One of Forrest's major responsibilities during the latter part of the war was harassing Sherman's Western supply lines as he moved southeast through Tennessee and Georgia. As a consequence, Forrest frequently operated in the same vicinity as Sam's unit. Because of his guerilla tactics and alleged brutality, Forrest was much despised by

Northerners. His name was further besmirched by the Fort Pillow Massacre (see note in Sam's letter of April 24, 1864) and his role as the first grand wizard of the Ku Klux Klan. Throughout the letters, Sam repeatedly spells his name incorrectly as "Forest." Jack Hurst, *Nathan Bedford Forrest: A Biography* (New York: Alfred A. Knopf, 1993), 4–6, 361.

⇢ SAM TO ANDREW ⇠
Memphis, Tenn. / Feb. 28, 1864

Dear Father,

Your kind Letter of the 18th came to hand on the 24th which gave me much Pleasure. The day upon which you[r] Letter was written was just [two] years since I Left The Old Homestead. Perhaps it was rather unexpected to you but not so much so by me as I had thought of going to the war whenever the 70th did. It would give me great satisfaction to see all of the folks at home and I do not doubt but that all would be pleased to see me.

"I would willingly be reinstated comfortably at home" if the war ended but could never be otherwise, I could not and would not Stay at home, 2 months, with health, and the war still going on. Home would be desolate, or seem so.

I may be fortunate enough yet to see the end of this war, with Peace and the Perpetuity of this glorious old Union forever, for which her gallant defenders have struggled so nobly to sustain. May God hide from me the day when such another struggle [sic]. May we be enabled to hand down to future generations this Glorious Union as it was to us Cemented by the blood of the fallen Brave. That Banner and that god that was a guide for Washington, Still is ours and will lead us to victory. I never want to see this government entrusted to recreant rulers.[1]

I believe you had some acquaintance with Maj Brown before he left camp Ripley. The Maj is considerable of a military man. Maj said when I left I left [sic] the 70 he did not know what he would or how he would do without me. Maj Brown, I understand, has been Promoted to Lieut Col, Cockerel to Brig Gen, [D. W. C.] Loudon to Col, &c&c. What is Carpenter's rank? I received a document from Everes of Brown yesterday, I like the document very well it offers information that can not be [illegible] else where. The Buckeyes here in the Regt all have to see it. I think Gen Grant's name should have been in this document, he was sent to West Point from our state, if I mistake not.[2] Sherman and McPherson are two as fine Gens are in this war. Smith, Rosecrans, and others, Ohio can boast of as good Generals as any other state and as many of them.

All is quiet here at Prison. Smith (Gen.) has returned from his tour round through Mississippi and has accomplished all he intended. I will enclose you Horace Manard's speech made at Memphis a few days ago, I think is good. Read it if you have not read it ere you receive it and hand it around that others may know how a Slave holder (Ex) talks.

Nothing more to write. I am quite well.

I am as ever,

Your son,

Sam

1. The word recreant means disloyal and cowardly.

2. This document seems to have been a list of Ohio Generals. Grant was born and raised in, and sent to West Point from, Ohio, but rejoined the military early in the Civil War as Colonel of the 7th District Regiment of Illinois Volunteers. Brooks D. Simpson, *Ulysses S. Grant: Triumph over Adversity, 1822–1865* (Boston: Houghton Mifflin Company, 2000), 10, 83.

⇻ AMOS TO SAM ⇺
Home / March 2, 1864

Dear Brother,

I rec'd yours of Feb 14th on the 21st it was thrice welcome & good. Now that Mothers inquisitiveness is for a time gratified, I will make a short apology for the manner in which I wrote concerning your affairs. Mother was always at me to write & make inquiry about you & not tell you she wanted it done for fear you would not tell her. You know a Mothers anxiety to see her Children do well. Pardon me for the act. I am far from being so medalsome, I am trying to protect the property & save all intrusted in my care. I am glad to see all do well, I have been forced into a responsible position in our family & I hope I may be enabled to prove worthy of trust. It is not my desire but I am not to be my own to choose. God has so ordained it.[1]

If you will give me the Name of the Express Co., The amounts & dates of the Money you sent home I will get it for you. If you delay too long it might be hard to get. You ought to have the receipts in your possession. If so send them to me & I will insure the money. I have collected considerable from Express since this war came. The Adams Express is about the safest. Use your pleasure about this but I do not like to see anyone loose money when there is no necessity of it. Not a cent has been recd by Express from you yet. Botners boys send all of their money by letter, but that is not safe. Will Sends his by State Agency or Agents. I do not charge you with neglect but I fear you will charge me with meddling. Brother I do not want to be so. I want to help you if I can.

I do not intend to leave our Parents unless times are more favorable. You know I need Schooling but I cannot get it without making our home look deserted & the family uncomfortable, that I will not do. I never intend to "marry a farm" if I should Sacrifice respect by so doing. I want to own a farm first then they often clap. Girls are making a very free use of leep Year but they can't make it pay until the war ends.[2] I want to be further South & get a good fruit farm. I Shall first aspire to an Education if I never [sic] get it. Enough.

We rec'd letters from Father, Will & George since writing. Father & Will are well. George is better. Father had just visited the big nursery at Columbus, he was highly pleased etc.

Our fruit prospect is much injured by the Severe weather. Peaches are nearly all killed. Wheat is at least 1/2 killed if not more. The weather has been very changeable, Rain, Snow, freeze & thaw all in 2 or three days. I have been milling this week, I ground 128 bu grist works Monday. I have got David King & Jacob Mitchell to work on the Sheep house, we will raise it tomorrow evening if nothing happens.

We hear Several reports that our Quota is filled in this township by volunteering. I would like to see some of our Val men Drafted.[3] I am very sleepy. Our folks are all well, Neighbors also, save old Patsy O Conner who is very sick. I have Sent you Several Advocates this year, did you get them & shall I still send them until you do get them?

All send their respects. I am very truly,

Your Brother,

Amos

1. Sam's letters to Amos from February 14 and 21 have not survived. Apparently Amos wrote Sam, at his mother's urging, to inquire about financial matters, and Sam indicated some resentment in his reply. Amos is the oldest son left at home and, with Andrew at Columbus, is the only male in the Evans household who is able to handle financial matters.

2. During leap years, women are traditionally allowed to propose to men, rather than vice versa; 1864 was a leap year.

3. For a note explaining the Union military draft, see Andrew's letter of August 3, 1862.

✥ AMOS TO SAM ✥

Home / March 17, 1864

Dear Brother,

Yours of march 2nd came to hand on the 12th. We were truly glad to hear from you. I rec'd letters from father, Will, George & Inda to night. All are well. George is at Feesburg on a Short leave of Absence. He is now in the invalid Corps [at] Cincinati.[1] Will has been in another battle & got through Safe. He is near or in Ringold, Ga. The folks here are all well — Some light Colds. I have a kind of big head to night.

Mrs. Ephra[i]m Martin died last Friday. Henry & Sam are both sick, also James' little boy, they are mending a little. There is no other sickness near us. Joseph Steward is up the hill, he got thrown from his horse & his leg broke. Miss Leoncy Darnell & Mr. James Fance were married last thursday—they took a bridal trip to the City [Cincinnati]. All is quiet here, no Candidates out yet for township offices. Men are trying to shun the draft in every way possible. The last 200,000 call is a damper on the butternuts. Times have got so that it is hardly possible to hire hands. We have no help at all & are trying to keep along with the usual amount of work. We cannot keep up much longer. The weather is so bad that we cannot do much on the farm.

Father went to the Express office in Maysville but did not find any money or learn anything of your money. Little Thom did marry—on the 3rd, his woman's name is Mary L. Riddings, he had her picture with him when he was here Christmas. She is a fine looking woman.

I do not get to splurge around any with the women & I guess some fellow is about try his hand with one that I have been eyeing. If he gets her there will be some left & I ain't in a hurry. Any way Cal & Mollie Thompson are coming out Saturday & will stay until Sunday Evening. And So it is. Davis has got another Boy. There is no news here of interest. Wheat is beginning to look better. I believe I never told you that we have got grand Ma's, Drs & John's tombstones up, they are very nice—the same as Grand Pa's.[2]

We levied a rent of one percent on wheat for Storage this year—
Nothing more but remain,
Yours,
Amos A. Evans

1. The Invalid Corps was composed of disabled soldiers. They were usually employed in garrison and other non-combat duties. Garrison, *Encyclopedia*, 121.

2. "Dr" (doctor) refers to Dr. Abraham Evans, Will's twin brother, who died May 4, 1862. For more about Abraham, see note in Andrew's letter of March 9, 1862.

❧ AMOS TO SAM ❧
Home / March 27, 1864

Dear Brother,

Your very interesting favor of the 12th came to hand on the 19th. This is not my regular time of writing but I am at leisure & I will write. I think mothers curiosity about your affairs are satisfied. Mary rec'd a letter from you yesterday & Little Jane one. I rec'd one from Will & one [from] father this week, they are well. Father will be home next Thursday. Will is at Ringold Ga. They are very busy at that point. George is at Cincinnati in the Invalid Corps. Inda & Morty were not so well as usual when we last heard from them. The general health here is good. Samuel Martin was burried last Sabbath, his mother about a week before him. Henry & Jane's child is better.

I think I have some idea how much you have to do, I Served 2 weeks on the different Raids about here or, as they should be called, "Scares".[1] I was gone 9 days when I was drafted. The Commissioners placed me in Command of the Co. which numbered 126 drafted & 40 Substitutes. I had to make all reports, Rolls, &c according to Army rules & regulations [and] also draw Rations, Call the roll &c. When we were Examined I clerked [took notes] for the Surgeon and I wrote all the discharges (they had no blanks) & etc.

Enough of this. The weather is pleasant now. We finished our sheep house this past week. It is 16 by 20 feet 2 story of 6 feet in the clear—a partition across below to seperate the flock at pleasure. It is set op[po]site the first spring up the hollow. It is well fixed for feeding & running. It is the best building of its size for sheep I Ever Saw, not because it is on my place or anything but it is so.

We are stirring the ground for oats & garden & pushing spring work generally. We have a Kentucky lad working for us but I think he wont do to bet on. I will now answer on your business Else you will think I do not care for you. Father called at the Express office when he was at home last but Could not find any money or information about it, Gaines never rec'd any. Neither did we receive any receipts, Armstrong never mentioned receiving any money or letter. I will be down to Riply Soon & will make Enquiries on the subject. Will always forwards by State Agents I will Send you a Copy of all Accts not Collected on a Slip of blank book.

The Mill is all in good condition as our work will prove. Your tools are as well cared for as our own. Your fine hand Saw is rusted some but not to serious injury. Your little Rifle is in as good condition as it ever was. I do not get to shoot often but keep the Guns all right. Your big Pistol is all O.K.

Mother Says all of your other things are all right. She Says come over & See how they are yourself & you will . . . says in Marys letter you do not care for your Property. I think you should care. I saw Cud Carrigan have a plow of your pattern a short time ago but could not drive the wagon fast Enough to catch up with him. He had it on his shoulder & was riding in a trot toward town, when we got within 50 yards he turned up the Pike at the Bridge. I will make him answer a few questions the first time I See him.

There is nothing strange about here. Very few Candidates out yet, none worth mentioning. There will be a big draft here I thing [sic]. Wheat is nearly froze out. Peaches are all dead—we have plenty on hand yet. We have about 700 bu of Corn yet & 100 lbs of apples & plenty to Eat. I have got out of conceit of the South.

Accept my regards. I am as Ever,

Your Brother,

Amos

[Notes written on letter] Mother says she is saving a can of nice Pears for you for when you come home. All is quiet here. Butternuts lay low & growl. Is the Small Pox among your darkies? Grant & Sherman are just where I have long wanted them to be.[2] Annie encloses a note to you. If you Capture any Southern Ladies Photos Send us one for Curiosity. I have Sent you Several Advocates, I do not know why you do not get them. There is not much to write about. Some of the girls are enjoying Leap Year.

Your brother,

Amos

1. Apparently Amos served two weeks on patrol during the panics resulting from the various raids of John Morgan into Kentucky and Ohio.

2. Here Amos is probably referring to Grant and Sherman's new positions. In March 1864 the Senate confirmed Grant as general-in-chief. With Grant's move to

Washington, Sherman took over the Military Division of the Mississippi, making him the leading Western commander. John F. Marszalek, *Sherman: A Soldier's Passion for Order* (New York: The Free Press, 1993), 256–57.

➤ SAM TO ANDREW ◆

Memphis, Tenn. / March 27, 1864

Dear Father:

I have had a good deal to do. Having been the only officer [fit] for duty in the Co. for a considerable time. I have received to [sic] speeches from you of Late. Thanks. They are good and sensible to the point. I received a Letter from Amos and you a short time ago. The freezing was done on the 1st day of Jan. That I wrote about. I may have written so as to convey a different Idea having written it in a hurry. I did not write as I recollect about it at the time, but I feel the effects very often now. My feet have hurt considerable for a few days since the weather has moderated a little.

You will notice by the heading of my letter that the name of our Regt. has been changed. Adjutant General Thomas has given us a national No. We should have had a no some where in the teens.[1] Address to me Co. A 59th U.S. Infantry (Colored). Gen Forest has gone up to Union City so the papers say. All is quiet here nothing of importance. I am still well but feel very dull and sleepy having been on picket or rather was on Last night and did not sleep any. I would like you to inquire what Smith & Wesson pistols sell at now. I mean the no. 3, 6 inch barrel they are selling for 26$ here. The same size of John's the one he bought of[f] Machabel. I still think I would Like to visit home, and will as soon as I can have an opportunity. Some of the officer[s] are gone home now on Leave. I have been getting bounties for orderly sergeants who have been out over 2 years. I have succeeded very well so far.

Well Give My respects to all and excuse haste I will write again soon.

I am as ever,

Your Affectionate son,

Sam

1. When all black troops were federalized, they were given USCT (United States Colored Troops) numbers that did not necessarily correspond to the regiments' lengths of service.

H.R. Columbus, Oh. / Mar. 27, 1864

Dear Son:

I have allowed myself to be so closely confined to business that I have neglected to write you as often as I had desired to do.

I find much more correspondence necessary with my constituents than I had supposed. I received many business letters, and, of course, have to answer them, both from citizens and soldiers, quite a number from the Army, asking some enquiry to be made of some of the military departments of the State.

I have, by attending to all such matters, become pretty well acquainted with most of the men at the heads of departments. These things, together with writing home twice a week, has kept me busy during the legislative recesses. I have nothing of unusual interest to write you, we are drawing near the close of our session.

We think of adjourning on the 30th. I think of going home whether they do or not, for I am extremely tired of staying here, and neglecting my business at home. My health is, and has been verry good for the last eight weeks, the general health of the members is good, but a few of them are sick at home, one member of the Senate is dangerously sick with Pneumonia, in an adjoining room to ours. The weather is verry fine now, which increases my anxiety to be at home. I got a letter from home last night, the folks were all well, I have nothing from Will in the last two weeks, he was well when wrote, he had been in another fight and was at Daulton in Georgia. I had a letter from Inda last week, she and Morty were neither well at the time.

I was at big "Aster high," last night. Saw a great deal of wine drinked & heard a great deal of noys [sic], but I came out, as sober as I went in. There were a few members who could not say as much in truth, but it is a common remark here, that this is the soberest Legislature ever assembled here. We have but one member in the house, that has been out of [illegible], or that indulges in "Ardent" [spirits] to any extent, and I think they have not one in the Senate. The liquor sellers cannot make it pay of this Legislature. When I get home, I shall endeavor to resume my regular correspondence with you, and shall expect a reciprosity in your part.

Our friend W W West has received an order to go into the recruiting service as soon as our session ends, he may not go to the front for some time, he has fattened this winter until his clothes are too small. He weighs near 200 pounds, and is some 20 or 25 pounds heavier than when he came here. Loudon & Dawson are well, and we four are rooming together yet, and are all right. You have their compliments tendered.

Truly your father,

Andrew Evans

➤ SAM TO ANDREW ◄

Head Qrs. 59, U.S. Inf (Colored) Memphis, Tenn. / April 3, 1864

Dear Father:

Your kind favor of the 27th came to hand on the 1st and was a welcome visitor. Yesterday I recd a letter from each Mary and Amos. In your previous letter you advised me not to write to you any more at Columbus. Consequently it has been some time since I wrote to you. But I think I can not be as closely confined for the Coming month as during the former and will endeavor to write home at my regular intervals.

I am glad to know that we have had one temperate Legislature and it might be termed a very peculiar and Isolated Case. I cannot say as Much for "The Military Dist. of Memphis." From appearances from and after today it will be bettered. Gen Hurlbut has issued an order that no officer or enlisted man shall visit Memphis unless bearing a pass from his commander and shall not be allowed to remain in town over nights without Special permission from the Gen Comm[an]d[in]g [the] District and has ordered a heavy Camp Guard placed around the different Camps to enforce the order. This order does not effect me in the least. I should think that Gen Hulbert [sic] is coming down to what is not his place to order. It is said he has become rich by swindling the government at this Post and likely is so, but I do not know that fact. Know one thing, he drinks a great deal more than a sober man could. He may be all right but I can not see it so. Gen. Buckland, the Post Commander or rather Dis'[tri]ct Commander is a "Man" sober and just, kind and frank. He commanded our brig at the Battle of Shiloh. I know he is "brave". At that time he was Col. of the 72nd Ohio, is now a Brigadier [General].

Sometime during week before lass [sic, last] Gen Forest sent in a flag of Truce to Gen Buckand that if he (Buckland) did not release some prisoners that were confined in the Military Prison at this place that he would take the place, Buckland told him to come in if he thought he could make it pay, but Forest did not wait a reply but moved on in the direction of

Union City, captured the place and undertook [to capture] Paducah but Col Hicks of the 40 Ills [Illinois] did not Scare much when threatened to have no quarters shown him. He did not surrender said he "did not see it". If the papers do not lie it was a considerable slaughter on the Reb side.

There is nothing of much interest in this vicinity. There is still some smuggling going on and quite a number are being detected in it. There is considerable horse stealing going on but have not yet been able to find who does it. With the exception of Small Pox, the health of the Army is pretty good. Some 10 or 12 Negros (Enlisted [men]) of this Regt. have died of it. As soon as a case is know the patient is sent to Small Pox hospital. Nearly all of the Regt. have been vaccinated. I have been vaccinated Several times since I have been in the Army but it never takes.[1] I don't go where it is any more than my duty requires. It might be with small pox as measles was with me, got it when I did not know any one had it. We are going along quite smoothly. The name of this Regt has been changed our designation is now viz, 59 Regt, U.S. Inf. (Colored). Our rank is higher, but the Regt went by the old designation while there were 58 national Nos. before this. Our ranking No. is now about 15 I think. All letters to me directed should be to the 59 US Inf (Colored).

I am well, have been. Will answer Amos and Mary's Letters soon. My Respects to all the Family.

I am as ever,

Sam

1. Union Army regulations required the administration of smallpox vaccinations. This regulation acted sufficiently to prevent widespread infection but there was a roughly 0.5 percent annual incidence of small pox among Union soldiers. Also, the importance of revaccination was frequently unrecognized and practiced only sporadically. Unsanitary and ineffective methods of vaccination also account for some of the instances of smallpox. George Worthington Adams, *Doctors in Blue: The Medical History of the Union Army in the Civil War* (Baton Rouge: Louisiana State University Press, 1980), 219–20.

⇢ ANDREW TO SAM ⇠
Home / April 10, 1864

Dear Son,

I was glad to hear that you are still in good health, which is more than I can say for myself. I came home in good health and found Amos quite sick in bed, and many things suffering for attention, I pitched in a little too deep for my strength, and gave out myself. I tended the mill two days of last week and let down again, since that time I have been "going slow" and am getting along pretty well, and am fit for light duty, and my health improving finely. Amos is going about and improving slowly. The residue of our family are in usual health, and looked about as glad as I felt, at my arrival at the old home.

We are having a backward spring, a good deal of rain and not much creek. There is but little ground broken for corn, and the ground will be too wet for several days if it rain no more.

The wheat has been injured by freezing during winter, so much so, that many fields are being put in other crops but these warm rains are reviving many lots that appeared to be dead, ours will be a half crop or more if nothing injures it hereafter . . . Our oats were sown when I came home and the flax ground ready, but it had been so rainy that we have not sowed it yet. We have but little garden made, some peas & some onions. We expect to plant a bushel of onion sets [slip or shoot for planting] as soon as the ground gets dry enough. We shall be very th[o]rough with out door work. We will tend the early garden too. We expect to plant all below the walk in . . . onions. Amos will plant 1000 or more peach trees in nursrey form on the upperside and we will sow the residue in potatoes &c. We will not plant more than 19 acres of corn this season, hands are scarce and high priced $20 pr month and that will not pay these days.

We have had many visitors today, A. B. and Dyas Gilbert, Nelly Housh and Sarah, Geo Sibbald, little Jane, Hannah Hiett &c. We had two letters from Will since I came home, he is in good health. Nothing very late from George or Inda. The general health is fair here, some cases on lung fever, but none fatal.

You would do well to keep at a fair distance from Smallpocks, tho I do not think you would be likely to take it. It has been [at] Columbus all winter and I did not take it.

I shall endeavor to write you once a week, if my health and condition will permit. If your convenience will permit you may reciprocate. I am caught so near in the dark with this that the lines are not in my way. The family send Love and compliments,

Truely your Father,
Andrew Evans

Home / April 21, 1864

Dear Brother,

I have unavoidably missed my regular time of writing, The reason why you are perhaps aware of ere this, I had a little touch of hemorage followed by cough & general debility which used me pretty roughly. I have had no physician & am now I think in the safe side of the ditch—I can get out & do light work, but lift nothing. My breathing is short & laborious yet, I cannot walk fast for 2 minutes at a time.

Father is not well yet, not much better able to work than I am. All the rest are about as usual. I rec'd a letter from George this Evening. He is in the City & very well, will go to the field as soon as transferred.

We have letters from Inda & Will of recent date, they are both well. Will is Still at Ringold, Ga. He Said it was rumored they would go to Richmond, but he doubted it very much. I have not rec'd a letter from you since I got sick more than three weeks ago. Father received one from you last week.

There is but little news here of interest. I believe no one has given you the Election news. I will give the result—John Buchanan (union), William Fulton & Jacob Cooper (Butternuts) Trustees[;] Jn O'Mitchel But[ternut], Treas[urer][;] Ezekiel Cooper But[ternut], Clerk[;] Samuel Hiett [illegible] (Union) Assessor[;] Elijah G. Holton (Union). Const[able][;] Father, Supervisor of No. 8, School Director No. 6 & Township Librarian. The School library is concentrated into a Township library So that Each Dist. can draw its No. of Books & by so doing affect an Exchange of Reading.

The Board (T[ownshi]p) have furnished father with a glass front Case to keep the books in. We will have School commence the 1st of May—by Amanda P Gilbert—(uncle Johns Amanda). Sallie E Housh is now going to the Decatur Academy. W. G. H. is clerking to the Comissary at Mount Sterling Ky. Perry Huron has sold his Stocks &c & gone to Bentonville to keep "Hotel".

We are farming a little Slowly. We have one of the slow boys at work for us, he don't plow much over an acre per day. Our wheat is badly froze out, we may have 1/3 of a crop. Some of our neighbors won't have a show. Grimes & many other Sowed Spring wheat & Barley. Our Oats looks as Well as I ever saw any, it is 2 or 3 in[ches] high now. The weather is nice now. We did considirable grafting to day, mostly Pear—Some Plum. I have now the best list of Pears to their no. in the State. We have about 20 kinds. Mother has a nice Can 1/2 gal She Saved all winter to Eat when you come. I dont know how long she will have to keep them. The winter injured my Peach Trees a little. We put out 1600 more in the nursery this Spring. Come over & help yourself when you please, we have plenty of good Apples yet. We will likely have a good moderate crop this year.

There is little doing in the mill now, we sell some times $5.00 worth a day. Since writing I have collected—James Paul & Samuel Hiett's accts. There is little else of interest. I feel dull and tired, hense better close for the present. Write Soon & oblige.

Truly your affectionate brother,

Amos A. Evans

⇒ SAM TO ANDREW ⇐
Memphis, Tenn. / April 24, 1864

Dear Father,

Your kind favor of the 17th came to hand yesterday, which was a very welcome visitor. I have not been very throng [sic] receiving letters from home for the last fortnight. I believe that I have only recd 3 during that time. I have written several the past week but none the week previous.

I am sorry to hear your health is not good. I hope you will soon recover your health. I am much obliged to you for inquiring about the Pistols. I have bought one. It cost $26.00 pistol Belt Scabbard and 100 rounds of Cartridges. It is a fine gun. Size of Johns but one (1) inch larger.

I thought I would not carry one but the Fort Pillow affair made me think if such things should occur as have, I would be persuaded to Leave Some individuals that frequent picket posts in a state of inertia [dead].[1] Such things they do, the only Plan for us is "Talionis".[2] How do you like the manner in which Gen. Grant is going to work about the Army of the Potomac less "balls", fewer visits by Staff officers to Washington, less baggage for officers, more vigilance in Picketing, &c&c.

Gen Grant informed Stanton that he was Commanding the Army. When Stanton said it was taking the power out of his hands and asked Mr. Lincoln to revoke Grants order, Lincoln said to Stanton that by a "Special" act of Congress Gen Grant was made the Commander of the forces of the U.S. and that he, Stanton, had better Let Grant alone.

Stanton will find that Gen Grant keeps his own secrets and does something to suit himself.[3]

There is nothing new here in the way of war news except that Gen Hurlbut is relieved from Command of the 16 army Corps. Gen. Washburn it is thought will take his command.[4] Washbern [sic] is from Illinois. I thing [sic] almost any boy could manage things as well as Hulbert [sic] has for Some time past. I think I could Prevent Forest with the force he has from going just where he pleases. Let me have the force that Hulbert [sic] had. Perhaps it is all right or will be in the end. I do not see that our Army has done much since the fall campaign. I think that the drafting business is going on too slow for our Benefit. This war will not end in 3 years more unless there is more activity on our part. It is very cumbersome to have so much goods shipped to the seat of Rebeldom as there are here. Forests whole army is supplied through this place at least in a great measure. This treasury Department, is a Government Swindle the agents become the gainers and not "Uncle Sam."

Small Pox are still pretty plenty and is killing soldiers in the ground as fast as any other disease. Officers of our Regt are all well. I am quite well and having a pretty good time just now, only on duty one [time] a week and then as officer of the day. I have written enough for tonight.

Love to all, I am as ever,

Your Son,

Sam

1. On April 12, 1864, General Forrest led an attack on Fort Pillow, on the Mississippi River in Tennessee. After their victory, some of Forrest's men murdered black soldiers after they had surrendered, forever blemishing Forrest's reputation. Thereafter "Remember Fort Pillow" became a battle cry of black soldiers. McPherson, *Battle Cry of Freedom*, 748.

2. Sam means to say "talion," meaning revenge.

3. Secretary of War Stanton and General Grant had a contentious relationship resulting from disputes over the chain of command. When Grant appealed to Lincoln for total control, Lincoln refused to formally subvert Stanton's authority, but assured Grant that de facto Stanton would not be allowed interfere with Grant's orders. Grant's authority was evidenced when Lincoln approved Grant's removal of forces defending Washington to bolster his field army despite Stanton's opposition, telling Stanton, "I think we better leave [Grant] alone to do as he pleases." Simpson, *Ulysses S. Grant*, 278.

4. Much of Sam's speculation is characteristic of the rumors that ran rampant within the army. Washburn was never appointed commander of the 16th Army Corps, which remained without a commander for six months.

Memphis, Tenn. / May 5, 1864

Dear Father,

Yours of the 24th was recd on the 30th an[d] Should have been answered Sooner but press of business Prevented it. I generally answer your Letters on Sunday, if not on duty. I received a Letter from Mary this Evening dated Apr 29. It is cheering to hear the health of the folks at home is improving. My health is still good. Notwithstanding for about a week our Regt have been doing over 2/3 of the Picket duty around this city, it makes two Reliefs bringing us on duty evry other day. The other Regts who have been doing Picket duty have gone out after Forest. We Learn that they have had a small fight and that Forest was slight worsted, retreated a cross Wolf River, burned the bridge—so ended the fight. There ar quite a No. of small running Parties that infest the neighboring country and commit depredations on soldiers and citizens at evry opportunity.

The Last impressment of the Rebels has Strengthened their army considerable in Tenn, Arkansas, Miss, and Missouri.[1] The squads of Rebels who have been roaming the country have gathered all the able bodied. Night before last one of the most noteable characters of mixed proclivities (Secesh and Union) attempted to run the Pickets. The night being dark, no one could Shoot to any certainty. 16 Shots were fired at him, 3 of which [had] effect respectively in the neck, shoulder and side. It was not known until next morning that he was hurt. Calvary was sent next morning to patrol when they found him dead about 3/4 of a mile from the line. He has been a Smugler of good[s] of various kinds. Our officers have taken two pairs of boots off him within the Last month and have arrested and sent him to the Provost Marshal's but by some means he always was cleared and permitted [to] return home. He lived about two miles from the Line. I have been thinking for some time he was playing The Spy.

Our Lines have been closed for the Last week, no one was allowed to pass out, but all could pass in who wished. Some few have undertaken to run the Lines at night. I do not approve the policy of admitting any in the lines when it is necessary to keep a move in the dark because if they are allowed to come in, it is possible to run almost any single chains [sic] of Pickets outward but almost impossible run in through. There is scarcely a citizen in West Tenn true to the old Union and her soldiers. There is a Regt of Cavalry here called the 1st Miss. Union. I would [sic] the whole Regt is a nuisance to the service. They would do as little harm in the

Rebel ranks as where they are. Most of them have been in the Rebel Army. There are about 20 men in the Regt who were in the Military Prison in this and were allowed to take their choice go to the Military Prison at Alton, Ill or go to this Regt, they chose the latter. Things are in Rather a bad shape somehow or other. But there have been darker hours since the Rebellion commenced. If Grant and Sherman cannot do something decisive this Spring, I think it will look rather dark in some respects.

Love to all the family,

I am as ever your Son,

Sam Evans

1. The last Confederate draft was passed by the Confederate Congress in February 1864. It reduced the minimum age to seventeen and required all men then in the army to remain in service. McPherson, *Ordeal by Fire*, 2:182.

⇥ ANDREW TO SAM ⇤
Home / May 8, 1864

Dear Son,

I will again give you a short offhand epistle, I have nothing from you since I Last wrote. My health has improved considerably within a week, I am clear of Diarrhea and improving otherwise, the residue of our family are in usual health, Amos is slowly improving, he works, hunts & fishes a little; dust, or damp air, disagrees with him, and sets him to coughing. The general health is fair, except Small pocks, which is prevailing considerably between dry run & Ellis' run. John K. Gray was buried yesterday from small pocks and there are several families in that neighborhood, said to be sore afflicted with the same disease.

We are daily looking for interesting Army news, Gen. Grant has moved the "Army of the Potomac," and it is said Lee is giving back. If he chooses to fall back to his entrenchments at Richmond let him do it, for Grant knows how to dig them out, he has got to fight or run certain for Grant is ready & moving. We have no news of Shermans move yet, but he is also about ready, and whereever he moves the wool will fly. Sherman & Grant are both highly pleased at the western States furnishing 100,000 100 days more, it will give them an Equal No. of Vetran troops who are on Guard & post duty. "Old Brough" says now is the time and that 100 days will probably decide the fate of the Rebellion and that it is of the utmost importance that we have plenty of men to insure a victory. Brough is likely to rival [Gov.] Morton of Ind. and that is saying a good deal. Ohio has now 40,000 in camp, armed & Equiped, waiting orders, the Gov only Expected 30,000 to obey the call, but he has been "disappointed". Our volunteer Militia system is perhaps the best in any state in the Union, for our Gov has 40,000 men in camp for duty before any other state had a man in camp. He is in favor of whipping them right now, and come home and see to their business. He says these 100 day men must be exempt from the present draft, which will draw on the copperheads, the more, & if they won't go, we will get their money, and "if they won't fish he'll make them cut bait." He's all right.

I see by the papers that your new Gen. is scouring things up about Memphis, something is needed to prevent Smuggling contraband goods to the Rebs at that place, and I think Washburn is making a very nice start. I hope all our armies will work for the interest of the Union for this season.

We did not get done planting corn last week, owing to rain, we planted 12 acres, and have 7 1/2 ready for corn which will close us out for this season. Our potatoes, melons and all the onions are planted. The weather is verry warm with indications of rain. Wheat is bound to be poor, oats and meadows look fair now. The fruit prospect is quite poor, perhaps 1/3 of our apple crop, no peaches, a few plums, Cherries &c, Currants, and Gooseberries plenty, Raspberries verry moderate: we have planted pumpkins, potatoes, onions &c &c to supply the family.

Nothing new in the local way, only that Michael & Big Jane have "done it", they are supposed to have married last Thursday evening, success to their [blank line appearing in text may refer to their family "line"].

Accept the love of us all.

Your father,

Andrew Evans

⇢ SAM TO ANDREW ⇠
Memphis, Tenn. / May 16, 1864

Dear Father,

Yesterday was my regular day for writing to you here. I was on duty and had not the opportunity to write. Yours of the 8 came to hand on the 14. I was glad to hear that all were well, and enjoying Life as well as possible. Small Pox is still here though it seems to be in a milder form than months ago. A "Darkie" is pretty sure to "go up" if he gets Small Pox. They are very easy discouraged when they are Sick. I believe this Regt. has Lost more than 200 Men since it was organized. Still we keep Recruited to more than maximum No. I am doubtfull whether the Fort Pillow Masicre [sic] will be retributed or not.[1] I Should love to have a chance at old Forest.

The news from Gen. Grant is still favorable to our arms, I am very anxious to have Grant give Lee and his forces a complete routing. Capture Richmond. If the papers do not Lie, Lee has been handled rougher than he has been a habit of, he did not Succeed in breaking Grant's Lines as he anticipated by massing his forces, dashing on the Lines. Would to God that I or anyone else could do enough to ensure Grant a complete victory and hurl confusion into the councils of our adversaries. I am afraid the news is too favorable to be altogether true. No man on the continent could do more than Gen Grant, I know of no man who has worked more earnestly for the government, devoted his entire time every [sic] to the cause of our government. If all the officer[s] and agents of the Government had the Good of Country at heart and not party strife or mercenary motives, this war would have Long since been closed. I am still confident of our ability to conquer this Rebellion. If nothing happens [to] me I intend to See the war ended.

My health is moderately good. My foot is still sore. Cannot wear a shoe or boot but can walk about. I do not know how soon it will be well. It is fine weather here now. There has been no very hot weather here this Season yet, very fine rains for vegetation, vegetables ar plenty. There are many very fine gardens, mostly tended by French, Dutch, and Italians. I think there are some of the nicest flower gardens here that I ever saw any where.

Gen Washburn is coming down pretty tight on Citizens of secesh Proclivities. Many are being sent south to remain while the war Lasts with forfeiture of all their property within our Lines. No one is now permitted [to] pass through these Lines without "Special permission" from Gen Washburn. I know but little about him. I think he is from the Potomac Army. I have nothing to do with any of the citizens, have never sought the acquaintance and any one who seeks my acquaintance goes off uninformed. I have no friendship for Rebels and most of the civilians are "[illegible]" Things are quiet in this vicinity. I would think they will remain so while Washburn is here. Old Hulbert [sic, Hurlbut] has made as much money as he needs for the present.

Excuse errors remember me to all the family I am as ever,
Your Son,
Sam

1. For a brief discussion of the Fort Pillow Massacre see note in Sam's letter of April 24, 1864.

❧ SAM TO ANDREW ❧
Memphis, Tenn. / May 22, 1864

Dear Father,

Your kind favor of the 8th came to hand on the 14 and was welcome, no Letters from home for more than a week which Seems like a long time because I have [been] in a habit of hearing from home once or twice a week, but I can do without a week or two if Grant and Sherman are only successful, that interests me more than all things else at present. So far as we have news Grant has proved a match for Lee if not more. I do hope he will continue to be. He is now the favorite of the nation and has more power in his hands than any man ever had in the United States. I am of opinion that no man in the Government is more sedulous or freer of mercenary motives: he is working for his country's good and nothing else. All is great in the vicinity of Memphis. Our lines are closed as to egress and all have to walk "the chalk." I have no more information as to our leaving as when I wrote to Mary. I am Still of opinion we will move. One thing certain, there are more troops here than are needed at this point. There are two Regts doing nearly all the picket duty around the town. Our Lines are about three miles from the City, about 9 miles in length, thus, you will see that there is labor in Guarding here. The militia of Memphis are drilling some, they have had our band playing for their parades. I did not suppose they would allow a Negro band to play for them but they came several times for it before Lt Col Cowden would let it go.

I stated that I would send some things home a short time ago. I think I will this week if can go to town. My foot hinders me from going about much. I thought one week ago that it would be well by this time but do not see that it has improved the Least in that time. I am doctoring it. It is kind of a carbuncle on the rise of the instep.[1] My health is good.

Weather is fine, rather warmer than I like. There is considerable of cotton growing inside our Lines this season and have been told citizens in the vicinity are raising considerable. So there will be perhaps plenty chances for Generals trying their Skill on Speculating the coming season. I will close as I have not much to write that would interest you. Give my best respects to all the family.

Your Son,

Sam

1. A carbuncle is an inflammation below the skin, similar to, but more serious than, a boil. Carbuncles can be accompanied by fever, headache, and loss of appetite.

⇉ JANE TO SAM ⇇
Huntington Township, Brown Co., Ohio / May 24, 1864

Dear Cousin Sam,

It is with pleasure that I now write you a few lines to let you know that I have not forgotten you. It has been sometime since I received your kind letter but I hope that you will excuse me for so long a delay. By some means I have neglected too long. It was not because I did not want to write. For it is more pleasure to me than anything else to receive a letter from one of my good cousins that is out fighting for our country and their loved ones at home. Cousin, it is hard, very hard to think about but we will have to take it easy as we can for it cannot be helped now. I do hope that it will not be much longer before this unholy Rebellion will come to close some way, either by fighting or a compromise. I don't see how it will be ended by fighting, if they don't do any better than they did of the late battles. The next thing that we know old Morgan and his crew will be over here again. The people in Maysville was looking for him in last night but I hope that he will get alarmed and not come.

I received a letter from your Brother Will, a few days ago! He says he is enjoying very good health. He says that he expects to come home some of these days! Will says that everything agrees with him down south very well except the women. He says that he don't like them at all. He says that they don't suit him. He said that he wanted me to pick one out for him again before he comes home. He gave me a full description. It beat anything that ever I heard of before.

Cousin, you said that you knew that I had some idea of marrying a soldier. I think that you will find that you are mistaken. It is not because I don't think that they are not good enough, I am a particular friend to all the soldiers. I guess that there is some that does not like me very well.

And for why I cannot say. Cousin, I think you are one among the best of the soldiers that is engaged in war if you would own to it. Big Jane is married at last and is gone to housekeeping. Don't believe that I would be in a very big hurry about marrying now and then be left by myself as apt as any may, for there is no telling how soon he would be drafted. How bad I would feel for my husband to have the name of being drafted. I would rather see them volunteer and go right then than to be forced to go.

Well, I believe that I will quit for the present. We all send our love and respects to you. Please write again for I do love to hear from my good cousin. I still remain as ever your true friend and cousin,

Jane Evans

> ≫ SAM TO ANDREW ≪
> Memphis, Tenn. / May 29, 1864

Dear Father,

Yours of the 22nd yesterday also one from Amos of the 20th and was very glad to hear from you and to know that you were getting a long pretty well. I do not [know] why you have not recd my Letters because I have been writing as many Letters as usual Since Forest left the River [probably the Mississippi River].

Tell Mother to give herself no uneasiness in regard to my sore foot, that I have marched and carried a Knapsack when both feet were worse than it is or has been. This thing of Laying up till my foot is well is played out. I can wear a slipper that does not hurt it. I have been doing nothing but light duty since it has been sore. My foot is doing well [better] though it is not well.

The war news is still good on our side. Grant will have to keep his eyes open or Lee will take Some advantage of him. Grant is fight[ing] under [difficult] circumstances, Lee having fortifications nearly all the way. I am of opinion that Sherman will not find near all of Johns[t]on['s] Army to fight where he is. I think Lee has a portion of it at any rate.

The ending of this war has been prophesied for the 4th of July for 2 or 3 years. I would like to see the war end on the next "4th". I am not tired of Soldiering but peace, an honorable Peace!, [is] preferable to war. You are mistaken about us being more tired of war than those who are at home. We came to conquer not to tire. Many of the report[s] circulated are untrue. It [is] almost Impossible to fight an enemy in his fortifyca-tions and not lose as many men. I think now that Gen Grant will take richmond with proper backing. If Gen Sherman could come up in the rear of Richmond with the army that he has, he could. Grant could make Jeff shake in his boots but that would be operating to[o] far from his [Sherman's] base of operations for Sherman's [army] to do that.

But a Short time ago it was reported that Forest was threatening Huntsville, Ala. Yesterday, report says he's not many miles from here, that I do not believe. His Supplies are cut off by Gen Washburn, by clos-ing these Lines and permitting no goods to pass. Citizens are working hard to get passes but no go. I suppose that you have heard that the "gun boats" of Red River have been brought out safely. That is more than I expected Banks has not done as well as I expected him to. Some report the cause of his defeat "Cotton on the Brain" Like to[o] many of our Generals.[1]

It is Something over a year since I came into this Regt. on the 3rd day May 1863. The 1st man was Recruited on the 6 of June, 5 companies were full and mustered into the service on the 27, the other 5 Co's were mus-tered hear. 250 men have died belonging to the 59[th USCT] yet it is almost as Large as ever. I suppose no Regt in the Service has done more Service in the same time.

I expect to go before a military board of examiners to know whether I am competent to hold the position of 1st Lt or whether I might not go a little higher.[2] I think I would bear an examination for the position of Capt. I made the application to be examined myself not [because] the Col thought that I was not competent but because I would be [found to be]. Our Col (Bouton) is Cmmdg brigade of darkies. Cowden formerly maj of the 59th U.S.I.C. [sic, USCI] has been promoted to Lt Col since Philips Risigned. By trade he was a Carpenter, Resident of Ohio and is one of the best men I have met with since I came and as good an officer as a great majority of men.

Remember me kindly to all the family I am,

As Ever I have been,

Sam

1. Union General Nathaniel Banks had been given the responsibility of moving up the Red River in Louisiana to capture a greater part of that state, up to Shreveport. On April 8, 1864, Confederate General Robert Taylor (son of twelfth U.S. president Za-chary Taylor) defeated Banks at Sabine's Crossing, thirty-five miles south of Shreve-port. The Union forces held off Taylor at Pleasant Hill the next day, but eventually had

to retreat. The Red River campaign was a great Union failure and resulted in little Union gain other than some small seizures of cotton. A Wisconsin colonel saved the Union gunboats by constructing several dams that enabled the fleet to retreat through the rapids intact. McPherson, *Battle Cry of Freedom*, 722–23.

2. When the USCT was established, the War Department created boards of examiners to test potential officers' "physical, mental, and moral fitness to command." The candidates were tested, sometimes for several hours, in a variety of subjects including military tactics, army regulations, history, mathematics, and geography. At their inception the boards were glutted with thousands of applicants to fill commissions in the new regiments. Afterward the boards apparently remained active, examining already commissioned USCT officers seeking promotion. Joseph T. Glatthaar, *Forged in Battle: The Civil War Alliance of Black Soldiers and White Officers* (New York: The Free Press, 1990), 48–54.

⇨ AMOS TO SAM ⇦
Home / June 2, 1864

Dear Brother,

I as usual occupy a few moments in writing to you once in 2 weeks. I have not got one from you some time. Father got several of late. Sorry to hear your foot is so bad.

We rec'd a long letter from Will yesterday. He is yet well & unhurt. They have been in severe fighting but are still bound for Atlanta. George has gone to Washington D.C., & is well. We are all as when father wrote. Think I am better, I work about 1/2 the time & loaf the rest. We are about done harrowing, our corn it looks fine. Wheat is slow heading out. Harvest will come about the Middle of July. We will work on the road the 3rd & 4th. There is nothing of any importance going on here now.

I like very much the way Grant & Sherman are getting along. I would like to See Grant take Richmond & Lee in it.

Samuel Hiett & W[ill]. S. Housh are both better. Hiett can ride in a buggy & Will is nearly able to work. Roses & Pinks are just beginning to bloom here.[1] We will have Peas & Beans in a few days to Eat. Currants are large Enough now. I have nothing to write to night. Write as usual.

Your brother as Ever,

Amos

N.B. Lid Jones (used to be) wants to know if you have forgotten her. Her Husband got killed in the Army & she is now a Milliner in Portsmouth.

1. "Pinks" are probably spicy-smelling flowers, one variety of which is the carnation.

⇒ ANDREW TO SAM ⇐
Home / June 5, 1864

Dear Son,

Look out for "partridge tracks" [poor handwriting] for my hand is so stiffened by the last two days work, that I cannot wield my pen decently.

I received a letter from you on last Monday, & one yesterday, also one for Ann, & one for Amos. We also had three from Will last week, he is in the front and is well. We are glad your sore foot is not worse, we admonish you to take as good care of it as you can, for you are in a hot climate, where more care is necessary than in temperate ones. You ought not to march or even walk enough to agrivate the sore, for you may thereby produce additional inflimation that would end in gangreenous superation.[1]

We are glad to learn that you are about [to] stand [for] an Examination before a "military board" to list your qualifications to hold office and for promotion. I hope you stand the test, and not only prove competent to hold the office you have; but to be compctent for any office in the Regiment. Clerks in business houses in Cinti, now get better wages than a Captain in the field. Our old friend Flickinger told Amos, he would give him a situation at $1,500 for the first year, that is a pretty good bid for a country boy, Will Hiett is hired with Tom Ellison at $100 per month as sutler clerk! Will Housh was getting $100 pr month clerking for a Quartermaster, until he got sick, (or at least he says so.)

Our Will saw the boys of the old Veteran 70th the day he wrote, they were well and unhurt thus far. Our war news is still cheering, our Grant has "retreated" almost to Richmond[2] and our Sherman is close to Atlanta (The Butternut papers here, say Grant has been retreating before Lee all the time and has been whipped in every fight.) Well if he backs into Richmond, it will do us as well as any way, I still believe he will go in, and that Sherman will take Atlanta, and that the Rebellion must fall, but whether the thing "can be slid," this season, is the great problem, the solution of which we are all, directly, or indirectly seaking [sic]. May the God of battles grant us a favorable solution, hastily.

We have nothing in local matters that would interest you, the health of the country is fair, the crops look well except wheat & barley, fruit crops will be verry light, corn is looking verry well, Oats unusually well—gardens & contents are flourishing. Our health is fair, Amos has improved considerably in the past week, the residue of us are as well as usual.

Goods & groceries are up a little here, Coffee 50,

Sugar 20 @ 30, rice 15, Tea $2.00, calico 25 to 30, sheating [sic] 40 to 60, such paper as this $2.50 pr Ream, "Daily Commercial" & postage $10.20—year. Farm products is also up some, but not in the same proportion. Flour is worth $7.00 pr bbl, corn 75 at crib [purchased at the farm], potatoes $1.00, bacon 15 to 17 &c&c.

It is so difficult for me to write that I will close for the present Accept the best wishes of the family. Affectionately,

Your father,

Andrew Evans

1. See definition of superate in note in Andrew's letter of July 3, 1862.

2. Unlike previous commanders of the Army of the Potomac who retreated north after being defeated, Grant moved steadily southward even after losses. Thus Andrew jokes about Grant having "'retreated' almost to Richmond."

⋙ ANN TO SAM ⋘
Home / June 5, 1864

Dear Brother,

I seat myself to write you a few lines. I have forgotten whether I answered your letter or not but I will write any how. We are all well as common. Amos is not well yet. We have a pretty nice garden. We got a letter from Will a day or two ago, he was well. It is very hot to day. I think it will rain pretty soon. We the girls went to Ridge to meeting to day. Sam I got a good long letter from you was glad to hear from you All so. Amos and father received one from you, said you went to the picnic at Memphis. If I was not so far off I would come over to see you and your darkeys awhile.

You ask if Cousin Amanda Gilbert is teaching school in our district, yes sir. You ask why I do not go to school. Mother can not spare us all at [sic, and] she said if I wood stay at home this school [session] she wood let me go the next school [session]. Sam I wish you wold come home and teach grammar school. I have not study grammar any yet. I think I will next school [session].

It is cloudieed up. I think it will rain. I have no news to write at present.

Goodby for today,

Ann D. Evans

Memphis, Tenn. / June 5, 1864

Dear Father,

Your kind favor of the 29 came to hand on the 4 inst. I was veery glad to hear from you and know that all are getting along fine. My foot is improving some little. I am left almost alone—The 59th (Cold) has gone out, leaving all the camp and Garrison Equipage behind in my charge with about 150 men, mostly convalescents. The Regt left the morning of the 1st at 6 A.M., went on the cars as far as Moscow, Tenn. and there waited the Supply trains and Cavalry which went by "Land". There was a very Large force Left here but we do not know where they are going. The report is they are going to Sherman, but that is all guess work. My impression is they will hunt Forests "whereabouts". There are three white men only Left, Surgeon, Q. M. Sergt, Sergt Maj. It is very Lonesome, I would rather be with the Regt than Left to care for all that is left here.

The news is still good from Grant. I would be well pleased if Gen Grant would make another 4th of July job.[1] I think Gen. Grant will capture Richmond. Quite a no. of the Red River men have arrived at Memphis and Some of them have gone on the Raid that Left here on the 1st inst.[2] They do not Speak very favorably of Banks as a General. I have talked with many very intelligent men who seem to think that Banks could have taken Shreveport if he had not waited so long. The Rebles concentrated all their forces in and about there, [Union] Gen. A. J. Smith is spoken of by all the men in his command whom I have heard Speak with great praise. There is nothing much of importance to write about Memphis.

Three Soldiers from the 2nd N. J. Cav. are to be Shot next Friday at 3 o'clock P.M., all the soldiers here not otherwise on duty are ordered to be present to witness the execution.[3] I would much rather it was that No. of Rebles.

It has been raining for the last 3 o[r] four days, just about enough to keep the air cool. Well I shall have to close as it is just about the time the mail goes out. Remember me to all. I am as ever,

Yours,

Sam

1. Grant had captured Vicksburg the previous July 4.

2. For general information about the Red River campaign, see note in Sam's letter of May 29, 1864. The men about whom Sam is talking were probably from the division of his corps that returned from the Red River campaign. Prior to the Red River campaign, Sherman had given Banks a division from the 16th Army Corps (to which Sam belonged) for a thirty-day period. The men took longer than thirty days to return, and General Sherman left for Georgia without this division. Marszalek, *Sherman*, 256.

3. Over the course of the war, over two hundred Union soldiers were executed for various crimes, but most commonly for rape, murder, or desertion. Executions were customarily carried out with great ceremony to make an impression on other soldiers. Often the condemned soldier's brigade or division would be required to form up prior to the prisoner's arrival, witness the execution, and march past the corpse. Bell Irvin Wiley, *The Life of Billy Yank: The Common Soldier of the Union* (1978; repr., Baton Rouge: Louisiana State University Press, 1991), 205–7.

⇾ SAM TO ANDREW ⇽
Memphis, Tennessee / June 11, 1864

Dear Father,

Yours of the 5 inst is at hand, recd today which gave me great pleasure. It is cheering to hear all are improving in health. You seem much concerned about my foot for fear that I will not take care of it. I think you need not give yourself any uneasiness in that matter. It has improved some since I last wrote and will perhaps be well enough to wear a shoe in a week as I take all the care I can. I have had a pretty bad foot. The Locality and nature of the sore were such as would cause almost any one to think it would become a chronic sore. It has now assumed a different form and is doing very well. My health otherwise is fare but not quite so good as it has been. I have not a very large amount of spare Strength, not hurt a great deal with fat.

Since I Last wrote you I have had a little sick spell, starved it out as I usually do; for a few days have been mending, think that there is or was nothing serious the matter. The examination I spoke of has not gone off yet. You spoke of QuarterMaster's Clerks getting $100, per month. I know of no such wages given to Clerks in the quarter master Dept. though I do not profess to know it all, only know that Clerks get no such wages here and this is about as Large a military post as our friend would be likely to get in. I am not positive that Ellison would give a new clerk $100 per month. His head clerk, book keeper &c only get 60, here.

Grants and Shermans "retreat" is still satisfactory. We Learn that Johns[t]on has out-Generaled Sherman got in his rear and taken a train of 240 wagons Loaded with supplies. This is Reble news through "Cin' Enquirer", was done about the 1st inst.[1] I would Love to see news papers that circulate that kind of Lies Suppressed. News papers talk of the "freedom of the Press" and all that kind of stuff. We would have had better Success in subduing this Rebellion if 49/50 of the papers had been suppressed in the beginning [and] the army "correspondents" been required to take a musket instead [of] the pen. This kind of warfare look[s] like tyranny, but justice to the Soldiers who are fighting the battles demands something of that nature. It is the soldier, the private soldier, who has suffered most inconveniences from these Scoundrels and are now losing their lives because, they have prolonged the war, beyond a time it would have been ended. The Editor of the New York World is very much chagrined at the president for Stopping this paper for publishing the "Forged Proclamation."[2] I do not think the President was to blame, in the case.

I like the nomination for president, vice president very well, and would be very glad to see them elected. I think them both honest and competent. Andrew Johnson is a Southern man but decidedly in favor of whipping the Rebles. If I am not badly duped, he is the man for that position. I know of no two that would please me better for the respective positions for which they have been nominated than they. May they be elected each to the office named and prove themselves worthy [of] the positions. I believe both have earnestly labored to conquer the Rebellion without a view to self aggrandizement or elevation.

When Buell Left Nashville he only left one small division to guard it. Johnson told Buell that before the Rebles should ever have possession of it again he would burn or die in the attempt. His property has been confiscated by the Rebles, at one time he was incarcerated, his family was taken away, after his imprisonment, he was threatened to be hanged if caught about his home. Many of his negros are in the Union Army. All that did not Run away he set at Liberty (if [I] mistake not), yet for all he has been faithful to the Union and its cause.[3]

The Scout that left this place on the first has not returned and will not likely for 15 days yet. I saw the execution of three of our soldiers yesterday for Rape and Robbery. I did intend to stay in Camp but received an order to take my detachment out, which of course I did. It is not a very pleasant sight. Every thing was done to make as much impression as possible on the troops present. The party that did the Shooting were very much touched but did their work with dispatch giving convicts no time to suffer, after the firing of the guns, all three falling back at the same instant, scarcely moving a muscle afterwards. I never want to see another Union Soldier executed. I would Like to see a[s] many Rebles hanged would double the number they murdered at fort Pillow. Military executions are very tedious and tiresome to me. I will send you the account published in the Bulletin which is a pretty correct one.

I will stop to night and finish tomorrow morning.

Sunday 12 / Since writing the foregoing some news has been received of a very discouraging character. The force that Left here for parts, not at that time mentionable, met Forest and have been badly defeated, very bad management [was] the cause of it. The Aggagate [*sic*, aggregate] of the 59th Rank and file was 650, nearly 50 of them have returned including officers, 23 officers are missing, Lt. Col. Cowden wounded badly and in the hands of the Rebles. Capt. Foster is missing the whole train and all the ammunition, 18 pieces of Artillery, about 180 wagons mostly abandoned and destroyed. I will give you a fuller account in my next.[4]

Am well at this writing,

Yours,

Lt Samuel Evans

1. Sam is correct in doubting this "Reble news." Sherman was steadily, if slowly, pushing Johnston back toward the defenses of Atlanta. McPherson, *Ordeal by Fire*, 2:432–33.

2. On May 18, 1864, the *New York World* and the *Journal of Commerce* printed a spurious proclamation, in which Lincoln called for a draft of four hundred thousand more men, inciting heavy Wall Street speculation leading to a drop in the value of greenbacks (Union paper currency). On Lincoln's order, troops temporarily shut down the papers and arrested their editors and owners. The editors and owners were eventually released and their sources were incarcerated. Despite criticism, Lincoln stood by his right to censor papers for irresponsible journalism. David Herbert Donald, *Lincoln* (New York: Simon and Schuster, 1995), 501–2.

3. Johnson called for the emancipation of all Tennessee slaves, the state not having been included in the Emancipation Proclamation's list of states in rebellion, in January 1864. It is unclear whether he personally freed any of his own bondsmen. Hans L. Trefousse, *Andrew Johnson: A Biography* (New York: W. W. Norton and Co., 1989), 172.

4. Here Sam is referring to the Battle of Guntown (also called the Battle of Brice's Cross Roads), Mississippi. Union General Samuel Sturgis commanded this disastrous defeat at the hands of General Forrest. Sam was absent from his regiment at the time of this battle, due to his injured foot. Hurst, *Nathan Bedford Forrest*, 192.

Home / June 12, 1864

Dear Son,

Yours of the 5th came to hand yesterday, and found us all in usual health, I cannot tell positively whether Amos is better, or not. His lungs, or bronchial tubes bled some twice last week, not fresh, but dark looking blood. He says there is no soreness in his lungs now, but considerable irritation in the bronchial tubes, that keeps him coughing considerably, if he exerts himself.

I console with you, in your lonesome encampment, but I am sure it is the best for your sore foot, and I am truly glad that you were not allowed to go with your Regiment for the [aggravation] of a march on [your] sore foot, might make a permanent cripple of you, if nothing worse.

Well we have our candidates before us again, What do you say for "Old Abe" and Andy Johnson? I say Amen: and that we must elect them. I am really glad to have so good a man as "Andy Johnson" for Vice Prest. One branch of the Copper Crats have nominated Freemont, and he has accepted the nomination; the other branch will probably take McClellan, or some body worse if they can find any of that kind.[1] We have an excellent State ticket & will triumphantly elect it when the Election day arrives.

I can give you but little more news from our "Maysville Raid," than Mary gave you, they left on Thursday evening with their horses &c, they were headed at Mt. Sterling by Union forces from Covington, who thrashed them out & got 150 horses back, I have no [illegible] but the horses were b[r]ought to Aberdeen.[2]

We have had nothing from Inda, nor George for several weeks, we are still looking for her, but she neither comes nor writes. We still get letters from Will, he is still tolerably well, and going "your way." Our Army news is megre [sic, meager] at present, no moves being made public in the vicinity of Richmond, we suppose Grant is proposing to dig [in]. Nothing of interest from Sherman. We are just in the hight of rose blooms and have rather fragrant home.

Accept the best wishes of the family and believe me,

Your affectionate parent,

Andrew Evans

1. In 1864, malcontented 1856 Republican Presidential nominee General John C. Frémont, whom Lincoln had failed to appoint to any important command, briefly mounted an abortive third-party presidential campaign, which drew modest support from opportunistic and disaffected members of both major parties.

2. In June 1864 Confederate General John Hunt Morgan led his final raid from Tennessee into Kentucky. Despite the anxiety provoked in Southern Ohio, Morgan's primary goal was the capture of Union supplies, most importantly the five thousand horses supposedly stabled in Lexington, Kentucky. Morgan was turned back by federal forces at Cynthianna, Kentucky, rather than at Mount Sterling, and the one thousand horses he had seized were recovered. Morgan's forces never threatened Maysville or Ohio. Thomas Edison, *John Hunt Morgan and His Raiders* (Lexington: University Press of Kentucky, 1975), 94–101.

⇒ AMOS TO SAM ⇐
Home / June 18, 1864

Dear Brother,

I rec'd yours of May 27th on the 4th June & one of June 8th on the 15th. I should have written sooner but had a severe headache Thursday, my regular day for writing & yesterday I went to the Examination of the Ripley School & did not get back until late. These are trifling excuses so I will not apologize further.

I am very sorry to hear of you being so lonesome & lame besides. I some times get so lonesome here that I don't know how to live. I do not know how I would do if I were away & lonesome.

This leaves us all as well as usual. My health is much improved. I have quit the use of all medicines Except that of slight Expectorants and help my breast some with [illegible]. This I have done for 2 months. We rec'd a letter from Will a few days ago, he is well Except much troubled at times with Dysintery. We have no word from George since he started for Washington. We rec'd a letter from Inda on the 15th, she & Morty were well. She has a Singer Sewing Machine & has a contract of making government Shirts.[1] Our Corn is growing fast. Wheat is much better than we rated it some time ago. We are getting along fine with our work. Harvest will be late . . .

The big meeting at Slickaway will be tomorrow. It was put off in May on acct of Small Pox which is now all dried up. Uncle Sam Carpenter is in Cincinnati working at his trade. I learned yesterday that John Thompson of Aberdeen is now a prisoner in the Rebel Army. The Morgan Raid in Ky I think was a good thing. We have nothing late from him. I notice we Suffered a heavy defeat near Memphis this week. I am anxious to know the truth of the matter. They are trying hard to cut off Shermans supplies, which are carried on a long line of Rail. Grant is not making any heavy demonstrations just now—I think he will soon.

There is no news here worth writing, the weather is fine & all is quiet. I am as Ever,

> Your affectionate Brother,
> Amos

1. The Union Army required large supplies of uniforms, bedding, and tents. Many Northern women who had been widowed or left alone by husbands and sons in the service needed additional income and eagerly helped to meet the army's demand by accepting government sewing contracts. Managed by often-unscrupulous contractors who ignored the government's recommended pay scale, women like Indiana ran the risk of being severely underpaid for their contribution to the war effort. Mary Elizabeth Massey, *Women in the Civil War* (Lincoln: University of Nebraska Press, 1966), 143.

⇥ ANDREW TO SAM ⇤
Home / June 19, 1864

Dear Son:

On Monday last, while I was mailing a letter to you, I received one from you, but mine was sealed & I could not acknowledge the receipt of yours. I was glad you did not go with your Regt. and we are all more glad since reading the fate of the troops that were with Sturgis that you were not among them, so your "sore foot" may have done you a favor. The last news we have from the 59th Colored, there were 200 men & 6 officers still missing. We are unabled [sic] to judge yet, whether the defeat was unavoidable, or bad management. But from whatever cause, I am glad you were not there. We have nothing from Sherman lately, but I have all confidence that he will do right. Grant is steadily & surely doing his job, he has got Petersburg together with its garrison & 13 cannon all right so far.

We had a letter from Inda last week, she & Morty were well, she is working on a Government contract, making shirts and drawers, she has got a sewing machine & is making 10 shirts per day, she thinks she can make 16 when she gets her hand in right, they send her 10 Doz at a time cut & numbered. Louis Muner & Mr. Bottner went her surety for the faithful performance of her contract. She has had no word from George since he left Cincinnati. We had a letter from Will last week, he was not verry well, some inclination to flux, but was on duty all the time.

Our Morgan Raid has subsided, and Morgan has come-off second best again, if he gets out of Kentucky at all, he will get out with less than half the strength he came in with. It is a notorious fact that Cal Rankin killed seven of Morgan['s] men in less than three minutes, in a "sabre charge" & doing so he cut-off 35 who were captured immediately by Capt Cal Rankin's men . . .

Small pocks have about subsided here, no contagious disease prevailing here, and the general health is quite fair. Our crops are looking verry well, (except wheat), our corn & gardens are well tended and look verry fine, we are still in the midst of beautiful & fragrant flowers, but we cannot enjoy them whilst our "flesh & Blood" are daily Exposed to Rebel bullets. God grant that you may safely return home in peace & enjoy a restored Union.

Our health is about as usual, Amos is looking better but has a tormenting cough at times.

Truly your father,
Andrew Evans

⇒ ANDREW TO SAM ⇐
Home / June 26, 1864

Dear Son,

Yours of the 4 & 12 came to hand on the 21st, and that of the 19 on the 25th (on six days from date,) I & we are pleased to learn that your foot is much better and that your health is still fair; Our health is nothing to brag of just now. I am as well as usual. Your mother is not well, she has some considerable derangement of the bowells just now. During the past week she has been plagued with rheumatism. Joe and Lee have each had a spel of vomiting recently. I presume it is caused by excessive hot & dry weather, the "Murcury" is standing at 98° in the shade, (2 oclock PM) and at 142° in the sunshine if you have it much hotter at Memphis I don't know how you get along;[1] Amos is about as usual, he had an Examination made on his chest yesterday, the Dr pronounced his disease bronchitis, and says his lungs are not affected.

We have nothing from George yet, we got a letter from Will yesterday only a few days old, he was well, and their Regt were in the front again and were skirmishing while he was writing. They have a great deal of rain and mud, but the general health of the army was good and a general anxiety to go a head on Atlanta, and with ful confidence of success whenever they moove.

"Grants Retreat," is plagueing the Rebs considerably about Petersburg & Richmond, he has got the last Railroad that leads to Richmond severed.[2] And Lee, his Army & the Citizens will have to bord from their own resources, or what is inside of Grant's lines, Fort Darling and Petersburg are closely beseiged if our news be true. I think the Gen. will not be able to close the sum on the 4th of July this year, the contract is too large for the time to work in, but I am still of opinion he will take Richmond and clean out Virginia, before this season ends. There will be frightful, losses of human life before those objects are affected [sic, effected], but nothing else can end the Rebellion. The Rebs are stubborn.

Our crops still look well, notwithstanding the weather is verry dry and hot. I cannot tell what such wether will do for the wheat, whether it will ripen it prematurely or not. Our early varieties are ripening quite fast. I am of opinion some of it will have to be cut the last of this week if it remain dry. Some of the garden crops are faiding pretty fast. Pea time unles we get rain soon. Beans are being hurt. Cabbage is looking well yet. The dry spel dont suit the Tobacco men, their plants will be too large if not set soon. We have all our growing crops in verry good condition, the ground clear of weeds, and deeply loosened, but there is plenty in sight of us not quite in the same fix. Tom's, Anjalines & Martins farms have (as usual) small corn and plenty of weeds. Tom & Anjaline have not cut the stalks in their wheat yet, Good farming perhaps!

We are making arrangements for a big celebration of the 4th at our fairgrounds, to consist of all the sunday schools in reach, a welcome to the 12th Ohio whose time is out, & citizens in general, &c &c.

I am about out of material for further composition and the weather is too hot to write the truth, & I have no desire to lie to you. Frank C. Porter has arrived safely at home & has paid us a verry agreeabl (to us) visit, his health is not verry good, but I think he will regain his health with proper care and rest, he talks like a true soldier and patriot.

Accept the best wishes of the family and believe me faithfully,
Your father,
Andrew Evans

1. Obviously, Civil War–era thermometers were not as finely calibrated as modern ones.

2. Here Andrew is referring to Grant's movement southeast following the battle at Cold Harbor on June 3, 1864. He crossed the James River and began his assault on Petersburg in the weeks that followed.

Home / July 10, 1864

Dear Son:

I received your short note of the 30th June from Lagrange on the 6th July, we have not been getting the usual amount of letters from you & Will, but we are glad to get any, for we know your chances to write are much abridged. We continue to start 2 letters per week to each of you such as they are.

I cannot promise you a well written one today for I have been harvesting and my hand is so stiff & swolen, that I can hardly wield the pen at all. We are within about 2 acres of being done cutting our wheat. The crop is verry poor, & wages verry high, so the thing won't pay, but we must do the best we can with it. $1.66 to 2 is the wages for harvest hands here, that won't pay on crops at 5 bu pr acre and poor at that. Threshers are setting their wage at 10 cents pr bushel.

Our health is something better than on the last [illegible] tho none of the flux patients are well. They are all going about. Jo is doing verry well but is too weak for business. Your mother is quite sore yet from the disease and has to be very careful. Peggy is about in the same fix. Amos is improving slowly but wont do in a wheat field. Ann had a hard attack of irritation of the stomach on thursday night last which lasted nearly all night. She has got well except soreness. Ibby is complaining today. The rest of us are about as well as usual. The general of the country is fair.

We had a letter from Will last week, written "under fire of the enemy," near Maryetta [sic], Georgia,[1] he is well but some what tired he has the care of two, and sometimes three Regts, Surgeons being rather scarce there for active duty. Dr. Crew is in charge of the Brigade Hospital and Purdum (the assistant Surg) & Will have charge of the Brigade in the field. Will don't entertain a doubt of Shermans success, and says they are going as fast as they can consistently without rushing.

I asked you some questions in my last about the Secretary of the Treasury, which would be out of place to day, for David Tod is not Secretary. We are in the dark yet, whether he declined the position or whether the Senate refused to confirm his nomination, but is certain now that Mr Fessenden of Maine is filling the position. He is a financier of tried abilities he having been Chairman of the Finance committee of the U.S. Senate for several years, and is believed to be second to no man in the Nation as a Financier not excepting S. P. Chase.[2] I hope it will all go on smoothly, for we do not want to see a financial crisis now.

We have but little news of interest from Grant, he had demanded the "Unconditional surrender" of Petersburg, of cource he was ready to [illegible] on the city when he made the demand. We are willing to leave the matter in his hands. "Old Abe" has declared Martial law all over Kentucky and suspended the privilege of the writ of Habius Corpus therein, that was much needed there and will bring some of the Rebs "to their milk".

Amos, Mary & our hired boys went to church to Ebeneezer today & have not returned yet, I will not close this til they return, I can then give you the afternoon news if any.

Evening, the folks safely returned from Church nothing new. We had a moderate rain since the above. We have verry warm weather and too dry yet tho we have had some small rains within a week, "evry little helps". There have been numerous hard rains went around us on either side, some too hard for the general wellfare of things thereabouts. I hope you will try to keep out of Forests hands for any who he may capture, may count on being murdered in cold blood.

With due respects,

Your Father,

Andrew Evans

1. On July 3, 1864, Sherman engaged Confederate General Joseph E. Johnston at Smyrna Camp Ground, four miles outside Marietta, Georgia, in an unsuccessful attempt to push Johnston across the Chattahoochie River. Marszalek, *Sherman*, 275.

2. In June 1864 Salmon Chase, who had made an abortive attempt to wrest the 1864 Republican presidential nomination from Lincoln, offered his resignation as secretary of treasury for the third time. Lincoln finally accepted and offered the position to David Tod, former Union Party Ohio Governor (1862–64). Tod declined, and Lincoln instead gave the post to Senator William Pitt Fessenden, who served for eight months in 1864–65 before returning to the Senate, where he chaired the Joint Committee on Reconstruction. Chase later became chief justice of the Supreme Court. McPherson, *Battle Cry of Freedom*, 713–15; John Sherman, *Recollections of Forty Years in the House, Senate and Cabinet: An Autobiography* (Chicago: The Werner Company, 1895), Vol. 1: 337–39.

⇻ ANDREW TO SAM ⇺
Home / July 17, 1864

Dear Son,

We have received nothing from you, since our short note from Moscow we suppose you have something Else to do, (if living) than to write letters. We have news in the "Commercial" of Gen Smith's forces having a fight with Forest, whipping his forces and killing him somewhere in Miss, we don't know whether to believe it or not, but are afraid it is not so. We continue our semi-weekly epistolary talk with you. We received two letters from Will last week, his last stated that he, (and Shermans Army) had been under fire for 61 days, or that there had been no day for that time without firing in some part of the Army, and on many of the days pretty heavy battles were fought. His health is fair, & he is tired.

We finished cutting wheat last monday, we have our oats cut & about 1/2 put up. Oats are generally good. We intend if the health & weather suits to put up as much as possible of the harvest crop this week. Many of the farmers finished cutting wheat yesterday, some are not done yet. The wheat is full, as poor as we expected. Corn is still looking well, where it has been well cultivated. We had a good rain on monday evening last, with wind enough to throw the corn so it cannot be plowed, but the rain did a great deal of good as well as some harm. The weather is still verry warm here, the water is still running in the creek but pastures are much parched up.

Inda is with us now on a visit. She & Morty are well. She says George is still at Washington City in better health he has been since he first got sick in the army, he is in 182 Co., 1 Bat V.R.C. Washington D.C.[1]

Our health; I had a rather sick spel last week, but am about square now. The residue of the family are mending & better than a week ago, Except Amos who, about holds his own.

Our army news is verry good if true, "Grant has taken Petersburg." "Sherman has crossed at Chattahooche & is within three miles of Atlanta," "Our forces at Washington whiped and drove the Rebs from that place" and "A.J. Smith whiped & killed Forest!" Too much good news to all be in one paper, hope it is all true, but have some doubts.[2]

Nothing local worthy of remark. Accept the best wishes of the family & believe me,

Your father,
Andrew Evans

1. VRC stood for Veteran Reserve Corps. In March 1864, the Union's Invalid Corps (see note in Amos's letter of March 17, 1864) was re-titled the Veteran Reserve Corps and reorganized to improve its effectiveness and standing. On rare occasion its able members were called to combat, the most notable example being in the defense of Washington DC against General Jubal Early on July 12, 1864. Garrison, *Encyclopedia*, 256.

2. Andrew is right to be skeptical about this army news reported to the home front. Grant had entrenched outside Petersburg, but he did not capture it until April 3, 1865. Sherman had gained control of the Chattahoochie, having forced General Johnston across it on July 9, but the main body of Sherman's army did not cross the river until July 17, the day this letter was written. General A. J. Smith did lead a Union victory over Forrest, who was wounded, but not killed (see note in Sam's letter of July 24, 1864). General Early was repelled by Union forces in his move on Washington, but his force escaped relatively unscathed. McPherson, *Battle Cry of Freedom*, 736, 749, 756–57. Marszalek, *Sherman*, 275–76.

⇒ ANDREW TO SAM ⇐
Home / July 24, 1864

Dear Son,

We have no letter from you since your short note from Moscow. We are exceedingly anxious for your welfare knowing that you [are] in the enemy's country which is filled with guerrillas of the darkest dye, who are bent on the annihilation of all colored troops, and their officers, if they are found in Federal uniform. You being in that capacity renders you liable at any moment to suffer all, or any tortures their hellish designs may see fit to inflict. May God preserve and protect you, and above all, may he enable you to keep free from the clutches of a foe so fiendish and hellish as are the Guerrillas of the so called "southern confederacy." We are fearful that your anxiety for revenge for past wrongs will lead you to do rash acts, and suffer yourself captured.

Our "war news" is favorable in general. Grant is not doing much visible active work just now, but is strategically puting the Rebs in a worse condition evry day. Those raiders who went into Maryland are likely to be sick of their trip before they get back to Lee's Army. They are getting whiped evry place our pursuing forces find them. We have already taken over 300 wagons heavily loded with stolen provisions. They were attempting to get to Lee's Army, and tis said that there is a fair prospect for none of them to ever get to Lee, with or without provision, as our pursuing force is far superior to them in numbers, and that Grant has so remodled his lines as to prevent their return to Lee's Army.

Sherman is bravely and steadily doing his work, and will have Atlanta in a verry few days, if not already in the city. He has a heavy force on to Macon to retake our prisoners confined there, and to destroy railroad, [im]press darkies, etc.

Our health is improved, Except Amos, who is not near so well, he is gone to Portsmouth, to see if Surgeon McDowell can do him any good, he says Mc told him when he was examining the drafted men in '62, that he never failed to cure "bronchitis". He therefore desires his proffessional skil, he went up last night, & will return tomorrow evening, unles the Dr. wishes to keep him longer. He is a good deal like you were in the summer of 1855 but has a worse cough, a sorer throat, and is more reduced.

We got a good long letter from Will yesterday dated 14 July, he was quite well & in the best of spirits, he had just visited the old 70th, had a good time with the boys, he says Dr. Philips is exceedingly popular, Doc rode a mile or two with him on his return. We have favorable news, from the expedition you are in, but no particulars, no casuality list and are therefore in great suspence for your welfare, knowing that Smith has had two or three fights! . . .

Accept our best wishes, and believe us unconditionally for the Union.
Andrew Evans

⇾ SAM TO ANDREW ⇽
Memphis, Tenn. / July 24, 1864

Dear Father,

It has been nearly 1 month since I talked to you. We arrived in Memphis Friday night about 2 O.Clk. Yesterday I was very tired and worn. I Should have written if I had felt qualified. I am as well as I could expect after so hard a trip—I am much better than when I left—I was quite sick all the way out but did not Leave my place—I was in command of "A", no other officer along. The expedition, to say the Least of it was entirely successful, Gen Smith out maneuvering Forest in evry instance. Tupelo, Miss. was the point we wished to strike. Smith, finding that Forest was in there and had his position, flanked him, pushed forward to Pontotoc. Forest then thought Smith was making for Okolona, which is 10 miles below Pontotoc on the R.R. We rested at the Latter place one day threw forward all our Cav, drove the enemy back considerable distance. Forest believing our intention was to press on to Okolona, drew all his Forces from Tupelo and occupied a high ridge beyond a Low Swampy bottom and fortified it, thinking Smith would rush his forces on through the bottom into a trap he had layed for him, as did Sturgis [in the battle of Guntown].

When Forest had evry thing fixed to suit him, Smith turned about for Tupelo and had not gone from Pontotoc more than two hours till Forest Cavalry began to press our rear, also to flank us on the right and left. The Black Brig. consisting of the 59, 61, and 68 and one 4 gun battery were in the Rear and were guarding the train or the principal portion till our brigade was Thrown in Line to fight back the Rebs. Then a white Brig. was ordered back with the train, while we were fighting in the rear till our train should pass out of danger. The Rebs. mounted Infantry, one Brig moved out on our Right flank, in about one hour they came in on our train in advance of us.[1] One Rebel Reg't was ambushed about 25 yds from our train and fired a volly into our train and a battery that was passing. But no sooner than this was done, the Inf. with train collected and drove the enemy back from the train, The whole Brig came into Line (White Brig) with the battery and fought the Enemy for about one hour when the enemy retreated leaving his kills and wounded without stand of colors on the field.

We lost 4 men killed 10 or 12 wounded The Enemy Lost 6 killed we know of and about 7 or 8 wounded. Brought of[f] our own wounded, burried our dead, left the rebs on the field. We lost 5 battery horses killed and 9 mules, 6 wagons were broken, [the animals] being scared and Running off. There being empty wagons along, the Stores were taken out of the broken wagons, changed to good ones, broken wagons were burned by us. The enemy did not ever make a "hard Tack" in the fight.[2] They still continued to press our rear but to no effect. They did not succeed in making any of them flank movements bear on us. Our movements were so rapid that we were out of their reach before they could get into position. The only thing they could annoy us with was their artillery which they would get in position in our rear & shell us at Long range. We tried to ambush the battery but found it was not safe because too strong a force was following. Consequently we only ambushed the head of their column, keeping them back, allowing our train to keep out of their Range. This was kept up till we passed over a bridge which we burned putting a stop to the shelling till the whole train reached camp at Tupelo where we arrived about 9 at night having marched distance of 20 miles and fought the enemy about 15 miles of the way.

On the 14th early in the morning the battle commenced.[3] Suffice to say our forces were entirely victorious. The enemy Lost 4 Cols, 3 of whom were Comdg. Brigs, Cols Folkner, Nelson, & Harrison. Col. Forest, lately promoted and Brother of Gen. Forest, report says Gen. Forest was wounded.

Prisoners Say so but I do not believe it. Several other secesh officers were killed. We lost one Col. Comdg. Brig killed 2 Surgeons 1 Maj., 1 Capt., 4 Lts. 500 would cover our loss in killed wounded and missing, while that of the enemy was at least 1000 killed in the battle of Tupelo besides those in the various other light battles and Skirmishes of the late expedition. I believe the loss in all could not be less than 1800 men, prisoners in cluded [sic]. Rebles say our loss is 600 but do not state their own, only that it was heavy. The white troops were in the hardest fight and fought with desperate valor. The Rebs made 6 different charges on our Lines but were met with a volly and a charge. The black troops were under fire several time, the only charge made on us was about 10 o'clock at night. They advanced pretty nearly our line and fired a volly and came on with a yell thinking we would run, but they were sadly mistaken, we were watching their maneuvers. As they came near enough, we let them have a volly, a "yell," and went for them. "They fled" not many of our men were hurt, they having over shot. Those at a distance looking on say the firing looked grand at night. During the time the infantry were fighting our Cav were tearing up the RR and burning Bridges. The R.R. was destroyed for 5 miles.

The Enemy dismounted one of [our] cannons but we brought it a way [sic, away]. One of their pieces of artillery was dismounted and fell into our possession. One other piece was [re]captured, one we lost at [illegible] Guntown. Smith gave Forest the roughest handling he has had for a long time. All of his troops came off feeling full as will those who came back after Sturgis's defeat. The white troops, if they ever have to go out with Sturgis again, they will kill.

On arriving I found letters from you from the 26 of June, 17 of July, 4 in No., one from Mary, 1 from Amos. Let this answer for a letter this time. Love to all the family,

As ever,

Sam Evans

I did receive a scratch in battle, no marks on My clothes. One bullet cut [a line] half its size off my hair above my right Ear. Did not notch the hide. I do not know that you [say] good pluck, but I can't run much.

Good by, S.

1. Unlike cavalry who fought from the saddle (at least in principle), mounted infantry used their horses to allow them greater mobility before engaging the enemy, but they still fought on foot. Garrison, *Encyclopedia*, 162–63.

2. Here Sam improbably uses a nautical term in describing a land battle.

3. On July 14, 1864, General Forrest and his seven thousand men were lured into an attack on fourteen thousand Union troops that had been sent from Memphis at Tupelo, Mississippi. The Battle of Tupelo was one of the only two major battles (the other being Shiloh) in which Sam participated. McPherson, *Battle Cry of Freedom*, 749.

⇀ JANE TO SAM ↽

Huntington Township, Brown Co., Oh. / July 25, 1864

Dear Cousin,

It is with pleasure that I now write you a few lines to let you know that we are all well at present, and I hope that these few lines may find you enjoying good health.

Cousin Sam it has bin sometime since I received your kind letter. I expect that you think that I have forgotten you entirely, but indeed, cousin, I have not. I think as much of you now as I ever did. There is some of the souldiers boys say that I don't care anything about them because they are gone so far away from home. That don't make any difference. I think as much of them when they are away as if they were at home, and I expect a little more so. Cousin I don't think hard of you for not writing sooner than you did, for I know that you have a great many letters to write, besides other work and camp duty.

Cousin Sam I expect you feel pretty tired and worn out those warm days when you have too [sic] march in the dust. Indeed it looks too hard but the way everry thing is, you have to put up with the hard ships [sic] the best way that you can. I don't think that the war will last much longer. If it does they won't be any man left too raise any thing, if there is 500,000 more men taken away. That is the last call. I don't no what the poor people will do if the times gets much harder than what they are now.

You say that your darkeys boys are good to fight. I am glad to here that, for they will save a good many [white] men's lives, and that is what we want to hear of. I do hope that Gen. Grant will take Richmond pretty soon. Some think that he is afraid to attact them. My opinion is that he is just getting a "good [and] ready" too [sic] blow them all out of there. I think they have bin there long enough.

You asked me how me and my 70th boy gets along. Cousin we don't get along at all. He is mad at me, for what I can not say. He says that he is a going to bring his woman home with him when he comes.

You asked me when I saw Cal. Cousin I have not seen her for some time, Cousin you must shurely be joking when you say that she is mad at you, I don't think that she would get mad at a good fellow as you are without you give her some cause to, which I don't think you would. I think she will get in a good humor when you come home. I expect that is the reason that she is mad, because you went away. I did here a week or so a go that Cal was a going to get married, but I don't think that she will till you get home. Cousin I want you to ask me too the wedding.

Well Cousin, I believe that I will close for this eavening, please write soon again for I do love to here from my cousins and friend that is in the army. I will try and answer [sooner] then I did this time. I still remain as ever,

Your true and faithful cousin,
Jane Evans

❧ SAM TO ANDREW ❧
Memphis, Tenn. / July 31, 1864

Dear Father,

I received a letter from you this week date I think the 17 of this month but I am not positive. I have misplaced it and cannot find it at present. I have not written many Letters since I came back from our Scout, 1 to you is all that I have written. The past week I have been very busy making pay Rolls, getting clothing [illegible] of soldiers, making ordnance returns, monthly returns of clothing, Camp and Garrison Equipage, and various other things too tedious.[1] I have transfered the company property to Capt Hensley, si[n]ce Cpt. Foster promoted to Maj. At the time of the Guntown fight or "defeat", my Co. property amounted to $3,500 including ord-nance and ordnance stores. There is not much news in this department. I am very sorry Gen. J. B. McPherson was kill[ed], he was one of the brightest stars of the Nation or age.[2] The Nation will morn his loss. You will recollect he was an Ohio Genl.

We are under marching orders again, expect to march tomorrow or next day, I cannot tell this time where we are going. I understand Gen. Washburn says we will be gone about 20 days. Some Say we will make a trip down on the Miss. Central R.R. down near Abbyville. I do not like to go in that direction, water is so scarce this time in the year.

My health is not as good as it has been but I need not complain, I have been confined too close for the Last week. I [have] not taken enough exercise. I received a Letter from G. W. Early the Last week, he says he is well and a little no[t] satisfied with his camping ground. Says he does not hear from Huntington [the township in which the Evans family resides] very often. He does not say any thing about the [attack] on Washington, or whether there was any or not. I am of opinion they made a good thing of it in the way of plunder, perhaps better than we did on our Late expedition because the country was much Richer. Rebles in this country have their meat, bacon, molasses, sugar, bed, clothing besides many other articles. Horses, mules, and cattle are also driven to the Swamps and River bottoms when ever we march through any part. There are enough of the [necessities] of Life to keep a small army from starving along the roads.

I guess I will not have an opportunity to be examined with refference to my qualifications for a higher position soon. I was thinking of trying to get a leave to go home but I do not think it will be necessary. I only have a year and 10 months to Stay till my time will be out. That will not take Long. I am getting tired sitting still so long. Will you please excuse this scribling and call it what we generally call papers in this shape. If we do not march tomorrow I will write again. Give my Love and best respects to all the family.

Yours as Ever,

Sam Evans

1. Typically used to designate a battery or group of guns, the term "ordnance" could also refer to vehicles used in combat, ammunition, or equipment. Garrison, *Encyclopedia*, 182.

2. General James McPherson of Ohio was killed in the Battle of Atlanta while commanding the Army of the Tennessee. He was shot from his horse after blundering into Confederate lines and refusing to surrender. Despite his own death, his army fought successfully and inflicted many casualties on Confederate General Hood's army. General McPherson was the only Union general in command of an army to die from battle wounds. McPherson, *Battle Cry of Freedom*, 754. Garrison, *Encyclopedia*, 16.

≫ ANDREW TO SAM ≪
Home / Aug. 7, 1864

Dear Son,

Yours of the 31 came to hand yesterday, we are glad to learn that you were still living & in tolerable health, but sorry that your duties are so onerous, as to impair your health to some extent, if you have all the duties of Captain to discharge why are you not promoted. I am fearful that you are taking so much duty on yourself, that you will breakdown. You have had but little rest since your "Tupelo raid," now to start on another (perhaps a worse one) without time to rest and restore sore toes &c is rather hard. I hope by the aid of divine Providence, that you may be enabled to endure your hardships and over come all obstacles you may meet, and return home [illegible].

We have a letter from Will date 31st, he is still in fair health, and entertains no doubt of their final success. The annihilation of Hood's army seems to be Sherman's ultimatum!, and not the mere taking of Atlanta, which he says he can do in two hours whenever he wishes it. May his designs be crowned with success. We don't know positively, what Grant is doing but are content to leave the taking of Richmond in his hands, as he has lost none of his confidence, in taking that great Rebel strong-hold "as sure as the [sun] rises." Recruiting, under the last call has started off tolerably well, I saw a number of men sworn in at Riply last Thursday (white & blacks). The Negros are coming over from Ky. and enlisting as substitutes, getting the hire, Bounty &c.[1] I can give you the name of but one from here, Alex Kitch, who has been living with Thompson Moddox. He goes as a substitute for Tom Maddox which exempts him if drafted. Many others who are not [yet] liable to the draft, are making arrangements to put in substitutes in time.

We have had our two letters from Amos since he left, both from Cleveland O.[2] The last one was written on tuesday last. He would go on board the ship "Meteor" at 3, P.M. that day and leave for the great Lake [Superior] that evening, a distance of 1100 miles. He was improved in his health. His throat and cough were both better. He thinks you need not try to correspond with him, as he will be mooving about in a strange place. He will write home once a week when he can, and we will post you as well as we can on his condition and "visa versa".

We have a letter from Inda, Recd yesterday. She and Morty were well, nothing new from George. Our health is about as usual, nothing serious the matter. Bell is not as stout as usual, she is slightly "Scorbutic" [affected by scurvy], again. Lee is not growing any, but as mischievous as ever. Jo is a verry good boy to work at anything he is able for, he & Ann are my assistent farmers now, but we dont make a strong team. We will have a hand before many days, "no preventing Providence".

We have had some slight improvement in weather. We had two light rains last week (not near enough) which helped the corn considerable. Potatoes will be a near failure. Corn will be considerably hurt, if [the weather is] seasonable from now out it may mak a 2/3 crop where it is well tended. Wheat so far as thrashed [*sic*, threshed] is making from 3 to 6 bushels to the acre, we have not thrashed [*sic*]. The weather is still warm but not so hot as before those rains. Pastures are improved, also stock water, and perhaps general health, for flux & other diseases were on the increase during the dry hot weather.

I believe we have nothing more in the local way that would interest you.

Accept the love and compliments of the family.

As ever your father,

Andrew Evans

1. Apparently blacks were fleeing slavery in Kentucky, which as a "loyal slave state" had been excluded from the Emancipation Proclamation, to join the army in southern Ohio as substitutes for draftees. The black substitute received a fee, or "hire," from the draftee as well as the bounty paid to enlistees.

2. Amos had apparently gone on a tour of the Great Lakes in an effort to recoup his health.

➤ ANDREW TO SAM ◄

Home / Aug. 14, 1864

Dear Son:

I have received nothing from you since I wrote, therefore you must put up with an offhand note. We are having a verry good rain today enough to soke the ground pretty well, and it fell & is falling slow enough to not wash the ground [away], this will help considerable of the corn. Some crops are beyond redemption, young grasses have been seriously injured, this rain will revive such as is not quite dead. We had intended to commence threshing our wheat tomorrow but it will be too damp. Dyas' machin is set at one of our stacks, the [illegible] does more good than we could, threshing poor wheat.

Our health is fair and we are progressing with our farm as well as we can for the force at our control. Our hand has got well and is with us, on duty again. He & I do make a good team to their size; but too light.

We have another letter from Amos, dated 5 Aug., he was then at the head of Saint Mary's River and to enter Lake Superior on the morning of the 6th. He said he was improving in health, and gaining some strength. We will hardly get another letter from him until he returns to the South edge of the big Lake, where he intends to remain some time, if his health improves.

We have nothing from George. Inda was well, Morty was not very well on wednesday last. We have a letter from Will of Aug. 2. He was well at that time, and located in a ditch before Atlanta, says the general health of Sherman's army is good, and that they are having about enough rain to keep the air good.

The "Old 70" suffered in their battle of the 28 [Battle of Ezra Church, three miles west of Atlanta], & since Capt. Jim Brown was wounded and sent home, Capt. Frank Summers killed. A few days after Maj. Brown was killed in a skirmish and now sleeps by the brave Cap Summers, both "noble men & officers". The casualties were mostly among the new recruits of the 70, Thomp Sheltons son badly wounded, Simon Reeders (Dan) wounded in the face, Boone Ferrick killed, my memory don't serve me further. I think you were not acquainted with many of the new recruits that suffered. Col Loudon is at home quite unable for duty. he is able to walk about with a cane. I am fearful the Regt. has lost its best stuff, Loudon, Brown, & Summers have a good reputation, Jim Brown & Cap Cooper are wounded and at home. Gen. Sherman is not giving much rest to his army, and less to the Rebs., I hope he will come out right. Grant don't appear to gain much in the vicinity of Richmond, I fear he has too heavy a contract, but I still believe he will work it out if it can be done by man.

Farragut has fooled the Rebs at Mobile to slick by passing their forts into the bay & taking their fort from "t'other side" Mobile is at his mercy; if not already taken.[1] We see by "orders" that Gen. Washburn's command is much enlarged, I hope your present raid will be a success without loss on our part. I wish you good luck through the "little time," ("only 2 years & 10 months,") you have to serve for I think you have no idea of coming home, unless the war should end before you time is out (and not then if you can get to stay longer).[2] We must allow you to be the judge in all such matters.

Will said some time ago that he would come home this fall, but it is easy to be mistaken in such cases. A soldier has no right to have either friends, or home to visit unless it suits his officers to grant leave, and they are doing but little of that kind of business now. We would be much pleased to have an honorable peace and have our Sons & friend[s] come home and enjoy the hospitality of home & friends that they have seen so little of for the last, nearly three years.

Accept the love and good wishes of the family and,
Your father,
Andrew Evans

1. On August 5, 1864, Union Admiral David Farragut led his fleet of fourteen wooden ships and four ironclad monitors into Mobile Bay and thrashed the Confederate flotilla, including the formidable ironclad CSS *Tennessee*. Within three weeks, Farragut's fleet, with the help of one army division, captured three forts on the bay, effectively closing the final remaining blockade-running port on the eastern Gulf of Mexico. McPherson, *Battle Cry of Freedom*, 761.

2. Andrew is needling Sam about his length of service and his apparent uninterest in returning home on leave. Notably Andrew misquotes Sam's letter of July 31, 1864, adding a year to Sam's remaining time of service.

↠ ANDREW TO SAM ↞
Home / Aug. 28, 1864

Dear Son,

Yours of the 14 from Waterford, Miss. was received yesterday, we were getting uneasy for your welfare having had no letter for some time. We are relieved to know you were still living and in fair health, you have verry many toils to undergo in those marches, besides the hazzard of being captured or killed by Guerillas. Forest made a raid on Memphis since you left, but failed to effect his object, got his forces thrashed and left.[1] I[f] he succeeds in getting all his forces together, and brings them against Smiths, he may give you a good deal of trouble and try the fighting qualities of your "Smoked yankees," (a new name for the Negro soldiers.) I hope you may succeed in your object and return safely to your HdQrters.

We have a letter from Will to the 11, he was still well & in good spirits. He says Sherman is plucking the heart strings [Atlanta] from the monster one by one, and Grant is knocking its brains out [Richmond] and by the loss of either vital [organ] it will die. Gen. Sherman is promoted to a Major Gen., in the Regular Army, a merited raise.

We have nothing from George since I wrote; a letter from Inda informs us of Mortys ill health, from Whooping cough. We have a letter from Amos the 14, he is improving slowly and seems in good spirits, says his skin has assumed the natural color, he is getting stronger an[d] heavier, I hope he may recover for he is a noble boy.

Our health at home is fair, the general health is poor. Amos' Jake is better today and in a fair way to recover, Laban is sick of flux, not dangerously so, I think there are many cases in the country.[2] We have had a great deal of wet weather for the last two weeks. Friday last, we had a wind with the rain which blew the corn down teribly. The weather is more pleasant. We have a great deal of thunder and the air seems much purified, and I think the heat will be improved.

Produce is higher here than in your country. Wheat is worth 2.00, corn 1.[00], bacon 20 to 30, sugar 30 to 40, Coffee 60, Tea 2.50 to 3.00, potatoes 1 to 1.25, eggs 10 @ 15, Chickens 3.00, Sheep 4 to 7 pr head, calico 45 to 50, brown sheetings 75 to 90, white flannels 1.25, Colored 1.35 to 1.45, Jeans 1.50 to 2.00, and so on.

Recruiting is verry slow, verry few have enlisted in this township. Only one more week and the draft will recruit them.

Our fruit is very inferior, the drouth hurt it seriously. It is falling prematurely and is small and knotty. The corn is so green that it will be in danger of frost. Pastures are growing rapidly, those rains will make our field pastures better than usual.

Accept the love and best wishes of the family and of,

Your father,

Andrew Evans

1. In a feint maneuver designed to prevent or delay General A. J. Smith's anticipated march into Mississippi, General Forrest led a raid on Memphis on August 21, 1864. Forrest's forces rode through the picket guarding Memphis, entered the city, and rode up to General Washburn's headquarters, but Washburn had already absconded to Fort Pickering. Having made a sufficient display to make Union commanders wary of sending forces away from Memphis, Forrest and his men rode off with numerous prisoners, but they did little material damage in Memphis. Ernest Walter Hooper, "Memphis, Tennessee: Federal Occupation and Reconstruction," Ph.D. diss. (Chapel Hill: University of North Carolina, 1957), 31.

2. Jake and Laban Evans are Andrew's brother Amos's sons, and Little Jane's brothers. At this time Jake was four and Laban was seventeen (calculated from 1860 U.S. Census for Huntington Township, Brown County, Ohio).

≫ SAM TO ANDREW ≪

Memphis, Tenn. / Sept. 1, 1864

Dear Father,

I again seat myself to pen you a few Lines. We (us & Co) arrived at Memphis night before last. Right Side [illegible] having done Some tall marching the last two days of our journey. From Holly Springs to Memphis is 50 miles. First day we marched 22 miles, last day 28.

One division of White troops was with us the 1st days march but they only came 18 miles the last day. Part of our trip was very hard. We did a great deal of marching backward and forward, hunting for the enemy but did not find him in force to offer us much Risistence. Oxford, Miss. was the furthest South we went. Part of the time our men were in want of Meat, they were without Meat 4 days at one time. Worse than all, there is no perceivable good we did but, if I am not mistaken, Forest rather out Generaled Smith & Washburn this time, made a flank movement and came into Memphis. Took some prisoners (200) is the Report here and Some few horses but left more Horses than he took away. Most he left were dead, Killed in the fight. I can not find the marks of a raid any place about here. There was no Government property destroyed. They did not free any thing. I do not know why [they] did not Liberate the prisoners in the "Irvin[g] Block", Nor rob the Post Office. They made an attempt to do both but did not succeed. I do not know how many either Side lost in killed and wounded. Several of their Stragglers were taken prisoners, I understand between 40 and 50.

There is but Little news of interest to communicate from this post. All is quiet. We will soon know who the Copperheads intend to run for President. I have not been studying Politics, I now think I never Shall. Abe and Johnson Will do me for President and Vice President.

I wrote to you from Watterford, or rather Mury. I found 2 letters here from you dated 14th and 21st Respectively, and one from Ibbe, I have forgotten the date.

I hope Amos will find some salubrious climate that will cure up his throat. I know of several cases having been cured by going to the war, my own for one but I do not mean by this that he had better join the Army or that it would cure him. I am Satisfied that no position I could [have] at home or out of the army could Satisfy me as well as a private in the Army. I can come as near being satisfied as any man with what ever comes. I hope you can get along with[out] Suffering too much without me at home but if you Should need my assistance to prevent you from worst or suffering, let me know. I will come if I can honorably. Otherwise I hope you will do as well without with me. I think I can do Some good for Uncle Sam. Do not fear that I will be killed. I have not felt that I would be killed, not even in battle. My health is good at this time. While out on the expedition I gaine[d] 8 1/2 Lbs. When I left my weight was 145 1/2. When I returned it was 154, is now my weight. You may know that I am not very fat. I was Some sick when I left.

I was a little uneasy when I heard the news of Forests Raid that he had taken my good Clothes and Watch and Green Backs. I do not mean to Say that I am a better General than Smith but what I told Some of our Officers [when I heard] that Forest had gone to make a Raid on Memphis, I Said if [he] did not he was "bigger fool" than I thought he was. He did not do as much as I thought he could, not as much as I think [I] could If I had been in his Shoes. His Great Errors was taking two pieces of ord[nance] cannon and firing in to Camp arousing all the Soldiers before he got in to the City. On the part of our commanders, I think they made a poor [show] out of heading [him off] after he had got in side our lines. Let this Suffice for the Raid.

Well I guess you will be tired of this ere you get the meaning. Give My Respects to all the family. I Remain,

Your Son as ever,

Sam Evans

➤ ANDREW TO SAM ◂
Home / Sept. 4, 1864

Dear Son,

Another week has passed without us getting a letter from you, we suppose the reason is because you are in the enemey's country without mail facilities in your [a]reas. Yours from Waterford is the last. We have letters from Will to the 22nd Aug, he was well at that time. We have one from Amos to the 19 Aug. He believes he is improving and is of opinion that country will do him much good. Nothing from George since I wrote, nothing from Inda. Our folks at home are in fair health. The general health of the neighborhood is much better than a week ago. Flux is subsiding, there have been several deaths, Joana Scott, old Peter Shaw, Judge C.F. Campbell, & Tip Martins Babe during last week.

We suppose the quota of our township in the 500,000 call is filled by volunteers, those men in this township who were subject to [the] draft want to work in Earnest & by reaching deep into their pockets raised the local bounty to $400. and on last Friday they raised the requisite No of men and went to Hillsborough to fill the quotas. This call will be filled more promptly than any previous call, for the fact that there is no 300 clause in the law.[1] If a man is drafted and is fit for duty, he must go or furnish a substitute, we will get the men this time & no dodging . . .

We are having considerable of rain these times, it rained all night and up to noon today. We have an ordinary high creek. We had quite a hail storm yesterday with a great deal of thunder and lightning, fall pastures are coming on verry finely, the potato crop was too far gone to be benefitted and will be short, the corn will be fair in quantity but much injured by blowing down. We will hold a fair on the 20th & [the] 3 following days of this month, if you will come up, we will put you on some important committee. Your Cuz' Mary Espy is nursing a girl of her own, name "Minnie Sherman".

I am exceedingly throug [sic, thorough] with law business. I tried 6 cases last week, and issued 23 summons for hearing this week. I will [have] but little time to do any thing until those cases are disposed of. They are mostly collection cases.

Well the Peace men had to take a War Democrat at last, if McLellan [sic] sticks to his doctrine, they would not gain much if they should chance to Elect him (which I cannot admit they are able to do), only that he might get hold of bad advisers, and do as old Buchanan did, I don't propose to try him. "Old Abe" will do me this time. The "Cops" [Copperheads] expected a large vote in the Army for Mack [McClellan] which I don't believe they will get.

The canvas is fairly open now and "stumping" going on lively, we believe we can knock them in this County, we will try hard. We will have a mass meeting in Aberdeen on Tuesday night to hear our candidate for Congress Mr. [Reader Wright] Clark[e] & others.

Accept our best wishes,
Andrew Evans

1. In the Federal Conscription Act of 1863, a conscript had three choices: to serve, hire a substitute, or pay three hundred dollars. After facing heavy criticism, the three-hundred-dollar commutation fee was eliminated as an option for draftees in the July and December drafts of 1864, excepting for rare cases of conscientious objectors. McPherson, *Battle Cry of Freedom*, 601.

➤ JANE TO SAMUEL ◄
Huntington, Township Brown Co. Ohio / Sept. 11, 1864
Mr. Samuel Evans,

Affectionate Cousin It is with pleasure that I now write you a few lines to let you know that I have not yet fogotten you. Cousin it has bin some time since I received your last letter. I suppose you think that I never intend to answer it. Cousin I have not had much of a chance to write untill now. I hope that you will excuse me for so long a delay. We have all bin sick since I heard from you. Little Jake come mighty near dying with the flux, but he is now most well. We are all tolerable well, Laban is not stout at all, he has bin spitting blood at times for times for more then a year, it is still growing worse on him, he looks pretty pale. Although he will run around every place, and expose himself in the nigh[t] air which he ought not to do. He has a very bad cough now of which I am afraid will get him down. I was down at your Fathers this eavening. They are all tolerable well except Amos he is at home sick, he looks very pale and bad, more so then I expected to see him. Cousin Lina Evans came out from Ripley while I was at your house, she is a going too teach School in our Destrict. She is going to commence tuesday 13th!

You said that you was glad that there was a going to be another draft in the north; I cannot say that I am very glad. For I would not like to see all the men taken away, and no one left to support the mamas and children, what will become of them? I rec[k]on we will all have to starve to death. I am glad that Laban is not old enough for this draft. I would a great deal rather see him die at home than to go out and fight to free the negro and no telling but what he would be buried by the side of a Negro as a white man, who would know.

If you was fighting for the old Union as it was I would be in for it. But such a union as some of you are trying to make of it! I can not hold up for it. I would not mind freeing the negros if they could be sent off and not come back here again. Cousin how can you send a free man away and make him stay away with out he wants too? Could any body make you stay any place without you wanted to stay. You may call me a Rebel secesh or a butternut or copperhead or any thing that you please, I am for peace. I am getting [tired] of this war. I want to see the end of it as soon as possible and that will never be as long as old Abe Lincoln is president. There is no true hearted Democrat that will vote for him. Who would vote for any one that has bin the cause of as many lives lost as he has, and still calling for more? He will do anything though to be an expence to the Government. Cousin Sam, never did I think that you would vote for old Abe. Cousin, do you mind [remember] how you use to talk to Jake Botner before the presidential Election four years ago. I have not forgotten yet. When you boys use to come up here and argue for two or three hours, do you mind of calling Jake a Negroamus and every other name that you could think of, and Jake would laugh at you and take it all in a good humor. You said that you would not vote for no such a black hearted old rip as he [Lincoln] was.

I think you have changed your notion verry much since then. Everyone can vote for who they please. I will never change my politics as long as I live. This thing turning from one side to the other, I don't believe in it. Cousin Sam, you turning don't make me think any the less of you, I love all of my cousins in the army and at home. You asked me who I heard that Cal was a going to marry. I heard that her and T. Hill was a going to marry soon but I don't believe it. I think that she is a waiting for the Lieut. S-E: Please write soon, this from,

Your true and faithful cousin,

Jane Evans

⇒ SAM TO ANDREW ⇐
Memphis, Tenn. / Sept. 16, 1864

Dear Father,

I wrote a letter to you Last Sunday but by some means I neglected to put it into the office. I found today that I had not mailed it and for fear the news would be a Little "Stale" I will try it again. I have a letter from home of the 1st is the latest.

We have again gone to picketing here. Commence about 2 weeks ago. The (100) day troops have gone home, their times being out, and many others are gone else where. There is nothing new in the military line, except the authorities have concluded to fortify some other points in the vicinity of Memphis and are making heavy details to work at fortifications. Trade is being opened up with the Citizens outside of the Line, (except) to Mississippians very few of them get anything—Some of them get a Small quantity. Lt. Col. Cowden has come back from Ohio. He was wounded at Guntown Miss. (Sturgis Defeat) and went home on sick leave, is now well of his wound. His home is near Bucyrus Ohio and is by the way one of the best men I have become acquainted with since I came into the Army. He is by profession a "Carpenter", was a Douglas Democrat but never much of a polittion, is for "Abe" and "Andy" as all of us down here are who can vote. The Memphis Bullitin is for them, has their names at the "Mast Head". I think Like you that Abe and Andy will do me although I do not expect to make any stump Speaches in their behalf. Neither of the other "Platforms" will do.[1] Mac has got into bad

Co. It was to be hoped that he would not accept the Chicago nomination but has accepted the nomination. If he does not stand on the Platform it is all the same so far as I regard the matter.[2] I would be pleased if you could roll up a nice majority for Abe & Andy in our Township and Co.[unty] Next Nov.

Winter is coming and I would like to know what a good heavy Calf boot (double) would cost at Ruggles' at this time. The above named article only costs $20.00 in the City of Memphis and then they are not quite as good as Ruggles'. Will you please inform me by next. Ask Mother what she can pack 50 lbs. of her own make of butter at per lbs. I mean if she makes any to sell. 7 of us board together, our butter alone to date has cost $20, this that is from the 1st of the month.

I will try to come home the coming fall or winter, It may be like my trip home Last March.[3] Most of [the] Men have been at home at least once since they came into the service. The Pay Master has not come this way for some months.[4] If I am paid and can get a "leave" I will bring my money home. I have more here than I want but do not like to risk Expressing it from here . . . I am carrying one of the best American Lever watches "out". I have one of "Smith & Wessons 5 inch Revolvers" (Copper Cartridge) Same pattern of John's only 1 inch Larger.

The health of the Army here is now much better than it was a year ago. My health is pretty good and I think is getting better. I have just received a notice from my Last "Ordnance Returns" that they were correct. They were for the 2nd Quarter, consequently included the Sturgis "loss" at Guntown. I do not Like to say it much but . . . I made the only set of papers that stand the test at the Ordnance Bureau at Washington that went from this Regt. I have the name of being the best in the Regt. at a difficult paper, and now am taken almost as "Law and Gospel" in [that] part of the Service in This Regt.

I hope you will not take this a boast because I do not intend it as such. Well you will be very apt to be tired of this ere you get through. Give Love and compliments to all. I have the honor to be Very Respectfully,

Your Obt. Serv't,

Sam Evans

1. Sam is referring to the Democratic platform and Fremont's radical Democratic platform. Fremont withdrew from the race on September 22, 1864. See note about Fremont's 1864 candidacy in Andrew's letter of June 12, 1864. McPherson, *Battle Cry of Freedom*, 776.

2. As Sam suggests, many of McClellan's views contradicted the Democratic platform. McClellan repudiated one plank that described the war as "four years of failure" in a September 8, 1864, letter in which he refused to "tell [Union soldiers] that their labor and the sacrifice of [their] slain and wounded brethren had been in vain." Instead of categorically supporting peace negotiations, as many Peace Democrats did, McClellan insisted on the Union as the one and only condition for peace negotiations, a requirement that seemed unlikely to be acceptable to most Southerners, and thus unlikely to bring an immediate start to peace talks. McPherson, *Battle Cry of Freedom*, 776.

3. This is another infrequent instance of Sam's sarcasm. He made no trip home in March 1864.

4. See note about payment processes in Sam's letter of May 1, 1862.

⟫ ANDREW TO SAM ⟪
Home / Sept. 18, 1864

Dear son,

I having the headache considerably, you will have to accept a short, and perhaps poor letter this time. We are in usual health, except Mary, who has a cold accompanied with considerable cough, she is on duty as usual but not so well. Amos is much better than he was last Sunday, his Cholera morbus is entirely quit[t]ed, and he is gaining strength, he is able to walk around some but looks verry bad. My sick head is but temporary. I think Mrs. Scotts family are about all sick, some of them dangerously low. The general health is improving. We have nothing from Will since the battle of Jonesborough and taking of Atlanta, hope he's well.

Our draft is appointed for tomorrow-week, if the quota is not previously filled, there are many more men gone from our township than would have filled her quota, but when our men ceased to pay $400 local bounty, they sold themselves to other townships for $430.00. Well, the draft won't hurt at our house, let it come. Fill our depleted Regiments make them effective, crush the rebellion at once; then all can come home. I am of opinion the draft will be small in our County, it need not [have] been pending at all, if the men who will not want to go had forked the money.

Our fair will commence on Tuesday next, I can't tell what it will be, til I see it tried, but I predict that it won't be much. I still have the honor of the chair and will endeavor to do my duty, but whether the people will come & bring articles to show, is in doubt.

We have had several days of good weather for curing corn, our corn is all too green for the season and is subject to serious injury from frost. Our fall pastures are unusually fine, and the ground in good order for work, people have not commenced seeding yet, some plowing done in the neighborhood. I shall seed but 7 1/2 acres, that will be as much as Jo and I can harvest. The people growl at the idea of the mill not running the coming season, they will have to growl on, for I cannot run it and stay at Columbus, nor could I, if I were home without hiring.

Bens Anjaline is teaching our school she is a "live teacher" she is bording with us, she is energetic & of good morals.

The compliments, love, & good wishes of the family are tendered to you by,

Your father,

Andrew Evans

P.S. Sept 19 at the P.O. A letter from you & one from Will. Both "all right" AE

≫ SAM TO ANDREW ≪
Memphis, Tenn. / Sept. 19, 1864

Dear Father,

I Should have written to you yesterday but was on Picket, but today will perhaps answer. I have nothing very interesting to write, everything is very quiet in the Military Line. There is a subject that I would Like to mention to you! Col. Bouton of this Regt. is a very worthy man. He has been Recommended for promotion to the next higher grade by Maj's Gen. Washburn, Smith and Hulbert [sic, Hurlbut] and By Brigadier's Gen. Buckland, Mower, Hatch and Grierson, and perhaps some others. I would if you could procure a Letter of Recommendation from Gov. Brough to President Lincoln. Consistently I am of opinion that it would have a great weight, I cannot exactly tell why I think thus. If you know of any honest way that you could get a letter from the Gove[r]nor it would be a great weight in the Col's favor. He is a very worthy Officer and has by Good conduct on the "field" and else where merited the position. If properly represented to the President [he] would be likely to receive the appointment I have only suggested the forgoing, if you do not see that you can do any thing, all right, that is all I have to say about it.

There is another thing going around here. I do not know how it Started. I have in my possession some Recommendations to the Gov of Ohio for promotion to a field office. I think there was a talk of here that the Gove[r]nor of Ohio intended to make field Officers of men who had been out in the Service from the commencement of the war, Col. Bouton and Lt. Col Cowden expressed a desire that I should Send a Recommend[ation] through you to Governor Brough but finding that the experiment is too Late I will not make any fu[r]ther exertion. I am not in the Line of promotion in Ohio because I hold an appointment from the President [in the USCT]. I send you my recommendations. You will please Keep them for me. Should you see an opportunity for a promotion, I hope you will send me a Line. These documents will do no harm to keep at home, I do not aspire to a much higher position although I know of men holding such who are not better qualified.[1]

My health is good. No letters from home for more than a week. Love to all.

Yours as ever,

Sam

1. The recommendation that Sam's commander, Lieutenant Colonel Robert Cowden, had Sam transmit to Governor Brough read:

To His Excellency, John Brough, Governor of the State of Ohio:

Sir: As a citizen of the great State of Ohio, and feeling a just pride in his good name and reputation, I take great pleasure in attesting to his excellent character as an officer, and as a man, and to his regiment, First Lieutenant Samuel Evans, an Ohioan. I have known him quite well since May, 1863, when he, with others, organized this regiment; I have noticed his good behavior, good conduct and high morals on all occasions of duty. Never a word of reproach has been brought against him. I consider him fully competent to fill any field office, or to command any regiment with credibility to himself and with honor to the State and Nation. I hereby beg, if consistent, that you appoint him to a field office in one of the Ohio Regiments now being organized. I have the honor to be,

Very Respectfully,

Your Obedient Servant,

Lieutenant Colonel Robert Cowden, Commanding the 59th U.S.C.I.

As Sam correctly stated, he did hold a commission from the president and would have first had to have been relieved of that commission before he could accept a position under an Ohio commission. Sam never received a commission from Governor Brough and remained a first lieutenant in the 59th USCI for the remainder of his service. Carl N. Thompson, *Historical Collections of Brown County, Ohio* (Piqua, Ohio: Hammer Graphics, 1969), 768.

Memphis, Tenn. / Sept. 24, 1864

Dear Father,

Your kind favor of the 12th came to hand today. I was very glad to hear from home. I am very Sorry to Learn that Amos is so ill, I was in hopes that his visit to the Lakes would have a Salutary influence on his health but by your letter it seems that it did but little good. I would like to hear of his restoration to health.

I received a very unwelcome letter from Little Jane. I never thought she was so much Reble. We have as loyal women in the "Irvin[g] Block" as she is. It would be a good thing for her if she were sent South for a month or two with the more honorable of her proclivities. It is very insulting to me or any other Union soldier to have their "would be friends" to write such sentiments to them while they are Striving to protect their Homes, periling their lives, and enduring a great many hardships. I will give you that portion I refer to just as she has written.

[Sam quotes at length from Jane's letter of Sept. 11, 1864: "You said that you was glad . . . I love all of my cousins in the army and at home."]

This is verbatum as far as I have gone. Well I am mad. How do you like this for a Northern Lady? Good Night.

Sunday Mornin 25 / I feel in some better humor than I did last night. Now I feel disposed to accredit some of the above to ignorance. I mean to answer it and quit correspondence with [her] unless She acknowledge the "Cor[rectio]n." There is no news of importance. A rumor Says Mobile has surrendered to our Gun boats but it is not believed. The weather is very fine, a fine rain fell Friday night. Produce continues high. Citizens and soldiers are making preparations for winter. We expect to remain here, but there is always an uncertainty in war. We expect to be reviewed by Maj Gen Howard in a few days and are making preparations for it.[1]

The health of the Army here is very good, better than usual for this season of the year. My own health is very good and my weight has increased from 146 1/2 (the day I Left on last Scout) to 163 lbs. my present weight. I am quite nervious this morning, can scarcely write at all. Respects to all the family.

As ever,

Sam

1. Nicknamed the Christian Soldier for his piety, General O. O. Howard was commander of the Army of the Tennessee, which included Sam's regiment. McPherson, *Battle Cry of Freedom*, 754.

Memphis, Tenn. / Oct. 2, 1864

Dear Father,

In obedience to previous arrangements I will devote an hour in Scribling you a few items. Nothing from home since the 15 of Last month, there should have been one since. I wrote some time about the price of boots, butter & c. The price here is $22.00 @ pair for such Boots as Ruggles made for me. Butter is selling at 75 cts @ per Lb. It may be that the Storekeepers add Something for the "Strength" of the article.

Price and Forest have been making some excitement in the war "business." I am not much uneasy about Price because he will be very apt to get trapped or stopped in his "wild career." Forest may succeed in doing a vast deal of damage, yet he cannot hurt Sherman much. Forest is pretty sharp and very mean. Gen Rousseau [Major General Lovell H. Rousseau of Kentucky] will be likely to make Forest's position a little uncomfortable. Nothing would please me much better than for Forest to get taken in. He has a good train of wagons mostly taken in the Guntown fight, or were rather left in the mud.

I think as I did while we were out on our Last Raid that we should have "put for" Grenada, Miss. as fast as possible. I think that was the way to do because we knew well that there were not enough force any where within reinforcing distance that could have periled our situation. My idea was that we could have destroyed all of his transportation or the greater part, because Forest with 3,500 men and they were best he had were at least 75 miles from us and a big stream between. The Road we were on was as direct as the other to Grenada. I might be mistaken, but thus it looks to me 10 days more would have taken us the whole trip. Gen. Smith went about as far as he was ordered and that is enough.

Last evening there come orders for us to be ready to march at a moment's warning. 2 Brigades of Rebel Cavalry were at White's Station, 7 miles out the Memphis & Charleston R.R. We have some Cav. out there. There were but few of our men out there. Gen Hatch's Div of Cav were out there, and that is their station but at present they are out to see what is going on. I would tell but caution says no. My Letter might be captured.

Gen. A. J. Smith is up to near St. Louis, Price will find him a hard horse to run against.[1] One Regt of our Brig is up there some where. That makes duty come a Little hard but that we are willing to stand if the Rebles get well tanned.

The "Milish" of Memphis are making pretty good show. They drill pretty well for "Milish" but not like Regulars".[2] I would Like you to see our Darks in a Dress Parade. I am Sure you would Say they work to gether mightily Like "Clock work." At least it is thus believed by all who witness our parades. I think we have more Spectators on Parade than any other Regt. here. There have been as many visitors as we had men in Ranks on several Parades.

The fortifications about here are progressing; a month more good weather would make them very effective but to complete them would take half a year with a 100 men working on each, evry day . . . There are being Barracks built inside the Fort (Pickering). We expect to build Barracks if the timber can be had. They are much better in winter than tents. Tents of each Co. cost about $800.00, for a Regt would be $10,000. The cost of the Lumber to the Government would not exceed $5000. Confiscate the logs and saw them on a confiscated sawmill, Uncle Sam's boys do the work. Tents last about 1 year when they are in the weather all the time.

My health has not been quite so good for a few days. Nothing serious, just the effects of measels

My compliments and best wishes to all the family.

I am still,

Sam

1. With widespread support from local anti-Union guerrillas, Conferate General Sterling Price led twelve thousand of his cavalry into Missouri. Despite initial victories, Price's invasion ultimately failed, ending organized Confederate resistance in Missouri. McPherson, *Battle Cry of Freedom*, 787–88.

2. By "Milish," Sam means the militia, made up of Unionist white men of Memphis.

≫ ANDREW TO SAM ≪
Home / October 9, 1864

Dear Son,

I again resume my weekly duty. Mary received a letter from you last week. Nothing from Will, George or Inda. Letter writing has slightly slacked off here, on the part of our girls, neither of them wrote a letter last week. I continue to write you each sunday and will unless providentially hindered. Our health is about as usual, I can see no change in

Amos' condition at least, none for the better, he is almost confined to the house, tho he Expects to go to the election Tuesday next if the weather shall be favorable at that time. I hope evry man will vote who is entitled to a vote. I have no fears of the results, we are pretty well warmed up on Election and feel able to do the work that will settle the Copperheads for a while at least.

With respect to our draft, I can give you but little more news than I did last Sunday. I will give you the names of those who have furnished substitutes viz: Dyas Gilbert, John Brookaver, Danl Kerr, Saul Wilson, Robert Howard, D. S. Guthry, Wm Riggs , Oscar Bricker, Moses Torres. Lewis Paul & John Brittingham went to Cinti and volunteered after they were drafted, and John M. V. Stewart & George W. Howard went to Canada! Poor cowardly devils!! They are unworthy to live among a patriotic people, I pledge you my honor, that if I live to get into the next session of the Legislature, I will report a bill, and use my utmost endeavor to have it passed into a law, to for ever disfranchise them in the State of Ohio. George W Davis & John Howell are exempted on account of "over age", Phineas Allen for "disability", Glasscock put his son in as a substitute. That is all the draft news I have at present.

We are having clear, cold windy weather, a heavy frost this morning which cut down the Tomatoes, Beans, Dahlias, cotton, and divers other week kneed vegetables. We will probably commence seeding tomorrow, in corn that is green and all down. Fall work is very backward owing to so much rain; I hope it will dry out for a while, at least until we seed.

Are you not afraid that Forest will whip Sherman & his Army or do you think he will fall into good hands? My opinion is, if he don't look sharp, Sherman will stop the hole behind him, and he will find more trouble in getting out, than he did in getting in, I coinside with you in wishing him [Forest] "bad luck." And the worse his luck, the better I will be pleased.

We have nothing local that would interest you, hands for work are verry scarce and high priced and a great throng of work at present, prices of goods and produce are hardly as high as they were some weeks ago.

Accept the love & good wishes of the family and believe me,

Your Parent,

Andrew Evans

P.S. Yours of the 2d was Recd on the evening of the 10 (yesterday), all was well as usual. Amos will go to the election. Yours, A. E.

Memphis, Tenn. / Oct. 25, 1864 [sic][1]

Dear Father,

Your kind favor of the 16 came to hand yesterday, am happy to Learn that all are getting along reasonably well, also that you have elected nearly all good Union men to office in Ohio, Brown has done well. The next main hit at the Rebles is Elect Lincoln and Johnson. We have ceased fortif[y]ing for a short time. All hands are now building Barracks nearly all the Regiment[s] here are building just now, I am bossing the job building ours. This will be a fine camp . . . I am Sorry you have to work more than you are able to stand. I hope you and mother will do with as Little as you can get along with. Is D. S. Guthry one of the meanest kinds of "Copperheads" or a conservative? Do you know any one who wants to run the mill who would do justice to all concerned? If so strike a bargain.

I have not written Little Jane an answer but will as soon as I have leisure. I will then copy it for you. I am not yet in a good humor about the one she wrote me. I will make her feel red, if she has any feeling.

I thought I ordered a pair of boots made but not sent till I would order. You will please have me a pair made as soon as you can conveniently and I will send you the money soon as we expect to be paid for 4 months soon. Six months are nearly due, we have not been paid since in Jun. Forest is again causing field to rise very early these morning[s]. Morgan L. Smith Commd Dist of West Tenn while Washburn is away. Tommorrow morning at 9 Oclock we will be inspected by Brig Gen Marcy of the of the [sic] Regular Army, I do not know whether he is the Old Secretary of State or not.[2] I think he is "Would be Pres McLellan's [sic]" father in Law. The weather is fine, dry and cool, some quite cool mornings and much Sickness about. I have been exceeding busy for a few days doing official Business.

I have been Selected as one to Square up the Lost Ordnance in the Sturgis [command]. The only papers that have stood the test were those I made out or directed. The other officers are charged with about $600, worth of Lost Ordnance. I have an answer from the Chief of Ordnance at Washington that what I was responsible for was found correct with orders to retain the Letter for a voucher in future. Some of our officers thought that the documents were too much work to get up, that less work would do as well.

It is now 11 Oclock. I am tired, you may be able to read this but I think it a little doubtful. It was done in haste, I have not time to proof read . . . Love to all the family, hope to have more time to write soon.

Yours as ever,

Sam Evans

1. This date on this letter was apparently accidentally changed to October 25, 1864, when it was recopied. The original, with the correct date, has not survived, but this letter was clearly written on or before October 15, 1864, the date of Sam's reply to Jane.

2. This was not former Secretary of State William L. Marcy, who served from 1853 to 1857. He died on July 4, 1857. The man inspecting Sam's camp is Brigadier General Randolph B. Marcy, who served as inspector general of several departments in the U.S. Army from 1863 to 1878. George B. McClellan, who served under him while exploring the Great Plains in 1852, and as his commander during the earlier part of the war, was indeed Marcy's son-in-law. "Marcy, William Learned" *Biographical Directory of the United States Congress*, 1501; Thomas W. Cutrer, "Marcy, Randolph Barnes," *The New Handbook of Texas* (Austin: Texas State Historical Association, 1996), Vol. 4: 502.

→ SAM TO JANE ←

Memphis, Tenn. / Oct. 15, 1864

Miss Jane Evans,

Your note of the 11 of Sept. came to hand in due time. I will reply to it. A portion of your letter is very unlady like. I could scarcely have believed you guilty of so treasonable language as that contained in your note of the date above referred. I have never given you any cause to speak so snearingly of me. In the first place you say "I would not like to see the draft go on, &c and all the men go off. Leave none to support the women and children, rec[k]on we will have to starve." You need not be uneasy about starving while there is ground to till and you keep your health. It is no disgrace to work. For that matter you can call on your friend Jeff Davis, he will admit you into his kingdom. There you can have your favorite Institution (provided the "abom[i]nable yanks" do not interfere with you.)

You say again ["]I would rather Laban would die at home than to see him go out and fight to free the Negers (you mean Negros).[1] There is no telling but what he would be buried by the side of a Negro as a white man." It would be more honorable to be buried by the side of "a brave Negro" who fell fighting for the glorious old banner than to be buried by the side of some cowardly Cur [dog] (in human form) who died for fear he would be drafted and who had proved himself recreant to the Boon of Liberty consecrated by the Blood of our forefathers.

Again you say "If you were fighting for the Old Union as it was" Was when? When the Star of the West was fired into![2] Or was it when Fort Sumpter fell? Or was it when the Government Mints were seized and large armies were raised in the South and marching North to wrest the National Capitol from us? All this and more was done, ere the murderer (Lincoln) as you class him, had called for a single volunteer. If you mean the Union before the South rebelled, we would have had no cause of war and would not be fighting because we are Democrats and love the Union. Not such as you, Jeff Davis, Vall' and Co. but of the cast of Jackson, Douglas, Grant, Sherman, Butler and hosts of others; who were willing that the South should have her rights. That is still what we are working for, but since she rebelled her rights have diminished. Once they were privileged to own thousands of acres of land and millions of slaves. Now we would willingly consign each of them to a space of 1 1/2' by 6', and nary slave!

You say you want to see peace and that you are tired of this war. I believe as a general thing all Rebels are. Again you say "no true hearted Democrat would vote for Lincoln." We do not expect that Democrats, true to the South as you and Jeff Davis, would. If you are going to make stump speeches for your friends of the new "Fangled Democracy" (properly styled Confederate Democracy), you had better procure you a lower garment usually worn by male sex, but seldom by the female. It is very much more convenient for your new business than that of your sex. I wonder if President Lincoln would not feel very bad if he knew what names you call him. You say too many hard things of him for a young lady of your caliber. I remember well all I said to Jake Botner about Lincoln except calling him "black hearted old rip" which strikes me very forcibly as cloth manufactured from yarn of your own spinning.

Now to your closing remarks. "This from your true hearted cousin." How can you talk of being true to me? What mockery! Can you profess Christianity and spout such falsities? God forgive you! I once thought you were right, alas! The change. I fear your associations have not been of the true grit for the last year.

Here is a verse that suits me. How do you like it?

No Slave beneath that Starry Flag
The Emblem of the Free!
No fettered hand shall wield the brave

That Smiles for Liberty!
No Tramp of Servile armies
Shall shame Columbia's Shore
For he who fights for Freedmens rights
Is free for Evermore!
I am very respectfully,
Your obt. Servant,
Sam Evans[3]

1. Sam misquotes Jane here. She wrote "negro," not "Neger."
2. The *Star of the West* was a steamboat that President Buchanan sent to resupply Fort Sumter. It had to retreat without completing its mission when fired upon on January 9, 1861, by batteries at Charleston Harbor and Fort Moultrie. Garrison, *Encyclopedia*, 238.
3. Not surprisingly this was the last letter between Sam and Jane.

➤ SAM TO ANDREW ◄
Memphis, Tenn / Oct. 16, 1864

Dear Father,

Nothing from home since I wrote to you. I have been anxious to know what is going on. The election news is good if it is not a news paper "lie". It would look much like the "confederate Democracy" has "gone up". I am somewhat undaunted as to the success of the Union Candidates for President and Vice President, but where much anxiety prevails, Some intripidity will. I never was so uneasy about the success of any candidates. The election of Union men (War men) will be as great a defeat to the Rebles as they have ever had and on the other hand, victory to the "Confed Democracy" better than a Bulls Run to our enemies in arms, The quickest peace for all. The Election of Lincoln & Johnson "vigorous prosecution of the war", "Arbitrary arrests" of traitors North and South.

I ask in the name of reason that you and all other Union men do all within your power for Lincoln and Johnson. On their election hangs the hopes of an honorable conclusion of this war. Life could never be [illegible] to a soldier or any true Patriot who will in quire [sic, inquire] into the immense cost of life and property already expended; With the triumph our Enemies, all would be lost, not a single benefit derived.

"Victory or Death". How could we live in a country like this would be, were the south to conquer after we had them within our Power? (Oh! Heaven, may such a calamity never befall a Free and Brave People.

Then fight on! fight on!! I must say.
The battle we ne'er will give o'er;
'Till vict'ry Crown our rugged way,
Then Peace shall reign instead of war.

Well I will have to lay down the pen for a few minutes. I have just learned that the small force that left here some time ago in pursuit of Forest received a thrashing from him, lost 4 pieces of Artillery. The particulars not known. Report says Forest is marching in the direction of Memphis. Our authorities expect him to make a raid in, or that he will attempt it.

The 59 have orders to go to Fort Pickering tomorrow morning before day light. I will wait till tomorrow to finish for fear there may be something [that] transpire[s].

Monday evening / Nothing serious has transpired during the day. This morning there was some skirmishing with the enemy, only to feel whether all was ready and on "the lookout". It would not astound me if this place would be attacked. We were in fort Pickering till noon to day and then I was on duty in the afternoon till now. Consequently I could not finish this letter. You need not now look for a long letter.

I am sleepy although it is not 8 oclock.

I would like for you to have me a pair of nice light boots made tand [tanned?] calf double footed and double soles, No 10's, tight fit for you. My fine boots (at home) are just right, particularly the right one. Want heels well nailed on the out quarter. You need not forward them to me unless you have plenty of means. I do not expect to send any money home because I have been [illegible] often enough. I think it probable that I will come home this fall or next winter and carry it myself. If you should send them, Express them through Adams' Express Co. I am moderately well. Good night!

Love to all &c.

Your[s] sincerely,

Sam

≫ ANDREW TO SAM ≪
Home / October 23, 1864

Dear Son:

Yours of the 16 arrived on the 22d. The patriotic sentiments therein contained, cause many involuntary tears to flow from, and down faces that were thought to be "hard" not only by your parents and other near & dear friend[s] at home, but by others of the "True Grit" to whom I handed the letter after I read it. Let me say to you that such letters from soldiers of known reputation & stamina, have a happy influence on our elections. Your Rebel simpathising (ought to be) friends here, of course, hate your patriotism, and fear your wrath, some of them have expressed themselves was that they would like to see you, but were afraid you would kill them, Poor cowardly fools. They are a misery to themselves, and would be but little loss to the community if they were in "Dixie" or that other place where they are being sent to by our Union Soldiers.

Our Election news is no "news paper lies" but a stern reality, and I have no more fears of the Election of "Abe & Andy" than I have of the Sun of Heaven ceasing shine. Mc & P [Democratic presidential and vice presidential candidates, McClellan and George Pendleton of Ohio] will not get a State in the Union unless by per chance by Rebel interferrance, they may get Missouri. Pennsylvania, Ohio, & Indiana, have already settled that election, nothing left, but for the day to arrive, and the formalities to be gone through and the thing "will be did". Coperhead-ism is at a lower ebb in the North now than it has ever been since the war began. Treason cannot be uttered here, as in days gone by, for they know they will be punished. Evry victory our Armies gain is a victory to us, and evry political victory we gain here is a victory to our Armies in the field, and a defeat to the confederates both in & out of arms.

We have had another draft 22 more men in our township are drafted . . . all butternuts but two . . .

We are well, except Amos who is sinking pretty fast, he is unable to help himself in or out of bed, and often cannot speak above a whisper, he cannot stay with us many weeks, unless a great and unexpected change takes place. The general health is good.

I ordered your Boots immediately on the receipt of your letter. John Mitchell says he has your measure and can fit you right. If you wish me to Express them to you, please say so at once. You say "If you should send them, Express them, Express them through Adams Express Co." but do not say whether you desire me to do so or not. I will do anything in my power for you that you may ask. If you can come home this fall, you would save the risk and know whether the fit was good or not, tho your will shall be done as near as I can do it, so be frank & explicit in your requests.

Our war news is good, Ohio is wearing the Laurels. Sherman and Sheridan are teaching the Rebs that they are in Earnest. "Phil Sheridan's" victory of the 19th [at Cedar Creek, Virginia] is a glorious one, and Sherman is teaching Hood a hard lesson, for his raid in Sherman's rear. I fancy I can see the sunshine of peace, already breaking through the dark clouds of war. I agree with you on "Elections, on a vigerous prosecution of the war, and arbitrary arrests of Traitors North & South" and desire them hanged after they are arrested.

Love from the family,

Your Father,

Andrew Evans

⇒ ANDREW TO SAM ⇐

Home / Oct. 26 [sic], 1864

Dear Son,

Yours of the 10th came to hand yesterday (the 14), a quick trip (the ink hardly dry!) in which I am pleased to hear that you are still well, and more pleased to hear that you are on the fortifications in the capacity of a superintendant. Your experience in that capacity will enable you to do justice to the Union, and honor to yourself, and you are enabled to get your rest at night, which I think is good for health.[1] I have no anxiety, that you should change the service you are in, unless you can better your condition in doing so. You are under good and tried Officers who have proven their regard for you, as an Officer and man! You might fall into worse hands, and perhaps into a worse climate. You are located where we can hear from you frequently which is a great satisfaction to your parents.

Our health is about as usual. Amos, hardly as well as a week ago. He went to the Election and stood the trip verry well, but on the two succeeding days he was much worse but is improving now and is sitting up. Necessity has compelled your Mother & I to do work that is too hard for us, we have been cutting up & shocking corn, to Enable us to winter our stock properly. Bell, Jo & Ann helped us, Your Mother stood the job better than I. My kidneys are Easily unfixed and when that is the case I have to let down, for I am growing more feeble, as there are greater demands on me.

In Election news, it is Glorious!! Our Congressmen are 17 for the Union, to 2 for Jeff Davis. Alec Long, Sam Cox & C. A. White are elected to "stay at home", Pugh is beaten. Our whole County ticket is carried by an increased majority, (the home vote don't Elect) but by the soldiers' vote old Brown will have driven the last "rotten Egg" out of our Court house. "Esto Perpetua".[2]

I can add but little "draft news" that my last did not contain, Davis Evans has runoff! D. S. Guthry was discharged for physical disability, a number of them have not reported, and under the law, are deserters. They have not been hunted up yet, therefore I cannot tell you who will be held to the service. We have nothing from Will or George in the last week. We have a letter from Inda. She and Morty were well. She is on soldier's clothing again; She informs us that George is still in Pennsylvania in fair health. Georg[e] Evans is still lurking about home hiding deserterlike, when he sees anybody, that family is making a nice record, two deserters!—

Well; I had much rather hear of any of my sons "falling" beneath their country's banner than hear that one of them had deserted; "Death before dishonor," is the motto of the true soldier, for such, there is a blessing. Wood [sic] to God, I were physically able to help you end this Rebellion, that I might deal telling blows to the enemy, instead of words.

The weather has been mostly fair this week. We have had several hard frosts. We have our seeding done, and are well along cutting up corn, potatoes are to dig yet, our force being weak, we progress slowly; I have wholly abandoned the idea of running the mill this season. It would be a profitable season to run it for grain is high, but I can't stand it myself, and have no one else to do it.

Have you given "little Jane" her dose? I hear to day, that she told a neighbor "she had got the blackest letter from Sam, that she ever saw," You ought to have retained a copy, for your friends will never hear its contents, she deserves a hard one.

Accept the love and good wishes of the family tendered by,
Your father,
Andrew Evans

P.S. Such boots as you wish, are worth $10.00 here now. I do not understand you to have ordered. AE

1. See Sam's letter of July 25, 1862, and note in Sam's letter of July 22, 1862, about Sam's "experience in that capacity" (i.e., working on fortifications).

2. What Andrew probably means in his bastardized Latin is "May it be so forever."

House, Mon. morning / Nov. 7, 1864

Dear Son:

Owing to company being here during the day, I failed to write you yesterday, but this will reach you as soon as if written yesterday. I wrote you Sunday of last week and failed to get the letter to the P.O. until Friday, and the girls did not write during the week. You will therefore have a blank in the usual amount of letters from home. Our health is fair considering the amount of sleep we loose. We sit up with Amos all night, and have for over two weeks. He has not declined so fast, for the last week as he had before, but he is steadily growing weaker, and is but seldom able to sit up while his bed is being made, his night sweats are terrible, no prospect of him remainning with us long. He speaks only by whisper. He would be pleased to see you all that are absent, before he departs, but has little or no hopes of doing so.

We are doing but little besides waiting on him and feeding the stock, we have no help at all, your mother, or one of the girls help me gather corn to feed with, and I haul the firewood. I have the promise of some help to gather the corn when ever it will do, it is not dry enough to put up in the husk yet.

We have letters from Will, Inda & George. Will is in Alabama, George in Chambersburg, Pa. Sherman is still after Hood, they are about [at] Florence, Ala. Hood was said to be fortifying at or about Florence at last news, and it is considered "Contraband" to tell where Sherman is or what he is doing.[1] But he is considered "all right".

John Hiett [Andrew's brother-in-law], Griff [Andrew's youngest brother, Griffith Evans] & others from the old 10th have arrived at home in good health. John has called with us twice, I have seen none of the others yet. John is looking very well. Your boots are perhaps done by this time, and if your order comes for me to forward them to you, I will start them as soon as possible. Don't send the money, it may be lost, I am not strained in money matters.

The weather has been unfavorable for out door operations for a while, rather wet but not very much rain. We have had ice 1/2 inch thick and very sharp white frosts. I know of no one that I would trust to run the mill, that I can get. I will not trust an incompetent one to run it, unless I could be with him, and that is out of the question. This season I will do your will so far as I can with all, or any of your matters here, but such as

I cannot do, I must expect to be excused. I verry much regret that I must leave the family this winter. I would rather give up both, the honors and profits, but duty required the sacrifice. It is near daylight and I must close for present.

Accept the love and best wishes of the family and still believe me,
Your father,
Andrew Evans

1. Hood had moved into Northern Alabama, hoping to draw Sherman after him. Andrew is correct that accurate information about Sherman was unavailable. In fact Sherman had gone in the opposite direction, heading east from Atlanta in his March to the Sea. It seems that Will deliberately gave Andrew misinformation. McPherson, *Ordeal by Fire*, 2:463–64.

⟶ SAM TO ANDREW ⟵
Memphis, Tennessee / Nov. 13, 1864

Dear Father,

Your very welcome letter of 23 came to hand yesterday, the first letter I have had from home for nearly 3 weeks. I do not blame you or any one at home, I do not know whose fault it is. We have Some election news that relieves me some yet I am not satisfied.

The Papers contain interesting news from Sherman, he has taken another bold course; he is risking considerable. But his competency to go where ever he wishes cannot well be questioned. Some of our authorities are not very Sure that Hood will not pounce on this place, if he should we will give him the best we can. Nearly all of our officers went home to vote. It makes duty a little heavy, not much heavier on me. I am on evry day and off at night. I had a fatigue out to day (Sunday).

I Still think of trying to get home this fall or winter but will not Get any time. Would like to be at home during Christmas. I am very sorry to hear Amos is not prospering. I hope he has not the spirit of despondency. Tell him to "be of good cheer", I hope to hear of his convalescence.

Well about the boots, I will have to buy a pair here. I cannot wait till they could be sent from home. You will keep those made for me till I order them or come after them. I will Enclose you ($50.00) fifty dollars in this letter. You will please let me know if it arrives safely. You may pay for the Boots out of if or keep it if you would rather. It is an interest bearing Note payable semi-annually, by presenting it at the expiration dates named on Coupons attached to National Bank. The note explains itself.

My health is good, nothing more.

Yours as ever,

Sam

Home / Nov. 14, 1864

Dear Son:

Owing to a number of visitors being with us yesterday and last night I had no opportunity to write to you. Our health is fair, except Amos, who is getting weaker. He is now unable to sit up to eat his victuals, he don't appear to suffer verry much pain, but is unable to help himself in any way, consequently requires a great deal of care at our hands, day and night. It is not likely that he will see another Monday. His voice is gone, he speaks, only in a whisper, and his cough is quite tormenting at times. He seldom laments, but stands his trouble with Christian fortitude. Our Rebel neighbors don't visit us, let them stay away, their company is not verry desirable to us; Wm Armstrong & Alex Jolly (from Ripley) visited us yesterday. Aunt Diane is with us now, she is a splendid Nurse to the sick. Sarah Housh helped us last night.

I have a pretty hard road to travel now a days, wood, & corn to haul and feeding to do besides the errands and other Etcetera [chores] belonging to a farm at this season of the year, besides my share of the nursing, and no boy to help me. Ann & Jo help me all they can, but they are going to school, & I do not let the work keep them from school. They & Lee are learning fast. I will get some help if possible to gather the corn. We have nearly enough wood cut to do through the winter and I want to have it hauled before winter if possible, but I shall have to drive the team myself. We had a verry cold night for the season last night, the ground was frozen quite hard this morning but it is more pleasant now (at noon). I wish the weather would set in good now, so we could get the corn in. I assume your boots are done, they were to be done last week. I have not been to town since the Election & it rained so much that day, that I did nothing but vote and come home, & I have but few chances to go any where at this time.

Well; the Election is over, the work is done, the children are born, and their names are "Abe & Andy!" Glory Enough for one day. The Northern Rebels are beaten, Mack is nowhere, 21 votes out of 231. Lincoln 500,000 ahead on the popular vote! There has been many a pretty good dog killed for being caught in bad company, that's Mack's fix—he is worse beaten than the Rebs beat him in his attempt to take Richmond and he has made a worse retreat, he has resigned his office and retreated to the Presidency of a R.R. Co. I am fearful the soldier vote will not elect all our County Officers, it will be a verry close vote, if any of the Regts fail to return their votes the Probate Judge & maybe the Auditor will be Butternut. I shall verry much regret that, if it should prove true, the idea of Dave Tarbell for Probate judge is more than I want to stand.[1] The Auditor is a clever man and a good officer but a most inveterate Copperhead, he was but one vote ahead on Saturday. I think we will win.

Do not think it strange if you fail sometimes in getting two letters per week, for the girls don't get to write in the middle of the week. Some times, they loose a good deal of sleep these nights, and cannot write [because of] waiting on Amos, we will do the best we can for you, & you must excuse us for that which we cannot do.

We have a letter from Will dated 30 Oct., he was at Rome, Ga. at that time but did know how long he would stay there, as Sherman's troops were on the wing, he was well at that time.

Nothing from George or Inda. The general health of the country is good. The weather has been excessively wet, in the last week in particular. We had high creeks tuesday & wednesday and ugly wet and cold weather to the end of the week. The prospect is better now, the sun is shining.

Accept the love and affection of the family tendered by,

Your father,

Andrew Evans

1. See note in James Burke's letter of April 8, 1862, identifying Dave Tarbell.

⇢ ANDREW TO SAM ⇠
Home / Nov. 21, 1864

Dear Son:

I write with a trembling hand this morning, perhaps caused by loss of sleep & exposure. Yours of the 13th came to hand Saturday containing $50. "7–30" with coupons attached all safe.[1] I am of opinion your letter, containing your answer to Jane, an article for the Bee &c are lost or miscarried, it is lost or miscarried for which I am truly sorry. Should it come to hand, I will do your will, with pleasure.

Our health is fair, we are somewhat worn by loss of sleep & exposure, I was mistaken in my last, saying "Amos would hardly see another

Monday." His condition is such that a few minutes time may end his existence at any time, he is exceedingly low, but does not suffer more than he did formerly, he is perfectly rational, calm, and resigned and is deeply interested in the welfare of our Country. Inda arrived here last night as Eleven O'clock. Dyas Gilbert went for her yesterday. The roads are so bad that he could make it no sooner. She & Morty are well.

We have a letter from Will date 8th Nov, he was well, and was at Kingston, Ga. He is in "Sherman's new moove." Inda has late news from George, he is well and is at Carlisle, Pa. John Carpenter is at Columbia Tenn, Adjutant of the 175 O.V.I. Thom. Carpenter was at Atlanta Ga. at last news, they were both well at last news.

Davis Evans got tired of running off & hiding & voluntarily reported at Hillsboro, was examined and exempt, poor calf, he now has nothing to live on, Nance sold the corn, cow, potatoes, onions, hens &c. in order to moove to Ky.[2] They are in a fair fix to beg, steal, or starve! I wish they would leave the neighborhood. I have got them well mad at me by refusing to trust them for anything. They are abler to work than I, and I could not support my own family without their assistance. They all help me, and I don't feel disposed to give the fruits of their labor to the support of idlers—would you? We have a hand again that relieves us smartly. He can cut wood, feed &c which is considerable relief to us. The boy who worked for us through the summer is with us again (Frank Yazle.)

We have had no weather yet to gather corn, it will all be rotton by the time we gather it. This month has been the wettest Nov I ever saw. We have our hogs about fat, will kill them as soon as the weather & circumstances will permit. I have but one to sell this year but it will bring between 40 &50 $ at present prices $13.50 to 15 per hundred lbs. I would like to sell two head of horses but they are not such as the Government is buying . . .

I will get your boots the first time I go to Aberdeen and bring them home and keep them subject to your order, or arrival. I am sorry you have to buy, if you had ordered me to procure & Express them to you when you first wrote, they might have been there, if not lost.

You may rest assured that the Election news is all right. Mc only got 21 out of the 231 Electoral votes, New Jersey 7, Delaware, 3, and Kentucky 11. "Abe & Andy" 210, enough to Elect I think. E. M. Stanton will be made Chief Justice of the Supreme Court, and old Ben Butler will be Secretary of War, then the Rebs pills will not be sugarcoated.[3]

The girls failed to write the middle of last week, they have verry poor chance to write while Amos is so bad, they are verry attentive to him and loose so much sleep that they are (as well as I) in poor mood for writing.

I am rather fearful that Hood & Beauregard will strike at Memphis while your forces are too weak to resist them.

Accept the love and good wishes of the family, and come and see us if you can.

Truely your father,

Andrew Evans

1. By "7–30" Andrew is probably referring to government bonds issued during the war paying 7.3 percent interest. Phillip Shaw Paludan, *A People's Contest: The Union and Civil War 1861–1865* (Lawrence: University Press of Kansas, 1996), 115–16.

2. Andrew mentions Davis fleeing the draft in his letter of October 26, 1864.

3. Andrew is mistaken. Lincoln appointed former Secretary of the Treasury Salmon P. Chase chief justice as a gesture of reconciliation to Chase and the radical wing of the Republican Party. McPherson, *Battle Cry of Freedom*, 841.

➤ ANDREW TO SAM ❤
Home / Nov. 27, 1864

Dear Son:

We are having a very gloomy day. It has thawed out and is raining. We are all in usual health, the exception that I have made for many months is no more an exception. Kind Providence has removed from among us our dearly beloved son, Amos A., whose suffering ended and his spirit departed from the body at 12 o'clock n. on Thursday, the 24th, Thanksgiving Day. He had been, for 48 hours previous to that morning, under high nervous excitement (produced by spinal affliction), during which time he slept none but was in continual motion and flighty talk, tho, in the whole time, an indecent or immoral word never passed his lips. His fruit & ornamental trees, shrubs and flowers, his living & deceased friends, the condition of his country and its defenders were deeply impressed on his mind. He said at one time, "Mary, John has come, & is waiting for me to go with him. Why don't you hurry and get me ready?" about daylight on his last morning, he became entirely calm and rational, and remained so to his death. He breathed his last as calmly and sweetly as a babe falls asleep, under the fullest faith, of a blessed immortality in Heaven.

We spaired neither labor nor money to restore his health and, when we had lost all hopes of his recovery, we did evrything in our power to make him comfortable. Mary was his favorite nurse and she gave him evry attention; and from her Motherly, kind and sweet Angelic turn, there are but few so well qualified to minister to the wants of the sick. He gave her his watch for her kind care. I cannot write you his eulogy. Suffice it to say, there is vacancy in our family that can never be filled! We feel that we have no strong arm on earth to lean upon in hours of trouble. Such is the way of this world of trouble. God's will be done, not ours. He was decently intered at John's right side in the new cemetery in front of "Ebenezer" on Friday, the 25th, at 3:00 o'clock P.M., in the presence of a large concourse of friends & relatives. Peace be with him.

Rainy weather, sickness, want of a hand etc. has got us considerably behind with our work tho we do not complain at our lot, your Mother & I were almost exhausted, (Physically,) at the time Amos died, from cares, loss of sleep etc., but a few nights rest has given some relief. We expect our hand will be able to help us in a few days, he is mending. Jo & the girls help me all they can, with the work. We will butcher our hogs as soon as the weather will suit, that will end part of our troubles.

We have no letter from you during the past week, nothing from Will for a longer time. Inda & Morty are with us in good health, they will remain with us for some time. We would be glad to see you "about Christmas," come and see us if you "honorably" can. We have but little news of interest.

Sherman, is progressing South as well as could be desired so far, nothing new from Richmond. Butler has his Comd now and we may expect a stir there soon. You are perhaps better posted in the mooving of Hood & Beaurigard than I, for they are much nearer to you, I have an idea they will be waited upon soon, by Thomas from the East side, and A. J. Smith from the west. I may be mistaken, but it looks so to me now. Smith was at Paducah a few days since, going up the Tennessee River,[1] and Thomas was concentrating his forces in the vicinity of Decatur [Alabama].[2] I think they will meet about Florence [Alabama] if Hood stays there.

Accept the love and affection of us all tendered through,

Your father,

Andrew Evans

1. Going up the Tennessee River at this point would actually mean moving south from Paducah, Kentucky, on the Ohio River, down into Tennessee.

2. Andrew is incorrect again. Thomas remained in Nashville with half of his army, while General John Schofield commanded the other half, skirmishing with Hood in northern Alabama and southern Tennessee. McPherson, *Battle Cry of Freedom*, 811–12.

"I Am Ready for Them to Give Up"
January 1865–April 1865

Dear Father,

Your favor of the 18 comes to hand on the 28 of last month. I write pretty often at least once a week. I have made you my Regular correspondent for nearly 3 years. I think I have written on an average 1 per week during that time making over 1 hundred & fifty letters. Since I Left Home, I have written 903 letters.[1] My correspondents have thrown off on me or rather I have got mad at some of them and quit.

Well, another year has come. We can now look back an[d] see what has transpired during 64. Some mealancholy things have passed, many dear ones have gone the way of all the world. Look at the bright side of the picture. Many [are] the glorious achievements of our arms. It would be needless for me to refer to the various successes knowing that you "read the News." Gen. Sherman's Christmas Gift to the Pres. is a good thing.[2] Hood seems to be in a bad fix. Forest has been well tanned. I think he ventured in too deep water for so small a band. I must admit that he has done more for the rebles than any other man with the same no. of men, but few of these Gens have taken more prisoners although he has [yet] to defeat any of our great movements. Sherman['s army] was a little too large [illegible] for Hood, and [illegible] I hope our friends in his army are all safe. They represent that they had a fine time on their journey through Georgia. I would like to have been in that army. We can live well here but a man can show but very little of his abilities here. Cannot get to see the country. I would prefer active campaigns under skilful leaders than the monotony of a station or garrison duty. Notwithstanding that, I have become used to it. I am somewhat inclined to stay here now [that] we have been here so long that it appears like home, and yet Memphis is a very mean place . . . All is very quiet here. This seems to be a kind of depot for one horse, broken down Gens, those who have proved of little consequence in the field.

I suppose you have noticed that I have not come home yet. I cannot help it. No leaves yet, don't know when there will be any. My boots suit me "muchly." Socks are splendid.

I have been writing at payrolls all day. This is a busy week for officers who are in Co's. I have made all the Payrolls except 2 since I came in to this company. I do not know why the Captain does not. It is his place to.

Well I am tired of writing for the night. I will write more when I have nothing else to do.

Love to all the family. I am as ever,

Your son,

Sam

1. Only 110 of these 903 letters by Sam have survived as part of this collection. None of the Evans's letters of December 1864 have survived.

2. On December 21, 1864, after marching from Atlanta to the sea, Union forces occupied Savannah. Sherman sent Lincoln a telegram that read, "I beg to present you, as a Christmas gift, the city of Savannah with 150 heavy guns . . . and about 25,000 bales of cotton." James M. McPherson, *Battle Cry of Freedom* (New York: Ballantine Books, 1988), 811.

ANDREW TO SAM
Home / Jan. 1, 1865

Dear Sam,

I have a letter from you but cannot tell the date from the fact that it is not dated in full, only "Dec. 1864" and the post mark is so indistinct that I cannot determine when it was mailed.[1] You acknowledge the receipt of mine of the 4 Dec. I, have written every Sunday; why you have you not received them, & why I have but one from you, in four weeks is more than I can tell. I started your boots and socks on the 12th and mailed my letter of the 4 containing a receipt from "Adams Express Co." on the same day which ought to have reached you in a week or less. I explained the reason of the delay in a previous letter, which I supposed would be satisfactory. I am glad you are satisfied with your position fair &c. for contentment is very essential to happiness. I do not wish you to violate a rule of the service in order to visit your friends.

We have nothing from Will since the 8 Nov. a few letters have got around from Savannah but none from Will. I[nda] still gets letters from George he is well & still at Camp Curtin, Pa. Yur cousin-in-law has got home & looks well. He was in the 1st. [Battle] of the 11 Cav in the far west.

Jake Botner has got back in good health, but is of opinion he will go into the service again after he rests a little. He says he will hire as a substitute if the price is made to suit him.

I have to leave for Columbus tomorrow and will be pleased to hear from you occasionally and will continue to write to you, but cannot give you much home news, Our girls are not very punctual correspondents, therefore I shall not be kept very well posted on home news . . .

We have a snow of about 7 inches deep (fell Friday night), the ground was in very good condition to receive it, it is pretty cold, but nice weather. I put the mill in as good condition to leave as I know how, cleaned both bolts and fixed things in general, but parted from it reluctantly for I had rather be tied to it, than to have a seat in the Ohio Legislature.

Miss Lina Evans was married to John Bently on thursday night last. Ripley has been holding a Sanitary fair for the last 8 days, closed last night, and is said to be quite a success.[2] Inda expects to go home tomorrow. The family at home will be lonesome.

Accept the best wishes of the family and believe me,

Truely your father,

Andrew Evans

P.S. Jake Botner sends you his best wishes and kindest compliments.

AE

1. None of the Evans's letters from December 1864 survived.

2. See note on Sanitary Fairs in Amos's letter of December 31, 1863.

⇒ ANDREW TO SAM ⇐
Columbus, Oh. / Jan. 8, 1865

Dear Son,

I cannot quit my old practice of writing to you when Sunday comes, I received your letter of (I have forgotten the date,) as I came through Aberdeen on last Monday, I read it, was pleased to learn you had got your boots & socks and that they gave satisfaction. I read the letter and gave it to Jo to take home that the family might read and be satisfied. I arrived safely here on Tuesday 10 1/2 O'clock and am Enjoying verry good health, but cannot have contentment while absent from my family, and they in so helpless a condition, I had much rather be with them than in the "Legislative Halls". I like legitimate Legislating verry well, but there is so much time spent in useless motions, &c that I had rather [be] at home tending to my business.

We had a most terrible snow storm here on Friday night, I cannot tell what debth it would have been without winds but the wind blew hard from the North the whole time the snow was falling and in the morning, it was three feet deep in many places in the City, some few places were almost bare, it took a great deal of shoveling to let people to their business. The weather is clear and beautiful now and Sl[e]ighing seems to be the principal amusement. The Street Cars cannot run, the tracks are buried far under the snow. All the trains that run to this place were many hours behind time yesterday, but I have heard of no accident yet among them. They all had to use the "Snow-plow," & back out, & come again, many time before the track was clear.

There is quite an anxiety among the numbers to make a general increase of salaries of State & County officers, which I take the liberty to oppose in all cases, and shall do so.

I have had nothing from Will yet, and am quite uneasy about his wellfare, he has always been so punctual in writing home that I am fearful he has been lost in the long march, many letters have come from Savannah, but none from him unless received at home since I left. I have not heard from home since I left, hence I can give you no news from there. I urged on the girls (before I left) the necessity of their punctual correspondence with you, but I cannot tell whether they will write as punctually as I did, while at home.[1]

We have tolerably good boarding at $6.00 a week, but have to walk considerably further than last winter. Many members are paying 10. and many 15. per week with no better fair [sic, fare] than we have. West has not come yet, he was in Thomas' army the last we heard of him.

Accept the best wishes of your father,

Andrew Evans

1. Now that Amos is deceased, correspondence with the "girls" has taken on new importance for Sam as his only way to receive news from home, while Andrew is at the legislature. This also explains why the next letter is addressed to Sam's mother, Mary, a rare occurrence among these letters.

→ SAM TO MARY (MOTHER) ←
Memphis, Tenn. / Jan. 8, 1865

Dear Mother,

I find myself seated and write you a few lines. I received a letter from (Father) dated Jan. 1st 1865 today in which he says he has received one letter from me for 4 weeks till the one before him. Said he could not tell the date as it was not dated in full I wrote it on the 18th of December 1864, and dated it thus, Dec 18/64 meaning the date above. I have received the Boots an 2 prs. socks on the day before Christmas all in good order. All are mighty nice. I thank you kindly for the Socks. They fit very nicely and seem to be of good quality. They all came in good play just about now.

The weather is quite cold and disagreeable. There has been but little snow here yet this winter.

I have been doing well for sometime, have not been on picket for 3 week[s], but the job I have been working at nearly complete, I will have to try picket again soon.

We have a good house to stay in now, nearly as comfortable as any place you can find in the army, I suppose you have been looking for me at home but did not see me. There are two ways that a man can get home, either of which I do not wish to do. The 1st get sick the 2nd be dismissed dishonorably. I presume you do not want to see me so badly as to have me come either way. I would like to come home very well now. It has been nearly 3 years since I left home and seen some service. My back will never be as stout as before I had the measels at Paducah. My throat disease and pain in the breast is entirely well. I have better health than I had at home for the past few years.

Why do not the girls write to me? Father has done all the writing for some time. I like to read letter[s] from home and will write as many as I have opportunity. I feel sleepy to night, I must finish this note. I think I am very much the same Sam as I formerly were. Good night Give my love to all the family and reserve a share for yourself.

Your affectionate Son,
Sam Evans

➤ SAM TO ANDREW ◄
Memphis, Tenn. / Jan. 12, 1865
Dear Father,

I received yours of Jan 1st Last Sunday and wrote home that night now that I have some Leisure time. I write you though I promise in the start that it will not be very interesting, because I do not feel very interesting myself; or rather I am a little mad, guess no one will be hurt. I hope by this you have heard that my boots and Socks have arrived. I received yours containing the receipt, came Tuesday before Christmas. The package [arrived] Christmas eve, bot articles in good order, much pleased with both, all fit nicely.

War matters here are all quiet, only a few Guerrillas about. Our Gen' here is doing as much for citizens as any Gen we have had but is coming down on officers and having a great many arrested, and I think he is producing quite a dissatisfaction a mong "Shoulder Straps" [officers]. The fact is there is a German and his Staff who run the whole machine. I do not complain as I have not been arrested yet and will not if I can a void it. There is a great talk just now about Resignations. I do not know how many will actually tender them.

I would like to have some [news] of our own state war matters if you should find any of such documents (for distribution) of interest, similar to that you lent me last spring. I have been feeling very well for sometime. I still like the service and would like very much to visit Ohio (not officially) nor as exhibition. Turner Hook is down here Suttlering for Ellison. I think Ellison intends to start him in some kind of business.[1] This is a good place for "[illegible]".

I will not detain you much longer. Our months business is down. Just now there is quite a run on me to show and to write military Histories of Officers as required by the war dept. I will think ere long that I am quite a military man if this war does not stop. Several officers have had the stupidity to say that I was the best posted officer in the Regt in regard to military matters. I am not so vain as that. I am aware that some officer[s] aren't as well informed as they might be, it's so with myself. Well enough of this. Is W. W. West with you this term? If so extend to him my highes[t] regards. "Good Night".

I remain your affc son,

Saml Evans

1. See note in Sam's letter of October 12, 1862, for an explanation of sutlers.

✣ ANDREW TO SAM ✣

Home / Jan. 15, 1865

Dear Son:

I write you from my old quarters having come home to see how the folks were getting along. I found them all in good health and getting along admirably. My own health is very good, very much better than it was last winter, but my enjoyment is no better, perhaps not as good as it was last winter, for our family is in a more helpless conditions. Therefore I feel that I ought to be with them; they are doing better than I supposed they could, I found everything satisfactory when I got home, but it necessarily exposes your mother and the girls more than I wish them to be, tho they meet it all, with the proper resolution determined to carry out their purpose faithfully.

We are having a very disagreeable winter, so very changable, that we cannot get used to any one kind for [sic, before] it is gone and a new one on hand. It looks like such weather would be disastrous to health, but the general health is good. The health in Camp Chase is said to be not good, particularly in the Prison. There are about 10,000 Reb. prisoners there now, over 5,000 arrived there since I have been in Columbus, I am not particular about their Sanitary, or hygiene condition. They are a shabby looking set. I have not been to camp, but can see them, as they are being taken through the city, they are from Hood's Army, mostly, and are better off than those in the field, for they get "sow belly & hard tack" enough to keep from starving or even suffering hunger. But they are poorly clad, for such weather as we have about Columbus.

W. W. West has not appeared yet. I cannot tell the reason. He is in Thomas army we suppose. He has not written to any of us. He is Major of the 182 O.V.I. Their are many other members absent, low wages and high boarding is perhaps the reason. There is some anxicty there to raise the Bounty law to 200 instead of one, as it passed last winter. I vote No everytime, and told the house I would like to vote to repeal the law that passed last winter, there is also a great anxiety to increase all fees and salaries of State and County officers, I vote No on that, State and County officers have just as good a right and are under as much obligation to bear their shares of the burdens of this war as any other class of men! and while I have a vote it will be "No."

Accept the love of the family and of,
Your father,
Andrew Evans

⇒ SAM TO ANDREW ⇐
Memphis, Tenn. / Jan. 27, 1865

Dear Father,

Your kind favor of the 15th came to hand in due time. I am very glad you found home in good condition and that your health is good. I wrote home Sunday, gave all the consolation I could, asked them to expose themselves as little as possible. I suppose your enjoyment is not very great, but your services are needed where you are sufficiently, to set conscience right. That you are not willfully absenting yourself. You speak of a proposition [to] raise the Bounty to Two hundred. That I do not approve of. I would ask you to reflect well upon these matters. It surely is rather a critical point to handle. I know of several Regt[s] who have sent a memorial to Congress praying that the wages of officers in the army might be raised. There was a meeting of the Officers of the Regt to do the same. I opposed it very strongly. The consequence was the thing fell through. My reasons were these: patriotism does not require to be hired. Wages are now equal to the emergencies and when economically use[d] sufficient to allow a small savings. To raise officers wages 20 per cent would increase "public debt" a great deal, and in many cases would tend to profligacy and wastefulness. It was not my intention to make money by leaving home but to serve my country. It would seem at present that Union arms would be victorious. What a pity! that Grant "Drinks," and Sherman, is Crazy. I should think it rather an enviable kind of "craziness" (of Sherman). I say God! Grant! Sherman! Victory!

For 7 or eight days the weather has been very cold. Snow has been lying on the ground about that long, and no moderation yet. Ponds are frozen hard enough to bear a horse, I am still on duty building for the Regt, have not been on picket for several weeks, but my job is nearly done. I have one 20 by 30 house to build and 36 window frames to make and set in. I have 12 hands but can do more than 3 of them when I work. There are several good workman in the Regt. I have a darkey here I wish you had at home to do the heavy work, but I suppose you do not care about employing the "American Citizens of Color," I think a good one is a very "good shade" in hot weather. The fellow that I speak of has offered to go home with me if I would let him and do whatever I wanted him to do, for his Board and Clothing. He has been with me two years, came from the 70th.[1]

I am having a very good time now reading. We have a Regimental library, composed of a hundred and fifty volumes.[2] I have been read Irving's *Washington* in 5 volumes 480 pages in each. It is a fine history. Each Book is as long as "Jone's Chimistry" (in your Lib). Irving is a fine writer and indeed very interesting. Among the other eccentricities of our camp are a "Piano," "Sewing Machine," and "Cook Stove."

Well there is but little news here, not worth detailing. Your attention is called to a word you almost invariably spell incorrectly: "verry", too many r's. If I Spell incorrectly cite my attention and oblige Sam.

Accept my best wishes for your welfare. I am as ever,

Your affectionate Son

Sam

1. This was apparently one of the ex-slaves employed by the 70th Ohio to work on Fort Pickering.

2. The officers of the 59th USCI had previously raised $125.00 and sent their chaplain to Cincinnati to buy books for a circulating library. Colonel Robert Cowden, *A Brief Sketch of the Organization and Services of the Fifty-Ninth Regiment of the United States Colored Infantry, and Biographical Sketches* (Dayton, Ohio: United Brethren Publishing House, 1883), 59.

⇸ ANDREW TO SAM ⇷
Columbus, Oh. / Jan. 29, 1865

Dear Son:

I have become so used to writing every Sunday that it appears to me my duty is not performed until something is written to you.

My health is very good, and the weather is cold, during nearly all last week the thermometer stood between 0 & 10. It is not quite so cold today, and there [are] indications of more snow. The sleighing is still good here, and any amount of it is done here, we arc hardly out of sound of Sleigh bells except from 12 to 4 or 5 Oclock A.M. There is no sign of a thaw here. It thawed some last sunday but snowed that night and became colder and remained so until this morning.

I have a letter from Will, date 17. He was well and would start on a new march on the next morning, for Charleston, perhaps. My last from home is to the 22d. All were well at the time. One from Inda to the 25, she & Morty were well. Nothing from George since I came here. I have become acquainted with an old gentleman here (Judge Brown), who has been our Ohio's "State agent" for several years. He has spent a good deal of his last year in Memphis and expects to go there in a few weeks again. He has a son in that place who is practising law there. When the old Gent starts back, I will give him a letter of introduction to you. He desires your acquaintance, and I am fully satisfied you would be pleased with him. His morals, sobriety, and gentlemanly demeanour would please all lovers of the good, and his love for the Union is beyond questioning. He has been nearly everywhere that Ohio soldiers were. He will start to Washington City tomorrow and return by here on his way to Memphis in one or two weeks.

There are many Peace rumors Extant now, we can't tell whether they are true or false, but I am of opinion, such peace commissioners as Sherman & Thomas are commanding, and such pointed arguments as the "boys in the Blue" are using, is all the kind and the best Peace commissioners we can send in to the Confederacy to treat for peace, and that kind is bringing them to their senses faster than all the civilians in the North, could do. It is the popular opinion here, that the Rebellion cannot stand Ninety days now, I hope that may be so, but I have not been one of the ninety days men generally; it does look now very flattering to our side. They must go under. I just learn that Georgia has seceded from the Confederacy.[1] If that is so, other States will follow and the thing will be wiped out. God grant that a speedy & honorable peace may be restored, that the many fond and seperated hearts may be brought together.

Legislature is progressing slowly. There is not a very great deal of good being done, tho the two branches are busily engaged. There is nothing in the local way here that would interest you. Things look like I will not go home Friday (our regular day to go home) the Navigation on the Ohio River is suspended. Such being the fact, I will have to stay here, for it is too far for me to walk.[2]

Accept the best wishes of,

Your father,

Andrew Evans

1. Andrew is incorrect. Georgia did not secede from the Confederacy.

2. In the nineteenth century, the Ohio River frequently froze during the winter. Andrew probably traveled the established stage route from Columbus to Cincinnati and then by boat on the Ohio to Brown County.

⇒ SAM TO MARY (MOTHER) ⇐
Memphis, Tenn. / Feb. 5, 1865

Dear Mother,

Your kind favor of the 22nd Jan. came to hand some 5 days ago I was very happy to hear all were doing so well. You speak of a long letter from Will. That kind of letters do very well if one has enough material on hand to manufacture them in good style. I could write mine longer than I do, but I always thought when one wrote all he had to, [he] had better stop. So it is with me, I have not time to write very lengthy.

I received a letter from father a few days ago. Stated he had been sick but is now quite well. I think from his letter that he does not like to stay a way from home much. It has been almost 3 years since I left Ohio, the time seems short, not withstanding very many changes have taken place. I have no doubt that it appears lonesome at home now. Life is uncertain. To meet Death prepared, always be ready. In regard to our future life, I suppose you have no doubt. I am assured that there is a future State. Of that I am as confident as I am of the present. We know not the time when we shall be called to render up our account for deeds done.

The weather has been very nice for several days, but today is rather rough, cool and very windy, has been sleeting. I wish you could see our nice Camp. It is as clean as can be. All the officers have a good house made of planks and floored. All the barracks are as white as can be. Everything goes on fine. I rather expect we shall be ordered away from here soon. I think so because we have [been] here more than a year. Landed here 25 day Jan. 1864, [that] one Regt. of Our Brig' has been ordered to New Orleans is my reasons for thinking we will go too. I would as [soon] leave [as] stay here as any way [sic, where] for a while yet. It has been some expense to us to fix as we have. So far my health has been very good here. I[t] might not be so other places. I been finishing up camp for some time, do not work much myself, I only boss the job, I am not stout enough to stand a heavy march but can stand any ordinary tramp and feel the better of it. I live very well now adays but not dainty. I miss good butter very much. Can get something that looks like butter, but it is too strong to suit my taste. If good butter from home could be had on a certainty, I could order some. Such packages do [not] come on any certainty.

I have been watching [for] an oppertunity to go home but have not seen any yet. As soon as I can I will come home. You need not look till yonder [for] me because I might not come. How are my watch and gun doing? I have a nice Album full almost of Pho[tos]. I want to send it home. Some time I will tell you ere I send it, that you may look out for it. I asked sometime ago about my taxes but did not hear about them. I suppose the letter was lost.

If any one wants to give you $30.00 for my watch you may sell it for cash. I have a good watch with me. I do not need two. I needed one here and did not like too send for the one at home for it would get lost. Turner Hawks is here, he is all the men that I knew before the war that is about here. Well I gues you will be tired reading this ere you get through with it.

My respect to all the family,

I am very respectfully and Affectionately,

Your Son

Samuel Evans

PS. How much do Each Joe an[d] Lee weigh? E,S.

⇻ ANDREW TO SAM ⇺
Columbus, Oh. / Feb. 5, 1865

Dear Son:

I have this minute Received and read your letter of the 27-Jan. and am much pleased to learn that you have continued good health and that you are enjoying yourself. With respect to the raise of wages of Officers, Military or civil, I coincide with you in "to.to." as my record will show both last winter & this. I am on the committee on "Fees & Salaries," and we have a great deal to do. All petitions, memorials, & Bills, for the purpose of raising fees or salaries are refered to us. In all cases, (except Township assessors & supervisors, whose per diem is below the wages of common laborers) we have not consented to any rise of "per diem" and in those two, we only add 50 cents per day. We desire to equalize the burdens. Men can fill civil, as well as Military offices these days through patriotic motives, it is as much the duty of the civilian to make sacrifices, as the "Militarie" and he that neglects, or refuses to do so lacks Patriotism! or at least that is my opinion and that opinion governs my options both on Committee and in the House.

The "Cops" [Copperheads] in the House are anxious to raise all salaries to the highest pitch, such as $6. per day for members and a proportionate rise on all others, they know the majority in the Legislature would be responsible and that they could make political capital of it, and use it in the next election. They would do any thing for success, they feel that they are going down, with their friends & allies, the Rebs.

I do not believe there is a "Cop" in the house who will vote to ratify the amendment to the Constitution of the U.S. abolishing Slavery. I am proud to tell you that I will, and am proud of the privilege. Next Wednesday is the day we will put ratification through. Then listen to the thunder on the reception of the news of is passage through Congress. We had a

Joint meeting of both branches in our hall to congratulate the Governor &, through him, the citizens of Ohio. It was a happy meeting. The addresses by our speaker and the Governor were fine and to the purpose, ending in loud & long cheers, followed by a salute of 100 guns on "State Square". When we ratify the amendment, the guns will [be] out again, and perhaps [be] followed by a jubilation.

It has been thawing slowly here for 4 or 5 days, but the snow & ice is not nearly gone. I have nothing from home since last Sunday, all wer well then. Nothing from Will since. I got a long letter from George on the 2 Feb. He is still at Camp Curtin Pa, in moderate health.

My health is good. I am lonesome, the members are nearly all gone home. I could not go "in consequence of navigations being suspended on the Ohio River by ice["]. I cannot tell when I will get home, maby not for three weeks, unless I can get a "leave of absence". The members will be back tuesday next. We will then go to work and do the legitimate business as fast as possible.

I accept your correction on "orthography" [the art of spelling] verry kindly, if you do not find many other words misspelled in my writing I shall think my self in luck, for I have words often, which I see are spelled wrong, rather than to blot them in correcting the error, if I have used the word you refered to, in this letter it will be spelled the same way from habit. Nothing new here worth your attention. The weather is verry pretty today, and thawing slowly.[1]

Accept the best wishes of,

Your affectionate father,

Andrew Evans

1. Here is another of Andrew's attempts at humor. Having apologized for misspelling "very," Andrew deliberately does it again in the same sentence and two sentences later.

<hr/>

❧ SAM TO ANDREW ❦
Memphis, Tenn. / Feb. 12, 1865

Dear Father:

I [have] become so accustomed to write evry Sunday that [I] do not feel well until I write. Yours of Feb 5th came right along in 4 days from date it was mailed. I am pleased to learn that your health is fair. I hope you enjoy yourself. enjoyment I believe is essential to good health. I am very much please[d] with Ohio, the way She is driving along. At one time there was a feeling among some of the soldiers to sully the fair name of Ohio and her Soldiers, but, now there is no State whose fame is greater or who can bo[a]st of having done more to crush this Rebellion. Ohio now has the name that was due her from the begining. But few states have furnished Regiments better than Ohio's. The 70th is a favorite of Sherman and has done much service. Col Phillips as leader is second to but few Regimental commanders in the field. I think deserves a "*" [star, for generals] and could wear it with greater honor than 2 thirds of those who do wear them. No State in the union can more justly be proud of her sons than Ohio, nor can it be said with Truth that any have furnished more Gens of high merit than She. I would love to see my native state, the banner state in all the essential Requisites, to conclude a lasting peace in our "glorious old union".

Am highly satisfied with the Pres[ident's] answer to the peace commissioners.[1] Our "peace men" were sent out in '61, and I am fully aware that they with proper direction will accomplish their purpose. Let us hold the Rebs to their "Ditches" and the day is not far distant when they will be conquered. It can be ended this year if all who can will try. I am not tired of sold[i]ering but "war" is Expensive and Demoralizing and must produce a great amount of suffering that could be alleviated in "Peace."

I have been thinking of going into a new Regt. that is being organized here, I have a shot at a majorship. All my officers say they would like to have me stay with them. I like to stay where I am and have a good Regt. and a good man. By joining the new Regt. I join for 3 years more. I would like to get home inside of 3 years. I sometime[s] think of staying my time out or till the war ends. I have never been before the Board of Examiners yet, I might not be able to stand an Examination for a majorship. My own officers say I could pass for it for a higher position. I am not fearful as to my qualifications for the position so far as Tactics Regulations orders and general Knowledge is concerned.

What would you think of me taking this position? You thought I "acted very rashly" by accepting the position I did. I am well satisfied of the choice I made. No news of interest here. Gen AJ Smith and his Corps have been lying at Memphis for 2 or 3 day, destination down the Miss. The candle is nearly out and I have none here. I finish in the morning.

Monday Morning / "All is well". We now have all the vacancies full in our regiment except "prisoners of war", none of whom have returned.[2]

We have letters from 2 who are now at home, one in Ohio who was paroled a short time since, one in Iowa who escaped when Sherman was in
Georgia. One 1st Lt is yet gone. We do not know whether he is alive or
not, have heard nothing of him for 6 months.

I will close. I am well as usual.

Accept my highest regards for your welfare and believe me as ever,

Your affectionate Son.

Sam Evans

1. This refers to the February 3, 1865, peace conference held at Hampton Roads,
Virginia. The talks were brief and fruitless, with the Confederate representatives demanding independence and Lincoln insisting on surrender, reunion, and emancipation. Garrison, *Encyclopedia*, 104.

2. Sam is referring to members of his regiment who were captured by the
Confederates.

⇒ SAM TO ANDREW ⇐
Memphis, Tenn. / Feb. 19, 1865

Dear Father,

Your kind favor of the 13th came to hand on the 18th and was a very
welcome visitor. Glad to hear you were well and hope you enjoy yourself
as well as I do. The weather here at the date of your writing was very fine
Thermomer stood at 40 in morning 56 at n[oon]. Since that, the weather
has been fine, the mercury has been as high as 65 and no time under 40.
Today it was warm working. I have been in the woods for 5 days getting
out timber to finish our officers kitchens and make a Hospital and Bath
House.

I do not place much confidence in the rumors of the evacuation of
Richmond or Charleston. It is my opinion they are trying to concentrate
a force to try to crush Sherman. How they will succeed if they try it will
require time to determine. I think they are anticipating heavy works. A
great effort will be made in some direction by them. I hope it will prove
as successful as the "Flank Movement["] of Hood's on Sherman.[1]

If you can find out who stole the wheat from the mill I hope you will
use every measure to have the individual punished. I would like to have
him here. We know how to punish from the least to the greatest offense
committed. I think we have as good dicipline here as any Regt you ever
saw. I am a very tight diciplinarian myself.

Still the boys of Co. A think more of me than they do of the Capt. He is a very clever fellow but is not a military man, too careless about nearly all he does in a military way. He is something like a bad machine, does not work to the mark. Consequently, bad fits, bad joints &c make a rough job.

I have not been reading the proceedings of the Ohio Legislature for sometime. The Commercial did not come Regularly. I quit taking it, my funds run a little short too. We have not been paid for a long time. It is thought we will be paid about the 20 next month. Then I will try if I cant tell how much property I have here, how much money. I do not think any one could say justly that I ever was a spendthrift or penurious user of money. I try to keep in the bound of economy. I use it for necessities and throw but little at the birds. What I wrote to you concerning Gen Smith taking command here did not prove true. I was informed of what I wrote by an officer who said he had it from a good authority. He has gone down the river, we have not yet moved. Some how or other I can not think we will stay here the coming spring. I hear no dissatisfaction about the manner we do duty. Inspectors tell us we are the best Regt here. They perhaps tell others the same thing about their Regts. I am getting a little tired writing I have written a pretty long letter home to-night do not feel as well as I have been. I have a very severe cold but think it is breaking, have had some symptoms of Bronchitis. It is likely to be nothing more than an inflammation of the throat produced by cold. Legs sore tonight . . .

Accept my best wishes for your prosperity and believe me as ever,
Your affectionate Son,
Sam

1. Sam is again being sarcastic. This refers to Hood's unsuccessful attempt to cut off Sherman during the Georgia campaign.

⟶ SAM TO ANDREW ⟵
Memphis, Tenn. / Feb. 28, 1865

Dear Father,

I write this time without having received anything from [you] since writing to you last. I received a letter from Ann today she is very hard on "butternuts" as she calls them.[1] She says "She wishes I was at home to shoot some of them." I suppose she thinks I am [the only] person author-ized to do such work as that. I would not think disloyalty in our old neigh-bors make them take things that do not belong to them; another trait of character must be involved (Stealing). If Laban [Jane's brother] has become so regardless of honesty, at this age his end will be anything but enviable.[2] I have known that he was not a very great medium for truth. I hope no one of our family will ever be regarded as having entered the State of deprivation of which he seems to have, better they die ere they arrive at the state [of] accountability. I think a close application with the wielding of a 10 lb. Sledge 10 hours per day would be an effective antidote to his wicked nature. Close application will give less time for such work.

Ann says she is affraid some body will burn the mill. I think there is no danger of that. That would do them but little good and me but little harm. Some of the folks in the neighborhood think that I swindled Grandfather and have talked that I never paid all I agreed to, or if I did, the money was squandered by those who had charge of the estate.[3]

A general move has taken place since I last wrote you. We were ordered to New Orleans as soon as we could prepare, but the order was revoked before we had made ready. The rest of the Col'd Brigade went last Saturday. But, we, still hold our old place on the picket line, and are still in our barracks. Col Kendrich, the man and I spoke of in a former letter as having done a little under hand work against Col Bouton (our Col), is at the bottom of this last trick! We should have gone with the other part of the Brig and Col Bouton been in command of the Brig as he is the Ranking officer. Kendrich wants a * [star] worse than any man about. He knew that it would not do to let the 59 go. Consequently, he did everything he could to have it remain by lying & he succeeded. [Disciplinary?] charges have gone to overtake him at [New] Orleans that will be very apt to knock him from under his "Eagles" and have a slight tendency to defer "Stars." I presume you understood these terms. (Eagles denote the rank of Col. stars, that of Generals.)

Our news from Sherman is still good. He is awaking things up down in Dixie. He's a terror almost to the Rebles and I think he can gain a decisive battle with Lee's force and less resistance than any Gen. in the field. We have dispaches from Richmond stating that Grant took Richmond but was himself taken in the end.[4] This last fact I hope is not true, but the former I hope is so. Charleston could not hear Sherman in its rear. I suppose if Richmond is evacuated, that force will pounce on Sherman and try to crush him. If they do, give the "corporal" 100,000 of his kind of men and they cannot do such a thing. "What a pity! Sherman is crazy".

I am almost tired of Dutch [actually German] officers, our commander is dutch.⁵ The Dutch did big thing in the beginning of this war. Nearly all of the German [officers] have played out. The Engineer here is a German and if I were to guess he does not know what he wants himself. He has been at work on this fort a year and more. He has had at his command 300 men everyday he could work. Today he had about 1400. all he has had done does not amount to more than what 300 men could do in two months if it were done in the right place. He is now having part of the old Fort torn down, has had about a dozen small ones built half to a mile and half out side. Block houses build [sic] all round the picket line, ditches cut a cross roads and various other Tom Foolery too tedious to mention. Such block houses as he has had built does not amount to a row of pins these times. I can march a hundred men in line up within 50 yard[s] and not have a man hurt, and they may stay inside and shoot at me all they can. All I would ask to do as good engineering would be a tow string, yard stick, and a piece of chalk.

Well I have said enough on this point I will close I am in moderatly good health.

I am as ever,

Your affectionate Son,

Sam

1. This letter has not survived.

2. Here we learn that Laban was the culprit in the wheat theft mentioned in the previous letter.

3. Sam bought the mill from his grandfather in 1858, the same year his grandfather died. Carl N. Thompson, *Historical Collections of Brown County, Ohio* (Piqua, Ohio: Hammer Graphics, 1969), 767.

4. Neither of these were true. The Confederate government did not evacuate Richmond until April 3, 1865. McPherson, *Ordeal by Fire*: Vol. 2, *The Civil War* (New York: Alfred A. Knopf, 1982), 481.

5. It is not clear to which officers Sam is referring.

⇒ SAM TO ANN ⇐
Memphis, Tenn. / March 8, 1865

Dear Sister Ann,

I received your kind letter of the 19 [illegible] one week ago. I should have answered it sooner but could not get an opportunity on account of business. I had letter from Belle on the 5 inst. Have not had a letter yet from father, that is since he was at home, I expect one today.

The weather has been very fine for a week. I was on picket a week ago, it rained very hard all day and all night. Since that I have been in camp. It seems I have been in camp longer than my time. We have permission from the General to make garden for ourselves. There is a great question what we had better plant that we may be able to get the most benefit from it. Should we remain long enough to allow it grow, the worst thing will be to get the seeds, seeds are scarce and not very good at that. We do not intend to put anything in that will not be fit for use by summer.

Gen Washburn has been sent back to Memphis and is now in Command. He is liked much better than Gen Dana who has just been Relieved and is not near the rascal. We have good news from the army in the South East, I hope it is so. I hope I could be with Gen. Sherman. I am not very certain that I would be stout enough to stand as much as some of his men have had to. I know that I could [stand] considerable.

Some of our officers talk of resigning soon. I don't know whether they will or not. We have not been paid yet, there is talk we will about the 20th of the month. The health of the army here is very good. I feel all right again. The River is very high but is now falling some. All is quiet about here, no Rebles have been about for a long time. I expect they will come around some of these times.

I suppose you are now trying the farming business. I hope you will not be under the necessity of doing much work. I must close for this time.

Love to all.

Your affectionate brother,

Sam

⇒ ANDREW TO SAM ⇐
H.R. Columbus, Oh. / March 11, 1865

Dear Son:

I have got a little out of time in my letters to you. After this one I shall endeavor to write on my usual day. Yours of the 28 Feb came to hand on the 6, Mar. in which you speak of some of the requests of your sister Ann and some of her requests of you. I am proud to inform you, that she is a noble, highminded, patriotic, warm hearted little girl! Such a one as any parent, or brother ought to be proud of. She hates a "butternut" at home, worse than you do a Rebel in arms. Since you have been gone, she looked to her noble brother Amos, as her protector; (for they were more afraid of him than the Devil). He is gone, and I am absent, hence her wishes for you to come home. She is sincere, don't doubt her.

I have talked kindly, advised her to treat them like other neighbors. She would say "Pap, I want to obey you. (there a cry!) I can't associate with them for they are Rebels, and I know Sam would shoot them if he is ever here." Therefore, I shall not try to make her love Rebels, for I have no love for them myself. Bell & Mary are of the same stripe, but can restrain their feelings a little better than she can.

My health is very good and has been for some time. The Weather is quite cool but pleasant. Business is progressing rapidly, whether for good or evil I am in some dout [sic]; there is no present prospect of adjournment before April. I have news from home to sunday. The folks were well, nothing from Will nor George, one from Inda of the 5th, she & Morty were well. George had been quite sick again, but was better. I am of opinion I shall be at home next saturday & Sunday, I will write from there.

Our war news is still all right Sherman is going along just as he pleases, and is fast closing the "last stitch." If they can't stop him within two weeks, he will have Lee stopped in Richmond, for it is certainly no secret now that he is going to that point. And if he gets there before Lee leaves the City, it will [be] "good by John". With [the] thaw, we have something evry day from our Armies. Things are brightning daily for a speedy peace. The tone of the Southern papers is decidedly softening. Some of them almost give up as "all lost." Well I am ready for them to give up.

I am sorry to inform you that our Vice President, "Andy Johnson" has been so drunk for several weeks as to be a fool. What a pity, so fine a man should be lost to his country, at the time we need his services. He was so drunk at Cincini on (his way) that he could not speak with "sence."

I started you two good documents yesterday. I hope they may reach you safely. The Secretary of States' report is a convenient Doct in a political sence. It has all the statistics of our last election, which I presume the Ohio boys at Memphis would be pleased to see.

Then the Gov's Message & accompanying Docts will be of interest to you. They were late in being delivered to us, is the cause of delay on my part.

Business requires me to close for the present.

Accept my best wishes, and believe me,

Affectionately your father,

Andrew Evans

⇢ SAM TO ANDREW ⇠
Memphis, Tenn. / March 14, 1865

Dear Father,

I received your very excellent letter of the 3rd on the 9th was quite glad to hear that your health is good. I rece'd a letter from Belle a short time ago written the day you left home (I think she says). I have had nothing from home since you left.

Matters are assuming a lively form for somedays past. Trade is brisk. Citizens seem better disposed than formerly toward the government. Gen Washburn has returned and all are better pleased. He promised to be liberal and just to the Citizens just so long as they are fair and honest toward the Government, and says when ever they are not he will be their worst enemy. Washburn and Dana had a fuss before Dana left about an investigation that Gen Washburn is having made. Washburn has put some of Dana's staff in arrest about some speculations that have been going on since Dana took Comd here.[1] It was found that an investigation would perhaps implicate some more of the staff, and perhaps Dana himself would not bear a very strict search. One day this week Dana went into Washburn's Office and told him that he had better stop that investigation and then [Washburn] took him by the shoulder and turning his face toward the door gave him a kick in the stern and sent him out the door. Since then Dana has not troubled Gen Washburn. He is now gone to Vicksburg.

I am glad to see that Ohio is filling up her quota with so little trouble. If the new call get in the field soon we will have no need of many more to send the Rebs. to the "Last ditch," that is, judging from what we see now. Gen Sherman is still driving along as usual. I have understood the Rebs intend to bag him and his force. I should think it would take a pretty strong bag, to hold him, if he was Bagged. I hope he has force enough to stand anything the Rebs can bring against him. I think he has the best army in the world to the size of it. It will be quite an honor to any man to say he had been with Sherman in the "great Campaign." I should be very glad to be with him now. We are now having hard enough work to do, but still there is no honor attached. A man nearly as well be dead as be nothing. I suppose a private of Sherman's veterans ranks nearly as high as a commission officer in some places. I know what hardships are but have never experienced such as that Army has. I perhaps could not. But I would be willing to try it.

The Miss River has been very high. In fact it is so now, though it has run down a little. Night before last there was the most sudden change in the weather from warm to cold I ever saw. The thermometer fell from 86° to 32° in 12 hours. The weather moderated almost as sudden.

We have commenced to garden We will try to raise our own needs if we remain long enough. There will be some difficulty to get seeds of the best quality. Unless it is guarded all the time, things will be stolen.

My health is good enough I am little sleepy to night. Was on picket last night and did not sleep much.

I will be on duty tomorrow again in camp. I will close.

I am as ever,

Your most Obt Serv't

Sam

1. Many Union officers and even some enlisted men saw opportunity for profiteering in the disorganized economy of the occupied South, most commonly by speculating in cotton. Many of their speculations violated civil and military law. Lawrence N. Powell, *New Masters: Northern Planters During the Civil War and Reconstruction* (New Haven, Conn.: Yale University Press, 1980), 11.

⊱ ANDREW TO SAM ⊰
Home / Mar. 19, 1865

Dear Sam,

I am at home on "leave" and expect to return tomorrow, we expect to adjourn sine die on the 30th. I am in fair health, and found the folks at home well, except colds. I only wrote you twice since I was at home. I have not had a letter from you lately. I got a letter from George thursday last, he is not very well but is on duty, I found one from Will on my arrival at home at date 2d mar. He is still at Savannah in good health. He is Steward of the 14 AC.[1] Whether he gets better wages or not, he don't say, he is on duty in the Corps Hospital. The weather is very pretty here, looks like spring, I ought to be here pruning the Orchard, making garden, etc. instead of staying at Columbus Legislating.

Ann sends you some garden seeds you speak of gardening this season you will find one paper [of] lettuce and one of best early raddish seeds, enclosed, they will mature early, and are good and wholesome.

I am hardly well enough posted in local news here, to give you an interesting sketch, John Daulton and George Anderson are both dead, both were volunteers under the last call, and both died at "Camp Chase." No others of your acquaintance have died there, it is a terible mud hole and is producing a good deal of sickness. They are being organized and sent away as fast as possible, 10 Regts had left before I left on friday last. They will organize 6 more which puts us to 200 OVI [regiments]. The residue of our quota will be sent to the old Regts in the field. There will be but little drafting in Ohio. A few places are awaiting the draft, they will be attended to.

If the session don't end [by Spring], I propose to quit and come home. My business is suffering for my presence now. You had better not send any more letters to me at Columbus for I am determined to leave there the last of this month.

Accept our love and best wishes and believe me as usual,
Your father,
Andrew Evans

1. See note about the position of hospital steward in Andrew's letter of April 5, 1863.

ANDREW TO SAM
H.R. Columbus, Oh. / March 26, 1865

Dear Sam:

I received a good and long letter from you yesterday date 19th glad you are still well. My own health is good but I am quite tired of legislating, at least while my business at home is demanding my attention. The garden, the nursery and the orchard are all pressing me for attention. My time seems to be as much in demand here, and there seems to be no prospect of an adjournment before the 10 or 15th of April. Therefore, I think I shall take my trunk and go home next Saturday and attend to some of my business and, if required, I can come back for a few days & help close out.

This war is making an immense amount of legislation necessary, but my private opinion is that some members are enclined to overdo the thing. We have now, at this late day of the session, some 120 bills pending in the house that don't look like getting done by the 1st of April. There is a great deal of business that never ought to have been introduced, but, as it is before us, we must pass, or kill it before we adjourn. There are a few bills of great importance before us that must be passed, or the wheels of State Government cannot be kept in motion, so [as] soon as these are passed, I would be in favor of smothering the residue as quickly as possible. We put 25 Bills through their second reading yesterday & refered them to appropriate committees, and there were over a Doz. new ones introduced.

Our War news is still bright, Our "Bulletin board," says this morning that Lee asked a peace on the terms offered by "Old Abe" to [Confederate] V.P. [Alexander] Stephens, during the [Hampton Roads] Peace conference viz: "Reconstruction" without slavery, Obediance to the Constitution & laws of the U.S. &c, if this is a fact, we shall soon have a peace; if not, Sherman will soon bring them to terms such as Grant generally asks.[1] They are in a hard condition, and will soon be compelled to "give up the ship" or sink with it. The prospect is certainly bright for an early Peace. Be it so!

The weather has been quite cool here for several days. We had quite a hail storm here on tuesday evening, since which it has been rather cool. It is clear now and more pleasant. Buds are not as forward here now as they were a week ago in Huntington.

I have nothing from Will or George since I wrote you, they write home more than to me, that is right, for I get the news twice a week, the folks at home were well on the 22. Well I must close and take a walk, I do not get enough exercise to harden the muscle. Be assured of my best wishes for your welfare and safe return to your many friends and the embraces of,

Your father,
Andrew Evans

1. This information is incorrect. Lee, still entrenched around Petersburg, Virginia, had not yet sued for peace.

Memphis, Tenn. / Mar. 26, 1865

Dear Father,

Your kind favor of the 19th came to hand yesterday containing 2 packages of garden seeds. Thanks for them. I am very glad to hear all are well. I have no letter from home but yours for a week. The girls have been writing pretty regular since you left, but I would like to hear from home at least evry week. I have just come in off of a week's duty on picket. I wrote my last to you while I was on picket. Day after tomorrow, I will be on picket again. Duty is heavy, but the weather is now good. Reble deserters are coming in fast. I think most of them are coming in good faith they say the "Confederacy" is gone up and that there is no use of contending any longer.

Grant seems to think Richmond is in a pretty tight place and will have to fall pretty soon. I think matters on our side are encouraging. The sooner the Rebles concede, the better for them. I have no particular love for killing men, but, if necessity says to, the wool must fly. I think if the war were to close tomorrow about a 1000 of the Reble Leaders [should] be executed, or imprisoned for life.

We have nothing new about here. All is very quiet and looks more like peace that anything I have seen since we landed at Paducah [Feb. 1862]. The citizens seem well disposed toward us. That haughty selfish disposition changed to a smile. It may be for a purpose. Trade is free all most. Cotton is down here, it is only worth 28 cts and buyers are not anxious at that.

The paymaster has come to pay the troops here. Perhaps we will be paid tomorrow or at farthest next week, no body is very sorry. I do not know whether I ought to express what I have to spare or keep it with me.

Col Bouton has been appointed a Brevet Brigadier since I last wrote. I do not think he will receive full appointment unless he has another chance at the Rebles with good success. If he is made a full Brig there will be a big contention for the major ship [sic] of the Regt. Several of the Capt's claim ranks, but before they receive appointment they will have to pass a military Board. Then some junior may stand as good a chance as any one of the Ranking Captains.

I have written about enough. Love to all. I am as ever,

Your Son,

Sam

H.R. Columbus, Oh. / April 9, 1865

Dear Son,

I shall attempt to write you one more letter from this place. I did not write you last sunday for I was at home and Ann was writing to you and I supposed she would give you all the news. My health is still very good I arrived here safely on Thursday morning, and from present indications we will adjourn on Thursday next, which will make this session 101 days, which is 13 days more than the last. There is a new case brought before us yesterday evening that I am fearful may detain us a day or two, it is the impeachment of "Vantrump", an associate judge in the Lancaster district.[1] The Sergt-at-arms will serve notice on him, his case will come up tomorrow.

The farm is in grass. We will try to sell off some useless strech and make some collections. I cannot farm, and wages are so high it won't pay to hire much. Hence we are trying to get things into such shape that we can manage them ourselves. The orchard & nursry's will take about as much work as I can stand.

Our war news is glorious. Ohio is still carrying off the laurels Grant! Sherman! Sherridan! are names that will forever be held sacred in the memory of all friends of good govern't; names that will shine with untarnished lusture so long as the "stars & stripes" shall wave. Millions yet unborn will be proud to lisp their names and honor the State that reared them. Richmond has gone under, and Lee's Army is almost annihilated, we have nothing official since Friday. At that time it was believed that Lee would be compelled to surrender the residue of his army. 30,000 prisoners had already been captured, Ewell, Kershaw, Button [*sic*, Barton], Custus Lee [George Washington Custis Lee, son of Robert E. Lee] and some other prominent commanding Gens. were captured, 200 wagons, many cannons, Casions, &c. &c. were among the trophies![2] The Rebellion is fast being closed out.

Accept my love and best wishes and believe me as ever,

Your Father,

Andrew Evans

1. Philadelph Van Trump served as a judge of the Court of Common Pleas starting in 1862. He was not removed from that office in the proceedings discussed here and continued to serve until 1867, when he was elected as a Democrat to his first of three terms in the U.S. Congress. "Van Trump, Philadelph," *Biographical Directory of the*

United States Congress, 1774–2005 (Washington D.C.: U.S. Government Printing Office, 2005), 2084.

2. Here Andrew probably means caisson, a two-wheeled cart used to carry a field gun's ammunition. Garrison, *Encyclopedia*, 41.

⇸ ANDREW TO SAM ⇷
Home / April 16, 1865

Dear Son:

I am most happy to inform you that I again address you from the "old Blue table," and am in very good health tho I cannot complain of being stout. I am quite lean and think I cannot stand hard work. I arrived at home yesterday morning and found the folks in ordinary health. Bell is smartly afflicted with Scurvy, but I think I can fix that up in a few weeks, the folks at home did not know what ail'd her and had done nothing for her, she is not laid up, but is somewhat under par. Mary is in very good health from appearances, so is Ann & Lee. Jo is hardly as stout as he has generally been, tho he is still on duty at school & at home. Your mother is about as usual, moderately well.

Spring is fast opening here. Many of the fruit and other trees are in bloom and many are leafed out, gras[s] and other vegetation looking fine. We are a little slow with our farm work no corn ground broke yet, but we will try to get ready by the first of May & that is as early as I care about planting corn. When I get the plow started I will pitch into the garden & orchard. I wish you would up and help me plow a few days, I am afraid I will be lonesome; the war is about over and they will not need all hands much longer. All drafting & recruiting has stopped by Gen Order, and surplus officers are to be "mustered out." This looks like closing out, for we will soon have nothing to fight. Lee's Army is gone, Forest's & Johns[t]on's is at Sherman's mercy. Then what is left for such armies as we have, to pursue? They can't stand to the first of May.

We have shocking news today, (if true) that some Demon in in [*sic*] human shape has assasinated President Lincoln and Secretary Seward!!![1] If this be true, what should be done with the perpetraters of a deed so foul and fiendish? If it is true, the Rebs will not profit by the operation for old Andy Johnson will hold them flatter and give less leniency than Lincoln did. He has been among them enough to know their ways & what they deserve, and I am of opinion they cannot get as good a bargain of him [as] they could of Lincoln. They still have Ohio's three great Generals to contract with in the field, Grant, Sherman and Shirredan [sic]. I am willing to abide by any contract the Rebs can make with them, or any one of them, their names will never die. "Pap Thomas" [Union General George Thomas] is one of the same stripe. He is a most glorious officer, [even] if he is a Virginian he's all right.

I found a check, payable to me, (on my arrival) for $900.00, which you request me to use if I need it. I am very much obliged for the offer but am happy to inform you that we have plenty to answer our present wants and some laid up to meet immergensys [sic, emergencies]. Therefore, so soon as I can have time to go to Ripley, I will turn it into 7/30 as the 5/20 are 10 percent premium & I would not deal in them at that price. I will take care of, and manage your affairs, the best I can until you come home, but I have been away so much that you must allow me to start things to going at home first, for a few days. I will notify you what luck I had as soon as I make the deal.

Accept the love and good wishes of the family and,

Your father,

Andrew Evans

1. Unlike Lincoln, Secretary of State Seward recovered from the wounds inflicted in the Booth assassination conspiracy.

⇢ SAM TO ANDREW ⇠
Memphis, Tenn. / April 17, 1865

Dear Father,

I did not write yesterday because I was on picket. I have received nothing from you for 2 weeks and nothing from home since the 10th from Ann.

We have very mournful and unexpected news. No nation in the world ever mourns the loss of its chief more deeply than ours. We know his worth, he was honest. I do not mean to say that mere honesty without the exhibition of real ability would be doing him justice but I reckon the unquestionable stainless integrity and the pure patriotism of Mr. Lincoln, in his conspicuous position and under the severest tests perhaps that a public [figure] has ever endured, have caused all to believe he was trustworthy. He aimed at no personal aggrandizement, he made no industrious use of his vast opportunity for building up fortunes for himself, and a store of favorites and dependents; he has been gratifying no mere party grudges. He has diligently and faithfully, with simplicity and prayerful dependence on God, aimed to do his duty and honestly strived to lead the country through the greatest crisis in its history, [the] end of which he almost lived to see. Thank God for such a quality in public men at any time. Thank God for such a President in times of unparalleled trial. Thank God for a people that recognizes, honors and were willing to retain him longer.

He has fallen by the hand of the most foul inhumain wretch of the continent. (I do not think there are enough adjectives in our language to express my incense toward the assassin). The good old man is no more. Taken from us at a time we were least preparred, while in full vigor and body and mind makes us mourn. Now that Mr. Johnson is our Chief Executive, our hopes and prayers shall be that he be guided by the same patriotic motives that his immieate [sic, immediate] predecessor was and that he will in no way prove recreant to the trust reposed in him by placing him in that exalted position.

I suppose you would think it strange that a very large portion of the secesh citizens of Memphis are very sorry and say that they have lost their best friend. They loved him because he was honest and human and while he was trying to crush the Rebellion he did [not] wish to harm his enemies more than was necessary to the restoration of the Union. Almost every house in the City was draped in mourning. I am persuaded to believe they are truly sorry. It is useless for me to comment as many have done so with more ability than I possess. Yet I think no one can feel more deeply the loss of "Honest Abe."

The war news is still very encouraging to the Union. If there is not some very powerful influence brought to bear that we cannot now foresee, peace will again be drawn upon our Country by the 4th day of July next. Citizens who have always felt some sympathy for the Southern cause—yet, never since we have been here have they done anything for or against either side—come out and say since Lee has surrendered, Richmond taken and defeat every where so evident, the hopes of a Southern nation have no foundation, and that it is worse than nonsense for further contention on the part of the South. It will only be creating suffering with no hope of success.

The weather here is now most beautiful. We were, previous to hearing the death of the President, feeling fine. All officers and soldiers will wear the prescribed badge of mourning for 30 days next ensuing. Our garden looks fine and will pay the trouble.

I am a little vexed today with all things, I feel dull. My Capt has gone off to town (as he generally does when there is anything to do) and left me alone to trim the company in mourning. I have made evry paper since I came into the company except what Lt Demott made during two months that he was here. I am about tired. Shall not work much more unless he pay me the 10.00 dollars [more] per month for commanding the company.

All are well. I hope to feel able to write you a more interesting letter in the next I write.

I am as ever,

Your affectionate Son,

Saml Evans

P.S. Sent a $900.00 check home please let me know whether it has gone safely or not.

⇒ ANDREW TO SAM ⇐
Home / April 23, 1865

Dear Sam,

I will use Sunday afternoon as I did in days gone by. I wrote you last Sunday afternoon and had not received the heart rending news of the fiendish ass[as]ination of our noble President until after the letter was closed.[1] I have received no such shock during the war. A noble, benevolent, christian, philanthropic and virtuous President has fallen a victim to the accursed doctrine of secession. I can truly say, A Loyal nation is in mourning; True, he was but a man, but he had just received the endorsment of his fellow citizens for a 2d term in testimony of their approval of his course and we desired him to out live the rebellion and hapily retire to private life to wear the Laurels he had won, but God has decreed it otherwise and we should not fault our Creator's decrees. My opinion is that they have killed their best friend in our executive department. "Andy Johnson" is now our President. I hope he will draw the strings of the Rebellion in such a way that they may be made to regret the whole affair, from the firing on Sumter to the murder of our President. If I do not mistake his "grit," they will have but little to thank him for when the rebellion is ended. I hope so at least. I still hope for the best, and still feel an abiding confidence that peace is nearer to us than the 4th of July is.

We received letters yesterday from Will, Inda and George, they were all well. Will had got to his Regt at Goldsborough N.C. George was still at Harrisburg, Pa., and Inda is helping Nats wife to keep [from] "Widow's distress", gardening &c.

Our family &c at home, we are moderately well. Bell is much improved in a week, her scurvy is yielding nicely to the treatment. Jo is also improving but not fit for active duty yet. I am first-rate when I do nothing, but I have found it necessary to cut cornstalks for a few days. That has made me feel like I am "soft", my hands and muscles are generally very sore. Your mother, Mary, Ann & Lee are all right. Lee has enough mischief in him to do most any family. The general health is very fair. Sam Hiett jus[t] died on tuesday last, and was buried on wednesday, his funeral sermon was preached at the house, and then the "Odd Fellows" took charge of and intered his remains agreeably to their rules, orders &c.[2]

I have hardly become naturalized to East fork yet, but have assumed the reigns of farm government & mus[t] put it through. We had a very windy cold day yesterday. Last night it snowed considerably & this morning there was snow plenty on the roofs, fences, leaves &c, and still falling, but it is gone now and the sun is shining verry nicely. Some have planted corn, but most folks have some plowing to do yet. We will be ready by the 1st May if we meet no backset, and that is early enough for us.

The family join me in love and good wishes to you.

Truly your father,

Andrew Evans

1. Andrew forgot that he gave Sam this news in his letter of April 16, 1865.

2. The Odd Fellows is a fraternal organization of long standing that remains popular in Midwestern communities.

> ⇒ SAM TO ANDREW ⇐
> Memphis, Tenn. / April 25, 1865

Dear Father,

Since writing you last, I have received 2 letters bearing 9 and 16 of April. The letter came yesterday. I did not write Sunday, was on duty. I am very happy to know all are quite well.

We have news that does not suit me very well. It is rumored here that Johns[t]on has surrendered to Sherman. If so, on the terms stated, I regard it as having acknowledged the of the [sic] "The Southern Thieves." The allowing them to take all their arms with them to respective States and store them, all the advantage we have is their honor that they will not take up arms against the U.S. Government. I regard their honor or oaths as worth nothing.[1]

In the first place they showed their nonconformity to the Constitution and laws of the United States, to their oaths and to evry thing that is sacred or obligatory upon any people, by the act of secession. Tell me where they have ever fulfilled any agreement since the commencement of the war. They have imprisoned our soldiers in places known by them to be most destructive to health and life, neither fed nor clothed as prisoners are by any half civilized people on the globe. It is almost a universal fact that our prisoners have been strip[p]ed of clothing and personal effects and, when the wants of our prisoners have been attempted to be supplied, what was the result? Were the articles forwarded to alleviate their suffering condition by our friends North delivered according to agreement? No! Besides all this, they have been murdered in a wholesale manner too [odious] and heart rending to bear description.[2]

All the secret intrig[ue]s that they could devise have been employed against us. When we consider all these things, it does not seem to me that it would be justice to our brave soldiers whose bones [we] see bleaching on evry State in the South by thousands and whose blood cries for a just retribution. What injustice to all loyal citizens it would be to adopt such measures as that offered by Gen. Sherman to Johns[t]on. There is something wrong. Sherman has been my favorite, till now. For this one act (if true) causes me to loose confidence in him as a statesman of these times. I have said make them conk [break down]. I still say so if we have to fight much longer. We have commenced the job, let us do it and do it well. No compromise was our motto years ago and is still mine. Whenever they lay down their arms and sue for peace on our own terms, then I am willing to cease firing.

My own conscience says Execute the Leaders, confiscate their property of evry kind; confiscate all property of those who have held commissions in the Reble Army; banish for life, all of the grade of General. Of the grades subordinate to these for ever disfranchise, except it be those who have taken the leniency of the President's Amnesty Proclamation.[3] All aiders and abettors should have their property confiscated in evry instance where there is a shadow of doubt as to their innocence. The same doctrine to extend to enlisted men in the Reble Army as that to aiders and [abettor] (by these [I] mean citizens North and South). Pardon me for giving you so extended an article on this subject. Nevertheless, I feel it would [be] nothing but justice and right [that] they bury the sole cause of this gigantic murder, or war, to use milder terms.

Love to all.

Your affectionate,

Samuel Evans

1. Sherman's April 18 terms were considered too generous, since they allowed Southern states to keep their arms and receive minimal punishment. Outcry in the North forced a renegotiation of the terms.

2. Sam is clearly responding to the widely publicized horrors at the Confederate prison camp of Andersonville, Georgia.

3. In Lincoln's December 8, 1863, Amnesty Proclamation, he extended pardon and amnesty to any Confederates (excepting government officials and high-ranking military officers) who swore an oath of allegiance to the United States and its laws and proclamations, including those concerning slavery. According to Lincoln's proclamation, once 10 percent of a state's 1860 electorate took the oath, that state could form a new government that the president would recognize. McPherson, *Battle Cry of Freedom*, 699.

"To Lay Aside All Prejudice"?

May 1865–January 1866

⇒ SAM TO ANDREW ⇐
Memphis, Tenn. / May 7, 1865

Dear Father,

I have received no letter from Home since yours of the 25th, I don't know what is the reason. I have not written hom[e] since the 28. I have been expecting a letter from home and have not written partly on that account. I shall not write much to night but [will] write again soon.

I should like very well to be at home now but one thing prevents. I want to see the end of the war. I am not in good humor with Rebles yet. They have caused too many [losses of] valuable life to be easily forgotten. I suppose I might resign, but I have something more to do yet. Then I can come home and stay in peace . . . I could make more money at Home but I am not altogether after that.

I have seen fit to bestow charity on the suffering soldiers of Sultana disaster.[1] I cannot bear to see our soldiers who have suffered as they and not help them when it is in my power so to do. Their wants could be seen we are willing to divide [our share] with our fellows in want.

Weather Hot, It is now raining. I am well as usual. We still have heavy duty. It's thought the lines will be thrown open pretty soon and free trade admitted. Except to munitions of war. I think [there] is but little doubt of it.

Love to all the family.

I am still,

Sam Evans

1. While carrying liberated Union prisoners of war up the Mississippi, the badly overloaded steamboat *Sultana* blew up just north of Memphis on April 27, 1865. This explosion killed nearly 1,800 men (more than the *Titanic* forty-seven years later), making it the largest marine disaster in American history and among the worst in world history. Both corpses and survivors floated down river to Memphis, whose citizens provided great assistance in relief for wounded survivors and in making final arrangements for the deceased. James M. McPherson, *Battle Cry of Freedom* (New York:

Ballantine Books, 1988), 853; Jerry O. Potter, *The Sultana Tragedy: America's Greatest Maritime Disaster* (Gretna, La.: Pelican Publishing Company, 1992), ix–x, 116.

➤ ANDREW TO SAM ◄

Home / May 7, 1865

Dear Son,

Yours of 25 April was received May 3rd. I coincide with you in to the sentiments therein. There were several of your old stand bys present, Jim, Helen, Sharp, Canan & others besides some of our Ex "Copperheads." After reading your letter to myself, I handed it to Sharp who read it aloud to the Company, the boys squirmed considerably while Helen commented, thus: "Sam Evans is worth a ten acre field full of the d-d butternuts. They are not fit to wipe Sam Evans a-s. Sam may do my talking and I will stand to any settlement he may make with the d-d traitors." Not one of them put in a word!

Mary received a letter from you yesterday date 30 April in which we are pleased to learn your health is still good. We regret that you still have too much duty to do. Is there any remedy? Why are you required to do the duty of others whilst they are receiving the pay? I do not want any Son of mine to do less than his whole duty, while able to for duty; but I do protest against them doing double duty in order to let some scalliwag loaf away his time whilst under Govt pay. I hope I love and respect my sons as much as any man does his: Even more, they have given me just cause to be proud of them as noble and faultless defenders of their bleeding country in her hour of need. They have beared their bosoms to the lead and steel of a desperate foe! God knows I am proud of them! and am earnestly anxious for their welfare and that they may be safely returned to their parents, that we may in our fe[e]ble efforts attempt to do them honor in some degree commensurate to their worth, and should it be God's will to call them home before reaching us, may the green sod press lightly on their remains, whilst the never dying soul may rest in Eternal Bliss.

We have letters from Will to the 21 April. He was very well & with Sherman. Expected to be mustered out soon. I see by the papers that the War Department has ordered 600,000 blank discharges. They will be used as fast as possible. It will take some time to muster out and pay so large an Army, but it will be done as fast as possible, in order to stop expenses. The 14 A.C. is one of the discharged, or rather ordered to be discharged. Will is in the 14. The 15th & 17th are also under orders for muster out. I am of opinion Will will be at home in [the] next month. Can't you come home about the same time? Will requests his mother to have a "chicken shaved & some taters biled" and "Pap to have the cigars & we will eat & smoke." We would be much pleased to have your company on that, or any other agreeable occasion. We have but little local news that would interest you. G. W. Wiles has let his better judgement be overruled & is sued in court for $2,500 for Bastardy Marriage contract, etc. by Miss Amanda Donalson.

Our health is about ordinary. Your Mother & I cannot conseal the fact that we are both declining considerably in weight, strength, vigor and most of the essentials that constitute the man or woman, or in other words, we are considerably schriveled up and good for nothing. Bell & Jo are improving, but not well. The rest of them are quite well.

We are having wet weather. We are done plowing but have planted no corn. We will do it up in a few days if the weather will permit. We had a letter from Inda Friday. She is well. George was well at his last writing.

The family joins me in love and good wishes to you, and in desiring you to quit the service and come home as soon as you can honorably do so, without prejudice to the well fare of your country.

Truly your Father,
Andrew Evans

➤ ANDREW TO SAM ◄
Home / May 14, 1865

Dear Son:

Your short note of the 7 May came to hand yesterday, Why our letters don't reach you promptly is more than I can tell, we write you no less than once a week, sometimes twice. I still write evry sunday. The girls do a great deal of letter writing, but not verry much to you. They correspond with Will, Inda, George, "Lida", Lill. and other of [Andrew's brother] Ben's family, besides an occasional letter to many of the soldiers of their acquaintance. They write to Will more than I do, to you less; I write to you more, & to Will less: It is from custom, not partiality.

We get many letters from Will, tho they are generally old when they come, they are new & interesting to us. He writes interesting letters, they mainly all contain interesting history & incidents. I have reason to believe (from paper news,) that Will is in Washington City today to be mustered out. His A.C. passed through Richmond last Sunday, and were marching 30 miles per day, or at least that was their average speed from Raleigh to Richmond. The rainy week may have retarded their march, they are on a race with the 20 A.C. The 14th beat to Richmond, and it said the 14 & 20 of Sherman's Army, will try to beat the 2& 5th of Grant's Army to Washington. That will amount to a small trial of speed & endurance between the Western and Eastern boys. They had better "go slow" or some of them will have tired legs, if nothing worse.

Well, the War is over, Peace has come and civil government is fast being reestablished in the Rebellious states. All the Rebel troops East of the Miss River are surrendered & disbanded, and a general order out, that "all Rebels found in arms shall be treated as outlaws." The government will retain enough of the troops to enforce civil law, and we will be on the peace platform anew. Free trade is open to all the states except for goods contraband of War. Thus, the many heavy duties you have heretofore had to stand are at an end, and you will have to quit the service in order to get something to do. Well, there is still plenty to do here, so if you get out of a job just come up and see us, and if we cannot find you [a] job we will agree that you may go back.

John Griffith & Mary Beasley were married last sunday. We have a terrible amount of rain during the past week, we have "nary corn" planted yet and the ground is still too wet to work, but verry few have planted, many that did will have to plant over, the Ohio River is verry high, was out of the banks yesterday and still rising, I have not heard from it today.

I saw John E Carpenter last week at Ripley. He came back to Cinti on some business for his post, and came home on short visit. He started back thursday night. He is "Post A.A.G." [Assistant Adjutant General] of the Post of Columbia Tenn. He is looking tolerably well.

Your friends & relatives here are generally well. Nothing from Inda or George since I wrote you. One letter from Will last week, he was still well. Jo, is about well, Bell is not so well, her scurvy is not yielding to the treatment as well as at first, she is on light duty, the rest of the family are well. I do not wish to dictate to you, but would much rather that you come home as soon as you can honorably and consistently do so.

Love and good wishes from the family &,

Your father,

Andrew Evans

Home / May 21, 1865

Dear Son:

Yours of the 15 came to hand yesterday, (containing the Photo which is a good one, thanks for it,) which gave us great satisfaction to learn that you have some remote idea of coming home someday after the war is over. Well, we have waited a good while with deep suspence & anxiety, when you were in greater danger than you are now. We will therefore wait your pleasure in less painful suspence, hoping that you will avail yourself of the earliest honorable convenience to give us a call.

Our health is better than it was a week ago. Jo is quite well, he covered corn a day last week. Bell is improving quite fast, she is nearly well. They all helped to plant the corn except your Mother, who cooked for the company. We did get done planting corn &c &c the past week, and have a great deal of rain since, perhaps washed some of it out. This has been a splendid time to bring grass along, that sown this spring is safe, and the pastures are verry fine. Wheat in this vicinity is not a verry bright prospect, but it has come out amazingly. I never saw corn planting streached [sic, stretched] so much as it is this season, a few planted as early as the 15 Apr. and many are not done yet, some are not done breaking up. That which was planted early is a poor prospect, it came verry unevenly or not at all and looks weak & yellow; garden crops are in fair condition, we hardly ever fail on a vegetable garden, & our Floral department is attracting some attention. Our girls take quite an interest in pretty flowers, I am glad to see it, for in my opinion it indicates a taste for refinement, and furnishes them pleasant employment.

I did not burn my hat, tear my shirt, or do any rash or foolish act on the arrival of the news of the capture of Jeff Davis, but I did shout some and felt awful good. If it is not christian like, to wish him hung, I am no christian, for I frankly confess before God, and man, that if Jeff had 10,000 lives and was in my power, I would have each one ignominiously taken by the halter on the gallows which would not half attone for the loss of human life he has caused. If they don't hang him, Treason is no crime! Hemp & the gallows useless!!

We received one letter from Will the past week, instructing us to write no more to him for the letters would not find him before he would get home, he was well & in fine spirits. He requests me to tender you his compliments & best wishes, please accept. I got a letter from Jake Botner yesterday. He is at Winchester Va., he send you his compliments. He is in a pioneer corps again and is in good health & spirits.[1]

You need not wait for the fight you propose. You could not hire 2000 Northern Copperheads to face 500 of your Niggers in an open fight. They are too afraid their valuable lives would be sacrifised. They are down without shooting. The successful closing of the war on our terms, has taken the wind out of their sails! You could hardly get on[e] of them to jaw back to a union man. They can find fault yet, they don't want any body hung, object to military trials and find fault generally at the way things are done, are verry sorry Mr. Lincoln is dead and are afraid Andy Johnson will deal harshly with the rebels: (I am not afraid of that.) I hope Old Andy will "give them fits" . . .

The love and best wishes of the family are tendered you herewith, in connection with those of,

Your father,

Andrew Evans

1. Pioneer companies were frequently drawn from the Veteran Reserve Corps or the USCT and were assigned to clear roads, build bridges, and work on fortifications. Web Garrison and Cheryl Garrison, *The Encyclopedia of Civil War Usage: An Illustrated Compendium of the Everyday Language of Soldiers and Civilians* (Nashville: Cumberland House, 2001), 192.

➤ SAM TO ANDREW ◄
Memphis, Tenn. / June 25, 1865

Dear Father,

To day finds me back at my old stomping Ground and in fair health. I arrived on the evening of the 23rd. I left Aberdeen the evening you brought me down.[1] Stopped at Ripley till next day at noon; remained in Cincinnati 24 hours. I visited several of my old friends. I was with W. R. Shaw several hours, did not go to his residence because I did not find him untill the time was most to short. I saw several of the 70, 5 of the wild cats who were on a short "French" returning to Louisville.[2] I only knew three of them—Amos Hamar, Elijah Penoe, Sam Dryden and 2 others whose names I have forgotten. The travel by rail was very disagreeable on account of dust and heat. I met our Q. M., Lt. John Leach, where we parted on our homeward trip. We came down the river together, arrived as above. All seemed glad of our return. None of the Resignation[s] sent up have yet returned, but are expected soon.

The weather is very hot but not dangerously so. Health is quite good. there seems to be no prevailing disease. There have been a few cases of Flux and some Typhoid Fever. I cannot tell whether we will remain at Memphis or not. Col Bouton has gone to report to Gen Conby and will perhaps return Friday or Saturday next. It is rumored that he will be assigned to the commission of a Brigade or Division. If so, he will have his own Regt with him if he can get it.

Military matters are very quiet. There are some few Guerrillas about but they are no worse on Soldiers than citizens. I received the news of Gen [Jacob] Cox's nomination for governor before I left Cincinnati. Copperheads talk of bringing out Gen Sherman (that is about all it will amount to). I think him too "honorable" to sully the bright lustre of his magnanimous name by associating with such ignoble Traitors whose infamous crimes are scarcely less than those of the darkest ages of the world. Our Garden is still furnishing plenty vegetables. I have not been able to discover that the butter we use down here is any better than that at home.

I told you that the name of the ink and we're using was Clark's. The best I have tried is Smith's American Ink as good as the best Foreign Ink "Made by Wm. Manlius Smith Manlius, N.Y." Butler's is next best. "Smith's American Ink" is put up in stone bottles similar to "Arnold's". We have been using the Ink nearly 5 months. If the dust is kept out, no sediment forms nor does it seem to get any thicker. My old watch does not run too good. I am affraid that it will have to be over hauled before I can trade it to advantage.

I found a letter here on my return from you and George to day. I read one from Sarah Housh. This is the first that I have written since I returned.

Give my respect to all the family,

I remain as ever,

Your affectionate Son

Sam Evans

1. On May 25, 1865, Sam was given permission to take a twenty-day leave of absence, commencing whatever date he left his department. Head-Quarters Department of the Cumberland, Nashville. Special Field orders No. 41. May 25, 1865. *Official Army Register of the Volunteer Force of the United States Army for the Years 1861, 62, 63, 64, 65* (Washington, D.C.: Adjutant General's Office, 1865).

2. The term "French leave" was used to describe soldiers who were absent without leave but were expected to return. Because of the difficulty of obtaining formal leave,

these soldiers were not considered deserters, and often received only the mild punishment of extra picket duty. Garrison, *Encyclopedia*, 87.

⇢ SAM TO ANDREW ⇠
Memphis, Tenn. / July 9, 1865

Dear Father,

As usual I am trying to fulfill a duty. A high privilege. Nothing of importance has transpired since I last wrote. The weather is quite hot, though I hear no cases of "Sun Stroke." We are at the same business we were doing when I left. We are now trying to gather all the Government property. We take the smallest piece we find in citizen's possession and turn it in for sale. I am not as well satisfied as when the war was going on & I cannot realize that I am doing the good that I was before, though the government will not let us out of the Service.

I shall not complain very loudly. Though it seems that we have fulfilled our contract the Government reserves the right to decide who shall remain. I think it very likely we shall leave this place in a short time. There are more troops coming in here, two Regts. have already come, and I learn at least 2 more are on their way. I cannot see that so many are needed here, there is not much to do, unless the Fort (Pickering) is to be leveled to the ground. This is talked of pretty strong.

The health of this place is still good. The work of Restoring civil government is going on lively but not to suit me at all. I think Treasonable Speeches are too frequent. No Reble should be allowed to utter a word of treasonable language. If so there must or should be a just reward meted out to the men [in] evry case.

Now that Rebles have been allowed to hold prominent offices, I am quite displeased and would say in the language of the "big Boy," "I want to go home." Ex Governor Campbell of Tenn. in a reccent speech, made use of language that I could not bear to hear. He is, I believe, a candidate for some office.[1] He said he was opposed to the Emacepation Proclaimation, that [neither] Lincoln nor Congress had any right to abolish Slavery, that evry thing in refference to the abolition of slavery was unconstitutional, consequently null and void. That he was in favor of putting union men and Rebles all on equal footing. He further said that Jeff Davis should not be punished.

I think such union men should be furnished with transportation to a small farm six by eight. Rebles are not giving us much trouble in the way of fighting. Those who have been in the army are seemingly well convinced that it is futile to contend further.

My health is good and I am again trying to content my self, I shall close. I have yet received no Bee. When I was at Ripley I never thought of paying the postage on the paper. If is not too much trouble, I wish you would pay the postage of a quarter and charge it to me till I send you some money.

Respects to all, tell them to write

As ever your Son,

Sam

1. In the summer of 1865, former governor and pro-slavery unionist William B. Campbell ran for Congress. His campaign argued that the Nashville Convention, which emancipated slaves and set up a Union Party state government, was unconstitutional. Campbell eventually withdrew from the congressional race, taking an oath of loyalty to the state constitution under the threat of military arrest. John Cimprich, *Slavery's End in Tennessee: 1861–1865* (Tuscaloosa: University of Alabama Press, 1985), 119.

⇒ ANDREW TO SAM ⇐
Home / July 9, 1865

Dear Son,

I shall attempt for a few minutes, to amuse you with my weekly visitor. I have received nothing from you since my last. We are in usual health and doing our summer work with moderate success, we have our onions, potatoes, vines, garden & all cleaned out & in good growing condition. Our corn has received its last plowing and is about half nicely hoed, a day & a half or such a matter will close it out. We will then be ready for the grass of which we have about 13 acres. I will get a machin to cut it if I can. It will be hard enough to get hands to put the hay up, but I think we will be able to take care of it. If so we can winter without cutting up corn.

We have but little in the way of general news that you cannot see in the papers: The "hanging" of four of the conspirators against the President's Life on last Friday suits me. And the "imprisonment for life," of four now also suits me, and "Andy Johnson" suits me for making short work of the job. Since writing the above, I have received yesterdays ["]Commercial," in which I learn that the sentences have all been faithfully executed & the parties have paid the earthly penalty for their more than

Hellish deeds! The world [may hear] (if not too foolish to learn,) that President Johnson is not afraid to hang such Rebels as ought to be hanged, after they have been found guilty, I hope he will keep on with the good work while his hand is in. I hope they may put old Jeff on trial soon, find him guilty, sentence and hang him, and the Devil will have his own.

Well, I adjourned for dinner and we have had a nice shower of rain. Vegetation is looking bright, we have some splendid dahlias in bloom over six feet high. Will & Mary are gone to visit Esqr Games who was unfortunate enough to get his Clavicle broken a few days ago by his horse. He was leading the horse out, he rared and struck him with one fore-foot.

The general health here is still good, I have not been to Ripley since you left, nor to Aberdeen but once. Will has not gone to Feesburg yet. George expects to get home about the 10, Inda & Morty are well. Will is getting fat, he is visiting considerably these days.

The old "70th O.V.I." will soon be mustered out & come home, the Army is being reduced pretty fast, the "Army of the Tennessee" are all to be mustered out as soon as it can be done. Won't you feel lonesome when the white troops are all gone home. I am of opinion all will be disbanded except Regulars, before winter.

Tell me how you "Buckeye Boys," who are commanding "Smoked Yanks["] at and in the vicinity of Memphis, feel on the "Negro suffrage question?" The traitors here are determined to force the issue on us in the present campaign. I for one feel disposed to meet it square, for I had rather stand by and vote with a Loyal Black man, than a white Traitor!

Accept our best wishes,

Truly your father,

Andrew Evans

⟶ ANDREW TO SAM ⟵
Home / July 16, 1865

Dear Son,

Yours of the 5th was recd. on the 13, & that of the 9th on the 15 (yesterday) I have written to you each week since you left, the Girls have not written at all. Will wrote once, I will endeavor to have them do better. Will and Mary started for Feesburg on Friday afternoon and expect to return tomorrow evening, they expected to stay with May Jolly Friday night, and visit the Russelville folks on their return trip. We have reason to believe George is at home, we heard of him in Cinti a few days ago on his way home. Will or Mary will report the facts to you on their return, they may be detained on account of rain, it has been all this day, and the weather has been pleasant for several days. I will enquire into your "Bee" case the first time I go to Ripley, tho I am sure postage is not due on News papers where mailed, but at the place of destination on their arrival. I presume that Tom Snippis [?] neglected to carry your name on the "mail Book", he made the entry on the subscription Book which should have been transfered to the mail book. I will see to it soon.

Nothing of exciting interest has occured here since you left, the soldiers from different Regts are occasionally coming home. I notice this morning that the "old 12" is mustered out & will soon be home, There are a great many at Camp Dennison waiting for their pay, the 175th has been there for 10 days John E. Carpenter has been promoted to Captain; There are a great many cheap promotions being made just before "muster out," it costs nothing and I suppose will look well on parchment.

With respect to Judge Campbell of Tenn. and his Rebel sentiments such is to be looked for, from such men, but Gov Brownlow is after him and all such in Tenn. (see Brownlow in the Commercial of the 14th). Secesh may gas, but they cannot hold an office, nor can they vote, if Brownlow carried out his doctrine (& he will) for there are soldiers enough & officers too, in Tenn. to see the election properly conducted and that Rebels shall neither vote for, nor be elected to Congress: "Campbell," might as well undertake to reinstate King George as owner of our continent, as to undo President Lincoln's Emancipation and Amnesty proclamations. They are part of our code sealed by the precious blood of many patriots and will endure to the end of time. Our party are completely reconciled with our State ticket and will triumphantly carry it at the election. The Cops are trying to make Gen Sherman their candidate for Governor, but he "can't se[e] it." Sherman said in Columbus last week, that he would not give his Commission for the Presidential chair! That he has about as much Military honor as he wants, and that he will have enough to do to take care of it, without hunting among politicians for a civil office.

We are ready to put up our wheat & grass when ever the weather will do. We are progressing verry [well] in Cheese making. We have made six of various weights from six, to 12 pounds, we make three a week besides keeping our supply of milk & butter on hands. How good they will be is yet to be tested, we make them by "the Book" & suppose they will be good when of sufficient age.

Accept our love & best wishes tendered by,

Your father,

Andrew Evans

P.S. Wednesday, all well & raining, creek up. Will & Mary back, folks all well at Feesburg and Russelville. Your Coz Mary Chambers is dead. AE

❧ SAM TO WILL ❦
Memphis, Tenn. / July 21, 1865

Dear Bro Will,

I did not write yesterday as I thought I would because I did not think I was in a writing humor, hover [sic, however] now I will try to fill my appointment. A Bee has just come, the only one since I cam back . . . I should very much liked to have seen Lafayette Parker and W. W. West. My stay was too short to see all of my friends that I would liked to have. To day is tremendously hot. I hear of no Sun-Strokes among the soldiers. I have nothing of much interest to communicate to you. Things are gliding along pretty slowly.

There is now less rowdiness in the city of Memphis than I have ever known. Citizens say that they never saw so little crime, not even in days of peace. Outside of the lines there is a great deal of thievery and robbing, particularly among the citizens. They think that the Government is being very harsh on them and among the citizens, and Reble soldiers all think they ought to be allowed all the privileges of the most loyal citizen to the U.S. Government. Losing their negros hurts them terribly. Some say that they can not manage the darkies, that they will have to turn over their plantations and lands to Yankees for they cannot get hands enough to work them.

Almost all of the negros have a strong hatred against their old masters, and, in some cases, a fear that the Rebles will not treat them [fairly]. In many places in the South, Rebles are trying to impress [on] their old slaves (or rather formerly slaves) that they are not free, that the Government has no power to liberate them. Citizens have more privileges than soldiers.

About this time there is considerable talk about colored men having the right of suffrage. Since they are free and some have been employed as defenders of liberty and right, it would be a logical conclusion to arrive at, that they should be permitted to have the right to vote. It is indeed very hard for any of us to lay aside all prejudice against the Negro race and look with as impartial an eye at this subject as on many other subjects upon which are brought into connection. I have thought considerable upon this subject and have concluded it was a question which would naturally solve itsself in the course of time. Consequently, if call[ed] to the ballot box to say whether [blacks] should now have the right afore said, I should vote in the negative. But if the question was presented in a different form, thus, shall the[y] ever enjoy that right, I would vote in the affirmative. My reasons for these two propositions are, [for the] first, the unsettled [state] of our country would be augmented for the minds of the people are not prepared for it. Neither is the darkie prepared for it. [For the] 2nd, in justice to the colored man who has proved loyal in almost evry case and further, under a free government, all loyal citizens are those who have not violated the provision of the Government by some crime or other, should enjoy the privileges extended by that Government. If this be not the case then they must be classed with the enemies and criminals of our law.

It is time for mail. All's well. Love to all.

Your brother,

Sam Evans

⇒ ANDREW TO SAM ⇐
Home / July 23, 1865

Dear Son,

Again, my hour writing you a short epistle has arrived. I have received nothing from you since I wrote and I have reason to suppose you are in the same fix for I did not get my last to the P.O. until it was three days old.

Our folks are in usual health and condition, except Jo, who cut his knee badly with a scythe on last Tuesday, since which time he has been quite "laid up". His cut is not a dangerous one, tho quite a severe, it is directly on the right knee cap commencing near the center and cutting upwards nearly to the upper end and nearly taking the piece out, he is doing well.

We have a terrible rainy week, tuesday being the only day dry enough for harvesting. We stacked our wheat that day and have been trying to mow a little since, but can do no good, for it rains again before the grass gets dry enough to put up.

Growing crops are in flourishing condition, corn, peas, potatoes &c are all well grown and a fine prospect for good crops. Garden vegetables are fine. I was mistaken in saying to you that Will or Mary would write to you on their return from Feesburg, they got home tuesday evening but neither has written yet. They made a general visit, Ripley, Georgetown, Feesburg & Russelville, found the folks quite well and had no mishap.

I have not been to Ripley yet. We will be quite throug [sic, busy?] for a week if the weather shall be good, we are anxious to get the hay up as soon as we can.

Political matters are grinding along slowly, neither party have made their county nominations, the Cops will nominate on the 2d Saturday of August, we will wait and see who we have to beat before we nominate. We have four names in the papers for Representative, Dave Dixson, John Henry, Alex Campbell & Evans, if none of these want the position worse than I, they will have an easy time. I read one of the best speaches to day that has been made for a year, (Gen Logan at Louisville) he is a wheal horse in politics, as well as in the field of battle, It is just the speach for the times.[1] Read it carefully when you can. The soldier boys are still getting home evry few days: the 182nd & 175 boys are at home. I think they will soon all be discharged except the "Gen[t]s of Color" & their officers.

The general health here is still good, the weather is quite hot between shours. I have strained pretty hard for something to write thus far, and inasmuch as my present stock is exhausted you will certainly parden me for the early close.

Accept our best wishes.

Your Father,

Andrew Evans

1. This is probably John A. Logan, later Republican senator from Illinois and unsuccessful vice presidential candidate on the Republican ticket in 1884.

>> ANDREW TO SAM <<
Home / July 30, 1865

Dear Son,

Yours of the 18 came to hand on the 26th and was a welcom visitor. It found us well. Jo's cut leg is mending verry fast. He can walk on it without the assistance of a crutch, but we do not allow him to do so, only for a few steps. We have an immense amount of rain. Our wet weather lasted to Friday last, but it does not right for clear weather. It has been verry hard on wheat, oats, grass (hay), etc. but verry favorable on corn, potatoes, tobacco, garden stuff, etc. We have not commenced cutting our meadows. We have the orchard in cock. We have the promise of the mowing machin on tuesday. If the weather should be favorable, we can soon put ours up. I have hired another hand to commence working tomorrow. We expect to progress faster with our work.

I was at Ripley yesterday but did not see Tom Sniffie[?]. I saw his partner and the boy that mailes the papers. They say no papers have been sent you from the fact that your name had not been put on the P.O. Book. They promised to remedy the evil at once and say that "prepayment" of postage on newspapers to subscrib[ers] is unnecessary and unusual. I was mistaken when I told you that John Carpenter was mustered out. I saw him yesterday. He is at home but not out. He is commissioned as Adjutant General of Volunteers on Brig Gen Dan McCoys staff and has to get out through the "War Office." He has to go to Cincinnati tomorrow and fix up the documents preparitory to getting out. They may be held to further service. Tom Carpenter has to serve his time out for taking a "French" from Louisville.[1] They court-martialed him and cut 3 months pay.

We have but little "Political" [news]. David Dixson has declined being a candidate for Rep. and Maj McIntire has been added to the list during the past week. I cannot give you an idea who will be nominated, neither do I know whether any of them are canvasing, shaking hands, gassing, etc. I am not, nor do I intend to.

We had a short visit by Aaron Lory today. He is out of the service after serving 3 years & ten months. He is looking quite well.

I sold my old wheat yesterday for $2.00 per bushel by delivering at Ripley this week. It will make a throug [busy] week for us but we will have to stand it. Will, Mary, & Bell are visiting "Old Ephraim" today. We are still progressing in cheese making, about 3 per week. We have made 12, eat[en] two & sold one. They are good so far as we have tested them. Come over & try a slice.

Accept our compliments,

Andrew Evans

NB If you have any prospects of getting home this fall, and will so inform me in time, I will have the mill race cleaned out, otherwise, I won't promise. A. E.

1. See note in Sam's letter of June 25, 1865, for an explanation of "French leave."

Memphis Tenn. / August 10, 1865

Dear Father,

Your kind favor of the 30 July came to hand on the 7 with a small note from Will. Glad to hear all are getting along well. I should have written sooner butt did not feel that I could write of interest. I do not feel much like writing. I have been sick of Fever about 8 days. I think I am improving again. There is but little news. There is a great deal of Sickness and disease, but this seems to be some thing more than ever since we were organized.

Politics is quite [sic, quiet], did not hear of any one being killed on Election day. You spoke of John E. Carpenter being on G. McCoys Staff. It is all a mistake, for the[re] is no such rank known in our army. There is but one such officer [Adjutant General] in our army and he is of higher rank than Gen McCoy himsel[f].

Is Maj McIntyre any body but a militia officer? If I were a citizen I should make it a rule to oppose all candidates that went about electioneering.

You say if there is any prospect of me coming home this Fall you will have the race cleaned out. I do not know that I shall. I may get a recommendation to be mustered out of the service. I am now in temporary command of Co A. I am rather a worse scribe than usually, I think I would be doing a good thing to close.

Love to all the family. I am as ever,

Your Big Boy,

Samuel Evans

Memphis, Tenn. / August 18, 1865

Dear Father,

See your kind favor of the 6 of Aug. came to hand on the 15. I was very glad to know all were well at home. We have not had so much rain as you for some considerable time: the 6 we had a severe rain but not to damage much. I was on picket that day, the only time I have been on duty for about 4 weeks. I took a back set, but I am almost myself again. I feel pretty well to. Stay in the shade and do nothing. The weather is quite hot. There is considerable sickness here mostly of a miasmatic character. I do not think there is so much fatality as 2 weeks ago. The Regt lost about 50 men in a month. The aggregate is now 813. About 100 of whom are on detached duty and about 125 are sick. Our duty is not now heavy.

There is not much news of a social or general character. The citizens I believe are growing more contempt[u]ous all the time. They are trying to evade the policy of the Government. A few days ago some citizens were confined by the military authorities. The civil authorities issued a writ of Habeas Corpus. Gen Chetlain, commanding Post & Defences of Memphis, when the demand was made for the prisoners immediately released them. Col Bouton, Provost Marshall, did not act quite so rash when the demand was made upon him for a prisoner he had confined. [He] informed [the] Sheriff "To take him if he could, that he had put him in prison to remain there untill his case was disposed of and that he had the bayonets to keep him there, and, if he did not go away from there he (Sherriff) would him self get into prison." He concluded he did not want the prisoner very badly and "took with a leaving."

There is being some trouble with the Rebles and the Freedmen. The Rebs employ them to work and after they get in debt to the darkies, try to drive them off with out paying them. The military have taken it in hands and hear their cases and decide the cases without the civil having anything to say about it. The Citizens, a great portion of them, are continually complaining [about] the negros being freed and always saying that the negro cannot be made to do any good with out a driver. There are some cases where the Employer endeavors to exercise that privilege and have had to pay some pretty high fines. It seems that they are determined to defeat the policy of the government, There is another thing they are complaining of; that is the disfranchising act of the Legislature of Tennessee and some think the confiscation of their property is very inhuman and unjust &c!&c!!

There are a great many new houses going up in Memphis and vicinity. The place has improved very considerably since the war ended. I hear that 14 officers have been recomended to be mustered out of our Regt. I may be one of those. If that should be the case I may be at home in September I am guessing partly at this from what I have heard said about board of Examiners. I understand they have made very unequal examination. Some officers were examined rigidly while others were scarcely examined at all.

Today there was a great heavy shock from an earthquake it made the houses shake very considerably more than I ever felt before.[1]

Well I have written more now than I thought I would when I sat down consequently I had better close Accept my love and best wishes for your wellfare.

Very Respectfully,

Your Obedient Servt,

Saml Evans

1. On August 17, 1865, the largest recorded earthquake to ever have its epicenter in Tennessee shook the ground strongly enough to bring chimneys down in Memphis. Carl W. Stover and Jerry L. Coffman, *Seisimicity of the United States, 1568–1989 (Revised)*, U.S. Geological Survey Professional Paper 1527 (Washington: U.S. Government Printing Office, 1993), 358.

> ANDREW TO SAM <
Home / Aug. 20, 1865

Dear Son,

Yours of 10th came to hand on the 18, and found us all in ordinary health. We were sorry to learn that you had been sick again, you do not inform us what kind of fever you had last time, or whether you were able to be up or to walk. I had much rather you would give us more particulars of your condition, at least while you are not well, for we feel a parental anxiety for your welfare.

We are done our hay work, we have some twelve tons of good hay well put up. I bought Wile's interest in the cornfield, he tended on our farm. We now have twenty four acres of corn, which, together with the hay, will enable us to winter our stock as it ought to be done.

Will, John Swisher, Marry & Bell are gone to large Union [illegible] meeting on the Bennington Ridge to day, it is called "Union" because there is a union of several religious denominations in the congregation. Your Mother & I attended the funeral of John Buchanans youngest child this morning, it died yesterday evening of Brain disease. Your cousin Sarah Hiett died on Wednesday last and was buried on Thursday, her child will perhaps, not survive her many weeks.[1] The Flux appears to be subsiding considerable, no new cases for several days, and the old ones about well. There is an occasional case of fever but not alarming, nor fatal, The weather is rather assuming a fall appearance, the nights are quite cool and the days verry warm . . .

Politics are started. The Cops have made their nominations, both State and County, they have taken the loudest Rebels for their candidates viz: Aleck Long for Gov. & Chilt A White for Lieut Gov., E. M. Fitch for Representative & old Bill Norris for Treasurer![2] How do you like it? They ought to be popular in the south, for they have favored that clime during the whole of the war. They are deeply in sympathy with the Soldiers, (in a hour) [?] but they had "nary" soldier as a delegate nor did they nominate one for any office to be filled at the Oct election. Our Union primary meetings were held yesterday. I have heard from none but our township. It is said to be unanimous for Evans for Rep & Hays for Treas. I was not present, nor do I intend to go to the County convention on Tuesday next. I am no office hunter, and do not desire the nomination.

I am not full enough of Military tec[h]nicalities to attempt to raise a quibble with you on the position J. E. Carpenter held on McCoys staff. I am not responsible for the error if the Secretary of War commissioned Carpenter to a position on Gen McCoys staff that is not known in "our army", nor shall it make any difference to me which is right.

With Parental anxiety and affection,

Your father,

Andrew Evans

1. It appears that Sarah Hiett died in childbirth, which was very common during this era.

2. The nominations to which Andrew is referring are not those of the Democratic Party proper, which did not hold its nominating convention until August 24. A small group of rabid states-rights Democrats held their own convention in Columbus on August 17 and nominated a ticket headed by Alexander Long, a Democratic congressman from Cincinnati from 1863 to 1865 whose antiwar views were even more extreme than Vallandigham's. Long had turned down a presidential nomination a year earlier from a similar extremist offshoot of the national Democratic Party. In 1865 the regular Democratic Party organization nominated General George W. Morgan for governor. Long ultimately received only 360 votes statewide. See note identifying Chilton Allen White in George's letter of December 11, 1863. Eugene H. Roseboom, *The Civil War Era*, vol. 4 of *History of the State of Ohio*, ed. Carl Wittke (Columbus: Ohio Archaeological and Historical Society, 1944), 433–34, 451–52; "Long, Alexander," *Biographical Directory of the United States Congress, 1774–2005* (Washington D.C.: U.S. Government Printing Office, 2005), 1463.

❧ SAM TO ANDREW ❧
Memphis, Tenn. / Aug. 21, 1865

Dear Father,

I have received nothing from you since I wrote, however I expect a letter from home today. News is very scarce. Things are very quiet in this vicinity at present. The weather is very hot, a great deal of sickness, mostly ague and fever not so much fatality as formerly.[1] I have not Straitened up, but I am improving slowly. There has been no rain for 10 days or 2 weeks of importance, and the ground is getting very dusty. Duty has been quite heavy for a week. We have not been paid since I sent the $900 check. It is thought we will be paid during next month, I think it probable. I have been commanding a Co for 12 days I get along well except writing. Since I was sick I have been very nervous. We only have 12 officers in [the] camp belonging to the line [captains and lieutenants].

I have not received that letter of Will's that he was going to write me. Cotton is coming in, in small lots and bringing a good price. Nothing has yet been heard from papers sent up for the discharge of officers upon the recommend of the Examining Board. I will close this note.

Remember me kindly to all the family.

Accept my best wishes for your welfare.

As ever your son,

Saml Evans

1. For a definition of ague, see note in Sam's letter of March 16, 1862.

❧ ANDREW TO SAM ❧
Home / Aug. 27, 1865

Dear Son:

I received a letter from you on the 23 and one on the 25 dated 17 & 21 respectively. In both of which I learn that you are considerably below par in point of health, I had much rather you were at home, where we could minister to your wants. You will have to be verry careful towards your condition, stay off duty that will expose your person, or in your weak condition you may become a valetudinarian if nothing worse.[1]

We are not in so good health as when I last wrote, on Friday evening last, your mother was attacked with "conjestion of the liver," from which she is yet confined to her bed, tho better this morning, she sat up in the bed a while, she is weak & sore. The rest of us are in ordinary health. I find this morning that I have committed an extraordinary oversight. I wrote you last sunday and put the letter in the usual place for P.O. delivery with instructions to the family to forward it, it got misplaced and is here yet.[2] I verry much regret that such is the fact & I cannot help it now. I will enclose this with it for it has some news in it, even tho it is slow to reach you.

Our nominations are over. Gen. Loudon is for Senator, I for Representative, Maj. Hays for Treasurer & c. I regret that I am the nominee, but since it is so, I will not let the "Union Banner" trail in the dust while I am able to keep it up. They had a splendid mass meeting at Ripley yesterday, I could not go, owing to your mothers ill health. Will, Mary, & Ann went. They speak in verry high terms of the nice meeting & of Gens Cox & [Congressman Robert] Schenck as fine & appropriate speakers.

Well, Tom has sold 100 acres of his farm to Bill Grimes at 50 per acre, reserving 20 acres where he lives for a home, Money will circulate for a while . . .

The S.B. [steamboat] on which the 70 OVI were returning to Ohio for discharge, made a blow up, at the head of Flint Island on the Ohio, 15 or more were scalded badly & 40 jumped overboard in the fright—8 of whom were drowned, among them "John McDaniel Co F", we do not know whether it is "Slick" or some other of the same name.[3]

Gov Brough is still in a verry precarious condition. The latest news is that amputation of one foot was determined upon in consultation of the bord of surgeons.

We have two excellent hands at work putting the fences in good order, John Swisher & Bill Thompson. (He worked for us several years ago.) He has been in the Army over 4 years, and has grown as large as you are, I don't know that it will pay, but I hate bad fences, besides spoiling stock, which it is certain to do.

Our best wishes for your health and wellfare are tendered throug[h],
Your Father,
Andrew Evans

1. A valetudinarian is an invalid, especially one overly concerned with his health.

2. Andrew is probably referring to his letter of August 20, 1865, which has been inserted into these letters in its chronological place.

3. This and the *Sultana* disaster illustrate the danger of Civil War–era steamboat travel.

Memphis, Tenn. / September 3, 1865

Dear Father,

I have just received 2 letters inclosed in one envelop, very glad to hear from you. I have been [illegible] sick a little myself, I have just got over a pretty bad spell, had [the] spell 5 days ago, feel pretty well now. I do not know of any imprudence on my part. You folks at home are thinking that we are, or I am, doing very badly, but it is as I say to you. You seem to think that that [sic] I do not tell you about being sick . . . I feel if I write, that if I tell you the truth, it is as good as a doz lies. I cannot do more, I am no doctor. I don't like much now, cant, I have Intermittent Fever with Erisypelas some on left side of face and head.[1]

I am glad you were nominated again. I learn that governor Brough is dead and burried.[2] I am sorry of it and would much rather he lived his term out. You speak of [sic, in] your letter to me [of] the one I wrote about a week ago, I think I wrote to you. I wrote it, put in an envelop, adressed it and did not put the State on, at least so it seems to me now.

Cotton is being put up [illegible] nice cotton. I saw the first gin[n]ed today that I ever saw. I[t] looked as fine as the dow[n] on young goslings. I am sorry John Slick has met with so bad an accident as the one you spok of for &c. It is too bad for soldiers who have stood the Iron hail, when they are all most home to perish, the explosion of and [sic] old Steamer.

I will send a small Box by Adams' Express to you, care S. Hembell & co. Riply Ohio. This Box contains 1 Claw hammer, 2 blouses, 1 pr old pants, 1 old sash, and some Boots. There are 2 small [illegible] Books, give them to An, Joe, and Lee. Give the good[s] to Mother and tell her to do what she pleases. The old papers, details &c are of no value, I put them in just for fun. I am well and feel like I would have no more trouble now. I will write soon and again and let you have more particulars.

Yours Truly,

Samuel Evans

1. See note about erisypelas in Andrew's letter of April 5, 1863.

2. Governor Brough, who had earlier announced his intention not to run for reelection, died from a combination of gangrene and generally poor health on August 29, 1865, several months before the conclusion of his term. Lieutenant Governor Charles Anderson served out the remainder of the term. Roseboom, *The Civil War Era*, 444.

Home / Sept. 13, 1865

Dear Son,

Yours of the 3d was received yesterday evening the only one from you in nearly 3 weeks, we were getting quite uneasy for your wellfare, but learn in your last that you are again convallescent which relieved our anxiety considerably. I certainly did not charge you with "lying" about your condition, I only meant to convey the idea that you were with holding part of the truth, about your condition, which I hope is not so. You have written to us so punctually in general that we naturally think you are sick if we do not get at least one letter each week.

I did not write to you last sunday from the fact that Will did, and I thought it useless for the two of us to write on the same day. Why he took my day is more than I can tell, I shall claim it hereafter. Our health is only moderate I am bond with an annoying diarrhaea today, from exposure. I was caught in a verry heavy rain on Monday evening and had to wear my wet goods for some time before I could change it will be all right in a day or two. Your mother is improving, but is not stout, the "Young uns" are well, the general health is fair.

We are having wet weather yet, it has rained evry day this month except today. We expect to commence sowing wheat tomorrow, the weather permitting. We will only sow 12 acres, we want to get done before the fair, which will come off next week. Our prospect is for a verry interesting fair. Our Booth privileges sold for $468.00 and the general prospect indicates an interesting fair.

In political matters I can give you but little information. Our canvasers are not thoroughly organized, when they report, we can give you a pretty correct idea. I have not gassed any, nor do I intend to, I may attend some of the meetings over the County but not many. I am told Fitch is "gassing" considerably, but I think to little purpose for I think he cannot deceive many of the voters. He is trying to convince the soldiers that he has been their steadfast friend during the war. Well if voting for "Val" Chilt & Co. makes a soldier's friend he is certainly one, but I am told the soldiers "can't se[e] it". John Slick is at home well, it was Jo McDaniels son John who was drowned, we did not know when I wrote you.

Gen Slocum is down on the Mississippians in the right shape, he don't want the Rebles armed yet & he is right.[1]

Accept the love of the family &,

Your father,

Andrew Evans

1. Major General Henry W. Slocum tried to prevent the formation of a new Mississippi militia, for fear it would be comprised of ex-Confederates who would treat freedmen and Unionists unfairly. President Johnson overrode Slocum and allowed the
militia to be created. Eric Foner, *A Short History of Reconstruction* (New York: Harper
and Row, 1990), 89.

⋙ SAM TO ANDREW ⋘
Jackson, Tenn. / Sept. 16, 1865

Dear Father,

I have not had a letter from you for more than 2 weeks. I do not know
when you have had a letter from me. I have done the writing. It [may]
seem a little strange to you that I write from Jackson. I hold fort here. I
left Memphis on the 8th, arrived here the 13. I am now provost Martial
[*sic*, Marshal] of Refugees, Freedmen and Abandoned Lands.[1]

I have not done a great deal here. I have the Ague since I have been
here. I don't like it much. I don't mind the shakes much but the fever is
rather rough. I think about one more chill will be the last this spell. This
is a bad place for mail. It does not seem to come at all, in fact the country
here is not doing very much. They feel the effects of the war worse then
we do, but they was not whipped hardly bad enough [bottom of page
missing]

I am boarding at a very good place. They have everything that I ask
for, and done up in good style. I came up here be cause I was not very
well, thinking this was [a] more healthy place. The water here tastes much
better than that at Memphis. The reason I write this letter with a pencil
is I have no Ink here. I will close.

You must excuse this short note.

Love to all the family.

Your affc Son,

Sam E

1. The Bureau of Refugees, Freedmen, and Abandoned Lands (often referred to as
the Freedmen's Bureau) was created by Congress on March 3, 1865, to aid ex-slaves'
transition to freedom. The bureau was fraught with many problems throughout its
short existence, one of which is illustrated in this letter about Sam's appointment: most
bureau employees were military men with widely varying commitments to the freed-
people's well-being. At this early stage in the Bureau's existence, titles varied. It appears
that, as provost marshal, Sam had all the duties of other Freedmen's Bureau officers
titled "assistant sub-commissioners," usually just called "agents." Foner, 31–32, 75–77.

Home / Sept. 17, 1865

Dear Son:

Notwithstanding I wrote you on Wednesday last (out of time,) I propose to resume my usual day. We had rain the first 15 days of this month accompanied by verry hot weather, yesterday & today have been dry. Tho verry warm, we had a heavy rain friday evening that made the ground to wet to seed. We sowed about 8 bushels thursday & friday & will endeavor to finish tomorrow if the weather should suit.

The fair will spoil the rest of the week. We will contribute something to the show, I shall show wheat, onions, & currant wine. The girls will perhaps show some flowers & preserved fruit & Mary will show a fine shirt, she has several bids of $5.00 for the shirt. She put nothing ornamental on the job, it is a plain, fine, substantial job. I shall perhaps be in attendance each day. It will be a good place to shake hands with the "dear people," and do some electioneering bushwacking.

We have not received your letter giving a more detailed history of your sickness & c, and of any prospect you may have of getting home; if you are not fit for duty, sickly & c, would your resignation be accepted, if you offer it? I do not urge such a cource on your part, if you prefer remaining in the service, but the war is ended and the sooner our people resume civil life the better for our government. You may be making more money than you could at home and just as honorably, but in my opinion, civil society has a pressing demand on our best civillians to enable things in general to float along in their proper channels. I look on many of our past troubles, as things that were! The great bone of contention (Slavery) is for ever dead, & nearly buried, those great southerners who would "die in the last ditch" are hard to find & what few are left are anxious to get back under the old flag they attempted to destroy.

President Johnson will pardon most of them who remain here, and aspect of civil government is fast taking the place of the Military. All the Military camps in Ohio (except Columbus) are annulled, and will soon produce Corn & potatoes, instead of Soldiers.

I have not seen any of your communications in the Bee yet. Have you written none?

Our health is fair, I have got about well, the general health is good.

Good by for a week.

Your father,

Andrew Evans

p.s. Since the within was written, I have learned the sorrowful news of the death of Will Case, late of Co. F 70. O.V.I. He was shot last night in Aberdeen by a man named Young from Maysville, in some kind of a drunken Row, which is quite too common in Aberdeen. I have not the particulars.

Truly your father,
Andrew Evans

⇥ SAM TO ANDREW ⇤
Memphis, Tenn. / Oct. 8, 1865

Dear Father,

I have not been receiving letters from you regularly I reced 6 from you all at once. I come to Memphis a few days ago and got all in a pile, 6 from you, 1 from Will and several from other sources. I left word to have all the letter[s] that come forwarded to Jackson, but some way or other they were left here for me. I have written you every week since I left Memphis. After that I went to Jackson. I had the ague for about 10 days, but Ague Cure nocked it cold. I had the Ague exceedingly hard, I do not now feel any symptoms of it. I hope that will never return.

If you have received my letters you know what I am doing at Jackson, Tenn. I wrote you that I was a provost Marshall of Freedmen at Jackson, Tenn. This now my address:

Lt. Samuel Evans
Provost Marshall Freedman
Jackson, Tenn

There is but little news of interest. The 59 is now doing Provost duty at Memphis, all the white troops having been mustered out here. Citizens do not like Negro troops here, but Gen Smith does not seem to care whether they do or not. There is but one Regt of white troops in the Dist of West Tenn, that is the 10 Mich Cav.

I am some what of the opinion that Pres. Johnson is about to Tylerize.[1] I do not like his course much; he is not the man for the place at this time. Citizens of the South believe Slavery will be restored to them, that their debt will be paid by the Government. I believe myself there will be an effort made to rush a bill through the next congress by the South[ern] Members and our Northern Cops. I hope the Union people will use evry effort to elect the Union candidates. I know nothing that I can do that would assist them any. There is no disturbance here or where I have been in a war way, but there is opposition to the Freedmens' Bureau and the military. They think that the military have no right to interfere with the civil authorities.

As yet they have not been able to do any thing against the military here. Many of the citizens who have plantations have been throwing [obstacles] in the way of the policy of the Government to make free labor a success. The means used to effect this end are these, Discourage the Negro, try to organize to put down his wages, encouraging bad men to circulate false reports about the government and such like. I am very much disgusted with the southern chivalry. I do not like them. No I can not, I will not. Enough of this. My health is good at present. I will write as usual.

Love to all the family.

Yours Respectfully,

Sam Evans

1. Here Sam is referring to tenth president John Tyler of Virginia. Elected as vice president on a Whig ticket, Tyler assumed the presidency early in the term, when William Henry Harrison died of pneumonia. Tyler then pursued policies more favorable to the Democratic Party than to the Whig Party. Sam is fearful that President Johnson has begun rejecting the principles of the Union (Republican) Party, on whose ticket he was elected as Lincoln's vice president.

➤ ANDREW TO SAM ⬅

Home / Oct. 8, 1865

Dear Son,

No letter from you since yours of the 16 Oct [sic]. Of cource, you write if you are able, but your present is almost equivalent to cutting of communication between us. Our family are in usual health. We have nothing from George since I wrote you. The weather is beautiful, dry & pleasant, we have had a few frosts but not sufficient to do any injury. The corn is well along drying, quite out of danger from frost, and crops are generally verry good. Potatoes are good & [a]bundant and the price $1.00 per bu. is high for this season of year. Flour is worth $10.50. Bacon 18 to 30, live hogs gross 11 @ [?]. Cattle 4 to 7. Milck cows 40 to $80 pr. head, scarce, sheep 3 to 5. Lambs 2 to 3. Beef Steak 20 &c.

Our political campaign has become quite warm. Every honorable exertion (& some Dis. Hon.) is being made for success in each party. I am still of opinion we will beat them in our County but the Cops, seem to be full[ly] as sanguine of success as we are. I believe in neither party are verry sanguine of success. The great battle is close at hand, and a few days will give the decision that we must abide.

I went to Decatur yesterday to a free soldiers' dinner & welcome to all soldiers who might see proper to attend. It was a magnificent affair, a bountiful dinner and the best of order, good speeches, no whiskey and a general good feeling. I came home & your Mother & I rode to Aberdeen and listened to an excellent speech delivered by Maj. T. T. Taylor of Georgetown late of the 47 O.V.I.[1] He is all right and plagues the butternuts terribly.

Dian Cook requests me to write you concerning some of her old friends in Jackson, Tenn. She is of opinion her acquaintances there are all Rebels except Old Judge Reed & Wife. She desires you to become acquainted with them, & to remember her kindly to them, inform the old judge that you are a relative of John S. Cook who built his cistern & did other work.

I notice in the "Washington news," that it is expected an order will be issued soon to Muster out all the colored troops in the U.S. service.[2] If that's a fact you may get home this fall, which is much desired by us at home.

You have the love & best wishes of us all.

Truely your father,

Andrew Evans

1. This is Andrew's friend Major T. T. Taylor. This collection includes a letter from Taylor to Andrew on October 24, 1863.

2. As the white regiments were quickly mustered out following Lee and Johnston's surrenders in the spring of 1865, almost all of the active black regiments remained to serve as an occupying army in the conquered South. There was a degree of fairness to this unequal timing, as black troops, having enlisted later, had completed less of their terms of enlistment than most white soldiers. This combined with racial preference and paternalism to leave most black regiments in the service through the start of 1866, often doing unpleasant duty at distant posts, such as border policing in Texas. The final USCT unit was not mustered out until December 20, 1867. Noah Andre Trudeau, *Like Men of War: Black Troops in the Civil War 1862–1865* (New York: Little, Brown and Company, 1998), 455–61.

Home / Oct. 15, 1865

Dear Son:

Yours of Oct. 8 from Memphis was received on the 12, an unusual short trip. We are glad to learn that you are in better health, hope you will continue to improve until your health is quite restored. We are all well at home. George Early is still sick, tho on the mend. We have a letter from Inda, date Oct 12, she & Morty are well, but George is quite confined, was unable to be hauled to the election. Inda is of opinion he will not be able to teach for 2 or 3 weeks unless he mends faster than he has thus far. Jake Botner is in verry poor health. He is able to go about, but looks verry bad & is a bad color, he thinks of going home until his health is restored.

Well; I have been up "Salt river," and am safely returned home to business.[1] We are beaten in this Country by some 200 votes. I cannot give you the exact figures, but it is enough to insure the whole Copperhead ticket in this county and nearly so in Clermont. The Union Gov. & all the State officers, and a fair working majority in both branches of the Legislature, are elected. This will insure a U.S. Senator for 6 years more on the Union side. The idea of having our County offices filled by such men as Dave Tarbell, Old Bill Norris & others of the same stripe is rather a hard Bolus for me to swallow, but the thing is done and we will have to stand it until the people will it otherwise.[2] The soldiers voted the Copperhead ticket is what done the work, in my opinion for I know of no other changes.

We have a wedding occasionally, Calab Glasscock & Lizzy Maddox were married on last Thursday night. James Sweet & Mary S. Dodd (Bills daughter) were also married on the same night. I officiated in the latter case, and I assure you we had a verry nice wedding, verry numerously attended by the young & gay people, and evry thing went off with hapy festivities . . .

The weather is still fine, no frosts to injure vegetation. The corn will verry soon do to gather, unless it turns in wet. I will give the new addres on this letter, wod [sic, would] have done so sooner, but [you] told me in several letters not to change your addres until you ordered a change, your last is the first order for change.

Big John has moved into Toms sheephouse again. Tom Gray has moved into the old residence where John left. Jake Mitchell has moved down the River on Oconnors lands. Newtt Cunningham has moved to

Indiana, Bill Cunningham expects to move to Ky soon. John Acklin has moved to Toledo, W B Dennis expects to go there this fall.

Accept our best wishes and believe me,

Affectionately your father,

Andrew Evans

1. See note in James Burke's letter of April 8, 1862.
2. A bolus is a large pill or a small rounded mass of chewed food.

⇒ SAM TO ANDREW ⇐
Office Provost Marshall Freedmen
Jackson, Tenn. / October 16, 1865

Dear Father,

I have reced nothing from you since I last wrote while I was in Memphis. I have a few leisure moments to write to you. Buisness in this office is lively, that is there is plenty of it. I am working hard to make the labor question here in my district a success. It is a question that absorbs almost all other[s] at this time. I, for one, am put here to see that they (the Col[-ore]d people) do justice and receive justice in return. If the present system of labor should prove to be a failure, you could hardly estimate the suffering condition of the Freedmen. I want to see it a success for their benefit mostly and ours partly. I do not like the negro race as labor[er]s generally but I would like to see them do better than many of them are doing. Many of them are so ignorant that they do not understand why they are free and have to work for a living. They do not understand the force of a contract. The consequence is a difficulty to keep them at work till they fulfill it.

The people here are generally better disposed to do right than at Memphis. Though I believe they are Rebles. Some are in hopes that slavery will be restored to them. That is what keeps them quiet. I think they have some reasons to believe so. Our President wont do to lie to, at least in some particulars. If he dare I believe he would be a traitor to us. I cannot exactly rid my mind of the idea that he figured in the assassination [of] Pres. Lincoln.

I have little election news from Ohio, only that Cox is elected. I am afraid that our Reble friend[s] at home have been gaining ground, but I would be glad to know that such is not the case. I fear Brown ha[s] gon[e] Reble.

I have been entirely clear of Ague Symptoms for more than 3 weeks. I am afflicted slightly with Neuralgia, I think it is getting better.[1] I think I shall try to leave the service before my term of service expires, there is but little ground for expecting it now.

If you will direct your letters to me to Jackson they will come here, as the R R from Columbus Ky is now [running] regularly. I do not like to have letters almost old when they are received. I do not see why the[y] could not come here as quick as to Memphis. No more at this time.

Love and respects to all the family,

Yours Respectfully,

Samuel Evans

1. See note in Andrew's letter of February 8, 1863, for a definition of neuralgia.

➤ SAM TO ANDREW ➤
Office Provost Marshall Freedmen
Jackson, Tenn. / Oct. 27, 1865

Dear Father,

I have received nothing from home since I left Memphis except from Will date Sept 30 recd today. I did not write Sunday for the reason that I was not free. I took an official tour through the country for three days and just returned today. I am having good times but I have plenty to do. I am running this machine myself, I have no clerk now. My clerk was taken from me and [I] cannot now get one.[1] I have met with no serious opposition in the discharge of my duties.

It is rather unpleasant to have all the quarrels between men to settle, but I have undertaken to do my duty and I do not like to be conquered or run off is the plain fact for my staying here now. I think I have friends even here among (subdued) Rebles for transacting business on the Square [fairly]. I think I shall have a better time soon. My health is now good and I commenced gaining. I have no exposure. It is a little tiresome to sit in the office all day but that is better than exposure too rain and bad weather. I do not know what is the reason that no Bees ever come to me I neither get Bees nor letters lately. I am sure I have written my share. I think our post master are all of the right stripe.

Cotton is down again. The present crop is first rate, what little there is. The yield is large but the quantity planted is small. Corn crops in Tenn are good. They will have about 30 bushels per acre on an average, that would not be very large with us. They do not know how to raise it.

Citizen[s] are trying to induce Norther[n] mechanic[s] to emigrate here and start shops; think it will help build up the country. Land is very cheap. I had 1000 acres of fine land offered me for $5.00 per acre. Now that is very cheap for improved land. The house on this farm could not be built for less than 7 or 8000 dollars, but I thouth I would not buy. The terms were 1/3 down, 1/3 in one year, the other in 2 years with 6 pr cent on the defered payments on the farm. There is more than enough of the present cotton crop to pay for the land. There are 40 stout hands on the farm. Some of our Yankees who raise a 100 acres of cotton have made about $10,000.00. Char Ellison (our sutler) made about $5000 of 55 acres when cotton is wort[h] 40 cts.[2] There is money in it. Well I have written enough about the cotton trade.

I shall close for this time and hope before I write again I will receive a letter from home.

Give my love an best wishes to all the family

As ever your affectionate Son,

Sam Evans

1. Because Freedmen's Bureau offices were staffed by the military, the rapid mustering out of Union troops left too few enlisted men to assist bureau officers. Foner, *A Short History of Reconstruction*, 67.

2. See note on corruption and profiteering in the occupied South in Sam's letter of March 14, 1865. For a definition of sutler, see note in Sam's letter of October 12, 1862.

⇒ ANDREW TO SAM ⇐
Home / Oct. 29, 1865

Dear Son:

Yours of the 16 came to hand on the 24, we were all glad to learn that your health was improving. We are all in tolerable health. Ann is not quite well, but much better than she was a week ago. She rode to church today to Ebeneezer and stood the trip well. The general health is verry fair for the season of year. Corn gathering was pretty generally started last week, we are within two loads of done the field at "Old Neds", would have finished it yesterday, but were prevented by rain. When that is finished I think we will clean the race before we gather the field at home. I cannot get along without a hand, and with one I can do some good with the mill, at least, have it ready for you when you come home, as I hope you will soon.

We have nothing from Will since we left him at Ripley on monday evening, there may be a letter at town, but none yesterday evening.[1] Nothing from George & Inda, we are almost destitute of news of interest to write you. We earnestly hope you may succeed in getting out of the service before your term expires, that would be glorious news to us. Will is gone again and we shall not see him until spring, if at all. You can hardly immagine how lonesome it is to us, after having so large a family of grown sons, to be left alone in so short a time. It is of cource a part of our fate and we must endure it until the decrees of fate order it otherwise. You speak of getting no letters from us. We cannot help it for your letters are mailed properly and to your present address. Sometimes we meet delay in getting them to the office, but only for a day or two.

Our weather has been verry favorable for business this fall. It is quite cool today, yesterday & last night was cool & windy with spitting snow, today is clear & cool. Frost have been so moderate that our dahlias are still beautifully in bloom. Sweet potatoes, Tomatoes & Butter beans are considerably frostbitten.

I hope you are mistaken about President Johnson. I cannot approve all his acts, but his cource may be for the best. I hope so at least, he pardons more Rebels than I could, but that may be better; as Christ pardons the greatest sinners, is it not christian like for man in authority, to pardon the vilest Rebel on proper repentance? They are too proud and brave a people to lick the rod that smote them! Understand me, I do not like his course, but it may [be] the best policy.

Our love & best wishes are tendered you by,
Your father
Andrew Evans

1. In October of 1865 Will entered the Charity Hospital Medical College in Cleveland. The following February he returned to Brown County with the degree of medical doctor and began practicing. Byron Williams, *History of Clermont and Brown counties, Ohio, from the earliest historical times down to the present* (Milford, Ohio: Hobart Publishing Company, 1913), 2:214.

⇢ ANDREW TO SAM ⇠
Home / Nov. 12, 1865

Dear Son,

We have nothing from you during the past week. We have had beautiful weather and have been using it in getting the Mill ready to run, we are ready to run with the exception of some inside work such as packing bushes, picking stones, &c. The races are cleaned, the dam well filled, the waste gait & run-over well repaired and the old trunk packed nearly all over. It will take some coaxing to make it do a season. The boys will enter on the corn again tomorrow if the weather remains good, they can finish up in less than a week of favorable weather, then we will be ready for winter. I think I will keep but one hand during the winter, that will be Bill Thompson, John Swisher talks of going to school this winter.

We have one letter from Will since I wrote you, he is verry well, pleasantly located and verry much pleased with his faculty. Nothing from George or Inda for a week. Our own folks are well as usual. Ann had a little Heamorrhage of the lungs last week, it was not rapid and was of short duration. I am fearful she will prove weak in the chest, tho her general health is improving. Lee is quite well and is attending school. I have up under a good deal of work at the dam, waste gate & trunk, and as well as usual, my back has not let down although I have done considerable stooping and some lifting.

The general health is quite fair. Temperate habits about our towns (I am sorry to tell you) are on the decline, Aberdeen & Ripley are both sorely infested with drunkenness, Gambling and Revelry of allmost evry description. The Morals of both places are horribly shaken, this is all [w]rong surely!

I learn that it is expected at Washington that all the volunteer troops will be mustered out shortly, Colored as well as white, and do the Garrison duty with the regulars, thinking that such a cource would restore good feelings between the antagonistic parties, sooncr than to do the garrison duty by colored troops.[1] I think so myself, not that we owe the Rebs any favors, but the sooner we can get the whole civil machinry to running in good order, the better it will be for us, as well as those in the South. I hope your fears of Andy Johnson's inconstancy to the Govt has banished; the more I criticize his conduct, the more I am convinced that he is a great and good man, [illegible] attached to the wellfare of our government.

I am with the highest regards,
Your affectionate father,

[Andrew Evans]

1. Union victory presented the North with the problem of restoring order and civil government in the South. Because this restoration of order required more soldiers than

were in the regular army, some proposed that soldiers of the USCT be used. Many, both in and out of the military, like Andrew, felt that the use of black soldiers as an occupying army would antagonize Southerners and irrevocably complicate reunification.

⇒ SAM TO ANDREW ⇐
Jackson, Tenn. / November 17, 1865

Dear Father,

I have just returned from a trip in the country. I find on my return three letters from Ohio, 1 from you, 1 [from] Mary and 1 from John E Carpenter, all of which are welcome "guests." I am glad all are well at the same time. I am enjoying the best of health. I am now heav[i]er than I ever was in my life. My weight is 175 lbs. (that is without any unnecessary clothing, simple uniform).

You make an illusion [sic] to my leaving the service. I would like to "get out" about Jan. next. There is no certainty that such a thing can be accomplished at that time though I shall try as you all feel anxious that I should come home. I could conduct myself in such a manner that I could leave the service in disgrace but you are aware that I prefer not to do so as "honesty is the better policy."

I sent a paper to you, published here, before I left for the country. I remained absent in the discharge of my duty 5 days. I have forgotten the date of my last letter to you. In the paper you will see an article above my signature. There are a great many things in my line of duty that are rather vexatious but I have "patience and endurance." I am well treated . . . I am the only "Blue Breeches" here.

When Gen Smith was about to send me a guard, the citizen[s] petitioned to have it remain in Memphis, that they would be obedient to my summon, that they would assist me to discharge my duty when assistance was required. I do not know whether the Gen has consented to try them a while or not, but the Guard has not come and the citizens have come at my calling. Thus far, I have been able to handle them very easily. I believe they come to time [more punctually] better than when there were soldiers here. The Freedmen's Bureau has, by many, been regarded as a "Grand Humbug." . . .

I find Uncle Saml Carpenter has an idea of coming South to work this winter. There is a fine opening here now, not half enough carpenters to do the work that is asked to be done. About 1/2 of the best part of the town is burned and those who are able to rebuild are trying to have it done. I would think that a first class workman would do a fine business here.

They have the poorest Smiths here you ever saw. I have not seen one that could make a decent horse shoe. I was in a shop a few days ago, saw a man mend a double [illegible] clevis by simply splicing it, he charged 50 cts and did a poor job I thought.[1] I have not seen a job that was well done since I came to Jackson. Smith charges $4. for shoeing a horse all 'round and $2.00 for setting old shoes.

Remember me kindly to all the family,

I am as ever the same,

Saml Evans

1. A clevis is a U-shaped piece of metal with a bolt or pin through the ends.

⟫ ANDREW TO SAM ⟪
Home / Dec. 3, 1865

Dear Son:

I have received nothing from you in the last week, we still get one or two letters per week from Will. He is still in good health and pleased with his situation. We are in usual health. I am almost clear of rheumatism. Your mother has some rheumatic troubles but not serious. The rest of the family are well. The general health is fair.

George & Inda went home yesterday. I took them to Ripley. They took the boat for Higginsport, and expected to meet Esqr Early [George's father?] there to convey them home. I found things at Ripley rather on the secret order respecting "small pox." The citizens are disinclined to talk on the subject, but if pinned up they will admit that there are a few cases among the negros. Outsiders say it is heavy in town.

I went to Georgetown on Monday last, found our candidates ready to enter the contest against our Butternut competitors. We held a council, investigated the case and determined to go ahead, we all served the proper notice on our contestees, and appointed the 11th Dec for taking depositions. The clerk's deposition is all we want to make our case. The poll books of Perry & Lewis [townships] are both claimed to be set aside for informality, want of tally sheets, certificates & c., all of which we can prove by the Clerk of the court. Our party are quite elated over the prospect. Many of them say, "go ahead, we will furnish pecuniary aid." Well, my case will not cost much, as the House of Representatives will try my case; Each party has to pay for their own testimony, we will all have to pay counsel for drawing up the notices, taking depositions & c. It will cost something.

The weather is still dry, and pleasant. No water to grind [wheat]. Yesterday was verry smoky. Indian summer like weather. Today is cloudy & warm. We killed 8 of our hogs on Thursday and salted them up. Pork had fallen to 9 cents at that time. It is a little better now, we are feeding 4 yet. If the price suits when they are fat, we will sell them, otherwise we will salt again.

We are looking for Sam Espy & wife this morning, should they bring any news I will give it to you in a p.s. Will Housh is going a head strong on Blacksmithing. He had a heavy load of iron and other material yesterday. He will find out what ails him some of these days.

Accept the highest regards of us all.

Verry truely your father,

Andrew Evans

⇒ SAM TO ANDREW ⇐
Jackson, Tenn. / Dec. 18, 1865

Dear Father,

Your very kind letter of the 3 of Dec. is at hand. Glad to hear all are well and that your prospects are flattering for a seat in the Legislature. I can not feel well when ever copperheads have the ascendancy. I believe they would upset all the good if possible that we as soldiers have been laboring to accomplish during the last 4 years. Were it not for them, these people down here would not be so bold and impudent in asking for what they do. I want conservative men who will not go to extremes, but those that will stand up for us and right. Radicals on both sides will not be willing to set a proper value on our services for the last 4 years or estimate the suffering of our soldiers during this war. I do not claim one ioto [sic] more than impartial men would be willing to award. But as far our soldiers, I want them to be placed in their proper height before the world. Conservative men will have to bring about reconstruction. Radicals can not do it or at least they will not.

I will be under the painful necessity of shortening the days of a Reble captain if he does not behave himself. I should have kill[ed] him some time ago if I had not been held so I could not. I will not be insulted by such men as he. At the same time I will not molest him if he behaves him self. Your need not be uneasy about me being rash. He has asked pardon of me for what he has done, but I shall keep an eye on him.

I have made application to be relieved from here, and sent to my Regt. I ordered all my mail sent to Memphis sometime ago I shall not have it changed as I expect to be relieved some time during the next week or rather the present week.

My health is very fine weight 175 and not very fat. I am boarding with a very fine man who treats me with respect. I have a great deal of work to do here and no one to assist in doing anything. I have three case[s] set for the day, U.S. vs. some white men. I asked for a clerk to help me but as yet have none. Here is a sketch of what I have to do. Make contract[s] in triplicate, Indentures, master and apprentice in duplicate, Try and decide all cases between white and black, supervision of schools, Abandoned lands, see to the destitute, and various other things. The weather has been quite cold for a week, two snows during the week about 4 inches deep.

Well I shall have to close as it is mail time. My best respects to all the family.

As ever your son,
Sam Evans

ANDREW TO SAM
Home / Dec. 31, 1865

Dear Son,

I have nothing from you within the past week. I got Will to write last sunday, owing to my sore finger I could scarcely write. It is better now, but not well. We are in only slow health, Ann has bled no more, but is quite weak with considerable cough. She is mending in general, unless her lungs give way she will get along, she is cheerful and resolute.

I was attacked with diarrhaea last night which gave me a pretty hard jerk, but all is quiet now. The residue of the family are in ordinary health.

I shall change my base of opperations for a while by going to Columbus. Will and I start tomorrow, and be company as far as Columbus. How long I will stay cannot be determined yet. It will perhaps be decided in two weeks from the commencement of the session . . . If I fail to get my seat I will mend it [a part of the mill] soon after I return, if not there is no one to run the mill on wheat. I have drilled Will Thompson until he is a good and safe hand to grind corn, he will grind corn if the mill keeps in order. If not he is instructed to lock up.

Slavery is forever dead in the United States allow me to congratulate you on the event. I think the Southern members will be admitted to their seats in Congress, and let people with proper discriminations accuse any who were engaged in trying to destroy the Govt. There will have to be some concessions, perhaps on both sides, to affect a proper and agreeable Union of the extremes.

Tis said that Hannah Hiett and Will Grierson are married in Illinois, be it so. We got a letter from George and Inda last night. They and Morty are verry well. George has a large school, Inda still sews and cuts & c. If I have to stay long at Columbus you shall hear from me there.

Accept the love & best wishes of the family through,

Your father,

Andrew Evans

➤ SAM TO ANDREW ◂
Jackson, Tenn. / January 7, 1866

Dear Father:

I have received nothing from you for the last 2 weeks though I looked. The mails are in a terrible bad fix. In the first place the R Road runs with a great deal of irregularity. The track being in a very bad fix, the cars run off very often. I don't like these devilish Rebles any better than I use to. Some of them are very nice men. I don't know whether I can get off from here or not. I have asked several times to be relieved. I have had an exceedingly throng[ed] time for the past 3 weeks in making contract[s] and approving them. I have already made and approved about 500. They were made in duplicate. I don't think that I shall be thronged more than one week longer. I think I shall go to Memphis next week. I am going to bring some troops here. These Rebs have killed my Deputy Sheriff who served all my processes.[1] I cannot now have a process served without more trouble than it is worth. I had better do it myself than bother about getting them to do it.

My health is excellent my weight is still about 175 and [sic] 176 and feel fine. I have not time to write more.

Love to all the family.

Your Son,

Sam Evans

⇒ ANDREW TO SAM ⇐
House of Rep.
Columbus, Oh. / Jan. 9, 1866

Dear Son:

I did not write you on Sunday from the fact that I had no news to send you, nor have I much now, but such as I have "I will give unto thee". I am still here with my case undecided. Our speaker has been slow to announce the standing committees, nothing could be done in my case, but to present the papers until the Committee on "Privileges & Elections" were organized. They have the case referred to them now, but do not expect to report this week as they desire to thourily [*sic*, thoroughly] investigate the matter before they report. I should have gone home this morning, but the Committee desires me to appear before them in their investigations, which I have consented to do.

I shall go home Thursday or Friday and stay a few days, but will have to return. Many of the members speak rather sanguine of my prospect of success, but I will not venture an opinion yet. I rather think Fitch expects to be ousted.[1] There has not been much done in Legislating, the Inauguration of Gov Cox took place yesterday on the rotunda in an immense croud. He is a fine looking man and verry nice speaker.

There are a great many strange faces in the Hall this year, but I am getting acquainted with them pretty fast. I find it verry convenient to have plenty of reliable friends when one is away from home. Such is my fix here. I had the pleasure of seeing Bro. Fitch squat: (Out of Order,) in his first effort at Legislating. Such has not [been] my fate yet, nor do I expect it to be for I have studied the rules too well to violate them. Elijah is not enjoying himself as well as he expected to. He is not near so fast as he is in his own County, he seems cowed.

The weather is extremely cold, an[d] has been since Thursday last, no snow on the ground, but the river is frozen 8 or 10 inches thick, we have many indications of snow, but it is too cold to snow. I got a letter from home yesterday. They were all well but Ann, with no improvement in her condition. Will was well saturday. I have not heard from him since.

The candidates for U.S. Senator, Sherman & Schenck are here "Buttonholing" with members with about equal chances. There will be a "Union caucus" held tonight that will perhaps decide the matter between them.[2]

You need not write to me here until you know whether I stay here. I shall hear from you through home if you write home, they write me twice a week.

Accept the love of,

Your father

Andrew Evans

1. Fitch is the Democrat who defeated Andrew in the 1865 election for Brown County's seat in the Ohio House of Representatives.

2. U.S. Senators were elected by state legislatures until 1913. Since the Union Party constituted a majority of the Ohio state legislature, their caucus would likely determine Ohio's senator. The Ohio Union Party chose to return incumbent, John Sherman, brother of General William T. Sherman, to the Senate. General Robert Schenck, who had defeated Vallandigham in the 1862 congressional election, continued to serve in the U.S. House of Representatives. Roseboom, *The Civil War Era*, 402, 452.

⇒ ANDREW TO SAM ⇐
Home / Jan. 28, 1866

Dear Son:

Yours of the 17th came to hand on the 26, found us all well as usual except our dear Angelic pet, Ann Delia, whose spiritless body was still with her bereaved friends. She breathed her last at 7 1/2 O'clock Thursday evening after an illness of 50 days. She died as she lived, a lovely, obedient, agreeable girl, much esteemed by all her associates.

We saw fit, to procure for her last dress, a beautiful black silk dress richly trimmed and the residue of her suit was of the proper kind for the occasion. When dressed she had that same sweet Angelic smile that [she] wore in life. I never saw a more natural or sweeter corpse. We followed her mortal remains to its last resting place, (by Amos' side) where she was intered at 12 N[oon] yesterday. "Peace to her ashes." Her disease was more rapid in its progress than I have ever seen on any other person, she was sensible to within a few minutes of her death. She knew us all, expressed a desire to see you, Will, Inda, & George but could not, then said she would see Abe, John, & Amos. She called each of the family by name and then called Bill Thompson, he went to her. She reached her hand

and shook his, told us all to not cry, she then became calm and slipt [*sic*] away without a moan or a shrug of any kind. O Sam; is not Providence pressing heavily upon us? The youthful, the beautiful, the dutiful as well as the wicked and vain, are alike subject to the great call! We are well admonished in the book where it says, "be ye also ready, for in the hour that ye know not, the Son of man cometh."

I need not say to you that we are bereaved and disconsolate, we must bear our loss as well as we can, the loss is setting verry heavily upon us all at present.

I arrived at home on Tuesday night last, consequently can give you no news of my contest case. [Former colonel of the 70th Ohio] Doc Phillips said he would attend in my behalf before the committe[e] and would notify me of the result as soon as know. I shall not go to Columbus sooner than tomorrow week if I get the seat, if not I may not go at all.

I am glad to learn that you expect to come home the coming Spring. I hope you can find some employment that will satisfy you without leaving us so far. Our family is so small now, two girls and two little boys all told.[1] You may imagine that we feel lonesome, and desire the presence of those living of our family.

Accept the warm affections of our family and believe me,

Your bereaved & affectionate father

Andrew Evans

1. All that remained home were Isabella, Mary, Joe, and Lee. Over the course of these letters, sons Abraham, John, and Amos and daughter Ann had died. Indiana and Will had moved out, and Sam was just about to return from the army. At this point, only four of eleven children remained at home.

EPILOGUE

In the final letter of this collection, Andrew laments the small size of the family left at home with him. Of his eleven children, four had died during the war—Abraham, John, Amos, and Ann—and only four remained at home, as Indiana lived with her husband, George Early, across the county in Feesburg. Will was at medical college in Cleveland, and Sam remained in the field with the Freedmen's Bureau. The war years took a heavy toll on the Evans family, shrinking their numbers and alienating those still living from relatives and old friends. Through these letters we saw Andrew lose a daughter and three sons, one to illness contracted in the army (John) and another because military absences necessitated a grueling regimen for those at home (Amos). These tragic events, despite his soldier sons' luck on the battlefields, made Andrew especially desperate for Sam to come home.

The war not only took away family members, but also divided the Evanses from neighbors, friends, and even their closest relatives. Most dramatically, Sam and his first cousin Jane terminated their affectionate relationship because Sam could not stomach her racist opposition to emancipation and half-hearted support for the war. After this, the story of Jane, her ne'er-do-well brother Laban, and the rest of her family is largely lost to history. Jane's father Amos, accused of deserting his regiment in February 1863, after being left in a shipboard sickbed at Nashville, never returned home or otherwise reappeared in the historical record.[1]

Like the life stories of so many common Americans of any generation, what little we know about the Evans's history years later is necessarily anecdotal and fragmentary. The war, and the fact that Sam and Andrew Evans so fastidiously saved their letters, gives readers a unique window into the story of these people's lives, but only for the four years Sam spent in the field. Sam's return to the family homestead reduced the need for

---

1. Josiah Morrow, *The History of Brown County, Ohio, Containing a History of the County . . . General and Local Statistics; Portraits of Early Settlers and Prominent Men; History of the Northwest Territory; History of Ohio; Map of Brown County; Constitution of the United States* (Chicago: W. H. Beers, 1883), Biographical Sketches 158–59; United States Civil War Records, Amos E. Evans, National Archives, Washington, DC.

regular letter writing, and the end of the Civil War eliminated nostalgic or documentary reasons for continuing to save any correspondence Sam and Andrew might have found reason to exchange. Thus the details of their day-to-day postwar lives are largely unknown—a stark contrast to how much we have learned about their wartime experience. From various sources documenting Brown County local history, one extant postwar letter Sam sent a former commander, and Andrew Evans's last will and testament, we can trace an outline of the Evans clan's postbellum lives.

Andrew Evans died at age sixty-nine on September 12, 1879. His wife, Mary, survived him for thirteen years. All seven of their children still living at the completion of the wartime correspondence outlived their father. At the time of Andrew's death, the five eldest all were married and living locally, Indiana at Ripley and the others, Sam, Will, Mary Grierson, and Isabella Hawk, at Hiett (a new town in Huntington Township, presumably named after their mother Mary Hiett Evans's family). The two youngest, Joseph H. (Jo in most letters) and Lee, resided at home with their mother. Joseph H. Evans remained in Brown County for the duration of his life, which ended prematurely in 1892.[2]

Sam and Will lived full lives that extended long past the Civil War. Well after scenes of battlefields faded into distant memory, they remained deeply proud of their exemplary military records and continued to celebrate wartime achievements of fellow Ohioans. The depth of their adulation for favorite Ohio generals is demonstrated by the tribute both Evans soldiers paid in the names of their first sons born after the war, Sam's U. S. Grant Evans and Will's boys W. T. Sherman Evans and P. H. Sheridan Evans (twins like their father). Sam and Will never strayed from wartime loyalties. Passionate Democrats before their military service, Sam and Will followed their brother John in abandoning the party of Jackson for the Union (Republican and pro-war) Party.[3] They never turned back. With slaveholders just across the Ohio River in Kentucky, Brown County Democrats had long reigned, unthreatened by the national party's pro-slavery record. The war abruptly changed this, culminating in Andrew's two elections on a Union ticket, making him the first

2. Andrew Evans, Will, Brown County Probate Records, Brown County Courthouse, Georgetown, Ohio, 1879; Byron Williams, *History of Clermont and Brown Counties, Ohio, from the Earliest Historical Times Down to the Present* (Milford, OH: Hobart, 1913), 2:213.

3. For the first mention of John's political conversion, see Andrew's letter of November 2, 1862.

Republican incumbent ever reelected in Brown County. By the closing months of Sam's service, however, the region was already reverting to old allegiances, marked by Andrew's narrow failure at the polls in 1865. Although he attributed the defeat to voter fraud, and confidently contested the election at Columbus, Andrew never again served in the legislature. Unlike many of their neighbors, the Evanses could not return to the party of Vallandigham and Jefferson Davis. Sam and Will remained avid Republican partisans for the duration of their lives. Sam managed to overcome the county's Democratic voting base and repeatedly won township election as justice of the peace. Will, on the other hand, ran unsuccessfully as a Republican for sheriff in 1870 and for State Senate in 1881.[4]

This wartime political conversion, experienced also by their father, who had served many terms as a Democratic judge and local officer, pales in comparison to Andrew's other transformations. Of course this is most dramatically demonstrated by his shift from contempt for Sam's decision to serve with black troops in 1863 to joy at helping ratify abolition less than two years later. Andrew's newfound tolerance is best exemplified by his preference to "stand by and vote with a Loyal Black man, [rather] than [with] a white Traitor."[5] His metamorphosis epitomizes the Civil War's very real promise of revolutionary change. This kind of thinking, this sudden critical reevaluation of ingrained prejudices and worldviews, seems to come to Americans in moments of extreme crisis, and was perhaps most dramatic during the greatest national crisis, the Civil War. Beyond the blood and gore, and bitterness and mourning, this war was the kind of earth-shattering event that could catalyze major change, remarkably quickly. Andrew Evans demonstrates how long-held views can rapidly evolve when confronted with such intense strife. Much of the North joined Andrew in accepting emancipation as a war aim and later a moral responsibility. Many may even have matched Andrew in casting off intense racial prejudice. Unfortunately this broad shift in public opinion did not last. By the 1870s, most Northerners were tired of division in their country, forgetful of blacks' wartime services, and eager to return to business as usual. The moment for radical change had passed, but Andrew Evans reminds us that this moment did exist. This opportunity

---

4. Morrow, *The History of Brown County*, Biographical Sketches 158.
5. See Andrew's letters of May 18, 1863; February 5, 1865; and July 9, 1865.

arose in large part because of the self-assertion of thousands of African Americans who fled slavery and fought in Union regiments like Sam's.[6] This opportunity existed, however, also because the war led large swaths of the American public, ordinary men like Andrew Evans, to take seriously revolutionary social change, even if only for a fleeting moment.

Will and Sam both maintained the strong reputations earned during their devoted wartime service. Will and his twin brother, Abraham, who died early in these letters, forged the family's way into the medical field, and several members of the Evans family followed. Will completed his medical schooling in 1866 and returned home, establishing a medical practice in 1868, which he maintained for over forty-five years. Will's military and medical accomplishments earned him positions as an officer of the Grand Army of the Republic and as a local chairman of the U.S. Board of Pension Examiners during the administration of Republican President Benjamin Harrison. William's twin boys emulated their physician father, serving as attachés, respectively of the state hospital at Dayton and of a hospital in Columbus. Indiana and George Early's son Louis Mortimer ("Morty" in the letters) also entered the medical profession. Indiana and George moved to Columbus, and Louis Mortimer Early practiced there before his death in 1912. Young Lee Andrew Evans, who Sam always remembered with fondness during his years at war, went further afield. The only one of Sam's surviving siblings at war's end to settle outside of Ohio, Lee Andrew briefly taught school locally, and ultimately moved to Redlands, California, near Los Angeles. There he established himself as a veterinary surgeon.[7]

Sam returned to the old home place after the war and soon achieved local prominence comparable his father's. Sam opened a new blacksmith shop and also worked the old mill. He closed the mill in the mid-1870s when it ceased to be profitable. Despite financial losses from failed investments in banks and a piano factory, Sam attained significant prestige. He became locally renowned for estate planning and execution, developing a reputation that earned him the opportunity to administer numerous estates and serve as guardian for several wards. He also served as

---

6. For a discussion of how slaves' own action created pressure for general emancipation legislation see Ira Berlin, Barbara J. Fields, Steven F. Miller, and Joseph P. Reidy, *Slaves No More: Three Essays on Emancipation and the Civil War* (Cambridge, UK: Cambridge University Press, 1992).

7. Byron Williams, *History of Clermont and Brown Counties*, 2:211–16; Morrow, *The History of Brown County*, Biographical Sketches 158; "Death of Samuel Evans," *Ripley Bee*, June 8, 1910, in Carl N. Thompson, *Historical Collections of Brown County, Ohio* (Piqua, OH: Hammer Graphics, 1969), 683.

president of his township's board of education and numerous terms as township justice of the peace.[8]

As Sam grew older, his business and political success became increasingly important, because side effects from a minor spinal wound limited his capability for manual labor. In 1867 Sam married a local girl named Margaret Shelton who was nearly fifteen years his junior. Sam and Margaret had eight children, including their aforementioned first-born, U. S. Grant Evans. Samuel Evans died in 1910 at age seventy-six, and his younger brother Will followed four years later, dying in 1914 at age seventy-nine, and thus passed into history these last two soldier sons of the Evans family that had so vigorously done their patriotic duty.[9]

8. Robert Cowden, *A Brief Sketch of the Organization and Services of the Fifty-Ninth Regiment of United States Colored Infantry, and Biographical Sketches* (Dayton, OH: United Brethren Publishing House, 1883), 252–55; Morrow, *The History of Brown County*, Biographical Sketches 156–57.

9. Morrow, *The History of Brown County*, Biographical Sketches 156–57; United States Civil War Pension Records, Samuel Evans, Record Group 15 National Archives, Washington DC; Civil War Pension Records, William Evans, Record Group 15; "Death of Samuel Evans" in Thompson, *Historical Collections of Brown County, Ohio*, 683.

1737, Dec 1	John Evans (Andrew's grandfather) was born in Baltimore County, Maryland, to Thomas and Elizabeth Evans, both immigrants from North Wales who had first settled in New North Wales in Philadelphia County, Pennsylvania
1770, Nov 17	John Evans Jr. (Andrew's father) was born in Maryland
1775, Aug 10	Mary Housh (later Mary Evans, Andrew's mother) was born
1792	John Evans Jr. went west and settled near the Blue Licks in Mason County, Kentucky
1800, fall	John Evans Jr. came to Huntington Township in Ohio; he bought 535 acres and built a cabin, where his family would move the following spring
1809, Dec 9	Andrew Evans was born, the fourth of eleven children born to John Evans Jr. and Mary (Housh) Evans
1815, Apr 21	Mary Hiett was born
1819	Andrew's brother Amos (Samuel's uncle) was born to John Evans Jr. and Mary (Housh) Evans
1833, June 3	Andrew Evans and Mary Hiett were married
1834, Apr 18	Samuel Evans was born, the first of eleven children born to Andrew and Mary (Hiett) Evans
1835, Oct 8	William H. and Abraham Evans (twins) were born, Andrew and Mary's second and third children
1837, Nov 3	Indiana Evans was born to Andrew and Mary
1841, Mar 12	John B. Evans was born to Andrew and Mary
1843, Apr 2	Amos A. Evans was born to Andrew and Mary
1844	Jane Evans was born, daughter of Angeline and Amos Evans (son of John Evans Jr.)
1845, Sept 30	Mary Evans was born to Andrew and Mary
1847	Laban Evans was born, son of Angeline and Amos Evans (son of John Evans Jr.)
1849, Mar 25	Isabella E. Evans was born to Andrew and Mary
1851, Sept 30	Ann D. Evans was born to Andrew and Mary
1854, Feb 15	Joseph H. Evans was born to Andrew and Mary

1858, Jan 18	Andrew's father John Evans Jr. died at the age of eighty-seven
1858, Oct 16	Lee A. Evans, Andrew and Mary's youngest child, was born
1861, Oct 16	John B. Evans enlisted in Company F, 70th Ohio Volunteer Infantry; he was later selected to be a sergeant
1862, Feb 18	Samuel enlisted in Company F, 70th Ohio Volunteer Infantry
1862, Apr 6–7	Battle of Shiloh, in which both Samuel and John participated; Samuel sustained minor wounds
1862, May 14	Abraham Evans died at Aberdeen, having been brought there by William from Pleasant Hill, Indiana, where Abraham was practicing medicine
1862, Aug 12	William enlisted in Company E , 89th Ohio Volunteer Infantry; in this regiment's organization he was appointed a duty sergeant; William's brother-in-law and uncle, George Early and Amos Evans also enlisted in this regiment, though not necessarily on this date
1862, Oct 3	Amos A. Evans (Samuel's brother) was drafted
1862, Oct 14	Amos A. Evans was discharged on account of physical disability
1863, May	Samuel was recommended by his superiors for a position commanding black troops
1863, May 14	Mary (Housh) Evans (Samuel's grandmother) died at the age of eighty-seven
1863, May 27	John B. Evans (Samuel's brother) died at the age of twenty-two
1863, Jun 6	Samuel was sworn into service as second lieutenant of Company B, 59th United States Colored Infantry
1863, Aug 14	William was commissioned hospital steward of his regiment
1863, Oct 2	Samuel was promoted to first lieutenant and assigned to Company A
1863, Oct	Andrew was elected a representative to the state legislature on the Union ticket
1864, Jul 5–21	Samuel joined his regiment on General Smith's expedition from Memphis to Tupelo, Mississippi; during this expedition, Samuel and his regiment

	participated in the battles of Pontotoc on July 11–12 and Tupelo on July 14–15
1864, Oct	Andrew was reelected as state representative, being the first incumbent Unionist (or Republican) in that office ever reelected in Brown County
1864, Nov 24	Amos A. Evans died at the age of twenty-one
1865, Feb	Andrew voted for the ratification of the Thirteenth Amendment, which was supported by the Ohio House by a vote of fifty-eight to twelve
1865, Jun	After nearly three and a half years of service Samuel finally was granted permission to return home on brief leave
1865, Jun 7	William was discharged from the army somewhere in the vicinity of Washington DC
1865, Aug 23	Samuel was detailed as provost marshal at Jackson, Tennessee, and ran the Freedmen's Bureau there until Jan 25, 1866
1865, Oct	Andrew lost his reelection bid by about two hundred votes; he contested the election result unsuccessfully
1866, Jan 31	Samuel was honorably discharged from the U.S. Army
1866, Feb 21	William graduated from the Charity Hospital Medical College in Cleveland; he then returned home to Huntington Township and began a medical practice there
1867, Oct 24	Samuel married Margaret E. Shelton
1867, Dec 5	William married Maria Games
1868, Sept 24	U. S. Grant Evans was born, the first of Samuel and Margaret's children; U.S. Grant would be followed by Mary L., Andrew W., Joseph S., Charles H., John I., Elizabeth M., and Katherine
1868, Oct 1	The first two of William and Maria's five children were born, twins (like William himself) W. T. Sherman, and P. H. Sheridan
1879, Sept 12	Andrew Evans died at age sixty-nine
1892, Aug 10	Mary (Hiett) Evans died at age seventy-seven
1910, May 27	Samuel Evans died at age seventy-six
1914, Dec 9	William H. Evans died at age seventy-nine

The information used to compile the family timeline above comes entirely from a series of archival and printed sources. These include, first, the letters themselves.

Additionally we located a surprising amount of family data from biographical sketches that appeared in three local histories of Brown County: Josiah Morrow, *The History of Brown County, Ohio, Containing a History of the County . . . General and Local Statistics; Portraits of Early Settlers and Prominent Men; History of the Northwest Territory; History of Ohio; Map of Brown County; Constitution of the United States* (Chicago: W. H. Beers, 1883); Carl N. Thompson, *Historical Collections of Brown County, Ohio* (Piqua, Ohio: Hammer Graphics, 1969); and Byron Williams, *History of Clermont and Brown Counties, Ohio, from the Earliest Historical Times Down to the Present* (Milford, Ohio: Hobart, 1913). Finally, in determining the birth years of family members who could not be traced in local histories, we estimated their birth year based on their age as listed in the United States Manuscript Census of 1860. Official United States Military Records, stored at the National Archives, also helped fill in some gaps in the history of the Evans men's military service. Also Frederick Henry Dyer, *A Compendium of the War of the Rebellion* (New York: T. Yoseloff, 1959) enabled us to specify the exact dates of the July 1864 expedition of General Smith in which Sam participated.

BIBLIOGRAPHY

Primary Sources

Compiled Military Service Record of Amos Evans, 89th Ohio Infantry. Record Group 94, National Archives, Washington, D.C.

Compiled Military Service Record of Lt. Samuel Evans, 59th U.S. Colored Infantry. Record Group 94, National Archives, Washington, D.C.

Compiled Military Service Record of Samuel Evans, 70th Ohio Infantry. Record Group 94, National Archives, Washington, D.C.

Compiled Military Service Record of William Evans, 89th Ohio Infantry. Record Group 94, National Archives, Washington, D.C.

Samuel Evans File, Civil War and Later Pension Files, Records of the Veterans Administration. Record Group 15, National Archives, Washington, D.C.

William Evans File, Civil War and Later Pension Files, Records of the Veterans Administration. Record Group 15, National Archives, Washington, D.C.

Secondary Sources

Adams, George Worthington. *Doctors in Blue: The Medical History of the Union Army in the Civil War.* Baton Rouge: Louisiana State University Press, 1980.

Bailey, Judith A., and Robert I. Cottom, eds. *After Chancellorsville: Letters from the Heart: The Civil War Letters of Private Walter G. Dunn and Emma Randolph.* Baltimore: Maryland Historical Society, 1998.

Berlin, Ira, Barbara J. Fields, Steven F. Miller, and Joseph P. Reidy. *Slaves No More: Three Essays on Emancipation and the Civil War.* Cambridge, UK: Cambridge University Press, 1992.

Biographical Directory of the United States Congress, 1774–2005. Washington D.C.: U.S. Government Printing Office, 2005.

Burton, E. Milby. *The Siege of Charleston: 1861–1865.* Columbia: University of South Carolina Press, 1970.

Cashin, Joan E., ed. *The War Was You and Me: Civilians in the American Civil War.* Princeton, N.J.: Princeton University Press, 2002.

Cimbala, Paul A., and Randall M. Miller, eds. *Union Soldiers and the Northern Home Front: Wartime Experiences, Postwar Adjustments.* New York: Fordham University Press, 2002.

Cimprich, John. *Slavery's End in Tennessee: 1861–1865.* Tuscaloosa: University of Alabama Press, 1985.

Cleaves, Freeman. *Meade of Gettysburg.* Dayton, Ohio: Morganside Bookshop, 1980.

Connelly, T. W. *The History of the Seventieth Ohio Regiment: From Its Organization to Its Mustering Out.* Cincinnati: Peak Brothers, 1902.

Cooling, Benjamin Franklin. *Fort Donelson's Legacy: War and Society in Kentucky and Tennessee, 1862–1863.* Knoxville: University of Tennessee Press, 1997.

Cornish, Dudley Taylor. *The Sable Arm: Negro Troops in the Union Army, 1861–1865.* New York: Norton, 1965.

Cowden, Colonel Robert. *A Brief Sketch of the Organization and Services of the Fifty-Ninth Regiment of the United States Colored Infantry, and Biographical Sketches.* Dayton, Ohio: United Brethren Publishing House, 1883.

Cutrer, Thomas W. "Marcy, Randolph Barnes." In *The New Handbook of Texas.* Austin: Texas State Historical Association, 1996.

Davis, Keith F. "'A Terrible Distinctness': Photography of the Civil War." In *Photography in Nineteenth-Century America,* edited by Martha A. Sandweiss, 130–79. Fort Worth, Tex.: Amon Carter Museum; New York: H. N. Abrams, 1991.

Donald, David Herbert. *Lincoln.* New York: Simon and Schuster, 1995.

Dyer, Frederik Henry. *A Compendium of the War of the Rebellion.* New York: T. Yoseloff, 1959.

Edison, Thomas. *John Hunt Morgan and His Raiders.* Lexington: University Press of Kentucky, 1975.

Engs, Robert F. *Educating the Disfranchised and Disinherited: Samuel Chapman Armstrong and Hampton Institute, 1839–1893.* Knoxville: University of Tennessee Press, 1999.

———. *Freedom's First Generation: Black Hampton, Virginia, 1861–1890.* New York: Fordham University Press, 2004.

Faust, Drew Gilpin. "The Civil War Soldier and the Art of Dying." *Journal of Southern History* 67 (Feb. 2001): 3–38.

Fellman, Michael. *Citizen Sherman: A Life of William Tecumseh Sherman.* New York: Random House, 1995.

Foner, Eric. *A Short History of Reconstruction.* New York: Harper and Row, 1990.

Frohman, Charles. *Rebels on Lake Erie.* Columbus: Ohio Historical Society, 1965.

Garrison, Webb, with Cheryl Garrison. *The Encyclopedia of Civil War Usage: An Illustrated Compendium of the Everyday Language of Soldiers and Civilians.* Nashville: Cumberland House, 2001.

Glatthaar, Joseph. "Duty, Country, Race, and Party: The Evans Family of Ohio." In *Union Soldiers and the Northern Home Front: Wartime Experiences, Postwar Adjustments,* edited by Paul A. Cimbala and Randall M. Miller, 332–57. New York: Fordham University Press, 2002.

———. *Forged in Battle: The Civil War Alliance of Black Soldiers and White Officers.* New York: Free Press, 1990.

Hallock, Judith Lee. *Braxton Bragg and Confederate Defeat,* vol. 2. Tuscaloosa: University of Alabama Press, 1991.

Hooper, Ernest Walter. "Memphis, Tennessee: Federal Occupation and Reconstruction." Ph.D. diss., University of North Carolina, 1957.

Hurst, Jack. *Nathan Bedford Forrest: A Biography.* New York: Alfred A. Knopf, 1993.

Jones, Virgil Carrington. *The Civil War at Sea.* Vol. 2, *March 1862–July 1863, The River War.* New York: Holt, Rinehart, and Winston, 1961.

Kiper, Richard L., ed., *Dear Catherine, Dear Taylor: The Civil War Letters of a Union Soldier and His Wife.* Lawrence: University Press of Kansas, 2002.

Klement, Frank L. *The Limits of Dissent: Clement L. Vallandigham & the Civil War.* New York: Fordham University Press, 1998.

Luvaas, Jay, Stephen Bowman, and Leonard Fullenkamp, eds. *Guide to the Battle of Shiloh.* Lawrence: University Press of Kansas, 1996.

Marszalek, John F. *Sherman: A Soldier's Passion for Order.* New York: Free Press, 1993.

Marvel, William. *Burnside.* Chapel Hill: University of North Carolina Press, 1991.

Massey, Mary Elizabeth. *Women in the Civil War.* Lincoln: University of Nebraska Press, 1966.

McPherson, James M. *Battle Cry of Freedom: The Civil War Era.* New York: Ballantine Books, 1988.

———. *Ordeal by Fire: Vol. 2, The Civil War.* New York: Alfred A. Knopf, 1982.

Morrow, Josiah. *The History of Brown County, Ohio, Containing a History of the County; Its Townships, Towns, Churches, Schools, Etc.; General and Local Statistics; Portraits of Early Settlers and Prominent Men; History of the Northwest Territory; History of Ohio; Map of Brown County; Constitution of the United States.* Chicago: W. H. Beers, 1883.

Paludan, Phillip Shaw. *A People's Contest: The Union and Civil War, 1861–1865.* Lawrence: University Press of Kansas, 1996.

George B. Davis, Joseph W. Kirkley, and Calvin D. Cowles. *The Official Military Atlas of the Civil War.* New York: Crown, 1978.

Potter, Jerry O. *The Sultana Tragedy: America's Greatest Maritime Disaster.* Gretna, La.: Pelican, 1992.

Powell, Lawrence N. *New Masters: Northern Planters During the Civil War and Reconstruction.* New Haven, Conn.: Yale University Press, 1980.

Ramage, James A. *Rebel Raider: The Life of General John Hunt Morgan.* Lexington: University Press of Kentucky, 1986.

Rankin, Captain R. C. *History of the Seventh Ohio Volunteer Cavalry.* Ripley, Ohio: J. C. Newcomb, 1881.

Rawley, James. *The Politics of Union: Northern Politics During the Civil War.* Lincoln: University of Nebraska Press, 1980.

Roseboom, Eugene H. *History of the State of Ohio.* Vol. 4, *The Civil War Era: 1850–1873,* ed. Carl Wittke. Columbus: Ohio State Archaeological and Historical Society, 1944.

———. "Southern Ohio and the Union in 1863." *Mississippi Valley Historical Review* 39 (June 1952): 29–44.

Roseboom, Eugene H., and Francis P. Weisenburger. *History of Ohio.* Columbus: Ohio State Archaeological and Historical Society, 1953.

Sherman, John. *Recollections of Forty Years in the House, Senate and Cabinet: An Autobiography.* Chicago: The Werner Company, 1895.

Simpson, Brooks D. *Ulysses S. Grant: Triumph over Adversity, 1822–1865*. Boston: Houghton Mifflin, 2000.

Starr, Stephen Z. *Fort Sumter to Gettysburg*. Vol. 5, *The Union Cavalry in the Civil War*. Baton Rouge: Louisiana State University Press, 1979.

Stover, Carl W., and Jerry L. Coffman, *Seisimicity of the United States, 1568–1989 (Revised)*, U.S. Geological Survey Professional Paper 1527. Washington: U.S. Government Printing Office, 1993.

Thompson, Carl N. *Historical Collections of Brown County, Ohio*. Piqua, Ohio: Hammer Graphics, 1969.

Trefousse, Hans L. *Andrew Johnson: A Biography*. New York: Norton, 1989.

Trudeau, Noah Andre. *Like Men of War: Black Troops in the Civil War 1862–1865*. New York: Little, Brown, 1998.

Wiley, Bell Irvin. *The Life of Billy Yank, the Common Soldier of the Union*. 1978. Reprint, Baton Rouge: Louisiana State University Press, 1991.

Williams, Byron. *History of Clermont and Brown counties, Ohio, from the earliest historical times down to the present*. Milford, Ohio: Hobart Pub. Co., 1913.

INDEX

Note: Samuel B. Evans is the primary for determining family relationships among the Evans family. Military units are grouped by the state from which they originated.

Aberdeen, Ohio, 8, 15–16, 48, 69
  East Fork, 5, 164
Aberdeen Battery, 174
absentee ballots, 194, 205
Acklin, John L., 121, 184, 189, 375
Adams, F. W., 87, 89, 90
Adams County, Ohio, 203
Adams Express Company, 237–38
Alabama: 1st Colored Infantry, 158
Ammen, Jacob, 40, 41n2, 162
Amnesty Proclamation, 344, 345n3, 356
Anderson, Charles, 162, 166
Anderson, George, 335
Anderson, William, 8
Andersonville, Georgia, 344
antiwar movement. See Butternuts; Copperheads
Armstrong, William, 76, 308
Army of the Cumberland, 104, 212n
Army of the Potomac, xxi, 91, 94, 143, 157, 158, 203, 251
Army of the Tennessee, 212n, 279, 355

Banks, Nathaniel Prentiss, 102, 135, 165, 257, 261
Beasley, Mary, 349
Beauregard, Pierre Gustav Toutant, 29, 194, 311
Bently, John, 315
black laborers, 51, 52, 196, 357, 362, 375
black male suffrage, 355, 357
black soldiers, 140, 148, 249n1, 254, 379–80n. See also 59th U.S.C.T. Infantry; Tennessee military units: 1st West Tennessee Infantry of African Descent
  bounty system and, 280
  desertion among, 161
  final muster of, 373
  illness among, 186, 252–53
  prisoner of war exchanges and, 196–97

  recruitment technique for, 139
  as substitutes for draftees, 281n1
Blackburn, Joseph, 11, 11n1
Bloomhuff, John P., 162, 209, 210
blue lights, 192
Bonman, William, 25
Botner, Jake, 7, 47, 119, 126, 288, 315, 350, 374
Botner, William, 233
bounty system, 57n2, 59, 242, 286, 291, 319, 320. See also corruption
  black soldiers and, 280
Bouton, Edward, 136, 166, 257, 292, 329, 337, 352, 362
Bragg, Braxton, 65n1, 167–168, 170n1, 171, 175, 219
Brice's Cross Roads, Battle of, 264, 264n3
Brough, John, 162, 165, 166, 193, 194–95n2, 205, 251–52
  declining health of, 366, 367
  inauguration of, 229–30
Brown, Jim, 282
Brown, Major, 58, 74, 131, 236, 282
Brown County, Ohio, 203, 205
Brownlow, William, 356
Buchanan, John, 112–13, 247, 363
Buckland, R. P., 244
Buell, Don Carlos, 65n1, 263
Burboge, Elya, 70
Bureau of Refugees, Freedmen, and Abandoned Lands, 369, 372, 375–76, 377n1, 380, 385
Burke, James, 7, 8n3, 9n1, 41
  letters from, 8–9, 16–17
  quits as hired hand, 45, 47, 48
Burnside, Ambrose, 150–151, 162, 169, 173, 217–19
  Order No. 38 and, 146, 147n1
Butler, Benjamin, 61n1, 167–68, 310, 312
Butternuts, xviii, 125, 126n1, 131–32, 140, 328, 332

Camp Chase, 319, 335
Camp Dennison, 54, 356
Camp Young, Texas, 4
Campbell, Alex, 359
Campbell, C. F., 198, 286
Campbell, Cal, 1, 4, 7, 19, 33, 34, 35, 40, 48, 60–61, 119–20
Campbell, Calvin A., 231
Campbell, J. B., Jr., 7, 11, 16
Campbell, John B., 21, 35, 54
Campbell, Mary, 31
Campbell, William B., 353, 354n1
Cannon, Samuel, 7, 16, 27
Carpenter, Bill, 59
Carpenter, John, 7, 59, 75, 212, 361
Carpenter, John E., 310, 349, 356, 364, 380
Carpenter, Mary. See Espy, Mary Carpenter
Carpenter, Sam, 266, 380–81
Carpenter, Tom, 75, 98, 360
Carrigan, Bill, 115
Carrigan, Cud, 86, 241
Carrigan, James, 43, 110
Case, John, Jr., 7
Case, Will, 71, 74, 371
Chalmers, James Ronald, 130, 132
Chancellorsville, Battle of, 144
Charleston, South Carolina, 123, 132, 174, 191, 194, 327
Chase, Salmon P., 270, 271n2, 311n3
Chattanooga, Tenn., 212, 219
Chickamauga, Battle of, 198–99
Chulahom, Miss., 84–85
Cincinnati, Ohio, 11–12n3, 43, 65n1, 321n2
   Sanitary Fair at, 227
Cobb, Miss, 41
Cochran, Samuel, 74
Cockerill, Joseph Randolph, 70, 107, 236
Colfax, Schuyler, 225
conscription, 56, 57n2, 59, 67–68, 123, 128, 130, 175, 181, 238, 287
   marriages and, 209
   meeting quota in township, 286, 291
   substitutes for, 280, 297
   within Union camps, 216
contraband, 61n.1, 136, 235, 244–45
Cook, Dian, 373
Cooper, Captain, 282

Cooper, Ezekiel, 247
Cooper, Jacob, 247
Copperheads, xviii, xx, 97n.3, 223, 285, 287, 324, 351, 352, 374. See also Vallandigham, Clement
Corinth, Miss., 21, 23–24, 159, 225
corpses, misidentification of, 19, 22, 103
Corrigan, James. See Carrigan, James
corruption, 333, 376–77. See also bounty system
Corwin, Thomas, 169, 170n3
cotton, 18n.4, 38, 87, 254, 334, 365, 367, 376
Covan, Maurice M., 166
Covert, James S., 121, 130
Cowden, Robert, 254, 257, 264, 289, 293n1
Crain, Martin, 6, 71
Crook, George, 125
Curtis, Jane, 16
Cynthiana, Ky, 48–49, 266n2

Dadd, Joseph, 82, 85
Dahlgren, John Adolphus Bernard, 194
Daulton, John, 335
Davis, George W., 297
Davis, Jefferson, 350, 353
Davis, Will, 7
Dawson, Amos, 228, 244
DeBott, George, 56
Dennis, John, 53
Dennis, L. W., 26
Dennis, W. B., 116, 121, 184, 375
Denver, James William, 64, 82, 102, 117
desertion, 55, 58, 96, 161, 224, 305
   among black soldiers, 161
   bounty system and, 57
Devore, E. C., 41, 183
Dixson, David, 359, 360
Dodd, Dave, 107, 112
Douglas, Stephen A., 102, 103n2
draft, military. See conscription
Dragoo, Cris, 51
Dragoo, Lawson, 12, 40, 112, 133, 136, 148, 152
Drennin, James, 63, 74, 81, 92, 160, 188, 191
Dryden, Isaac, 198

Du Pont, Samuel Francis, 132
Duke, Basil, 175, 176n2

Early, David W., 56, 60
Early, George W., 6n1, 27, 43, 54, 59,
    61, 77
    letters from, 5–6, 25, 33, 223–24
Early, Indiana Evans, 3, 6n1, 124–25
    government sewing contract for,
    266, 267
    letters from, 77–78
Early, Louis Mortimer (Morty), 283,
    392
Early, Samuel Benjamin, 27, 33, 54,
    125, 146, 179
earthquakes, 363
East Fork, Aberdeen, Ohio, 5, 164
elections
    county, 41, 121, 203, 359
    presidential, 263, 265, 289–90,
    308–9
    state, 183–184, 305, 366, 374
    township, 4, 7, 11, 15–16, 189, 247
Ellis, Perse, 53
Ellis, William, 103
Ellison, Char, 376–77
Ellison, Tom, 259, 262, 318
Emancipation Proclamation, 95, 136,
    356
Espy, Mary Carpenter, 7, 35, 46, 54,
    100, 209, 287
Espy, Sam, 164, 209, 381
Espy, Tom M., 219
Eubanks, Elliot, 104
Evans, Abraham (brother), 7, 8n1, 14,
    26, 239
Evans, Amos A. (Tad) (brother), 8n3,
    45, 95, 100, 198, 308, 311, 332
    draft and discharge of, 71, 72
    1862, letters from, 10–11, 22–23,
    30–31, 39–42, 67–68
    1863, letters from, 90–91, 101, 109–
    10, 112–13, 137–38, 140, 149, 159–
    60, 174–76, 179–80, 190, 208–9,
    222–23, 227–28
    1864, letters from, 232–34, 237–41,
    247–48, 258, 266–67
    on handling of Samuel's business
    affairs, 62, 86, 110, 115, 227, 233
    overall health deterioration of, 152,
    167, 220, 245, 251, 265, 268

recuperative trip to Great Lakes,
    280, 286
Evans, Amos (uncle), 19, 61, 75, 77, 79,
    93, 100, 104, 119, 125, 126–27
Evans, Andrew, 9–10, 16, 109, 115–16,
    125, 183, 203, 247, 366
    1862, letters from, 6–7, 26–27, 36–37,
    61–62, 66–67, 74–75, 79
    1863, letters from, 93–94, 98–99, 104,
    107–9, 115–16, 120–22, 124–29,
    134–35, 143–44, 147, 150, 152–53,
    156–57, 161–65, 167–70, 172–74,
    176–78, 180–81, 183–84, 197–99,
    201–4, 207–10, 213–21
    1864, letters from, 228–30, 245–46,
    251–52, 265, 267–74, 279–84,
    291–92, 296–97, 302–7, 308–12
    1865, letters from, 314–16, 318–21,
    323–24, 331–36, 338–40, 342–43,
    347–51, 354–60, 363, 365–68,
    370–71, 377–79, 381–87
Evans, Ann Delia (sister), 165, 329,
    331–32, 335
    death of, 386–87
    letters from, 3, 53, 95, 114–15, 144,
    201, 212, 221–22, 260–61
Evans, Benjamin (uncle), 42
Evans, Davis, 305, 310
Evans, Diana (aunt), 30, 75, 204, 308
Evans, Elizabeth (Lida) (aunt), 32, 42,
    162
Evans, Griffith (uncle), 112, 306
Evans, Indiana Early (sister). See Early,
    Indiana Evans
Evans, Isabella (sister), 270, 280, 339,
    343
    letters from, 231–32
Evans, Jane (Big), 5, 6n3, 19, 34, 127,
    201
    report of the marriage of, 252, 256
Evans, Jane (cousin), xvii, 5, 6n3, 43,
    389
    antiwar sentiments of, 201, 287–89,
    294, 298, 305
    letters from, 19, 34–35, 47–48, 99–
    100, 119–20, 126–27, 255–56,
    277–78, 287–89
Evans, John B. (brother), xvii, 1, 2, 6, 8,
    13, 32, 34, 136
    abandons republicanism, 76
    death of, 149, 150
    letters from, 14, 17–18, 49, 59–61

letters to, 36, 41–42, 135–36
takes ill at camp, 27–28
Evans, Joseph H. (brother), 227, 358, 390
Evans, Laban (cousin), 283, 288, 299, 329
Evans, Lee (brother), 15, 67, 111, 163, 392
Evans, Lina (cousin), 77, 222, 288, 315
Evans, Mary (grandmother), 42–43, 51–52, 140
Evans, Mary (mother), 9–10, 27–30, 316–17, 322–24
Evans, Mary (sister). *See* Grierson, Mary Evans
Evans, Samuel B., xvii, xviii–xix, 96, 179. *See also* soldiers' life
1862, letters from, 2, 9–10, 12–13, 17, 21–22, 23–24, 27–30, 37–39, 50–51, 57–58, 62–65, 69–74, 80–85
1863, letters from, 85–92, 95–97, 101–3, 105–7, 110–14, 117–19, 122–24, 129–33, 135–36, 138–39, 141–42, 147–49, 151–56, 158–61, 165–66, 170–72, 178–79, 182–89, 191–97, 199–200, 211–16, 224–27
1864, letters from, 230–31, 234–37, 242, 244–45, 248–57, 259–64, 274–76, 278–79, 284–85, 289–90, 292–96, 298–302, 307–8
1865, letters from, 313, 316–20, 322–31, 333–34, 337, 340–41, 343–46, 351–54, 361–63, 365, 367, 369, 371–72, 375–77, 380–83
1866, letters from, 384
Evans, William H. (brother), 7, 47, 53, 54, 59, 98, 137, 255, 347–48
handling of Samuel's business affairs, 3–4, 29, 40, 59, 61
hospital stewardship of, 121, 150, 154, 169, 181, 187, 191, 207
letter to, 357–58
letters from, 1, 3–4, 35–36, 43–44
receives medical degree, 378, 378n1
reported rumor of his death, 197–98
Ezra Church, Battle of, 282

Farragut, David Glasgow, 132, 282, 283n1
fatigue parties, 24, 25n1

Ferrick, Boone, 282
Fessenden, William Pitt, 270
59th U.S.C.T. Infantry, xix, 239, 242, 261, 267, 326–27, 371
    at Battle of Brice's Cross Roads, 264
    at Battle of Tupelo, 274–76
Fitch, E. M., 364, 368, 385
Forrest, Nathan Bedford, 234, 242, 244–45, 249, 257, 264, 272, 295
    at Battle of Tupelo, 274–76
    raid on Memphis by, 283, 285–86
Fort Donelson, Ky, 2, 3n.2, 13, 30n1, 104
Fort Pickering, Tenn., 51n2, 52, 72, 74, 302
    construction of barracks at, 296, 298
Fort Pillow massacre, 236–37n, 248, 253
Foster, James C., 56, 92, 221, 231, 264, 278
Freedmen's Bureau, 369, 372, 375–76, 377n1, 380, 385
Frémont, John C., 265, 290
Fulton, Joseph, 190
Fulton, William, 4, 121, 174, 247

Galbraith, James, 21, 50, 74
Galbraith, Thomas I., 164, 168
Games, David, 2, 12, 32, 37, 40
Games, Euphemia, 209
Games, G. G., 109, 110
Games, Simpson, 12
Ganus, G. G. *See* Games, G. G.
Georgetown, Ky., 48
Gilbert, A. B., 7, 246
Gilbert, Amanda, 227, 232, 247, 260
Gilbert, Dyas, 40, 57, 58, 110, 281, 297
Gilbert, Robert B., 225
Gillmore, Quincy Adams, 188, 191, 194
government sewing contracts, 266, 267n
Grand Junction, 37, 117, 152
Grant, Ulysses S., 85, 103, 135, 211n, 224, 253, 254, 261
    Bragg and, 219–20
    campaign against Vicksburg, 117, 119n2, 142, 150, 168–69, 171, 177
    at Chattanooga, 219
    dispute with Stanton over chain of command, 248–49

paroling of Pemberton's army, 180–81
Richmond campaign and, 277, 280, 282, 283, 329, 337
war rumors of Petersburg campaign led by, 267, 269, 271
on Sherman, 213
Grantham, Nelly, 100, 104
Grier, Thomas, 74, 112
Grierson, Alexander, 5*n*2, 16
Grierson, Benjamin, 292
Grierson, John W., 121–22, 130, 198
Grierson, Mary Evans, 9, 9*n*1, 14–15, 53–54
Guntown, Battle of, 264*n*3, 276, 278, 295
Guthrie, Dr. John W., 47*n*3, 109
Guttery, Henry, 53

habeas corpus, writ of, 96, 97*n*3, 271, 362
Hall, Aleck, 59
Halleck, Henry, 94, 95, 147, 168
Hampton Roads Peace conference, 326, 336
Hart, William R., 114
Hawk, Phillip, 43, 47
Hawks, Turner, 323
Haynes, W. M., 103, 118
Hays, Major, 366
Hays, William, 56
Heaton, Doctor, 36, 107
Heitt, Griff, 74
Heitt, W. G., 7
Helm, James, 31
Henry, John, 359
Hensley, Captain, 278
Hiett, John, 3, 15, 28, 56, 110, 117, 133, 136, 137, 144, 306
Hiett, Samuel R., 4, 5*n*.3, 25, 27, 32, 40, 45, 54, 70, 247
death of, 343
Hiett, Sarah, 180, 363
Hiett, W. G., 121
Hiett, Will, 259
hired hands, difficulty of employing, 297, 310, 320, 379
Holly Springs, Miss., 50, 84–85, 130
Holton, Elijah G., 247, 385
Hood, John Bell, 306
Hook, Turner, 74, 112, 318
Hooker, Joseph, 135, 151, 158

Housh, Harrison, 56, 128
Housh, James H., 109
Housh, John, 128
Housh, Sallie E., 247
Housh, Sam, 76, 128
Housh, Sarah, 308, 352
Housh, Will, 258, 259, 382
Howard, George W., 297
Howard, O. O., 294
Howland, Jesse, 28
Hunt, Peter, 128
Hurlburt, Stephen A., 244, 253
Huron, Perry, 247
Hurrin, Lile, 109

Invalid Corps, 239, 240. *See also* Veteran Reserve Corps
Iowa: 13th Volunteer Infantry, 206
Island No. 10, Battle of, 13, 14n

Jameson, George, 3
Jewett, Hugh J., 125, 126*n*2
Johnson, Andrew, xxii, 263, 265, 332, 339, 370, 371
candidacy of, 289–90, 303, 308, 342, 351
Johnson, B. F., 103, 111
Johnson, Henry, 166
Johnson's Island, 215
Johnston, Joseph Eggleston, 175, 271*n*1, 273*n*2, 343–44
Jolly, John, 56, 116
Jury, Abner, 104

Kanawha River Valley, 75–76
Kansas, 7th Jayhawkers Cavalry, 231
Kendrich, Colonel, 329
Kimble, David B., 12–13, 68–69
King, David, 75, 86, 238
King, James R., 32, 40, 45
King, John W., 56
Kitch, Alex, 280

Lafabre, John, 146, 154, 162
LaGrange, Tenn., 38, 88, 130, 132
Lane, Cyrus, 56, 59
Lane, Presley, 17, 19, 22, 32
Lawwill, B. B., 7
Lawwill, Jack, 210
Lee, George Washington Custis, 338
Lee, Robert E., 168–69, 171, 253, 336
letterwriting system, 107, 109
Lexington, Ky., 48, 75, 266

Lincoln, Abraham, 60, 102, 208n, 225, 226n1, 264
  assassination of, 339, 340–43
  conscription and, 128
  dispute with Stanton over chain of command, 248, 249n3
Logan, John A., 359
Long, Aaron, 4, 6, 360
Long, Alexander, 305, 364, 364n2
Longstreet, James, 217, 218–19, 221
Lory, Aaron. See Long, Aaron
Loudon, Alfred, 183
Loudon, D. W. C., 18n2, 89, 92, 111, 131, 139, 282
Loudon, James, 183, 203, 228, 244, 366
Lowill, John, 59–60

Maddox, David, 43
Maddox, Thompson, 227, 280
Maddox, Tyre, 95
Manassas, Va, 9, 9n2
Marcy, Randolph B., 298, 299n2
Marcy, William L., 299n2
marriages and conscription, 209
Marshall, John G., 56
Martin, Samuel H., 4, 15–16, 31, 240
Maysville, Ky., 48, 62–63, 69, 160, 221, 255, 265, 267–68
McClellan, George B., 51, 95, 161
  nomination for president, 265, 287, 290–91, 303
McDaniel, John, 52, 92, 100, 148, 184, 366, 368
McDaniel, Joseph, 17
McFerren, John W., 18, 71, 71n1
McLawwill, James, 43
McNight, John, 6
McPherson, James B., 89, 119n2, 237–38, 278, 279n2
Meade, George Gordon, 169, 170n2, 171, 172n1
Memphis, Tenn., 37, 50–51, 63–64, 254, 357
  earthquakes in, 363
Michigan military units
  3rd Michigan Cavalry, 230
  10th Michigan Cavalry, 371
Midghall, John, 136, 137
Mills, William, 70, 184
Minor, S. S., 161
Mississippi, First Union Cavalry, 250

Mitchell, I. C., 7
Mitchell, Jacob, 238, 374
Mitchell, John, 7, 121, 129, 164, 168, 171–72, 303
Mockbee, W. L., 105, 111
Moddox, Thompson. See Maddox, Thompson
Moore, Isaac W., 36, 43, 110, 115
Moore, J. W. See Moore, Isaac W.
Moore, John, 59, 68
Moore, John F., 144
Moore, L. B., 168, 198
Morgan, George W., 364n2
Morgan, John Hunt, 48, 169, 182
  march through Ohio and Indiana, 173–74, 175, 177, 178, 180, 181
  news of escape from prison, 221
  raid into Kentucky, 266, 266n2, 267–68
Morgan, Richard, 176n1
Morrison, John, 70
Morton, Oliver Hazard Perry, 169, 252
Moscow, Tenn., 50, 86–87, 132, 261
Mount Sterling, Ky., 122–23, 247

Nashville Convention, 353, 354n1
Nelson, Captain, 58
Newman, Leige, 100
Norris, F. H. B., 56
Norris, William, 146, 151, 154, 162, 364, 374

Odd Fellows, Independent Order of, 343
Oglesby, Richard James, 158
Ohio military units
  3rd Independent Battery of Ohio National Guard, 4n.1
  7th Volunteer Cavalry, 121–22
  10th Volunteer Cavalry, 112
  47th Volunteer Infantry, 203–6
  70th Volunteer Infantry, 11n1, 17–18, 71, 72, 103, 105, 111–12, 182, 184, 282, 355, 366
  89th Volunteer Infantry, 56, 57n1, 70, 93, 102, 118, 187
O'Mitchell, John, 247

Parker, Lafayette, 60, 65, 100, 106, 211, 234
Pemberton, John C., 167, 171
Penola, Miss., 132

Phillips, H. L., 28, 82, 113, 115, 117, 129
Phillips, Robert E., 166, 257, 326, 387
Phillips, Wendell, 11, 11n3
Pierson, David V., 56
pioneer companies, 351n
Pittsburgh, Tenn., 14
Pittsburgh Landing, Tenn., 21, 22n1
Pope, John, 29
Port Hudson, 102, 171, 177–78
Porter, Frank C., 19, 61, 269
Power, Robert, 128
Price, Sterling, 295
prisoners of war exchange, 29, 30n,
    144, 177–78, 196–97
profiteering. See corruption
Proter, Elijah, 33

Queen of the West (steamer), 95, 97n1,
    112, 132

Ramsey, William, 137, 149, 159, 222
reconstruction, 225, 384
recruitment, 56, 57n1
Red River campaign, 256n1, 262n2
Richmond, Virginia, 51, 123
Ridley, Bob, 43, 59
Rosencrans, William Starke, 104, 106,
    123, 135, 150, 194, 197, 200, 202
    Bragg and, 167–68, 171, 175
Rousseau, Lovell H., 295

Savannah, Ga, 10, 13, 313, 314n2
Sawyer, 17, 45, 71, 74, 138
Scott, Jacob, 47, 56, 59
Seward, William Henry, 339
Sharp, Thomas, 7, 26, 32, 233, 347
Shelton, William, 138
Sherman, John, 386
Sherman, William Tecumseh, 38, 73,
    81, 85, 213, 306
    Fort Pickering and, 39, 52
    Joseph Eggleston Johnston and, 175,
        343–44
    march to Chattanooga, 211, 212n,
        217
    Nathan Bedford Forest and, 295,
        297
    pursuit of John Bell Hood by, 304,
        306, 307, 313, 328
    refusal of Copperhead nomination
        for president, 352, 356
Sherring, John, 109

Shiloh, Battle of, 17–18, 18n1, 23–24
Sibbald, James, 71
Sibbald, John, 45, 74, 105, 136
Simons, Joshua, 71
Simons, Thomas, 34, 50, 71, 74
Simpson, Thomas, 150
Simpson, Will, 2, 15
Slocum, Henry W., 368, 369n
Smith, A. J., 261, 283
Smith, Edmund Kirby, 65n1
Smith, Morgan L., 298
Smith, William S., 117, 123, 130, 140,
    158–59, 274–76
smuggling and smugglers. See
    contraband
Sniffie, Tom, 360
soldiers' life, 12–13, 21, 23–24, 38, 96.
    See also Evans, Samuel B.
    barracks, 296, 298, 323
    execution of soldiers, 261, 262n2,
        263–64
    furloughs, 13, 55, 103, 117, 123, 130–
        31, 194n2, 196, 360
    guard duty, 23–24, 88
    morale, 106, 318, 331
    payroll issues in a, 21, 22n2, 38–39,
        111–12, 113, 337, 365
    picket duty, 21, 23, 250, 289, 337
    restrictions on travel into Memphis
        instituted, 244
    tending a garden, 253, 331, 334
    vaccinations received during, 161,
        245, 245n1
    voting rights during a, 157, 221, 223
Somerset, Battle of, 128
spelling, 13, 16, 92, 104, 110–11, 325
Stanton, Edward M., 94, 248, 310
Star of the West (steamboat), 300,
    301n2
Stevenson, Carter L., 216
Steward, Joseph, 239
Stewart, John M. V., 297
Stoneman, George, 138, 139n1
Sturgis, Samuel, 264n4, 276
Sultana (steamboat), 346, 366n3
Summers, Frank, 282
sutlers, 71n.2, 216, 318
Sutton, Rac, 29
Swisher, Harriet, 201
Swisher, John, 118, 366, 379
Swisher, John W., 103

Tarbell, David, 4, 7, 16, 40, 41, 72, 76,
    130, 309

Taylor, John D., 204–6
Taylor, Robert, 257n1
Taylor, T. T., 203, 373
Tennessee military units
  1st Middle Tennessee Cavalry, 150
  1st West Tennessee Infantry of African Descent, 158, 166
Tennessee Unionists, 13
Tennessee Valley, 206
Thirteenth Amendment, 324–25
Thomas, George, 340
Thomas, Lorenzo, 141, 142n1
Thompson, John, 266
Thompson, N. B., 57–58, 112, 164, 165
Thompson, William (Bill), 366, 379, 384, 386
Tod, David, 126, 208n, 270, 271n2
Tomlinson, Will, 221
Tupelo, Battle of, 274–76
Tuscumbia, 199–200
Tyler, John, 371, 372

U.S. Sanitary Commission, 227–28, 228n, 315
Union Party, xx, 77n2, 208, 386

vaccinations, 161, 244–45
Vallandigham, Clement, 96, 97n3, 125, 144, 157, 186, 194. See also Copperheads
  rumors of conspiracy to free prisoners, 215, 215n
Van Trump, Philadelph, 338, 338n1

Veteran Reserve Corps, 272, 351n1. See also Invalid Corps
Vicksburg, Miss., 93, 95, 112, 118, 132, 150, 158
  Grant's campaign against, 117, 119n.2, 142, 150, 168–69, 170–71, 177

Waldron, J. C., 4, 4n1, 41, 49, 121, 129, 174, 207–8, 210
Waldron, James, 33, 34, 37
Waldron, P. W., 4, 4n1, 121, 160, 164, 175, 184, 189
Washburn, Cadwallader Colden, 249, 257, 278, 282, 284n1, 331, 333
  smuggling abatement and, 251–53
West, W. W., 67, 97, 107, 112, 319
  health of, 133, 134
  ordered to go into recruiting service, 243–44
  promotions of, 73, 112
  as state representative, 203, 228
White, Betty, 5
White, Chilton Allen, 224, 305, 364
White, George, 30, 32, 45
Wilson, John T., 136, 203
Wilson, Oliver Gray, 52
Wood, A. W., 164, 174
Wood, Andrew, 41
Wood, John, 59
Wool, John Ellis, 63

Zimmerman, Captain, 136